"Jeremy Lundgren's remarkably rich theology of safety offers Christians today a gateway into true Christian freedom. It is often hard to decide whether the modern world is safer than ever before or saturated with frightening risks earlier generations could never have imagined. Helpfully locating our experiences by tracing their historical genesis, Lundgren shows us how we came to be constantly bombarded by safety messages and risk warnings. What might it look like to live with confidence in Christ in such a cultural context? Christians living in developed nations today cannot afford to ignore the ways in which safety has become the idol of our time. Lundgren's work offers a long-overdue account of what true Christian freedom looks like in a world where we are constantly told that we are at risk."

Brian Brock, professor of moral and practical theology at the School of Divinity, History, and Philosophy, King's College, University of Aberdeen

"Socrates noted that it's impossible to avoid all risk, even in an ideal city, and especially in raising children. Our loss of such ancient wisdom has left us fearful, obsessed with safety, and cut off from the benefits that responsible risk can bring. In this deeply researched and expertly written book, Lundgren tells the story of this loss and outlines a courageous and hopeful theology of safety for all who confess themselves to be upheld by the fatherly hand of God."

Rob Price, associate professor of theology at the Talbot School of Theology, Biola University

"What difference does the death and resurrection of Jesus Christ as well as Christians' conformation to this pattern of life play in our pursuit of safety? We often order our lives around the desire to maintain a sense of security, loading it with moral weight. In this book, Jeremy Lundgren deftly situates concepts of safety, risk, and harm within the redemptive narrative and the call to pursue a life ordered to the cross. Paying careful attention to the text of Holy Writ and offering numerous helpful conceptual distinctions along the way, this book is a theological masterclass well worth reading."

Daniel Lee Hill, assistant professor of Christian theology at Baylor University

"Jeremy Lundgren has produced the right kind of theology book: insightful theory with an eye toward helping the life of the church. *The Pursuit of Safety* has uncomfortably confronted how I might be idolizing safety due to a misguided doctrine of creation, lopsided theological anthropology, or distorted view of God. Take a risk and read this book!"

Kevin Wong, assistant professor of theological studies at Dallas Theological Seminary

"Modern society is littered with 'signposts of safety.' From delivery packages and children's toys to roadways and hallways, there are inevitably warning signs looming nearby designed to keep us 'safe.' In this volume, Lundgren provides the reader with both apt descriptions of our supposedly ordered modern lives and biblically rich, theologically deep instructions on wisely navigating them as disciples of Jesus. May we all attend to the signpost of the cross—the best indicator of true safety—and find wholeness, soundness, and health (i.e., safety) in Jesus."

Ty Kieser, assistant professor of theology at Criswell College

"This is the book I didn't know I needed about a topic that proves to be immensely practical and applicable at the end of a global pandemic. It goes below the surface to help Christians seeking to figure out why people and governments reacted the way they did during those disorienting days. It's astonishing how easily Dr. Lundgren moves from a historical understanding of the theology of safety, through a biblical survey of risk, to why it is beneficial for leaders in the church to grasp these ideas today."

Jeff Brewer, executive director of WordPartners

THE PURSUIT of SAFETY

A Theology of Danger, Risk, and Security

◆◆◆◆◆◆◆◆◆◆◆◆◆◆◆◆◆◆◆◆◆◆◆

Jeremy Lundgren

Foreword by
Marc Cortez

An imprint of InterVarsity Press
Downers Grove, Illinois

InterVarsity Press
P.O. Box 1400 | Downers Grove, IL 60515-1426
ivpress.com | email@ivpress.com

©2024 by Jeremy M. Lundgren

All rights reserved. No part of this book may be reproduced in any form without written permission from InterVarsity Press.

InterVarsity Press® is the publishing division of InterVarsity Christian Fellowship/USA®. For more information, visit intervarsity.org.

Scripture quotations, unless otherwise noted, are from *The Holy Bible, English Standard Version*, copyright © 2001 by Crossway Bibles, a division of Good News Publishers. Used by permission. All rights reserved.

While any stories in this book are true, some names and identifying information may have been changed to protect the privacy of individuals.

The publisher cannot verify the accuracy or functionality of website URLs used in this book beyond the date of publication.

Cover design: David Fassett
Interior design: Daniel van Loon
Cover Image Credits: © Archive Holdings Inc. / The Image Bank / Getty Images

ISBN 978-1-5140-0801-0 (print) | ISBN 978-1-5140-0802-7 (digital)

Printed in the United States of America ∞

Library of Congress Cataloging-in-Publication Data

Names: Lundgren, Jeremy M., 1976- author.
Title: The pursuit of safety : a theology of danger, risk, and security / Jeremy Lundgren.
Description: Downers Grove, IL : IVP Academic, [2024] | Series: Studies in Christian doctrine and scripture | Includes bibliographical references and index.
Identifiers: LCCN 2024012200 (print) | LCCN 2024012201 (ebook) | ISBN 9781514008010 (print) | ISBN 9781514008027 (digital)
Subjects: LCSH: Risk-taking (Psychology)–Religious aspects–Christianity. | Christian life. | BISAC: RELIGION / Christian Theology / General | RELIGION / Christian Ministry / Pastoral Resources
Classification: LCC BF637.R57 L8 2024 (print) | LCC BF637.R57 (ebook) | DDC 155.9–dc23/eng/20240424
LC record available at https://lccn.loc.gov/2024012200
LC ebook record available at https://lccn.loc.gov/2024012201

To Kaci, Samuel, Evan, and Annie.

May you face danger with courage;

may you find safety in Christ.

Contents

Foreword by Marc Cortez — ix

Acknowledgments — xi

Series Introduction — xiii

Abbreviations — xix

PART ONE: SIGNPOSTS OF SAFETY IN THE MODERN LANDSCAPE

1 Tokens of Safety — 3

2 The Form and Status of Safety Today — 20

PART TWO: SOURCES OF DANGER THROUGH THE AGES

3 Humanity Against the Gods: Premodern Risk — 37

4 Humanity Against Nature: Early Modern Risk — 55

5 Humanity Against Itself: Late-Modern Risk — 73

PART THREE: AVOIDING HARM IN A FALLEN WORLD

6 Grasping the Future: Probabilities and the Promises of God — 91

7 Ordering Creation: Technology, Idols, and the Cross of Christ — 129

8 Guiding Action: Procedures, Forgiveness, and the Advantage of Wisdom — 174

PART FOUR: LIVING AND DYING UNDER THE LORDSHIP OF CHRIST

9 Discipleship and the Demands of Safety — 221

10 Putting Safety in Its Place — 251

Bibliography — 263

General Index — 283

Scripture Index — 287

Foreword

Marc Cortez

SHOULD WE SEEK SAFETY? Most of us live in a world in which the answer to that question is obvious. Of course we should! Who wouldn't want to be safe? And who wouldn't want the people they love to be safe? We thus have all kinds of regulations, stipulations, and policies against various violations, all of which seek to protect something we hold dearly: our safety.

Before encountering Jeremy Lundgren's work, that's certainly how I would have responded to such a seemingly simple question. However, as is often the case, there is tremendous complexity lurking just beneath the surface of that simplicity. What do we mean by *safety*? How do we pursue it? Why is it such a great value that we should all seek it? And what do we mean by *should*? Is this a moral obligation? Have we done something wrong if we *don't* seek safety? And how does all of this relate specifically to Christian discipleship and maturity? Should Christians pursue safety? Avoid it? Some combination of the two? And if that last question is the right way to frame things, how do we discern when pursuing safety is the right course of action?

If you haven't noticed already, these are all fundamentally theological questions. Although you won't find a lot of talk about "safety" in the history of theology, you *will* find plenty of discussion about the things we ought to pursue as faithful Christ-followers, the ways in which we ought to pursue them, and the moral obligations that pertain to those pursuits. In other words, any question that asks whether Christians should seek "X" is a theological question.

The problem is that we often have a hard time recognizing when questions are "theological." Ask us a question about the nature of the atonement, the persons of the Trinity, or the existence of free will, and most Christians will quickly recognize that they are operating in "theological" territory. However, ask us about how we should view food, whether sports are good, or if we should pursue safety, and most Christians won't even realize that they are being asked questions with all kinds of theological significance.

That is often the case with safety. Most of us will see a sign on the wall announcing how many days it's been since the last accident, and at best we'll think briefly about how well that place is doing with promoting safety. For Lundgren, though, that sign is an opportunity for theological reflection, another signal that a pervasive value is at work and is worth serious consideration.

I encourage you to accompany Lundgren on his theological tour through our culture's near obsession with safety. He ably demonstrates how safety is one of the dominant values of the Western world, encoded in countless practices and policies. With years of experience in construction, ministry, parenting, and other areas of life that are dominated by safety-related perspectives, Lundgren is well positioned to help us think well about the nature of safety, whether it ought to be the dominant value that it has become, and if so, how we ought to pursue it as Christians seeking to live faithfully in a broken world.

Should we seek safety? I think the answer is still yes. But by the end of this book, you will see that question in entirely new ways.

Acknowledgments

MANY PEOPLE HAVE HELPED me in writing this book. Numerous friends, colleagues, and acquaintances helped by showing genuine interest in its subject matter, sharing with me their own anecdotes, fears, frustrations, and questions regarding matters of safety, and, in many instances, sharing with me their desire to trust God and be faithful to him as they engage with the dangers and risks of this world. I am grateful for those many conversations—some brief, some quite lengthy—because they challenged me to think deeply and carefully.

This book began as my PhD dissertation at Wheaton College and had even earlier beginnings in my ThM thesis at Talbot School of Theology. At Talbot, I would like to thank my thesis adviser, Mark Saucy, and my ThM program director, Rob Price, for their support and direction. At Wheaton, I would like to thank the faculty who taught and mentored me. Marc Cortez has been a trustworthy adviser, colleague, and friend whose input helped give clarity and coherence to this project. Daniel Treier has shown unwavering support for both this book and its author, helping to strengthen my research and arguments in many important ways. I would also like to express gratitude for my fellow students at Wheaton who challenged me intellectually and encouraged me spiritually. In particular, thank you to Kevin Wong, Daniel Hill, Matt Monkemeier, Justin Zahraee, and Sam Ashton.

Thank you to all those at InterVarsity Press who worked to bring this book to publication. Zachary Gordon was patient, encouraging, insightful, and helpful as I worked to finish the manuscript. I am honored that Daniel Treier and Kevin Vanhoozer invited me to contribute to the SCDS series, and I am humbled that the things God has taught me about his faithfulness, goodness, power, and love might be shared with others. I pray that this book will help its readers cling a little less tightly to those things that can be shaken and a little more tightly to what cannot be shaken (Heb 12:26-29).

Finally, I would like to thank my wife, Kaci, and our children, Samuel, Evan, and Annie. I am grateful to my children for their companionship, hopefulness, and vitality. Kaci offered the original impetus for this book when she told me to start writing down my thoughts on the subject. Apparently, I had a lot to say! Along the way, she has been encouraging and supportive in all of the ways that I needed, many that I noticed and many more that I did not. But I am grateful for all of them.

Series Introduction
Studies in Christian Doctrine and Scripture (SCDS)

DANIEL J. TREIER AND KEVIN VANHOOZER

THE STUDIES IN CHRISTIAN DOCTRINE and Scripture (SCDS) series attempts to reconcile two disciplines that should never have been divided: the study of Christian Scripture and the study of Christian doctrine. Old walls of disciplinary hostility are beginning to come down, a development that we hope will better serve the church. To that end, books in this series affirm the supreme authority of Scripture, seeking to read it faithfully and creatively as they develop fresh articulations of Christian doctrine. This agenda can be spelled out further in five claims.

1. We aim to publish constructive **contributions to systematic theology** rather than merely descriptive rehearsals of biblical theology, historical retrievals of classic or contemporary theologians, or hermeneutical reflections on theological method—volumes that are plentifully and expertly published elsewhere.

The initial impetus for the SCDS series came from supervising evangelical graduate students and seeking to encourage their pursuit of constructive theological projects shaped by the supremacy of Scripture. Existing publication venues demonstrate how rarely biblical scholars and systematic theologians trespass into each other's fields. Synthetic treatments of biblical theology garner publication in monograph series for biblical studies or evangelical biblical theology. A notable example is a companion series from IVP Academic, New Studies in Biblical Theology. Many of its volumes have theological significance, yet most are written by biblical scholars. Meanwhile, historical retrievals of theological figures garner publication in monograph series for historical and systematic theology. For instance, there have been entire series devoted to figures such as Karl Barth or the patristic era, and even series named for systematic theology tend to contain figure-oriented monographs.

The reason for providing an alternative publication venue is not to denigrate these valuable enterprises. Instead, the rationale for encouraging constructively evangelical projects is twofold and practical: The church needs such projects, and they form the theologians undertaking them. The church needs such projects, both addressing new challenges for her life in the world (such as contemporary political theology) and retrieving neglected concepts (such as the classic doctrine of God) in fresh ways. The church also needs her theologians not merely to develop detailed intellectual skills but also ultimately to wrestle with the whole counsel of God in the Scriptures.

2. We aim to promote **evangelical** contributions, neither retreating from broader dialogue into a narrow version of this identity on the one hand, nor running away from the biblical preoccupation of our heritage on the other hand.

In our initial volume, *Theology and the Mirror of Scripture*, we articulate this pursuit of evangelical renewal. We take up the well-known metaphor of mere Christianity as a hallway, with particular church traditions as the rooms in a house. Many people believe that the evangelical hallway is crumbling, an impression that current events only exacerbate. Our inspection highlights a few fragmenting factors such as more robust academic engagement, increased awareness of the Great Christian Tradition and the variety of evangelical subtraditions, interest in global Christianity, and interfaces with emergent Christianity and culture. Looking more deeply, we find historical-theological debates about the very definition of *evangelical* and whether it reflects—still, or ever—a shared gospel, a shared doctrine of God, and a theological method that can operationalize our shared commitment to Scripture's authority.

In response, prompted by James 1:22-25, our proposal develops the metaphor of a mirror for clarifying evangelical theology's relation to Scripture. The reality behind the mirror is the gospel of God and the God of the gospel: what is revealed in Christ. In disputes about whether to focus on a center or boundaries, it may seem as if evangelicalism has no doctrinal core. But we propose treating what is revealed in Christ—the triune God and the cross of Christ, viewed in the mirror of Scripture—as an evangelical anchor, a center with a certain range of motion. Still, it may seem as if evangelicalism has no hermeneutical coherence, as if interpretive anarchy nullifies biblical authority. But we propose treating Scripture as *canonical testimony*, a God-given mirror of truth that enables the church to reflect the wisdom that is in Christ. The holistic and contextual character of such wisdom gives theology a dialogic character, which requires an evangelical account of the church's catholicity. We need the wisdom to know the difference between church-destroying heresy, church-dividing disagreements that still permit evangelical fellowship, and intrachurch differences that require mutual admonition as well as forbearance.

Volumes in the SCDS series will not necessarily reflect the views of any particular editor, advisory board member, or the publisher—not even concerning "evangelical" boundaries. Volumes may approach perceived boundaries if their excellent engagement with Scripture deserves a hearing. But we are not seeking reform for reform's sake; we are more likely to publish volumes containing new explorations or presentations of traditional positions than radically revisionist proposals. Valuing the historic evangelical commitment to a deeply scriptural theology, we often find that perceived boundaries are appropriate—reflecting positions' biblical plausibility or lack thereof.

3. We seek fresh understanding of Christian doctrine **through creatively faithful engagement with Scripture**. To some fellow evangelicals and interested others today, we commend the classic evangelical commitment of *engaging Scripture*. To other fellow evangelicals today, we commend a contemporary aim to engage Scripture with *creative fidelity*. The church is to be always reforming—but always reforming according to the Word of God.

It is possible to acknowledge *sola Scriptura* in principle—Scripture as the final authority, the norming norm—without treating Scripture as theology's primary source. It is also possible to approach Scripture as theology's primary source in practice without doing that well.

The classic evangelical aspiration has been to mirror the form, not just the content, of Scripture as closely as possible in our theology. That aspiration has potential drawbacks: It can foster naive prooftexting, flatten biblical diversity, and stifle creative cultural engagement with a biblicist idiom. But we should not overreact to these drawbacks, falling prey to the temptation of paying mere lip service to *sola Scriptura* and replacing the Bible's primacy with the secondary idiom of the theologians' guild.

Thus in *Theology and the Mirror of Scripture* we propose a rubric for applying biblical theology to doctrinal judgments in a way that preserves evangelical freedom yet promotes the primacy of Scripture. At the ends of the spectrum, biblical theology can (1) rule out theological proposals that contradict scriptural judgments or cohere poorly with other concepts, and it can (5) require proposals that appeal to what is clear and central in Scripture. In between, it can (2) permit proposals that do not contradict Scripture, (3) support proposals that appeal creatively although indirectly or implicitly to Scripture, and (4) relate theological teaching to church life by using familiar scriptural language as much as possible. This spectrum offers considerable freedom for evangelical theology to mirror the biblical wisdom found in Christ with contextual creativity. Yet it simultaneously encourages evangelical theologians to reflect biblical wisdom not just in their judgments but also in the very idioms of their teaching.

4. We seek **fresh understanding of Christian doctrine**. We do not promote a singular method; we welcome proposals appealing to biblical theology, the history of interpretation, theological interpretation of Scripture, or still other approaches. We welcome projects that engage in detailed exegesis as well as those that appropriate broader biblical themes and patterns. Ultimately, we hope to promote relating Scripture to doctrinal understanding in material, not just formal, ways.

As noted above, the fresh understanding we seek may not involve altogether novel claims—which might well land in heresy! Again, in *Theology and the Mirror of Scripture* we offer an illustrative, nonexhaustive rubric for encouraging various forms of evangelical theological scholarship:

projects shaped primarily by (1) hermeneutics, (2) integrative biblical theology, (3) stewardship of the Great Tradition, (4) church dogmatics, (5) intellectual history, (6) analytic theism, (7) living witness, and (8) healing resistance. While some of these scholarly shapes probably fit the present series better than others, all of them reflect practices that can help evangelical theologians to make more faithfully biblical judgments and to generate more creatively constructive scholarship.

The volumes in the SCDS series will therefore reflect quite varied approaches. They will be similar in engaging one or more biblical texts as a key aspect of their contributions while going beyond exegetical recital or descriptive biblical theology, yet those biblical contributions themselves will be manifold.

5. We promote scriptural engagement **in dialogue with catholic tradition(s)**. A periodic evangelical weakness is relative lack of interest in the church's shared creedal heritage, in churches' particular confessions, and more generally in the history of dogmatic reflection. Beyond existing efforts to enhance understanding of themes and corpora in biblical theology, then, we hope to foster engagement with Scripture that bears on and learns from loci, themes, or crucial questions in classic dogmatics and contemporary systematic theology.

Series authors and editors will reflect several church affiliations and doctrinal backgrounds. Our goal is that such commitments would play a productive but not decisive hermeneutical role. Series volumes may focus on more generically evangelical approaches, or they may operate from within a particular tradition while engaging internal challenges or external objections.

We hope that both the diversity of our contributor list and the catholic engagement of our projects will continually expand. As important as those contextual factors are, though, these are most fundamentally studies in Christian *doctrine* and *Scripture*. Our goal is to promote and to publish constructive evangelical projects that study Scripture with creative fidelity and thereby offer fresh understanding of Christian doctrine. Various contexts and perspectives can help us study Scripture in that lively way, but they must remain secondary to theology's primary source and soul.

We do not study the mirror of Scripture for its own sake. Finding all the treasures of wisdom in Christ to be reflected there with the help of Christian doctrine, we come to know God and ourselves more truly. Thus encountering God's perfect instruction, we find the true freedom that is ours in the gospel, and we joyfully commend it to others through our own ministry of Scripture's teaching.

Abbreviations

ACW	Ancient Christian Writers. 1946–
ANF	*Ante-Nicene Fathers*. Edited by A. Roberts and J. Donaldson. Buffalo, 1885–1896. Reprint, Grand Rapids, 1975
BBR	*Bulletin for Biblical Research*
BDAG	Bauer, W., F. W. Danker, W. F. Arndt, and F. W. Gingrich. *Greek-English Lexicon of the New Testament and Other Early Christian Literature*. 3rd ed. Chicago, 1999
BDB	Brown, F., S. R. Driver, and C. A. Briggs. *A Hebrew and English Lexicon of the Old Testament with an Appendix Containing the Biblical Aramaic*. Oxford, 1977
BECNT	Baker Exegetical Commentary on the New Testament
CBQ	*Catholic Biblical Quarterly*
FC	Fathers of the Church. Washington, DC, 1947–
HTR	*Harvard Theological Review*
IJST	*International Journal of Systematic Theology*
JBL	*Journal of Biblical Literature*
LCC	Library of Christian Classics. Philadelphia, 1953–
LCL	Loeb Classical Library
LW	*Luther's Works*. Edited by J. Pelikan and H. T. Lehmann. 55 vols. St. Louis, 1955–1986
NAC	New American Commentary
NICNT	New International Commentary on the New Testament
NICOT	New International Commentary on the Old Testament

NPNF¹	*Nicene and Post-Nicene Fathers,* Series 1. Edited by Philip Schaff. New York, 1886–1890. Reprint, Peabody, MA, 1994
NPNF²	*Nicene and Post-Nicene Fathers,* Series 2. Edited by Philip Schaff and Henry Wace. New York, 1890. Reprint, Peabody, MA, 1994
NSC	National Safety Council
NZSTR	*Neue Zeitschrift für Systematische Theologie und Religionphilosophie*
OED	*Oxford English Dictionary*
SBET	*Scottish Bulletin of Evangelical Theology*
ST	*Summa Theologiae*
TNTC	Tyndale New Testament Commentaries
TWOT	*Theological Wordbook of the Old Testament.* Edited by R. L. Harris, G. L. Archer Jr., and B. K. Waltke. 2 vols. Chicago, 1999
WBC	Word Biblical Commentary
WSA	*Works of St. Augustine.* Edited by John E. Rotelle. Brooklyn, 1990–2009
ZTK	*Zeitschrift für Theologie und Kirche*

PART ONE

Signposts of Safety in the Modern Landscape

ONE

Tokens of Safety

If with Christ you died to the elemental spirits of the world, why, as if you were still alive in the world, do you submit to regulations—"Do not handle, Do not taste, Do not touch"?

COLOSSIANS 2:20-21

O**N A TRIP SEVERAL** years ago, my wife, Kaci, and I shuffled our three small children out to the front porch of a restaurant to find a table and wait for our food. Once the children were settled, I ran a quick errand a couple blocks away and returned to find them sitting just where I left them. Something was wrong, though. The kids were subdued, and Kaci looked like she had something she needed to say.

After I had left, our oldest son, Samuel—a preschooler at the time—said he needed to go to the bathroom. Kaci could not haul all three children and our bags to the bathroom by herself, so she told him to wait until I got back. Soon he needed to go "really bad," though, so she told him to go inside and ask to use the bathroom. He returned and said it was around back on the outside of the building. They waited for me again, but the situation only got worse. After some deliberation with herself, she finally told him to go use the bathroom and then come right back. He ran off in search of relief, and she sat waiting with the younger two. The seconds ticked by. A minute or two ticked by. She wondered how long it had been. She told herself not to worry. At any moment he would come back, or I would pull up. More time passed. He did not come. I still did not come. Suddenly, a sense of urgency came over her. It had been too long. She picked up the toddler, grabbed the stroller, abandoned the belongings, and made her way to the back of the building. As she got closer, she thought she could hear noises. Her pace quickened. When she rounded the corner, the noises became louder and distinct. He was yelling, pounding, and crying for help from inside the bathroom. Horrible thoughts flooded her mind as she raced to the door.

To her great relief he was unharmed and alone in the bathroom. He was yelling and pounding because the door was stuck, and he could not get out. He was sitting safely next to me as she recounted the story, but horrible thoughts flooded my mind as well when I heard that he had been calling for help from inside the bathroom. My fists clenched. For my wife in the moment and for me as I heard about it, we were briefly but powerfully seized by the fear of what our child's cries might have meant. The event was troubling, not so much because of what happened, but because of what could have been happening during those tense moments of separation.

Humanity is affected by the harm that befalls it. That is obvious. Humanity is also affected by the harm that could befall it, and that is fascinating. When harm comes—when a child has a complicated birth or falls off a bike, when a woman is assaulted or diagnosed with cancer, when a worker loses a finger or crashes heavy equipment—life is disrupted. Things no longer fit together as they should. Damaged bodies need healing, damaged belongings need fixing, and damaged hearts need mending. Areas of life once navigated with ease are now avoided or tiptoed through. Perhaps there is a hole where there used to be wholeness, fear where there used to be innocence, or regret where there used to be contentment. Conversely, perhaps there is strength where there used to be weakness, hope where there used to be fear, or courage where there used to be cowardice.

When harm could come—when parents imagine a complicated birth or a child almost falls off a bike, when a woman hears of an assault or a worker narrowly avoids an accident, when students learn of another school shooting or citizens look at the likelihood of war—life is also disrupted. Anxieties and suspicions rise. Dangerous people and places are avoided. Risks are assessed and managed. Warnings are given. Precautions are taken. Fates are cursed, and guardian angels are invoked. We try to anticipate all the various ways that harm could come, and we look back at all the ways that it could have come, but we do not know with certainty when or how it will in fact befall us. In the face of such uncertainty, it is not harm itself but the possibility and proximity of harm that affect our lives.

Signs and Symbols

The world we inhabit is scattered with tokens of safety. These tokens—the warnings, notices, slogans, and labels that have been so thoroughly incorporated into the modern landscape—exert authority over our lives, mediating our interactions with each other and the world around us. The tokens of safety function as signs. They point to dangers and give instruction on how to avoid them. They remind pedestrians to watch out for traffic, alert consumers to the dangers of devices, and tell children how play equipment is to be used. When you start your car, little lights and bells remind you to buckle up. When you plug in a new appliance, a small tag advises you on the dangers of electrocution. The plastic that the appliance was wrapped in advises you that it can suffocate children and pets. When passengers check in at airports, kindly voices prohibit them from leaving their baggage unattended and direct their hands to the railings on escalators. Signs at jobsite entrances show workers what protective equipment to wear. When you board a train, grab a cart at the grocery store, or engage in any number of everyday activities, you are encountered by such tokens of safety. They fill the spaces, surfaces, and silences of our world with a steady stream of reminders that while we may want summers to be fun, journeys to be successful, and encounters with strangers to be enjoyable, we also want them to be safe.

The tokens of safety also function as symbols. Beyond their explicit messages, they carry implicit meanings. They connect their observers to fundamental ideas and beliefs about the very nature of safety. As symbols, the tokens of safety are echoes of a deeper power, reminders of an underlying authority on which a morality of safety has been built. The importance of these tokens lies not merely in what they claim or demand regarding the practicalities of safety but in their very presence, what they assume and imply concerning humanity and its relationship to the dangers of this world. They point to the concerns and habits of safety, but also to the beliefs that legitimize those concerns and the powers supposed to make those habits effectual.

The tokens of safety draw attention to the enigmatic relationship we have with danger, and then offer ways out. They shape the way we think about safety. They set the terms of the discussion, the rules of engagement, and the boundaries of the field in advance. They tell us what safety is, where it is located, and how to pursue it. These tokens are not alien to the modern world, though, as if they were being imposed from elsewhere. They are themselves fruits of our age, and while they are typically produced and plastered about by authorities, institutions, and bureaucracies, each of us bears responsibility for the ways that we interact with them.

There are probably many people who do not give much thought to the tokens of safety. Such people just look past them or through them. The tokens are part of the scenery, nothing more than background noise in a busy world, little annoyances to ignore, get around, or placate in order to get on to better things. Such an attitude would have been difficult to maintain during the Covid-19 related mandates and restrictions of 2020 and 2021. Signs, barriers, masks, and enforcements sprung up everywhere. Participation was not optional. The tokens related to that virus reduced significantly in the years since, but the events surrounding them brought to light an enduring feature of the modern tokens of safety: they are intended, by those who post them, to be given their proper due. Safety is meant to be the business of everyone.

When people do give thought to the tokens of safety, they often acknowledge and submit to them simply as signs. They do so without much deliberation or critical reflection, being motivated by a basic desire for safety, a basic fear of danger. The announcement says to stay clear of the closing train doors, so they take a step. The arrows indicate a sharp curve in the road ahead, so they slow down. The sign says masks are required to slow the spread of the disease, so they put them on.

There are times, though, when people engage with the tokens of safety as more than signs, more than basic sources of information or instruction for navigating dangers in this world. The tokens, and people's responses to them, take on symbolic significance. Sometimes, when the warning comes on about the train doors, a commuter who is already clear can be seen taking an additional and emphatic step. Sometimes a safety officer has more regard for his authority than the well-being of his workers. Sometimes violating the demands of these tokens is an act of selfish obstinance. At other times, it is a triumph of sanity and wisdom. Sometimes submission to the tokens of safety is an exercise in superstition. At other times, it is a calculated means of self-justification.

A utility worker parked his truck, half on the shoulder, half in the lane, of a rural highway, in order to perform repairs during an ice storm. On his side of the road were a ditch, utility poles, and a field. On the other side, a row of houses. He had stopped his truck in a blind spot, at the crest of a hill. Video footage showed the chaos that followed. Cars were sliding one way, hitting the ditch. They were sliding the other way, through front yards. Still more were spinning, skidding, and crashing into each other. He was in the wrong place. He was being dangerous. But when motorists pleaded with him to move, he coldly explained that he was acting in accordance with policy. His yellow warning lights were on, and he had put up hazard signals at the required distances. He insisted that if other people were harmed, it was their fault, not his.

I was at a campground with family and friends once, and on the morning of our departure, a park ranger came by and reminded me that the fire needed to be put out. I thanked him and he started to leave, but then hesitated, returned with a shovel, and started putting the dying embers out himself. After the fire was extinguished, after all the embers had been repeatedly dug up and smothered, he continued stabbing and stirring the ash and dirt for an astonishingly long time. People often think a fire is out when the embers are still hot underneath. One small spark can set an entire forest ablaze. The signs say to put fires out—dead out. It is better to go beyond that point than to stop short of it. I thought about all these things as he stirred and talked. The fire was far past death, but he continued on. As he did, his actions changed from the focused movements of a man accomplishing a task to the exaggerated gestures of a man proving a point. His fire-safety speech had become repetitive and tired, and his attitude toward us had become rude and condescending. When he finally gave his shovel a rest, he had long since stopped putting out a fire.

My daughter Annie spent the first half of one of her school years sitting in classrooms and walking down hallways with crowds of other middle schoolers who were all required to wear masks in order to "stop the spread of Covid." The masks came off frequently. They regularly sat below the nose or sagged beneath the chin. Students spent maskless hours together after school. If there was any chance that those masks could have reduced the spread of a respiratory virus, the behaviors of the children ensured they would do no such thing. Once the school district could no longer compel masks, Annie stopped wearing one. She showed up to one of her classes. It was deep winter. The teacher opened the windows, made any maskless students sit under them, and told the class to start bringing winter coats if they got cold. The actual spread of the virus in that teacher's classroom over the previous months, the question of how much harm it may have caused, the level of effectiveness of masks in that school, as well as the goodness of being kind to others—all those things were overwhelmed by this teacher's zeal for one particular token of safety.

Perhaps you disagree with my characterizations of these different scenarios. An interesting feature of conversations about safety is the ease with which they can turn in one direction or another, take on one mood or another. You may find yourself in a conversation in which safety is looked on as an enemy. It is a hindrance, a nuisance, an object of ridicule and contempt. The long procession through airport security checkpoints is intrusive, demeaning, and overwrought, an elaborate inconvenience for millions of travelers that should be replaced with focused, investigative security work. There is so much concern about the safety of children that they grow up not knowing the adventure of exploring the world around them, never allowed to take risks, never growing through pain and failure, never learning how to get out of a tough situation or find their way home after getting lost. The long-winded script read by passionless attendants while handing rental equipment over to customers is infantile and clearly given to satisfy the wishes of lawyers, not to aid in the use of the equipment. When a mother, who is recognized and well-known, comes to pick up her child from the church nursery, but is not allowed to because she cannot find the voucher given at check-in, the whole situation feels just a bit ridiculous. These types of conversations draw attention to the numerous ways that our efforts to keep ourselves alive suck the life out of us, the ways that safety measures often turn out to be unnecessary, ineffective, and even harmful.

Other conversations focus on the preciousness and value of what is at stake, the magnitude of the tragedy if a worst-case-scenario became a reality, the small price of safety in contrast to the great cost of its neglect, and the regularity with which it is effective. Most car trips end well, without a crash or the need for seatbelts, but it is good to buckle them every time because you never know when one of those trips will be cut short by an accident. Children naturally like to run around and explore, but safeguards need to be in place because they are unaware of the dangers they may face and because of how devastating it would be if something horrible, no matter how small the chance, happened to one of them. The procedures in the church nursery may seem redundant and may cause inconveniences at times, but how would a church body recover if a child was somehow taken? Modern industrial jobsites are complex and dangerous. Employers have a responsibility to adequately train their employees on the dangers and protocols of the jobsite and to make sure they are aware of the hazards that surround them.

I was talking recently with another father about safety, and the conversation went in both of these directions. He was involved with safety compliance at nuclear power plants, so he was familiar with both the devastation that could come if things went wrong and the aggravations that can accompany bureaucratic redundancies. We talked about our desires for our children to be strong, skillful, and competent. We talked about the various ways that our society, supposedly for the welfare of children, sabotages their attainment of these virtues. As we discussed the benefits that could come with giving children additional freedoms, he told me about a news story he had just heard in which a little girl disappeared from a park while her parents and friends were nearby. Her bike was found on the path, but she was gone. What if you gave your child some additional freedom, the chance to ride off a little ways by herself, and then something like this happened? Our conversation faltered. She was thankfully found a couple days later, but we did not know that at the time. It could have turned out differently. Perhaps he and I had been too cavalier in our earlier pronouncements. Perhaps it is just not worth it to allow your child to be alone in a park. But then we remembered all of the children in all of the parks, and all of the times that they safely play and roam and explore. The tokens of safety point to mundane matters of life, yet those matters evoke potent reactions and confound simplistic reasoning.

Why a Theology of Safety

Safety has a prominent place in our lives, but we often accept its influence uncritically. This is so in everyday activities—travel, business, industry, education—but also in the life and mission of the church. Christ calls his followers to die to themselves, take up their crosses, and follow him. He calls his church to walk in submission to his Word, make disciples of all nations, care for the least of these, and demonstrate love among its members and toward outsiders. The church has many dangers to navigate as it does these things. In fact, navigating the dangers of this world in a way that is faithful, hopeful, and honoring to God is itself one of the things the church is called to do.

The church has long known that it would face danger and harm as it fulfilled its mission. Jesus said so. Persecutions, tribulations, and martyrdom come from without; attacks, compromises, and betrayals from within. Amid such threats, though, there are missionaries to be sent to foreign lands, churches to be planted in new cities, and aid to be brought to areas of poverty and disaster. There are the vulnerable, sick, and weak to be cared for. There is malice and exploitation to be rooted out, times when those who ought to keep others safe are themselves dangerous, manipulative, and abusive. There are also youth events that need supervision, congregants with food allergies who need to be served the Lord's Supper, and church vans that need maintenance. All for the sake of Christ.

When I was a youth pastor in Arizona, I canceled a week-long mission trip to Mexico because of concerns within the church about travel warnings related to drug violence in Mexico. The small town where we were planning to serve was peaceful and calm, but we still decided not to go. Instead, I put together a last-minute trip to Los Angeles. While we were there, we served at a rescue mission surrounded by drug use, theft, drunkenness, and prostitution. We walked through neighborhoods rife with drug distribution and violence. We were much closer to a variety of dangers than we would have been in Mexico. The trip to Los Angeles turned out very well, and I still chuckle at the irony of it all, but as I look back, I wish I had been better prepared to work through that decision and the concerns involved. When Covid-19 hit, many churches were similarly ill-equipped, and as anyone involved in the life and mission of the church knows, other scenarios like these will arise and demand responses from us.

This world is filled with manmade rules and regulations that have "an appearance of wisdom" but offer no help in "stopping the indulgence of the flesh" (Col 2:23). A person's efforts to procure safety are not necessarily indulgences of the flesh, but the tokens of safety, with their strong warnings and clear imperatives, are often invitations for the flesh to indulge itself, while also justifying the indulgence. They appear to be the opposite. They appear to offer opportunities for caution, discipline, and self-control: "Do not handle, Do not taste, Do not touch" (Col 2:21). But the flesh, that residue of corruption, pride, and godlessness that abides in each of us, feeds on acute fears and vague worries, ascetic rigors and easy promises. It does not want to be bound to Christ or nourished by him, so it is held captive by "the elemental spirits of the world" (Col 2:20)—those dark powers that leverage the basic human desire for safety against the weakness of the flesh. The flesh is unsound and treacherous. The flesh compromises. It sells its birthright for a bowl of fleeting comfort. It does not wait. It does not trust. It does not hope. It is not a reliable guide to follow. Yet, we repeatedly listen to it and feed it in our pursuits of safety.

Therefore, the church would benefit from a clear understanding of what Scripture teaches about safety, danger, risk, and security and from firm convictions about how to live, worship, gather, and serve while facing possibilities of harm with hope, joy, and thankfulness. There is a pressing need for clear theological reflection and courageous moral deliberation on safety. Toward those ends, I will seek to develop a Christian theology of safety. I want to look at the dangers that the tokens of safety signify, but more importantly, the ideas that they symbolize. I want to follow these tokens to the fundamental conceptions of safety that lie behind them and consider what is found in light of the lordship of Christ and the fatherly care of God. Our conversations about safety, as well as our thoughts, affections, decisions, and actions, are too often guided by fleshly insecurity and worldly boastfulness. They need to be tethered to the Word of God.

Safety has to do with humanity's condition in this world, its capacities, limitations, strengths, and frailties in a world of splendor and danger, a world that both sustains and destroys life. God has endowed humanity with creaturely capacities effective in the avoidance of harm. Humankind is given dominion over creation. It can anticipate the future and shape the surrounding world. But there are limitations. The future is neither entirely clear nor entirely opaque. The world is neither entirely controllable nor entirely chaotic. Sin strains humanity's relationship with the world. Creation is a means of God's blessings but also of his judgments. Sin also distorts humanity's perception of its condition and standing in this world. John Calvin has famously said that true wisdom "consists of two parts: the knowledge of God and of ourselves."[1] To this may be added the hope that true wisdom, as bestowed through God's redemptive work in Christ, would also lead to the knowledge of creation not only as the theater of God's glory, but also as the arena of human life. For it is here, in this world, between the anticipated and actual future, between intention and result, that attempts are made to navigate a favorable path through the dangers that confront us.

Safety is a legitimate desire, but it is pursued on ground that has been cursed by God. Sometimes we can avoid harm. Sometimes it overwhelms us. Sometimes small dangers are greatly feared while great dangers are carelessly ignored. Sometimes complex dangers are easily avoided while simple dangers cause confusion and harm. The legitimate desire for safety as a creational good often becomes an idolatrous desire for safety as an ultimate good. Therefore, safety's relative worth must be viewed in comparison to the supreme value of walking with Christ, and humanity's sinful tendency to misjudge its relationship with danger must be acknowledged. Safety in this world must be considered in its proper place, in right relation to other good things, as well as to dangers that are of a spiritual and eternal nature.

Our world is filled with tokens of safety. It is also filled with reminders of all that could go wrong, all the areas of life where threats press in on us and fears rise up within us. By far, the most common question other Christians have asked me regarding safety has been whether we should be safe or trust God: "Should I keep walking my daughter to school or let her walk alone

---

[1] John Calvin, *Institutes of the Christian Religion*, ed. John T. McNeill, trans. Ford Lewis Battles, LCC 20-21 (Philadelphia: Westminster John Knox, 1960), I.1.1, p. 35.

and trust God to protect her?"; "Do we really need all these provisions before we begin? Shouldn't we move forward and trust God to supply?"; "I know I should trust God to take care of my husband when he's away, but is it ok that I feel better when I can see where he is?"; "When should I just have faith, and when should I be wise?"

The problem with these questions is that having faith and being wise are not opposites. Neither are being safe and trusting God, nor being in danger and trusting God. You can trust God when you walk your daughter to school, and you can trust him when you send her out the door on her own. You can trust God when he protects you, and you can trust him when he does not. You can trust him when he gives, and when he takes away. Seeking for safety in conformance to the pattern of this world, as a means of indulging the flesh, or as an exercise in worry—those are the opposite of trusting God. But if we trust him whole-heartedly, if we place our lives in his hands, come what may, if we remember that he has seated us with Christ in the heavenly places, then we would find much clarity, simplicity, and freedom in our use of the things he provides for our protection and security. We will not see each situation with perfect clarity, and there may be more than one acceptable way to handle any given situation. There may also be times when danger and harm are unavoidable. Roughly speaking, though, there are instances in which we ought to make use of the means of safety that God provides, other instances in which we are free to use or not use means of safety, and some instances in which we ought to let go of the means of safety for the sake of Christ and the work he calls us to do. However we handle the dangers that we face, "Each one should be fully convinced in his own mind" (Rom 14:5), and whatever we do as we encounter danger in this world should be done with thankfulness to God.

As I develop a theological account of safety, I will look into some historical questions: How did safety become so pervasive in the late-modern world? Why is it pursued in the ways that it is pursued? I will also look into some ethical questions: How should the church engage with the world's pursuit of safety? To what extent should the church affirm, encourage, and participate in this pursuit? To what extent does Christ reshape the church's understanding of safety and how it is pursued?

The above questions are raised, and their answers will be developed against the backdrop of the industrialized, modernized world. Yet, this theology of safety is further motivated and shaped by Christianity's answers to questions concerning the nature of human existence in God's creation. Life in this world is shaped by God's initial work of creation and humanity's subsequent fall, as well as God's work of redemption in Christ and its coming consummation. Theological reflection on humanity's relationship to the dangers of this world harkens back to the lost safety of Eden and points forward to the unshakable safety of the new creation, but it also draws attention to safety's present tenuousness.

Questions about why safety has become so important and why it is pursued in particular ways are answered, in part, by paying attention to the reasons, arguments, and justifications given by those involved in the pursuit. Therefore, I will interact with works on safety, risk, and related topics from various fields of study. Some of these sources offer perceptive critiques of late-modern humanity's pursuit of safety. Their overall arguments are inadequate, though, inasmuch as they attempt to understand humanity and its condition in this world apart from any acknowledgment of God, apart from any recognition that this world is his creation or that Christ is its Lord.

In recent years, a number of theologians have used risk as a central idea in their understanding of God.[2] These theologians typically reject the teachings that God fully knows the future or that he established a definite course for the world to follow. Instead, they say that God took a risk in creating the world, opening himself up to both intimacy and suffering. A risk-taking view of God then serves as a basis for understanding human risk. The future is not certain for God, so it is not certain for us either. We should be hopeful, though, and open ourselves up to risk because of the blessings that may come, even through suffering and wounds. A theology of safety is located at the intersection of the doctrines of humanity, creation, and God.

---

[2]Representative works include Niels Henrik Gregersen, "Risk and Religion: Toward a Theology of Risk Taking," *Zygon* 38 (2003): 355-76; John Sanders, *The God Who Risks: A Theology of Divine Providence*, 2nd ed. (Downers Grove, IL: InterVarsity Press, 2007); and Clark H. Pinnock et al., *The Openness of God: A Biblical Challenge to the Traditional Understanding of God* (Downers Grove, IL: InterVarsity Press, 1994). See Mikkel Gabriel Christoffersen, "Living with Risk and Danger: Studies in Interdisciplinary Systematic Theology" (PhD diss., Copenhagen: University of Copenhagen, 2017), 15, who lists Niels Gregersen, John Sanders, William Vanstone, Günter Thomas, Sharon Welch, and Karen Baker Fletcher among these "theologians of risk."

Why are human bodies so vulnerable to external forces? To what extent can humanity anticipate and shape the future? Why has God placed humanity, as such creatures, in such a world? Does he care about the dangers we face? Will he keep us safe? Answers to these types of questions will be sought, not by following the idea that God take risks, but with the confession that he rules supremely over all things. I will approach these doctrines from a broadly Reformed perspective, grounded in classical doctrines of God and divine providence, along with the affirmation that he is not vulnerable to but sovereign over the dangers of this world: "Who is this who comes from Edom, in crimsoned garments from Bozrah, he who is splendid in his apparel, marching in the greatness of his strength? 'It is I, speaking in righteousness, mighty to save'" (Is 63:1).

When reading the Bible in order to develop a theology of safety, a number of passages stand out because they address practical matters of safety. There are laws about ox gorings, infectious diseases, accidental deaths, and fall protection (Ex 21:28-32; Lev 13; Deut 19:4-6, 22:8). There are numerous admonitions to care for others in dangerous situations (e.g., Deut 24:21, Eph 4:28, Jas 1:27). Scripture has much more to say about safety, though, because it addresses fundamental themes regarding humanity and its standing before God in this world. Therefore, I will engage with passages that address matters of safety directly, as well as many that address these key theological themes. The dogmatic content of the Christian faith should shape the church's understanding of safety. Throughout this work, then, I appeal to Scripture as the authoritative revelation of humanity's condition in this world before God and of Christ's headship over all things. In other words, the Bible speaks to the matter today, and what it says is relevant and authoritative to all who desire safety in this world.

Signposts of Safety in the Modern Landscape

The tokens of safety are signposts. They point to a way forward in the pursuit of safety, and they point to the ideas and assumptions at the heart of that pursuit. Throughout this work, I will draw out those ideas and assumptions in order to consider how Christians should relate to the world's pursuit of safety. Two prominent features of safety today are its modernized form and elevated status. I will describe these features in the next chapter, the second half of part one. The concepts of risk and safety have become quite prevalent in our world today. They are used in all sorts of situations and for thinking about all sorts of things. As I describe the current form and status of safety, I will set the focus of this study on physical safety, while affirming its relevance for wider conceptions of safety, risk, security, and danger.

Sources of Danger Through the Ages

Safety is everywhere in our world. That is easy to see. But since safety is so prevalent, it is difficult to evaluate. It is hard to see the unique characteristics of safety today. In part two, in order to gain a fresh perspective on something that surrounds us every day, I will trace the historical development of the concept of risk through its premodern, early modern, and late-modern phases. The trajectory of this development begins with premodern humanity viewing the gods or other spiritual powers as the primary sources of danger, then moves to early modern humanity viewing nature as the primary source of danger, and concludes with late-modern humanity viewing itself as the primary source of danger. I will follow this story about the sources of danger through the ages, offering historical and theological criticisms along the way. The overall shape of this story is helpful in understanding how people today conceive of safety, but its fundamental flaw is that it takes itself to be a story of progress, getting closer and closer to the true essence of risk, instead of recognizing that throughout all of history humankind is in danger because of its estrangement from God and therefore from all three of these sources—itself, natural powers, and spiritual forces.

Avoiding Harm in a Fallen World

A basic image used in Scripture to describe human existence in this world, especially in its inescapably ethical quality, is that of a path traveled: "You shall walk after the Lord your God" (Deut 13:4); "Walk in the way of insight" (Prov 9:6); "Follow me" (Mt 9:9). When life is conceived in this way, time, the world, and the mobility of the one traveling present themselves as its three essential ingredients. Time provides a *when* for human existence. Life moves forward as the future opens up and the past closes in. The world provides a *where* for human existence. Life moves through creation, in dynamic relation to other people, creatures, and things. The *who* of human existence is given in the action and agency of the one traveling. Life moves forward in conjunction with the movements of the one who is walking.[3] Taken together, these three ingredients—time, creation, and action—provide a helpful recipe for theological engagement with safety. In the modern world, safety is pursued probabilistically in relation to time, technologically in relation to creation, and procedurally in relation to action.

Therefore, in part three, I will engage with the probabilistic, technological, and procedural tools of contemporary safety. These tools reflect humanity's God-given capacities to anticipate the future, shape the material world, and act purposefully, but those capacities, when not submitted to the lordship of Christ, become presumptuous overextensions of humanity's proper place in this world. Humanity relies on probabilistic predictions, but the future is seen rightly in light of the promises of God. As the ant in Proverbs 6:6-11 and the ravens and lilies in Luke 12:22-31 show, Christ calls his church to engage with the uncertainties of the future through faithful preparation apart from fruitless anxiety.

Technology is a form of power, a way to order the world. Dangers are anticipated probabilistically and then controlled technologically. A canonical study of the biblical phrase "work of one's hands" will contrast creation as the work of God's hands with technological devices and idols as the works of human hands. In the late-modern world, humanity's engagement with the material world is rarely explicit idolatry but it is frequently idolatrous. Humanity orders creation technologically in pursuit of safety, but it often does so without acknowledging that this world, in both its original creation and coming renewal, is ordered by Christ.

Probabilistic predictions and technological manipulations work best when related human behaviors are controlled and consistent.[4] Proceduralism seeks to guide human action down predetermined paths by anticipating problems and making decisions beforehand. Such an approach to

---

[3]These components are featured in the title and content of Oliver O'Donovan, *Self, World, and Time: Ethics as Theology, Volume 1, An Induction* (Grand Rapids, MI: Eerdmans, 2013). O'Donovan begins by asking what "practical reasoning" can tell us "of God, who stands behind and before our agency, and of our position in his world and time" (1). He later says that practical reasoning answers these questions as it "looks for a word that makes attention to the world intelligible, a word that will maintain the coherence and intelligence of the world as it finds its way through it, a word of God" (12).
[4]Brian Brock, *Christian Ethics in a Technological Age* (Grand Rapids, MI: Eerdmans, 2010), 72.

human action, as employed in the contemporary pursuit of safety, is limited by its inability to anticipate all dangers, its own susceptibility to accidents, and its reluctance to extend forgiveness. In contrast, the Mosaic law contains both instruction to avoid inadvertent harm and means of forgiveness when it happens, while Ecclesiastes 10:8-11 points to the advantage that wisdom affords in humanity's engagement with dangerous activities.

Living and Dying Under the Lordship of Christ

The arguments developed in part three on how God's people should engage with the world's pursuit of safety are based implicitly on the theme of discipleship. I will develop that theme in part four. Into a world where safety holds such an elevated status, the words of Christ echo loudly: "Whoever would save his life will lose it, but whoever loses his life for my sake and the gospel's will save it" (Mk 8:35). These words follow his call to discipleship: "If anyone would come after me, let him deny himself and take up his cross and follow me" (Mk 8:34). The path that Christ calls us to navigate through this world full of dangers is the one that follows him to the cross, but with the hope of life on the other side.

I will explore what it means to subject the demands of safety to the lordship of Christ. His teachings on discipleship provide a lens on the Christian life that highlights how all Christians should face today in light of his present and coming reign. When the seemingly radical commands of Christ are contrasted with the seemingly reasonable demands of safety, it turns out that Christ, not safety, guides us on a path of prudence and wisdom. The contemporary pursuit of safety is more of a defensive attempt to avoid harm than an active effort to pursue life. Discipleship is a pursuit of life by way of the cross. Christ calls his disciples to follow him in "delivering up" their lives, a key concept in the New Testament that will be explored in detail. Christ then gives wholeness, freedom, and life through fellowship with himself.

I will conclude by considering the proper place that safety should have in our lives. After the symbols of safety have been demystified, after the light of the Word of God has shone on the deeper powers behind the tokens of safety, the weaknesses of the world's pursuit of safety are laid bare. It lacks the conceptual capacity to acknowledge the spiritual realities of our world, it fails to recognize the constancy of humanity's vulnerabilities in this age, and it is thwarted by its own inherent limitations. Jesus is a more trustworthy guide through the dangers of this world.

Discipleship is a fitting theme for theological engagement with the pursuit of safety. Christ's juxtaposition of those who lose their lives with those who save them brings into sharp focus the ultimate futility of safety apart from him, while also presenting a clear path to life. He speaks of saving or losing one's life in relation to the physical condition of the body. He talks about suffering and death, denying oneself, and bearing one's cross. He speaks of rejection and shame. He speaks of gaining the whole world, whatever good things we may want in life. In so doing, he includes other aspects of safety along with the physical—social, relational, emotional, etc.—in the saving of one's life. But Christ contrasts all of this, all that can be gained or lost regarding the "things of man" with what can be gained regarding the "things of God": one's life and the vision of the kingdom of God.[5]

Discipleship is also a fitting theme because of its comprehensiveness. The demands of contemporary safety lack any pretense of modesty. They meet us in our inward thoughts and desires. They meet us in our hopes and anxieties, in our plans, memories, and intentions. They meet us in our outward behaviors, conversations, and interactions with others, in the structures, traditions, systems, and powers of this world. The pursuit of safety is a total pursuit, a way of life, a state of mind. But however extensive the pursuit of safety may be, however far its demands may reach, the call of Jesus is deeper and wider. Discipleship encompasses all those areas of life. Christ claims lordship over each of them. His voice is present, confronting the demands of safety wherever they may be found, even to the point of death and beyond. Death sets a hard limit on the pursuit of safety. Death is the very thing that safety promises to help us avoid, but when it comes—and it does come—safety's weaknesses and limitations are exposed. Christ's call of discipleship extends unashamedly through the doorway of death. He promises victory over it, not merely its avoidance or delay.

---

[5]The observations in this paragraph are based on Mk 8:31–9:1.

TWO

The Form and Status of Safety Today

> *"Safety first" is burned in our brains so that it is always "Safety first" and not second or third or fourth or last, but always safety first, then we do things.*
>
> R.C. Richards,
> First Co-operative Safety Congress

SAFETY TODAY HAS A particular *form*, one that bears the hallmarks of modernity. It is thought about and pursued in certain ways. Safety is commonly viewed today as mechanistic protection from physical harm or material loss.[1] It is shaped by the early modern hopes of grasping the future probabilistically, mastering creation technologically, and guiding human action procedurally. While the form of safety today is also shaped by late-modern uncertainties about things like the true nature of safety, differing perceptions of risk, and whether dangers can actually be conquered, it retains its probabilistic, technological, and procedural character. In other words, when confronted by danger, people today look to things like statistical models, technological devices, and behavioral restraints to find safety: eat fish to reduce the probability of a heart attack; wear this watch to track your sleep patterns; do not take strollers on escalators.

---

[1] See Carl Craver and James Tabery, "Mechanisms in Science," in *The Stanford Encyclopedia of Philosophy*, ed. Edward N. Zalta, November 18, 2015, https://plato.stanford.edu/archives/sum2019/entries/science-mechanisms. The term "mechanism" (or "mechanical philosophy") refers to a "mechanistic framework" with roots going back to Descartes that seeks to understand "the basic causal forces in the world." According to this view, scientific research can be described as the search for causal mechanisms, or the unknown connection between phenomena and their causes.

The observation that safety has taken this form may come across as unremarkable. How else would safety be conceived but as human control of the physical world? How else would it be pursued? The human desire to control the physical world is nothing new, of course, but the contemporary form of safety—with its probabilistic, technological, and procedural aspects—is a relatively recent development. It is part of modern humanity's relationship to the world in general and should not be overlooked or uncritically assumed simply because of its current prevalence and familiarity.

Safety also has an elevated moral *status*. In the early 1940s, German philosopher Ludwig Marcuse observed that safety is "the real obsession of an age which is not very obsessed at all." He says that earlier generations were enraptured by ideals such as "liberty and the pursuit of happiness"—with all the entailing uncertainties—but that the place once held by those ideals is now occupied by safety.[2] In an era typified by the lack of a cohesive moral framework, safety is something of an unquestioned, and therefore unifying, virtue. Its unifying power can be seen in the pervasiveness and homogeneity of the tokens of safety across all spheres of life. Safety has an authoritative ethical place in our world, influencing how we make decisions, interact with creation, respond to hardship, and relate with each other. Declaring something unsafe is generally equivalent to declaring it wrong. Safety has a distinctly modern form, but because of its elevated moral status, it is also pursued with a high level of stringency. There is a strong desire to see modernity's probabilistic, technological, and procedural hopes deliver on their promises. There is a widespread expectation that the demands of safety ought to be satisfied and disapproval when they are ignored. Those who do not fulfill safety's demands have done something taboo.[3]

When someone steps out of line, others will often intervene. On a family bike ride, my daughter Annie got ahead of us and disappeared around a corner in the bike path. She was not distressed or harmed in any way. She was happily pedaling, but when we caught up, a man was stopped next to her asking if she was ok, if she knew where she was, if she needed help.

---

[2] Ludwig Marcuse, *Das Märchen von der Sicherheit* (Zürich: Diogenes, 1981), 24.

[3] According to the cultural theory of risk, the categories of safety and risk function similarly to religious taboos, as mechanisms "for social categorization and division," instructing on which behaviors are acceptable and which are not. See Åsa Boholm, *Anthropology and Risk* (New York: Routledge, 2015), 75. I agree with this comparison, contra Boholm, who is critical of it.

Apparently, it was too dangerous for her to be on that bike path, so he stepped in. In another scenario, a mother of young children left them in the car while she went into a store to pick something up at the counter. While she was gone, someone noticed the children, the police were called, and a small crowd gathered around the car to make sure nothing troubling happened and to confront the mother when she returned. The children were frightened. There was probably a greater likelihood of harm traversing back and forth through the parking lot, but that did not matter. It was unacceptable for them to be in the car without their mother. When Child Protective Services visited their home, the children were further confused and frightened. And Lenore Skenazy was famously dubbed "Worst Mom in America" because she let her nine-year-old son ride the New York subway home by himself.[4]

The topics of safety and risk—especially risk—have gained notable standing in several academic fields. A distinction can be made between research that uses the conceptual tools of safety and risk in its engagement with other issues and research that critically engages with the conceptual tools of safety and risk.[5] Literature that makes use of safety and risk in its engagement with other issues is ubiquitous and can be taken as evidence of safety's elevated status in our culture. The array of literature that critically engages with the conceptual tools of safety and risk is narrower and part of "a distinct body of thought" that has developed in recent centuries related to "the academic study of risk."[6]

The concept of risk has gained a tremendous amount of traction in the late-modern age, so much so that there is a desire not only to understand risk or safety in light of the developments of modernity, but also to understand the developments of modernity in light of the concept of risk. Economist Peter Bernstein says that the "mastery of risk" is the "revolutionary idea that defines the boundary between modern times and the past,"[7] and

---

[4]Lenore Skenazy, *Free-Range Kids: How to Raise Safe, Self-Reliant Children* (San Francisco: Jossey-Bass, 2010), xvi.
[5]Matthias Beck and Beth Kewell speak of a similar distinction while rightly acknowledging the difficulty of drawing "precise boundaries around writings or intellectual developments that are primarily about risk and those where risk and uncertainty are peripheral." Matthias Beck and Beth Kewell, *Risk: A Study of Its Origins, History and Politics* (Hackensack, NJ: World Scientific, 2014), 11-12.
[6]Beck and Kewell, *Risk*, vii.
[7]Peter L. Bernstein, *Against the Gods: The Remarkable Story of Risk* (New York: Wiley, 1998), 1.

sociologist Ulrich Beck employs the idea of a "risk society," not primarily to develop a late-modern understanding of risk, but rather to understand late modernity itself by means of the concept of risk. He then raises the question: "Can the concept of risk carry the theoretical and historical significance which is demanded of it here?" The answer for many, including Beck, is yes.[8] Social anthropologist Åsa Boholm says that the concept of risk has become so prevalent in the late-modern age that it is "taken to be universally relevant: it is applicable to anything and everything of human concern."[9] Safety and risk may be applicable to all that is under the sun, but it will be helpful in further understanding the form and status of safety today to clarify what I mean by *safety* and other related concepts.

ABSOLUTE AND ORDINARY SAFETY

Within theology and philosophy, there are various forms of the idea that a person can be safe in a way that goes beyond bodily experience. Ludwig Wittgenstein describes "the experience of feeling *absolutely* safe" as "the state of mind in which one is inclined to say 'I am safe, nothing can injure me whatever happens.'" Such absolute safety, he says, "has been described by saying that we feel safe in the hands of God."[10] Socrates says that "a good man cannot suffer any evil either in life or after death."[11] Søren Kierkegaard says that the world, in all its strength, "can no more punish an innocent one than it can put a dead person to death."[12] The idea of safety in spite of bodily

---

[8]Ulrich Beck, *Risk Society: Towards a New Modernity*, trans. Mark Ritter (London: Sage, 1992), 10-20. Beck says, "In the nineteenth century, privileges of rank and religious world views were being demystified; today the same is happening to the understanding of science and technology in the classical industrial society, as well as to the modes of existence in work, leisure, the family and sexuality" (*Risk Society*, 10). Later he says, "To the extent that this transition [to a risk society] occurs, there will be a real transformation of society which will lead us out of the previous modes of thought and action" (*Risk Society*, 20). Eckart Conze says that safety (*Sicherheit*) is not a mere value, but has become the basis for an entire socio-cultural system of values. Eckart Conze, "Sicherheit als Kultur. Überlegungen zu einer 'modernen Politikgeschichte' der Bundesrepublik Deutschland," *Vierteljahrshefte für Zeitgeschichte* 53 (2005): 362.
[9]Boholm, *Anthropology and Risk*, 6.
[10]Ludwig Wittgenstein, "A Lecture on Ethics," *The Philosophical Review* 74 (1965): 8-10, italics his.
[11]Plato, *Apology*, trans. Harold North Fowler, LCL 36 (Cambridge, MA: Harvard University Press, 1914), 41.
[12]Søren Kierkegaard, *Purity of Heart Is to Will One Thing*, trans. Douglas V. Steere (New York: Fontana Books, 1961), 85. These quotations by Wittgenstein, Socrates, and Kierkegaard, along with similar quotes by William Shakespeare and Mark Twain are brought together in Peter Winch, "Can a Good Man Be Harmed?," *Proceedings of the Aristotelian Society* 66 (1965): 55-70.

experience or historical circumstance is found in Scripture as well: "Though our outer self is wasting away, our inner self is being renewed day by day" (2 Cor 4:16). In fact, the teaching that the troubles and dangers of this world cannot separate the believer from the love of Christ is a central hope of the Christian faith (Rom 8:35).

In contrast to absolute safety, there is also the ordinary safety of everyday life. Ordinary safety is not detached from bodily experiences and historical circumstances. It is defined by them. Wittgenstein distinguishes between absolute safety and "what it means in ordinary life to be safe." He says of ordinary safety, "I am safe in my room, when I cannot be run over by an omnibus. I am safe if I have had whooping cough and cannot therefore get it again."[13]

Ordinary safety, the safety of traffic, bacteria, and other such things, will be the focus of this study. Such safety is theologically important in its own right and ought to be explored in a way that properly relates it to inner tranquility or the hope of eternal salvation, but without subsuming it under such categories as absolute or eternal safety. The psalmist boldly asks, "What can man do to me?" (Ps 56:11), and Jesus warns not to fear those who kill the body, but rather "him who can destroy both soul and body in hell" (Mt 10:28). Such passages keep ordinary safety in proper perspective in relation to matters of God's coming judgment and the present comfort he gives to those who trust in him. But matters of ordinary safety are not lost from sight. Before asking his bold question, the psalmist laments his dangers and recounts his anguish (Ps 56:1-8). After saying not to fear those who can kill the body, Jesus gives a reminder that every hair on our heads is numbered by God (Mt 10:30). Therefore, the killing of the body or, in less extreme instances, the damaging of the body will be considered in light of Christ's warning about the destruction of the soul, but also in light of God's present care for his children.

Physical Safety and Other Kinds

Ordinary, everyday safety is most commonly focused on the physical aspect of safety. This is where its tokens draw our attention. At the physical level,

---

[13]Wittgenstein, "A Lecture on Ethics," 9-10.

safety has to do with the absence of harm to our bodies—avoiding injuries, stopping the spread of diseases, protecting against intruders, securing ample provisions. It also has to do with the absence of harm to those physical things that keep our bodies healthy and safe—food and water supplies, houses, vehicles, clothes, and property. The physical aspect of safety, which has to do with protection against the destruction of the body, is the primary focus of this study because it is the primary focus of everyday conceptions of safety.

However, everyday conceptions and discussions of safety frequently expand beyond the physical. Some tokens of safety draw attention to other facets of safety, other areas of life in which protective efforts can be made to avoid or minimize harm. Along with physical safety, there is emotional, relational, mental, financial, psychological, social, political, and spiritual safety, among others. The concept of safety is applicable to any area of life in which there are things of value that could be lost or harmed. This widespread applicability is a reminder of the inconstancies of this world and all the various ways that harm intrudes on our lives. It also shows that safety is a versatile concept that has made its way deep into the ethos of our culture.

To the extent that conceptions of human well-being are expanded beyond the physical to include other aspects of life, I think that is good. Contemporary safety is often reductionistic in its approach to human well-being, emphasizing its physical aspect to the neglect of others or failing to adequately account for the connections between them. To the extent, though, that the logic and methods of contemporary safety are being applied to these other areas of life, the expansive applicability of safety will be matched by limitations in its usefulness.

Danger and Harm

For Wittgenstein, absolute safety is an experience of safety in spite of circumstances. Others define absolute safety differently, as safety that is achieved through perfect control of circumstances. In these instances, absolute safety, or a total control of dangers, is distinguished from relative safety, or a tolerable control of dangers.[14] Since that sort of absolute safety is

---

[14] Max Boholm, Niklas Möller, and Sven Ove Hansson, "The Concepts of Risk, Safety, and Security: Applications in Everyday Language," *Risk Analysis: An International Journal* 36 (2016):

not possible in this world, there is an appropriate apprehensiveness about defining safety, in the everyday sense, as the complete absence of danger. There is always a chance, no matter how small, that a danger that has been controlled could get out of control again or that an unexpected danger could appear suddenly, seemingly out of nowhere. In everyday speech, safety is typically discussed in a comparative or relative sense, whether or not it is stated explicitly. If someone speaks of living in a safe neighborhood, we do not take it to mean there are no possible circumstances in which that neighborhood could be dangerous but that it is as safe as can reasonably be expected. If someone says that a building is fire-safe, we do not take it to mean that it is impossible for the building to burn but that it is relatively safe from fire.

While it is true in many cases that safety is implicitly discussed in a relative sense, it is important to notice that expectations and reactions easily slide from relative to absolute. We may be able to acknowledge that dangerous things sometimes happen in safe neighborhoods or that fire-safe buildings sometimes burn. But when something dangerous happens in our neighborhood or when our fire-safe building burns, the responses often shift to the absolute: "How could this ever have happened?" The tension between absolute and relative conceptions of safety is due, in part, to the future-oriented understanding of safety as the absence of danger, rather than a present-oriented understanding of safety as the absence of harm. There are important differences between *danger* and *harm*, even if our imaginations often lose track of those differences. Danger is the possibility of harm. It is not actual harm. Being in danger or being threatened with harm can themselves be harmful in their own ways, like "a deadly wound in my bones" (Ps 42:10).[15] But there is a very real difference between being in danger and being harmed, between almost crashing and crashing, between being threatened with violence and being attacked, between being exposed to a disease and being infected by it. A friend once said her worst nightmare came true when she realized she had forgotten to pick up her daughter from

---

320-38; Niklas Möller, Sven Ove Hansson, and Martin Peterson, "Safety Is More Than the Antonym of Risk," *Journal of Applied Philosophy* 23 (November 2006): 419-32.

[15]Sven Ove Hansson notes, "It is a debated issue whether a risk imposition is in itself a harm or whether there is no harm unless the risk materializes." Sven Ove Hansson, *The Ethics of Risk: Ethical Analysis in an Uncertain World* (New York: Palgrave Macmillan, 2013), 129.

soccer practice and she was alone in the field after dark. That is not a nightmare, though. A nightmare is whatever terrible thing my friend imagined could have happened in that circumstance. Not all dangers become harms. In view of the present, safety can be defined as the absence of harm. But inasmuch as safety is oriented toward the future, it will also be defined by danger in terms of what *could* happen, in terms of possibilities and probabilities, "the fuzzy world of potentialities."[16]

The forward-looking aspect of safety is unavoidable. Life moves into the future, and God has given humanity the capacity to anticipate what is coming. However, a place should also be found for conceiving of safety in terms of the present, and even the past. This may help foster thankfulness to God for the safety of yesterday and today, whether that safety is removed or used by God as provision for the dangers of tomorrow. It may help us to see safety, not only in regard to what may or may not happen next, but comprehensively, in regard to God's guidance through the entire course of life. Calvin notes that the godly person "will count it among the blessings of the Lord, if he is not destitute of human helps which he may use for his safety."[17] Safety in this world is often elusive. We may have it to greater or lesser degrees. We may have it one moment but not the next. Therefore, safety may be thought of as the relative absence of harm in view of the present and the relative absence of danger in view of the future, with an awareness of past provision.

Safety and Healing

Safety is primarily future-oriented. Healing is primarily past-oriented. When a mother says to her son, "Be careful with that knife," and when a doctor says to him, "Hold still. You are going to feel some pressure," they both have in mind the same goal—the wholeness of the son's finger. The mother's words had to do with safety because harm was possible but he had not yet sliced his finger open. The doctor's words had to do with healing because harm had already occurred and his finger needed to be sewn shut.

---

[16] Niels Henrik Gregersen, "Risk and Religion: Toward a Theology of Risk Taking," *Zygon* 38 (2003): 359.

[17] John Calvin, *Institutes of the Christian Religion*, ed. John T. McNeill, trans. Ford Lewis Battles, LCC 20-21 (Philadelphia: Westminster John Knox, 1960), I.17.9, p. 222.

Safety seeks to prevent harm, while healing seeks to restore health. While the focus of this study is on safety and the prevention of harm, it is worth acknowledging that the pursuit of safety has much in common with the pursuit of healing.

SAFETY, SECURITY, AND RISK

A recent analysis of the use of the terms *safety* and *security* in everyday speech revealed that the two are synonyms. In many instances they are interchangeable with each other. They do not carry the same meaning entirely, though, and the difference between the two is often related to the nature of the danger at hand. We tend to associate security with protection against intentional harm and safety with protection against unintentional harm. With intentional harm, one person or group is seeking through their actions to bring about harm to others. Murder, war, abuse, theft, and sabotage are examples of intentional harm. Unintentional harm has to do with things such as accidents, crashes, injuries, and mishaps, occasions when harm comes about through carelessness, chaos, or unanticipated events.[18]

Another possible way to conceive of the relationship between safety and security is in how one avoids being harmed. Safety has more to do with the avoidance of dangerous situations or protection from their harmful results, while security has more to do with subduing threats in an active manner. The safety on a gun is intended to protect against accidental firings, but the gun itself may be intended to provide security against violent assault. The distinction between intentional and unintentional harm could, perhaps, be carried over to natural threats as well to the extent that agency and intention are ascribed to the actions of animals and to the extent that the actions of God or spiritual powers are bracketed off. Hurricanes and lightning bolts seem like unintentional threats on the part of nature, while dog bites and bear attacks seem intentional on the parts of those creatures, and things like bee stings and mosquito bites fall somewhere in between.

Teasing out the differences between safety and security is helpful to some degree because it draws attention to the various ways that harms come on

---

[18]Boholm, Möller, and Hansson, "The Concepts of Risk, Safety, and Security," 322-30. Many other languages, e.g., Swedish and German, have "no lexical distinction" between safety and security.

us and the various ways that we seek to protect ourselves from them. The distinction between safety and unintentional harm on the one hand and security and intentional harm on the other is not hard and fast. Again, these terms are synonyms, with a high degree of overlap in meaning and usage.

As with the idea of safety, "the idea of risk," according to Danish theologian Niels Gregersen, "has increasingly dominated public perception of the world" in recent decades.[19] Therefore, this theology of safety will be shaped in important ways by its engagement with current conceptions of risk. A *risk* is typically understood today as "an unwanted event that may or may not occur."[20] Earlier notions of risk, rooted in the Renaissance, paired the possibility of harm with the possibility of gain, as represented in the classic formula: "Risk equals Probability (of events) multiplied by the Size (of the benefits and damages)."[21] In this venturesome understanding, a person *takes* a risk hoping to see gain but aware of the possibility of loss. However, understandings of risk have shifted over time. Currently, there is much more talk of *managing* risks than *taking* risks. In defining a risk as "an unwanted event that may or may not occur," the contingency of the event, as found in the classic formula, is maintained. The possibility of an undesirable outcome is also maintained. But the possibility of gain has been dropped, evoking a more defensive posture. Risk, in this newer sense, is therefore closely related to danger. We may say that driving has risks or that it has dangers, that a behavior is risky or that it is dangerous. In either case, we are referring to the possibility of harm or unwanted consequences. Risks are those things that hinder safety or must be managed in the pursuit of it.

Imaginary, Possible, and Actual Harm

Since safety has to do both with what does happen and what could happen, it is important to distinguish between imaginary, possible, and actual harm. Imaginary harm is harm that has no chance, or only a very small chance, of happening. Actual harm is harm that is happening. Possible harm occupies the space between those two and is harm that could happen or might happen. When we imagine harm coming upon us, we worry. When actual

---

[19]Gregersen, "Risk and Religion," 357.
[20]Boholm, Möller, and Hansson, "The Concepts of Risk, Safety, and Security," 321.
[21]Gregersen, "Risk and Religion," 362.

harm comes upon us, we suffer. When faced with possible harm—harm that is not actual, but could become so in the future—we respond, typically, by pursuing safety. This pursuit encompasses the entire range of activities meant to lower the likelihood that possible harm will become actual harm, whether by preventing a harmful event from happening or by insulating ourselves from its effects if it does happen. Therefore, we can differentiate to some degree between worry as a correlative of imaginary harm, suffering as a correlative of actual harm, and the pursuit of safety as a correlative of possible harm.

For example, a helmet is worn specifically for the sake of safety. It is not something you put on at home to help calm your worries about crashing your bike, nor is it something you put on after you crash to alleviate the pain in your head. It is something you put on when you ride your bike in order to lower the likelihood of harm if you crash. It would be difficult to draw clear lines between imaginary, possible, and actual harm, just as it would be difficult to draw clear lines between worrying, pursuing safety, and suffering. These categories overlap in complex and nuanced ways. The anxious anticipation of a harmful event can cause suffering even if the event does not occur. Safeguards are employed for harms that never come about, and harms come about that were never foreseen. Nonetheless, possible harm and the corresponding pursuit of safety have risen in prominence as distinct categories that play formative roles in humanity's engagement with the dangers of this world.

THE CONDITION AND PURSUIT OF SAFETY

The pursuit of safety encompasses a large sphere of human activity. When we speak of safety we are often speaking of engagement in those activities, as well as the hoped for results. But it is important to distinguish between the *condition* of safety and the *pursuit* of that condition. If safety is the absence of harm or danger, then the efforts made to attain that condition are part of the pursuit of safety but not safety itself. When the National Safety Council defines safety as the "control and elimination of recognized hazards to attain an acceptable level of risk," the "control and elimination of recognized hazards" is not safety, but a set of activities engaged in to procure safety. Safety, in this instance, is the attainment of "an acceptable level of risk."[22] In general usage, *safe* and *safety* often refer to both the condition and the pursuit of safety. So, when we say to someone, "Be safe," we have both in mind. The person should act in such a way that will help attain, or maintain, the condition of safety. However, it is vitally important to the proper development of a theology of safety to maintain a clear distinction between the condition and pursuit of safety. There is not a one-to-one correspondence between the two. Sometimes a person is being safe but harmed anyway. Sometimes a person is not being safe yet suffers no harm. In order to uphold this distinction, I will use *safety* in reference to the condition and *pursuit of safety* or an equivalent phrase in reference to the efforts made to attain that condition.

Individual and Corporate Safety

By saying that the focus of this study is on safety as physical protection, I have initially located safety primarily in the body of the individual. Again, I have done so because that is where the tokens of safety most typically draw our attention. Warnings not to suffocate on plastic packaging, fall off a train platform, touch the edge of a blade, leave belongings unattended, nor stick your hand out the window make safety about the individual's body and possessions. However, safety can be located in other places as well, particularly when it is thought about corporately.

First, safety can be conceived of corporately as an aggregation of the safety of individuals, perhaps a defined group of individuals such as the citizens of a town, the members of a family, or the employees of a business. The town, family, or business is safe insofar as the individual members are safe. On the one hand, this sort of safety could be thought of numerically, as a percentage or ratio. If most of the individuals in a group are safe, say ninety-nine out of one hundred, while only one is in danger, then the group itself is safe, or mostly safe. On the other hand, if the safety of any given individual within the group is connected to the safety of any other given individual or the group as a whole, as is often the case, then even if only one member is harmed or in danger, the group itself may not be safe. Its other members may be exposed to additional dangers. Perhaps a father is harmed

---

[22]Phyllis Crittenden, ed., *Supervisors' Safety Manual*, 10th ed. (Itasca, IL: NSC, 2009), 6.

and can no longer care for his children. Perhaps a member of a team is harmed and can no longer help the others complete a demanding task.

When safety is thought about corporately, the sources of danger may come from outside, but also from within the group. Members may be dangers to each other, dangers to the group, or in danger from the group. In recent years, a spotlight has shined on the harm that occurs in businesses, institutions, and churches through sinful actions such as sexual immorality, fits of anger, and deception, through ungodly outflows of the heart such as pride, lust, and conceit, and through self-interested compromises such as laziness, cowardice, and negligence. These behaviors and attitudes, which often include violence and abuse, are physically dangerous. They are also harmful emotionally and relationally because of the manipulations and coercions that accompany them. They are dangerous to the members in a variety of ways, and they are corrosive to the group as a whole.

Second, safety can be conceived of corporately as a function of the larger societal setting in which individuals and groups encounter dangers and pursue safety. For example, a person may seek to be a safe driver, but must do so in a vehicle designed by others, on roads engineered by others, alongside cars driven by others, and in accordance with regulations administered by others. Safety while driving, or doing any number of other activities within society, is dependent on a set of conditions that arises through the decisions and actions of many.

Third, safety can be conceived of corporately by locating it, not in the individual body, nor in the aggregation of multiple bodies, but in a corporate entity itself. A person can be safe, but so can a town, family, or business. Its ongoing existence, its relative strength and health, its ability to function as intended, can all be harmed, whether that harm occurs on a physical level to its members, property, land, or resources, or on some other level. So, along with the safety of an individual, we may also speak corporately of the safety of a family, church, city, or civilization. Dangers do not just threaten individuals, but institutions and nations.

Safety, Wholeness, and Worship

Safety relates to the absence of harm or the likelihood of harm, but the meaning of harm needs to be clarified. Christ asks the question: "Is it lawful on the Sabbath to do good or to do harm, to save life or to destroy it?" (Lk 6:9). Harm is that which destroys life. Doing harm to someone is the opposite of doing good to them (cf. Prov 31:12; Is 41:23; Jer 21:10). This raises the question of what is good for a person, of what is entailed in the flourishing of human life. Human flourishing is often assumed to entail such things as health, prosperity, and longevity.[23] But these are desired, or should be desired, as means to some greater end, parts of some greater whole. The goodness of life is a tree by streams of water (Ps 1:3), a sheep in green pastures (Ps 23:2), a face shining with oil (Ps 104:15). God provides all these. He gives life so that we would live with him, love him, and serve him. Harm refers to any deficiency or damage that hinders people from thriving in their proper environment.

A Christian understanding of what is good for human life affirms the ordered intricacy and wonder of the human body, the suitable place that God has established in this world for humankind alongside the rest of creation, the damaging effects of sin, and God's faithfulness to his children to ultimately bring good from harm and wipe away every tear. Safety and wholeness in relation to creation is a penultimate good to be enjoyed, but it ought to be directed to humanity's "true telos" of knowing and seeing God.[24] Furthermore, a Christian understanding of safety is fundamentally shaped by the paradox of the cross in which life comes through death, strength comes through weakness, and triumph comes through surrender. Safety is more than the absence of harm. It is health and wholeness, the presence of a positive good.

The desire to be kept safe is rooted in the desire to live, and the desire to live manifests itself as scorn toward those things that hinder life. According to Thomas Aquinas, "every man has it instilled in him by nature to love his own life and whatever is directed thereto." Inasmuch as life and the good things that accompany it are rightly loved and desired, the dangers that remove or damage those good things are rightly feared. This rightly ordered fear "implies flight," but is similar to what we might call scorn, disdain, or distaste, not cowardice or terror. It is a healthy repulsion of that which

---

[23]Charles Taylor, *A Secular Age* (Cambridge, MA: Harvard University Press, 2007), 150-51.
[24]Marc Cortez, *ReSourcing Theological Anthropology: A Constructive Account of Humanity in the Light of Christ* (Grand Rapids, MI: Zondervan, 2018), 65.

inhibits life. If the good things that promote life are loved "in due measure" instead of as ends in themselves, there will be an appropriate aversion to those things that cause harm and death. Aquinas cautions against too much love of life, which results in fear and inaction. He also cautions against too little love of life, referencing Aristotle, who says that if a person "feared nothing—not even an earthquake or rough seas, as people say of the Celts—he would be a sort of madman or insensible."[25] Calvin also addresses the scorn that we have toward things that cause harm. He says that the knowledge of God's providential care "will impel us continually to call upon God," who will "buttress our minds with good hope, that, with confidence and courage, we may not hesitate to despise those dangers which surround us."[26]

An aversion to the endangerment of life is not cowardly fear, but hopeful vitality. When the psalmists cry out to God to rescue them from trouble, the hope of deliverance is accompanied by antipathy toward whatever has encroached on their lives. They call out to God against the sources of affliction and are glad when he brings deliverance. Psalm 107 exemplifies this pattern. Those who cried out from the wilderness rejoice in the safety of the city (Ps 107:4-7, 36). Those who sat in prison thank God for breaking chains and shattering doors (Ps 107:10-16). Those afflicted because of sinful foolishness worship God for healing and deliverance (Ps 107:17-22). Those caught in a storm at sea are "glad that the waters were quiet" (Ps 107:23-32). The steadfast love of God is better than life (Ps 63:3), yet "life and whatever is directed thereto" do not fade from view. Instead, they find their proper significance in light of the love of God. Life, with all its dangers, is a gift from God. It is the occasion of our worship of him and satisfaction in his provision (Ps 63:4-5). When a person is "beyond the possibility of praising God, he is truly 'in death.'"[27] The psalmists scorn danger because they want to live, they want to worship: "For in death there is no remembrance of you; in Sheol who will give you praise?" (Ps 6:5).

---

[25]Thomas Aquinas, *ST* (London: Eyre & Spottiswoode), 2-2.125-126; Aristotle, *Nicomachean Ethics*, trans. Roger Crisp (Cambridge: Cambridge University Press, 2000), iii, 7.
[26]Calvin, *Institutes*, I.17.9, p. 222.
[27]Hans Walter Wolff, *Anthropology of the Old Testament*, trans. Margaret Kohl (London: SCM Press, 1981), 111.

PART TWO

Sources of Danger Through the Ages

Humanity Against the Gods
Premodern Risk

When a god sends harm, not even the strong can escape.

Sophocles, *Electra*

The Narrative Structure of Safety

When we pursue safety, we tell ourselves stories. They may be simple, as mundane as a passenger approaching a yellow line at a train station, or complex, as bewildering as a ship navigating a storm at sea. Yet these stories give shape to our encounters with danger. As with all stories, the stories of safety follow particular characters in particular settings through a basic plot structure with "a beginning, a middle, and an end."[1] There is movement from one state of affairs to another, perhaps from one place of safety to a new place of safety with dangers between. Conflict rises when the protagonist comes upon danger, and resolution follows as it is navigated safely, perhaps with some harm or other changes happening in the process.

This narrative structure is inherent to the pursuit of safety. It can be seen in the microcosms of life, in the stories of specific people encountering specific risks. It also appears in the macrocosm of human existence, in the overall story of humanity's relationship to this world full of dangers. The pursuit of safety is an "anthropological constant,"[2] yet it is narrated in

---

[1] Hervé Corvellec, "The Narrative Structure of Risk Accounts," *Risk Management* 13 (2011): 102.
[2] Emil Angehrn says that the pursuit of safety is an anthropological constant because it is a basic part of human existence, something that distinguishes humans from animals and is present in all areas of life, including relationships with others, nature, and divine powers. All people, in all

particular ways in the industrialized and secularized late-modern world, within a certain setting, with a certain set of characters, and with a certain understanding of the nature of the conflict. These features of the story—the settings, characters, and conflicts, or, more accurately, perceptions of them—have undergone significant shifts throughout the history of Western civilization. Understandings of safety have changed as understandings of the world have changed. Angels, for example, are no longer widely acknowledged for the role they play in guarding the lives of mortals. That is not to say that the actual activities of angels in this world have changed, but that perceptions of their activities, and therefore narrations of safety, have changed. A sailor kept safe by a prayer and an angel is a different story than a sailor kept safe by a compass and a weather forecast.

When Paul was being taken to Italy as a Roman prisoner (Acts 27), his ship was delayed by slow sailing and adverse winds. He told his guards and the captain what he had "perceived" about the voyage, that it would end poorly for the ship, its cargo, and its passengers (Acts 27:10). Paul's perception was prophetic insight, but it did not take a prophet to see that he was right. The time of year, the weather patterns, and their location were all clear signs that it would be a dangerous journey. Paul did not have a compass, but he gave a prudent warning based on the technological and predictive tools available. They sailed anyway. When the storm hit, the sailors used up all their strength and strategy. All hope was abandoned. In the darkness, an angel stood before Paul and spoke words of comfort. God had granted his life, and the lives of all on board. There was still more work to be done and more problems to be dealt with before the ship ran ashore, but all 276 souls were saved. As is typical of Scripture, this story highlights the limitations of human skill and technique, but also the mercy and power of God: "For he will command his angels concerning you to guard you in all your ways" (Ps 91:11).

The tokens that testify to safety's pervasiveness in our world also narrate the pursuit of safety in a particular way. The features of these narrations can

---

times and places, seek to protect themselves from harm. Angehrn contrasts the constancy of the pursuit of safety with historical variations in how that pursuit is understood and undertaken. See Emil Angehrn, "Das Streben nach Sicherheit: Ein Politisch-Metaphysisches Problem," in *Zur Philosophie Der Gefühle*, ed. G. Lohmann and H. Fink-Eitel (Frankfurt am Main: Suhrkamp, 1993), 218-19.

be seen, for example, in the "risk warning signs" that we so frequently encounter.[3] The texts on these signs may be brief ("Stand behind the yellow line"), yet they follow the basic narrative structure mentioned above. Attention is drawn to a certain danger, and whether implicitly or explicitly, the sign tells how the conflict ought to be resolved. In some cases, these signs are interpreted as establishing obligations as well. A case went before the Supreme Court of Canada regarding a woman who neither suffered nor caused harm, but was arrested and fined for not holding an escalator handrail in a metro station. One of the main issues in this case was whether the risk warning sign on the escalator legally obligated the woman to hold the handrail. Lower courts ruled in favor of the transit authority's position that the sign did impose an obligation, but the Supreme Court of Canada ruled in favor of the woman.[4]

The signs have a moral dimension to them. They "allocate blame as well as responsibility." They have a political dimension as well. Those in authority, who narrate these encounters with risk, "give themselves the credit" for warning of danger while also setting a behavioral "limit for transgression."[5] The tokens of safety, despite their pervasiveness, cannot be comprehensive. Therefore, the risk narrators, through the presence or absence of particular warnings, determine which risks are most important. However, the pursuit of safety is driven by what *could* happen. These responsibilities and obligations are based on contingencies. The signs may be imperative, but they are doubly speculative, telling what *must* be done because of what *might* happen *if* a certain set of conditions comes about.[6] Encounters with the dangers of this world are enframed in, interpreted by, and blurred together with narrations of safety and risk, whether those stories are told through risk warning signs or some other means.

These smaller stories of safety are set within a larger understanding of humanity's historical relationship to risk. Humanity's conceptualizations of risk and danger, as well as its methods of dealing with them, have changed

---

[3]Corvellec, "The Narrative Structure of Risk Accounts," 101.
[4]Lee Berthiaume, "Woman Arrested for Not Using Métro Escalator Handrail Awarded $20,000," *Montreal Gazette*, November 30, 2019, https://montrealgazette.com/news/local-news/woman-arrested-for-not-using-metro-escalator-handrail-awarded-20000.
[5]Corvellec, "The Narrative Structure of Risk Accounts," 101, 113.
[6]Corvellec, "The Narrative Structure of Risk Accounts," 106-7.

throughout history. One important and recurring question that this observation highlights is whether or not humanity is corporately becoming safer. Are we gaining ground in conquering risk itself, not just in conquering certain risks? Are we able to make any fundamental and lasting changes to how we stand in relation to the dangers of this world?

Humanity's pursuit of safety, in this larger sense, is frequently narrated today by presenting the conceptual development of risk as a historical progression from premodernity, when dangers are understood primarily in relation to the gods, to early modernity, when dangers are understood primarily in relation to nature, and finally to late, or post-, modernity, when dangers are understood primarily in relation to humanity itself. This secularized story of risk serves a number of purposes. It offers a compelling explanation for why humanity can now conquer dangers that had been insurmountable in ages past. It presents such advancements, not simply as progress within a static understanding of risk, but as outcomes of progress in conceptualizations of risk itself. It creates space, within the late-modern stage, for the entrance of new and unforeseen risks into modernized societies. Finally, it provides a larger, shared narrative by which individuals or groups can interpret the stories of their own encounters with the dangers of this world.

The conceptual development of risk and its application to life are part of the much larger story of modernity and its aftermath. Any historical narrative which tries to succinctly make sense of developments that unfolded through numerous nations, centuries, and cultures will be necessarily constrained. As sociologist Anthony Giddens says, "It is a risky business in itself to draw generalized contrasts between the modern era and the whole gamut of premodern social orders."[7] This threefold structure has some limitations that are apparent at the outset. It will struggle to account for the classical age as part of the bleak, premodern phase of humanity's relationship to risk, yet also a highpoint in human development and sophistication. It will tend to present modernity as rising out of the ashes of history while overlooking the medieval achievements on which it is built. Finally, it simplifies a complicated history and obscures enduring creational realities. The movement

---

[7]Anthony Giddens, *The Consequences of Modernity* (Stanford, CA: Stanford University Press, 1991), 100.

from "humanity versus the gods" in premodern risk to "humanity versus nature" in early modern risk to "humanity versus itself" in late-modern risk resonates as a helpful heuristic, but on further reflection, numerous exceptions and qualifications begin to appear.

Therefore, my engagement with this threefold structure regarding the sources of danger through the ages offers an opportunity to learn about how people from earlier eras conceived of danger, but it also offers an opportunity to reflect on where we have situated ourselves in the story of humanity's relationship to risk and how we view our own pursuit of safety in relation to those of other times and places. The current form and status of safety have grown out of the early modern hope that humanity could gain mastery over nature and have been chastened by the late-modern suspicion that humanity multiplies new risks while subtracting old ones. As we look at the story of humanity's relationship to danger, though, it will be important to keep in mind that it cannot be told fully within the confines of history.

ANCIENT ACCOMPLISHMENTS

> Surely it is obvious enough, if one looks at the whole world, that it is becoming daily better cultivated and more fully peopled than anciently. All places are now accessible, all are well known, all open to commerce.... No longer are (savage) islands dreaded, nor their rocky shores feared; everywhere are houses, and inhabitants, and settled government, and civilized life. What most frequently meets our view (and occasions complaint), is our teeming population: our numbers are burdensome to the world, which can hardly supply us from its natural elements; our wants grow more and more keen, and our complaints more bitter in all mouths, whilst Nature fails in affording us her usual sustenance.[8]

These observations were made by Tertullian eighteen centuries ago. As recorded on a bronze tablet from the first century BC, Julius Caesar enacted one of the earliest known traffic safety regulations: "After January 1 next no one shall drive a wagon along the streets of Rome or along those streets in the suburbs where there is continuous housing after sunrise or before the

---

[8]Tertullian, *A Treatise on the Soul*, ed. Alexander Roberts, James Donaldson, and A. Cleveland Coxe, trans. Peter Holmes, *ANF* 3 (Buffalo: Christian Literature, 1885; reprint, Grand Rapids, MI: Eerdmans, 1963), 210.

tenth hour of the day."⁹ This statute, which included civil and ceremonial exceptions, was apparently intended to ease congestion and make the narrow, crowded streets of the Eternal City safer for pedestrians.¹⁰ The Roman engineer Vitruvius, after noting the ill effects of lead on those who worked with it, advised that "water should not be brought in lead pipes if we desire to have it wholesome."¹¹ The Egyptians, according to Pliny the Elder, developed a civil works program to protect agricultural land from the flood waters of the Nile while irrigating their crops with those same waters.¹² The Code of Hammurabi held house and ship builders liable for loss of life or property due to faulty construction (§228-35), and Mosaic law required anyone who built a new house to include a parapet around the roof, so that "you may not bring the guilt of blood upon your house, if anyone should fall from it" (Deut 22:8).

While these programs and regulations offered protection by means of behavioral, social, and technological controls, methods of risk analysis were also developed in the premodern world. Priests in ancient Mesopotamia, when consulted about future events or risky decisions, would tally the results of their divinations in a ledger.¹³ Although the data and means of gathering it were decidedly premodern (looking for omens in the entrails of sacrificial animals), the calculative rationality used to draw conclusions from the data marked "the first recorded instance of a simplified form of risk analysis."¹⁴

Probabilistic forecasting, vital to risk analysis today, was understood conceptually long before it was calculated mathematically. It can be seen, for

---

⁹Allan Chester Johnson, Paul Robinson Coleman-Norton, and Frank Card Bourne, "Law of Caesar on Municipalities," in *Ancient Roman Statutes: A Translation with Introduction, Commentary, Glossary, and Index* (Austin: University of Texas Press, 1961), 94. This and several of the following examples from the ancient world have been drawn from Vincent T. Covello and Jeryl Mumpower, "Risk Analysis and Risk Management: An Historical Perspective," *Risk Analysis: An International Journal* 5 (1985): 103-20.

¹⁰J. Donald Hughes, *Environmental Problems of the Greeks and Romans: Ecology in the Ancient Mediterranean*, 2nd ed. (Baltimore: Johns Hopkins University Press, 2014), 170.

¹¹Vitruvius, *On Architecture* 8.6.10-11, trans. Frank Granger, LCL 280 (Cambridge, MA: Harvard University Press, 1934), 2:189.

¹²Pliny, *Natural History* 5:58, trans. H. Rackham, LCL 352 (Cambridge, MA: Harvard University Press, 1952), 2:263.

¹³A. Leo Oppenheim, *Ancient Mesopotamia: Portrait of a Dead Civilization*, rev. ed. (Chicago: University of Chicago Press, 1977), 210-12.

¹⁴Covello and Mumpower, "Risk Analysis and Risk Management," 103.

example, in the use of the Greek term εἰκός (likely).[15] Socrates used the term to distinguish truth from that which has a likeness to truth (ὁμοιότητα τοῦ ἀληθοῦς).[16] He thought it best, in accordance with his philosophical ideals, to speak of what is true instead of what is probable. Others did not share his concern. The Corinthian army, when contemplating war with the Athenians, boasted: "For every reason we are likely to succeed. First, because we are superior in numbers and in military skill; secondly, because we all obey as one man the orders given to us."[17] Antiphon the Sophist surmised that "any business that is started correctly is likely to end correctly too."[18] The Talmud applies probabilistic reasoning to a number of ethical dilemmas, such as determining whether meat that may or may not be kosher can be eaten (*b. Ketub. 15a*), addressing unconfirmed accusations of adultery (*b. Ketub. 9a*), and responding to unusual medical events that may or may not be related (*b. Ta'an. 21a*).[19] Domitius Ulpianus is noteworthy for developing life expectancy tables around AD 230, an extremely rare statistical undertaking prior to the seventeenth century.[20] In the fourth century AD, Arnobius put forth a precursor to Pascal's wager. When faced with the option of converting to Christianity or remaining in paganism, he argues, "We should believe the one which affords some hopes rather than the one which affords none at all."[21]

---

[15]Samuel Sambursky, "On the Possible and the Probable in Ancient Greece," in *Studies in the History of Statistics and Probability: A Series of Papers*, ed. Maurice G. Kendall and R. L. Plackett (London: Griffin, 1970), 2:36.

[16]Plato, *Phaedrus* 273d, trans. Harold North Fowler, LCL 36 (Cambridge, MA: Harvard University Press, 1914), 559. Socrates rejects persuasive techniques in which a speaker appeals to what is probable because that is what the majority will believe. He does not want to appeal to that which is likely, but to that which is true. He explains, "For in the courts, they say, nobody cares for truth about these matters, but for that which is convincing; and that is probability, so that he who is to be an artist in speech must fix his attention upon probability. For sometimes one must not even tell what was actually done, if it was not likely to be done, but what was probable, whether in accusation or defence; and in brief, a speaker must always aim at probability, paying no attention to truth; for this method, if pursued throughout the whole speech, provides us with the entire art" (Plato, *Phaedrus* 272d-273a, LCL 36:555-56).

[17]Thucydides, *History of the Peloponnesian War* 1.121.3, trans. C. F. Smith, LCL 108 (Cambridge, MA: Harvard University Press, 1919), 1:201.

[18]Robin Waterfield, trans., *The First Philosophers: The Presocratics and Sophists*, Oxford World's Classics (New York: Oxford University Press, 2000), 261; see also Sambursky, "On the Possible and the Probable in Ancient Greece," 36.

[19]Nachum L. Rabinovitch, "Studies in the History of Probability and Statistics. XXII: Probability in the Talmud," *Biometrika* 56 (August 1969): 437-38.

[20]Covello and Mumpower, "Risk Analysis and Risk Management," 106.

[21]Arnobius, *The Case Against the Pagans* 2.5, trans. George E. McCracken, ACW 7 (Westminster, MD: Newman, 1942), 116-17.

Mechanistic causality was also employed as a means of risk analysis in the ancient world. Vitruvius, as mentioned above, deduced that lead pipes make drinking water unwholesome. There was also a longstanding awareness of a connection between malaria and swamps, and correlations were established between various diseases and environments. Although these and other causal relationships were observed, the physical, chemical, and biological mechanisms by which they occurred remained largely unknown.

These ancient methods of analyzing dangers were matched with various tools for managing those dangers. Although they may have lacked something of our modern rigor and precision, ancient civilizations successfully employed a variety of political and economic tools designed to mitigate loss from occasional or unexpected calamities. The Code of Hammurabi was the basis for several ancient risk management institutions. The most important of these was bottomry, a system in which a ship serves as security against a loan. If a merchant sailor borrowed money for a voyage but could not repay, the ship would be taken instead. If the ship sank, both the sailor and the lender lost out, though the sailor more so! The idea of having numerous parties share proportionately the risk of both loss and gain served as the basis for an insurance exchange in Athens. Later, the Romans developed life and health insurance associations in which members paid into a common fund that was later used to pay for medical or burial expenses.[22]

Another important aspect of the premodern world's understanding of risk is the prevalence of gambling. Like people today, people in ancient cultures enjoyed playing games of chance, especially for money. Many ancient peoples, including the Greeks, gambled with *astragali*, or sheep ankle bones that can be rolled like dice. In the sixteenth and seventeenth centuries, such aleatory activities would become the motivation and inspiration for the theory of probability, but the Greeks and others, who were so capable of talking conceptually about certainty, doubt, and likelihood, never devised a mathematical approach to risk. They were unable to calculate the probability of a future event, or what is likely to happen based on what has happened.[23]

---

[22]Covello and Mumpower, "Risk Analysis and Risk Management," 108-9.

[23]As will be discussed in chapter 6, on the development of the theory of probability, a sharp distinction is made between *conceptualizing* and *calculating* probabilities. It seems rudimentary today, but the ability to *numerically* calculate the likelihood of rolling a certain number with

Modern writings on the history of risk highlight the large span of years between the rise of gambling during the classical age and the development of the theory of probability in the seventeenth century. The "late birth" of the theory of probability, and accompanying technological progress, is partially attributed to such historical particulars as the difficulty of doing math with roman numerals, but the bulk of the blame is laid at the feet of religion.[24] Therefore, in spite of these various ancient accomplishments, many of which are similar to risk management and risk analysis techniques of today, the absence of a mathematical theory of probability is consistently set forth in the secular story of risk as a distinct boundary marker between modern and premodern humanity's relationships to risk.

THE SETTING: A POROUS AND ENCHANTED COSMOS

Premodern humanity lived in a world where technology, knowledge of the natural world, and non-mathematical conceptions of the probable were used to greater or lesser extents in interactions with the dangers of this world. However, a distinct characteristic of premodern risk is that the natural causes of these events are less important than the moral or spiritual causes. Some level of order is to be found in the natural world, but its operations are overshadowed by the spirits, angels, demons, and fates that fill the cosmos. In the premodern world, "the direct physical agent that caused the harm was of considerably less interest than the moral status of the victim."[25] Boholm gives a modern day parallel. The Azande people of Sudan "do not fail to accurately assess the physical cause, such as termite attack or poor construction," when a granary collapses and kills someone, but since spiritual beings have "agency and power" over these events, the Azande people believe witchcraft is the ultimate cause of such "accidents."[26] Centuries before Isaac Newton, Jews in Jerusalem would have had an intuitive

---

dice or that a given procedure will be successful was a revolutionary mathematical development with far-reaching societal consequences.

[24] F. N. David, *Games, Gods, and Gambling: A History of Probability and Statistical Ideas* (Mineola, NY: Dover, 1998), 21; Peter L. Bernstein, *Against the Gods: The Remarkable Story of Risk* (New York: Wiley, 1998), 31. For a full discussion see chapter 3 in Bernstein, "As Easy as I, II, III." In 1259, an edict in Florence forbade the use of the "Gottlosen" arabic numbers. See Ludwig Marcuse, *Das Märchen von der Sicherheit* (Zürich: Diogenes, 1981), 171.

[25] Covello and Mumpower, "Risk Analysis and Risk Management," 108.

[26] Åsa Boholm, *Anthropology and Risk* (New York: Routledge, 2015), 3.

understanding of the physics involved in the collapse of the tower of Siloam. Yet they also had a moral explanation, believing that those who died were "worse sinners" than the rest. Perhaps if Vitruvius were there they would have talked architecture, but with Jesus, that event prompted a theological discussion (Lk 13:1-5). There is a place for natural causes in the premodern understanding of danger. Even premodern people have "folk sciences that they use to explain many of the ordinary, immediate experiences of their lives."[27] But those natural causes are enveloped in underlying spiritual causes.

This premodern world is a hierarchically ordered cosmos with "higher and lower levels of being" that reach their "apex in eternity." Whatever is at the apex, "the Ideas, or God, or both together," gives meaning and shape to the beings below.[28] This hierarchical pattern is carried out through spiritual, social, and natural spheres, so that gods shape the lives of people, ancestors shape the lives of the living, rulers shape the lives of subjects, and spiritual powers shape the course of nature. According to traditional African religions, as John S. Mbiti explains, humanity "lives in a religious universe, so that the natural phenomena and objects are intimately associated with God." The world bears "not only the imprint but the reflection of God."[29]

According to Charles Taylor, this premodern world is "porous." Beings, things, and forces within the cosmos are readily open to influence from each other. Natural events—floods, storms, droughts, and earthquakes—happen according to the purposes of divine beings. Objects in nature may in turn exercise influence over spirits or people. A rock may have magical powers to keep evil spirits away. A certain place may affect the moods of those who enter. People are porous and therefore "vulnerable, to spirits, demons, cosmic forces."[30] The porousness works both ways. People can exercise agency and seek to influence events in nature or the actions of gods through magic, prayers, and sacrifices.[31] This porous cosmos is not one in which the sphere of nature, as it might be understood today, is occasionally open to

---

[27]Paul G. Hiebert, "The Flaw of the Excluded Middle," *Missiology: An International Review* 10 (January 1982): 40.
[28]Charles Taylor, *A Secular Age* (Cambridge, MA: Harvard University Press, 2007), 60.
[29]John S. Mbiti, *African Religions and Philosophy*, 2nd ed. (Portsmouth, NH: Heinemann, 1990), 48.
[30]Taylor, *A Secular Age*, 27-35, 38.
[31]This point is largely missed by Bernstein, *Against the Gods*, and Ulrich Beck, *Risk Society: Towards a New Modernity*, trans. Mark Ritter (London: Sage, 1992), who characterize premodern humanity as passively helpless before these other powers.

beings or powers from a separate spiritual sphere. Instead, nature, animals, humanity, and these spiritual beings continually exist in the same "enchanted" cosmos.[32] Philosopher Lucien Lévy-Bruhl explains, "There is a blurring of the difference between natural and supernatural, and it tends to disappear. In many circumstances the primitive's thought and action pass from one to the other of these worlds almost imperceptibly."[33] It is important to note, of course, that Lévy-Bruhl's observation begins with the presupposition that the natural and supernatural are sharply divided from each other. From the perspective of premodern people, they are not blurring two distinct realms together. Instead, they would have thought that Lévy-Bruhl had curiously divided what is so clearly enmeshed together. This highlights an important weakness of the secular interpretation of the story of risk: the passage of time is conflated with the supposed development of certain ideals.[34] Terms like *primitive*, *ancient*, or *premodern* carry chronological and qualitative connotations that are often at odds with each other. People in modernized cultures still believe in angels and demons.

There is disharmony in the porous, premodern cosmos. Hostility, alienation, and tension exist between the beings, things, and forces within the hierarchy. According to Matthias Beck and Beth Kewell, this disharmony is symbolized in the fall of Genesis 3 and is manifested wherever evil spirits, angry gods, or ineluctable fates bring "danger, hazard, disaster, and catastrophe."[35] Other accounts of the origins of evil can be found in the ancient world, for example, in Babylonian, Egyptian, and Greek mythology, where the current condition and well-being of humanity are somehow tied up with the actions, preferences, and disagreements of the gods. Porousness or vulnerability to outside entities may be a source of salvation, healing, and joy or damnation, suffering, and sorrow. Actions may appease or anger the gods.

---

[32]"We are widely aware of living in a 'disenchanted' universe; and our use of this word bespeaks our sense that it was once enchanted" (Taylor, *A Secular Age*, 28).
[33]Lucien Lévy-Bruhl, *Primitives and the Supernatural*, trans. Lilian Ada Long Clare (New York: E. P. Dutton, 1935), 34.
[34]Mbiti critiques those who have "failed to understand" traditional African views of the physical and spiritual as "two dimensions of one and the same universe" (*African Religions and Philosophy*, 56-57).
[35]Matthias Beck and Beth Kewell, *Risk: A Study of Its Origins, History and Politics* (Hackensack, NJ: World Scientific, 2014), 1-2.

At the level of physics, chemistry, and biology—that is, the level at which modern humanity has made so many advances—the premodern world appears dark and mysterious. Vitruvius may have been able to draw a correlation between lead and health, but he could not have known how lead chemically works its toxic effects in the developing brains of children. Ancient civilizations may have linked malaria to swamps, but they could not have conceived that it came from a microscopic parasite carried by a mosquito. Martin Luther was aware that certain diseases were transferred when an infected person came into close proximity with others, but he was also of the opinion that "all the epidemics, like any plague, are spread among the people by evil spirits who poison the air or exhale a pestilential breath which puts a deadly poison into the flesh."[36] He says that God decrees all such things, that they are punishments to which we should submit, and that we should risk our lives serving our neighbors when they come. That service might mean staying away if you know you are infected or risking infection in order to care for others.

The Characters: The Gods, The Living, The Priests, and The Dead

There is a large and varied set of characters in the premodern understanding of risk. This often includes a supreme being who exists beyond the hierarchy of this cosmos, such as Aristotle's Unmoved Mover or a Creator who does not dwell in the unseen part of this world, but in a more remote unseen world. Then there are lower spiritual beings and powers. These may exert influence over the supreme being in ways that humanity cannot. They also exert influence over other spiritual beings, events in nature, and humanity. They may be angels sent to protect or demons sent to tempt. They may be benevolent or malevolent toward humanity. They might be indifferent to, forgetful about, or inconvenienced by the needs and weaknesses of humanity, as seems so often to be the case among the gods of Greek mythology. Whatever the personalities, inclinations, attributes, or actions of these various beings, the key element that they hold in common is the ability to affect the outcomes of humanity's encounters with danger, whether by guiding, or at times disrupting, the normal processes of nature.

---

[36]Martin Luther, "Whether One May Flee from a Deadly Plague," in *Devotional Writings II*, ed. Gustav K. Weinke, *LW* 43 (Philadelphia: Fortress, 1968), 127.

Premodern humanity finds itself at the center of its own story of risk, but not at the top of its order of being. Therefore, basic matters of human well-being—long life, health, safety, and community—must be sought in conjunction with the honor that these higher beings deserve and demand. Practical skills, spiritual knowledge, and moral virtue all play a role in the premodern pursuit of safety. Efforts to give higher beings the reverence they are due and efforts to acquire provisions for the needs of life are basically indistinguishable from each other. This makes worship, or at least religious activities, central to the pursuit of safety. Missiologist Paul Hiebert distinguishes between magic and worship at this point. Magic is "based on a mechanistic view" of the world and is a method by which people seek to "control their own destiny" through manipulation of the gods. Modern technological endeavors are also based on a mechanistic view of the world and are motivated by a desire to control the world. The key difference between technological hubris and magic is the spectrum of powers and entities thought to be at one's disposal. Worship, in the Christian sense, is "rooted in a relational view of life," in which worshipers "place themselves in the power and mercy of a greater being."[37]

In many early religions, a "low" or "natural" understanding of human flourishing, defined by such things as long life and health, prevailed. There were also "higher" religious or philosophical ideas of flourishing that went beyond such earthly circumstances.[38] These align with Wittgenstein's idea of absolute safety. Frédéric Gros describes one version of this higher type of flourishing based on the original meaning of the Latin *securus*, which he says describes one who is *sine cura* (without care). This type of security is "a state of the soul, a subjective disposition characterized by trust, tranquility, and quietude."[39] It is the "sérénité du sage," whether a Stoic safety of inner control, an Epicurean safety of disciplined desires, or a Skeptical safety of detachment.

These sages, who work to distance themselves from the vicissitudes of life and perhaps also the control of the gods, are the exceptions, rather than the

---

[37]Hiebert, "The Flaw of the Excluded Middle," 46.
[38]Taylor, *A Secular Age*, 17-19, 150.
[39]Frédéric Gros, *Le Principe Sécurité* (Paris: Gallimard, 2012), 10-51, "Un état d'âme, une disposition subjective caractérisés par la confiance, la tranquillité, la quietude" (15).

rule. They are a subgroup within a particular culture that serves a special pedagogical, formative, or mediatorial function for others. "Medicine-men, Rainmakers, Kings, and Priests," or what Mbiti refers to as "specialists," are also subgroups that serve special religious and political functions in a culture's encounters with risk and engagements with gods.[40] These are the people who make the knowledge of the gods their specialty. Their role is to guide others in their worship of the gods or magical practices, and therefore in their quest for security.

The dead are another unique subgroup in the premodern pursuit of safety. Saints from long ago are intermediaries between God and those who are still alive. They offer comfort and hope. Epic heroes inspire and encourage. Recently departed family members intercede before the gods on behalf of the living. The dead, since they were once as the living now are, can sympathize with their needs.

The Conflict: Humanity Against the Gods

The dangers that premodern people faced are similar, in many ways, to the dangers faced today. Premodern people could die from an illness, suffer harm from an accident, endure loss through violence, face cultural or economic instability through politics or war. Danger could come from nature, technology, animals, enemies, or accidents. However, if those sources of danger are under the control of the gods, and if humanity, through prayers, pleadings, sacrifices, and manipulations, can influence the outcomes of its encounters with dangers, then the conflict in premodern risk is between humanity and the gods. Whatever happens in the visible realm of nature is the outcome of a battle or drama taking place in what, for modern humanity, is the "excluded middle" of the cosmos, not the highest heaven where God dwells, nor the empirical realm of nature, but the place between, where divine beings intervene in human history.[41]

In this conflict, the gods are the primary source of danger, but they are also the primary source of safety. The gods are superior beings, and humanity's encounters with danger are in their hands, whether for good or bad.

---

[40]Mbiti, *African Religions and Philosophy*, 162-88. Taylor refers to them as "functionaries—priests, shamans, medicine men, diviners, chiefs, etc." (*A Secular Age*, 149).
[41]Hiebert, "The Flaw of the Excluded Middle," 46.

They bring victory as well as defeat, health as well as sickness, good fortune as well as bad. Matti Kamppinen, professor of religious studies, describes the "superior beings of religions" as "challenging antagonists for games of life."[42] Part of the challenge of these games, though, is that the gods are not always only antagonistic. Perhaps some gods are, but others can be placated. Their favor can be gained or lost. The disharmony in the cosmos may increase or decrease. Humanity may experience suffering or safety, but either way it does so under the inescapable purview of the gods.

Therefore, premodern humanity does not seek to defeat the gods, but to appease them. The gods demand reverence and incite fear. They are not conquered in the pursuit of safety, but "revered and ritually manipulated."[43] Of course, manipulations per se had their limitations. Instead, as Taylor explains, "These beings commanded our awe. There was no question of treating them as we treat the forces of nature we harness for energy." The conflict between humanity and the gods in premodern risk converges, to a large degree, on the religious activities performed to garner safety from the gods. In medieval France, for example, magic was combined with Christianity to form "a network of superstition" that was intended to "ward off danger or disease" by means of portents, pilgrimages, amulets, and offerings.[44] Religious beliefs and worship of the gods can be "a source of extreme anxiety or despair," but also a source of "security for the believer."[45]

Premodern Considerations

From Roman traffic regulations and Hebrew parapet walls to Babylonian construction liability and Greek life insurance, many features of premodern risk are familiar today. These precursors to modern risk analysis and management were developed in ancient societies, which in one form or another

---

[42]Matti Kamppinen, "Playing Against Superior Beings in Religion, Technology and Economy," in *Religion, Economy, and Cooperation*, ed. Ilkka Pyysiainen, Research and Reason 49 (Berlin: De Gruyter, 2010), 83.

[43]Kamppinen, "Playing Against Superior Beings," 83.

[44]Deborah Lupton, *Risk*, 2nd ed. (New York: Routledge, 2013), 2, referencing Robert Muchembled, *Popular Culture and Elite Culture in France, 1400–1750* (Baton Rouge: Louisiana State University Press, 1985).

[45]Giddens, *The Consequences of Modernity*, 103-4. Giddens sees religion as "something that generates a sense of the reliability of social and natural events" and as possibly "connected psychologically to trust mechanisms," but does not give place to the actual workings of supernatural beings or forces in this world.

believed that God, or the gods, or deceased ancestors, or fate are active agents in this world. This is a definitive feature of premodern risk. The range of possible cause and effect relationships in the cosmos includes not only the flow of history and the forces of nature, but the wills and powers of the gods. The gods may be appeased or incensed by the actions of humanity. The processes of this world, whether normal or spectacular, mundane or miraculous, are driven by the wills of gods. This is not to say that there was no place for mechanistic causation or technological innovation, nor is it to say that premodern peoples passively attributed the events of life to the gods, but it is to say that the course of history and the mechanics of the world were understood to be under the authority and direction of the gods.

In contemporary accounts of premodern risk, a shift frequently takes place from describing premodern beliefs that the gods are sources of danger to implicating those religious beliefs themselves as sources of danger or hindrances to safety. Lupton says, "As in pre-modern times, we may acknowledge that threats exist, but we like to think that something can be done to deal with them."[46] Kamppinen says that the "mental models of archaic contexts are more immune and less open to critical assessment" than modern mental models.[47] Life has become safer, according to Kamppinen, as "supernatural superior beings have been transformed into known and partly manageable lawful forces of nature."[48] Bernstein describes premodernity as a period when the future was viewed as a "whim of the gods," when humanity was "passive before nature," and when oracles and soothsayers "held a monopoly over knowledge of anticipated events." He presents these beliefs and associated views of life as hindrances to the development of the theory of probability and therefore to humanity's conquest of risk. According to Bernstein, premodern humanity navigated the dangers of this world "with no real understanding of risk or *the nature of decision-making*."[49]

Whether or not the human race is safer or more successful in its encounters with danger now than it was in premodern times depends on a

---

[46] Lupton, *Risk*, 3-4.
[47] Kamppinen, "Playing Against Superior Beings," 95.
[48] Kamppinen, "Playing Against Superior Beings," 88.
[49] Bernstein, *Against the Gods*, 1-4, italics his.

number of factors and the bases by which they are evaluated. We are quick in contemporary societies to note the drastic decline in infant mortality that has come with modern healthcare, yet we do not correlate that with the rapid increase in induced abortions that has also accompanied the spread of modern medical practices. In 1800 approximately 40 percent of children in Europe did not survive from birth to the age of five because of sickness, diseases, and other forces of nature largely uncontrollable at the time.[50] From 2010 to 2014, approximately 30 percent of children in a much more populous Europe did not survive from conception to birth because of the willful actions of authorities, parents, and medical practitioners.[51] This could hardly be called progress. The small pockets of violence in the modern world, as compared with the widespread violence of the premodern world (assuming this characterization is accurate), are of little comfort as we consider the speed, intensity, and efficiency of modern warfare. The weapons and techniques used today are far more deadly than the slow machinations of war used in previous centuries. At one level, then, statistically based claims of improved safety need to be understood and evaluated in a more comprehensive manner, while rightly acknowledging the many ways that modern societies have seen genuine improvements in safety. At another level, though, one of the weaknesses of the secular story of risk is its frequent inability to conceive of life before modern technology as good, enjoyable, or safe. By what standard do we decide if a peasant farmer in the twelfth century who died at the age of forty-two was less safe than a retail worker in the twenty-first century who died at the age of seventy-one? The obvious answer is the one who lived longer, but numbers alone do not tell the whole story. Even medieval peasants are capable of wholeness and contentedness.

It would be a misrepresentation of premodern people to say that they did not think something could be done about the dangers they faced or that their models of the world are closed to critical assessment. Premodern humanity was not passive before nature or the gods. What else were the innumerable shrines, temples, and altars but places of active engagement with

---

[50]Saloni Dattani, Fiona Spooner, Hannah Ritchie, and Max Roser, "Child and Infant Mortality," *Our World in Data*, 2023, https://ourworldindata.org/child-mortality.
[51]"Induced Abortion Worldwide," Guttmacher Institute, March 2018, www.guttmacher.org/fact-sheet/induced-abortion-worldwide-2018.

deities? When a rainmaker danced under the sky and flagellated himself to the point of exhaustion, how could that be called passivity toward nature? Premodern humanity, existing as it does in a porous and hierarchical cosmos, is strange to behold through the lens of modernity. Yet, in the story of humanity's encounters with the dangers of this world, there should be no question whether the ancients were active participants, but rather whether the tools that they used, the battleground as they saw it, and the conflict as they understood it were based on an accurate understanding of humanity's condition in this world before God.

FOUR

Humanity Against Nature
Early Modern Risk

> *All man can do to achieve results is to bring natural bodies together and take them apart.*
>
> Francis Bacon, *The New Organon*

Secularizing Risk

The modern world, in the eyes of many who occupy it, is safer than the premodern world. The premodern world is often seen as a dark place, afflicted by natural disasters, high infant mortality rates, low life expectancy, and endemic illnesses. Threats of violence abounded from "invading armies, marauders, local warlords, brigands, robbers, [and] pirates."[1] Rabid dogs, child-eating pigs, and murderous feuds made insecurity, with all its attendant fears, "rife and permanent" in the premodern age.[2] By contrast, the risks of the modern world are seen to be a bit more tame—or at least more tamable. These modern risks include "being the victim of a crime, falling prey to cancer, being in a car accident, losing our jobs, having our marriage break down or our children fail at school."[3] Instead of the widespread violence of premodernity, we are told that modernity faces "only relatively small pockets [of violence] within wider territorial

---

[1] Anthony Giddens, *The Consequences of Modernity* (Stanford, CA: Stanford University Press, 1991), 107.
[2] Deborah Lupton, *Risk*, 2nd ed. (New York: Routledge, 2013), 1-2.
[3] Lupton, *Risk*, 3. Lupton emphasizes the modern assumption that humanity is not helpless before these dangers, though she expresses a level of suspicion toward early modern optimism.

areas."[4] Cancer may be as deadly as the plague, a car crash as deadly as a wild beast, and war as deadly as ever, but the difference, according to the secular story of risk, is that humanity is no longer helpless before these dangers. This is so, not because the gods will intervene, but because dangers can be overcome through the mastery of nature. In the same way that smallpox, once so devastating, was overcome through a simple vaccination, so other dangers are being, or will soon be, overcome through the advances of modernity.

Modernity refers to the present era of human history, which started around the beginning of the seventeenth century. It also refers to certain modes of life and certain ways of thinking about the world—as guided by laws of nature—which emerged at that time. Premodernity is the long era of human history leading up to that point. Someone once observed that Abraham Lincoln, who was alive just 160 years ago, had more in common technologically with Abraham in the book of Genesis than with people who live today. Modernity refers to the relatively short period of time in which all those rapid changes have taken place. Late modernity or postmodernity began in the twentieth century and has many features in common with early modernity, but is distinguished by its turn toward critical reflection on modernity itself.[5]

In the beginning phases of modernization and industrialization, production moved from workshops, where safety developed alongside skillfulness, to factories, where the emphasis on faster production and cheaper labor far outpaced matters of safety. Some have argued that the initial increase in harm was inevitable, since the dangers of the tools of industry were unknown until they were put into use.[6] Perhaps that was the case, but perhaps this justification betrays the allurement of technology and the enticement of progress, as well as the destructive power of simple greed. Nonetheless, new modes of production, distribution, and transportation brought with them "an appalling rate of worker injuries and deaths."[7] Modern

---

[4]Giddens, *The Consequences of Modernity*, 107.
[5]When I use *modern* or *modernity* without qualifiers (early, late, post), I am speaking of modernity or the modern era in general, both early and late.
[6]Philip E. Hagan, John F. Montgomery, and James T. O'Reilly, eds., *Accident Prevention Manual for Business & Industry: Administration & Programs*, 14th ed. (Itasca, IL: NSC, 2009), 5.
[7]Hagan, Montgomery, and O'Reilly, *Accident Prevention Manual for Business & Industry*, 4.

industrial safety arose in response to these conditions, and with that early setback accounted for, the increased safety of modernity is tied to an accompanying increase in prosperity and opportunity. According to Giddens, the social institutions of modernity have spread throughout the world and are better suited to human flourishing "than any type of pre-modern system."[8] Bernstein says that modern risk management has led to "economic growth, improved quality of life, and technological progress," while also bringing "unparalleled access to the good things of life."[9] Modernity, according to Covello and Mumpower, has led to "overall improved prospects for a longer, healthier life."[10]

These improvements are often linked to the secularization of modern, Western, culture.[11] Philosopher Emil Angehrn says that modern, secularized strategies for the pursuit of safety emerged "after the fundamental safety of religion lost its viability."[12] If it was not the gods, but irrational beliefs about the gods that hindered safety in the premodern world, then one of the first steps in the early modern pursuit of safety is to overcome or remove such fearful superstitions.[13] The mathematical and conceptual advances that lie

---

[8]Giddens, *The Consequences of Modernity*, 7. Giddens warns, however, of a "sombre side" to modernity. He says that of the three founding fathers of sociology, Karl Marx and Émile Durkheim were more optimistic, stressing the "opportunity side" of modernity over its negative characteristics, while Max Weber was more pessimistic, yet did not fully anticipate "the darker side of modernity." While most late-modern authors recognize some of the darker aspects of modernity, they still consistently characterize it as brighter than premodern times.
[9]Peter L. Bernstein, *Against the Gods: The Remarkable Story of Risk* (New York: Wiley, 1998), 1-2.
[10]Vincent T. Covello and Jeryl Mumpower, "Risk Analysis and Risk Management: An Historical Perspective," *Risk Analysis: An International Journal* 5 (1985): 118.
[11]Secularization is traced in detail by Taylor, who defines it as the process "which takes us from a society in which it was virtually impossible not to believe in God, to one in which faith, even for the staunchest believer, is one human possibility among others" (*A Secular Age*, 3).
[12]Emil Angehrn, "Das Streben nach Sicherheit: Ein Politisch-Metaphysisches Problem," in *Zur Philosophie Der Gefühle*, ed. G. Lohmann and H. Fink-Eitel (Frankfurt am Main: Suhrkamp, 1993), 218.
[13]However, Michael D. Bailey critiques the enduring narrative that "in the history of European magic and superstition" there was a clear progression from the premodern enchanted world to the modern disenchanted world, "governed by scientific reason" (Michael D. Bailey, *Fearful Spirits, Reasoned Follies: The Boundaries of Superstition in Late Medieval Europe* [Ithaca, NY: Cornell University Press, 2013], 11). Bailey also helpfully distinguishes between religious condemnations of superstitions as heretical practices (e.g., Augustine, *On Christian Doctrine* 2.20, trans. J. F. Shaw [Mineola, NY: Dover, 2009], 31) and scientific criticisms of superstitions as factually erroneous (Bailey, *Fearful Spirits*, 14). During the Enlightenment, some thinkers began placing all religion in the category of superstition, but such secularizing developments "were never as complete as Enlightenment propaganda or subsequent notions of an entirely disenchanted and secularized Western 'modernity' might assert" (Bailey, *Fearful Spirits*, 25).

at the heart of modern humanity's relationship to risk "had to await the realization that human beings are not totally helpless in the hands of fate, nor is their worldly destiny always determined by God."[14] Therefore, the initial obstacle to be overcome in early modern risk is the premodern belief that humanity's encounters with the dangers of this world are at the mercy of unseen and unpredictable spiritual forces.

As a result, the pursuit of safety in early modernity is separated from the realms of the gods, the inescapability of fate, and the tricks of devils. This separation can be seen in Francis Bacon's evaluation of the historical trajectory of "philosophy and intellectual sciences" in comparison to that of the "mechanical arts."[15] According to Bacon, the mechanical arts, when they began, were "crude, clumsy almost, and ungainly," but as time moved forward they improved and refined, acquiring "new powers and a kind of elegance." He then voices frustration that the sciences, following the logic of ages past, had long been static—ancient yet puerile statues, sculpted in the Hellenistic age, to be "admired and venerated but not improved." Bacon's desire for the sciences is that they may "provide more reliable and secure directions for present and future generations." Therefore, the "sciences and philosophies" must remain neutral and avoid the mistake, found in superstitious practices, of celebrating outcomes that confirm a previously held belief while ignoring those that contradict it. By "a better and more perfect use and application of the mind and understanding," humankind can set forth on the long, yet fruitful task of mapping the "labyrinth" of the "fabric of the universe."[16]

Jason Josephson-Storm draws the same conclusion: "Disenchantment is a myth. . . . Secularization and disenchantment are not correlated" (Jason Josephson-Storm, *The Myth of Disenchantment: Magic, Modernity, and the Birth of the Human Sciences* [Chicago: University of Chicago Press, 2017], 304).

[14]Bernstein, *Against the Gods*, 20.

[15]Francis Bacon, *The New Organon*, ed. Lisa Jardine and Michael Silverthorne (Cambridge: Cambridge University Press, 2000), 7. The mechanical arts, in distinction from the liberal arts, "arise from 'some imitation or human devising,'" and include an array of technological and economic subjects including trades, craftsmanship, metalwork, and commerce (Steve Walton, "An Introduction to the Mechanical Arts in the Middle Ages," paper presented at the International Congress for Medieval Studies, Kalamazoo, MI, May 1993, AVISTA, revised 2014).

[16]Bacon, *The New Organon*, 7-11, 43. Bacon says that this task can only be done with God's help. He prays "that from a clear understanding, purged of fantasy and vanity, yet subject still to the oracles of God and wholly committed to them, we may give to faith all that belongs to faith." Yet, the task he sets forth, of acquiring knowledge of the universe through the mind and the senses,

Bernstein is among the most exultant in his descriptions of these early modern victories over superstition. He praises the modern pioneers of probability theory for their Promethean defiance of the gods. Those early thinkers, he says, "probed the darkness in search of the light that converted the future from an enemy into an opportunity."[17] According to Beck and Kewell, Bernstein's work is an example of "the much criticized but still very popular linear narrative in which accumulated progress amasses according to an evenly paced and seemingly predestined path of logical discovery."[18] Yet, Bernstein captures the early modern optimism that came with looking on the natural world as an object of study, predictability, and manipulation instead of a layer in a hierarchical cosmos. While premodern humanity may have been inextricably bound up in the drama of the cosmos, early modern humanity stands apart from nature, takes it in hand for observation, and seeks to dominate it.[19] Mapping the labyrinth of the universe is not intended to be an exercise in cartography. It is meant "for the uses and benefits of life."[20]

Therefore, the technological and scientific advances of the early modern era coincide with significant shifts in how humanity understands its relationship to nature, each other, and God. The physical world has been extricated from its place in a hierarchical cosmos. A distinction has been made between the immanent and transcendent, the natural and the supernatural. That is not to say that the transcendent, supernatural, and religious have been removed from modern cultures. They clearly have not. The significance of secularization, though, is that the work of God and

---

seems to be on a trajectory of secularization in which more and more of the oracles of God are either bracketed from this task as matters of faith or moved to the "fantasy and vanity" category.

[17]Bernstein, *Against the Gods*, 1. For a similar approach, see Isaac Todhunter, *A History of Probability from the Time of Pascal to That of Laplace* (Cambridge: Macmillan, 1865).

[18]Matthias Beck and Beth Kewell, *Risk: A Study of Its Origins, History and Politics* (Hackensack, NJ: World Scientific, 2014), 4. Instead, Beck and Kewell advocate for a dialectical view of the history of risk in which gradual developments take place alongside mistakes and setbacks. Forward movement comes about through a series of random rises and falls. Their view "mirrors in part the view of progress defined by Robert K. Merton as a series of serendipitous lucky breaks afforded to scientists and innovators already supported in their endeavours by way of beneficent Matthew effects, the patronage of generous sponsors and the support of civil society." See Robert K. Merton, "The Matthew Effect in Science," *Science* 159 (1968): 56-63, which makes use of Matthew 13:12, "To the one who has, more will be given."

[19]This is the purpose of a laboratory. See Bruno Latour, *We Have Never Been Modern*, trans. Catherine Porter (Cambridge, MA: Harvard University Press, 1993), 20-22.

[20]Bacon, *The New Organon*, 13.

the ministries of his angels have been bracketed off from numerous spheres of public life, including the pursuit of safety. God and his angels are not supposed to be taken into serious consideration as people make decisions on matters of safety. Instead, religious images and theological concepts have been "gradually evacuated from the various spheres of modern society."[21] Modern humanity evaluates risks and pursues safety in a "post-cosmic universe."[22]

The Setting: A Constant and Neutral Universe

Unlike the premodern cosmos, ordered by social and ontic hierarchies, the time, space, and matter of the modern universe are ordered by a neutral constancy of natural laws. This universe stands as an intricate and autonomous mechanism. Earth no longer sits between heaven and hell but orbits the sun between Venus and Mars. The motions of bodies, whether heavenly or microscopic, are no longer teleological, directed toward divine purposes, but free. Their movements are limited, as Newton tells us, only by encounters with other bodies or forces. Time had once been circular, or episodic, rising and falling through the centuries with the kingdoms of Daniel's prophecy, rising and falling through the seasons with the reversals and renewals of the sacred and secular. Now time is linear, moving steadily in the same direction. As such, modern time has been negatively characterized as "homogenous, empty time,"[23] just as the modern universe could be negatively characterized as homogenous, empty space. Yet, in relation to the pursuit of safety, the stability and consistency of the early modern universe has an appeal over the porousness and occasional disharmony of the premodern cosmos.

The transition from the premodern cosmos to the early modern universe as the setting for humanity's engagement with risk took place through a number of developments. Among them, the processes of *disembedding, disenchanting,* and *demythologizing* are characteristic of how modern humanity extricated the universe from the premodern cosmos.

---

[21]Jean-Louis Schlegel, "L'eschatologie et l'apocalypse dans l'histoire: un bilan controversé," *Esprit* 343 (March 2008): 88. ("Les anciennes images religieuses du monde, les concepts théologiques ou théologico-politiques, les comportements religieux ont été progressivement évacués des diverses sphères de la société moderne.")
[22]Taylor, *A Secular Age*, 26.
[23]Walter Benjamin, *Illuminations*, trans. Harry Zohn (New York: Schocken, 1968), 264.

First, the modern universe has been extricated from the premodern cosmos through a process of *disembedding*.[24] The various beings, forces, and objects, which were once embedded in a web of porous relationships, have been disembedded, or removed from their relational situatedness in the cosmos. They have been separated and distinguished from each other. The results of this disembedding can be seen along both social and cosmic lines.[25] Socially, disembedded humanity has been separated from its history, previous affiliations, and families of origin. Therefore, individuals can now place themselves, or at least imagine themselves, in any number of roles or cultural settings. Disembedded humanity now interacts directly with the natural world and the bodies therein, which have also been disembedded from their locations in the hierarchy of the cosmos. Like humanity, the objects, beings, and properties of the natural world can be placed, or at least imagined, in roles or settings different from those they are found in. New questions and new possibilities arise about how things should stand in relation to each other. If the cosmic web of relationships has been cut, connections can be redrawn or omitted.[26]

Second, the modern universe has been extricated from the premodern cosmos through the process of *disenchantment*. Angels, ancestors, gods, and demons, these beings and powers from other places in the cosmos, may be held on to as matters of subjective belief, but they are no longer afforded objective existence from the modern, secularized perspective. They are no longer viewed as interfering in the affairs of humanity, especially not in spectacular ways that go against the normal flow of events. As humanity seeks to understand cause and effect sequences, it looks within the natural world. Disenchantment, then, is "the historical process by which the natural world and all areas of human experience become experienced and understood as less mysterious."[27] Sociologist Richard Jenkins explains: "In a

---

[24]Taylor, *A Secular Age*, ch. 3, "The Great Disembedding."
[25]In premodernity, "human agents are embedded in society, society in the cosmos, and the cosmos incorporates the divine" (Taylor, *A Secular Age*, 152).
[26]Unlike feudal economic institutions or hierarchical religious institutions of premodernity, modern social institutions are shaped around this disembedding. As Giddens explains, "The modes of life brought into being by modernity have swept us away from *all* traditional types of social order, in quite unprecedented fashion" (Giddens, *The Consequences of Modernity*, 4).
[27]Richard Jenkins, "Disenchantment, Enchantment and Re-Enchantment: Max Weber at the Millennium," *Max Weber Studies* 1 (November 2000): 12. Jenkins is summarizing Weber's classical

disenchanted world everything becomes understandable and tameable, even if not, for the moment, understood and tamed."[28] In the transition from premodern to early modern conceptions of risk, the world becomes less mysterious, not through divine revelation, but through the rational and technological capacities of humanity. The New Testament may speak of the Spirit revealing the mystery of Christ to the apostles and prophets (Eph 3:5), but in the project of disenchantment, such revelations may be seen as unpredictable impositions from outside the natural world, and so remain relics of the enchanted world.[29] As supernatural beings are removed as causal agents in nature, early modern humanity finds new ways of understanding, predicting, and taming the dangers of this world. The theory of probability is significant as a mathematical accomplishment, but also as a non-religious means of predicting the future, something that had been "long denigrated as a waste of time at best and a sin at worst."[30] Other advancements in science and technology have been increasingly and successfully employed against the dangers of a disenchanted world. According to the logic of disenchantment, the discovery that an infection is caused by bacteria may be understood as the simultaneous confirmation that it is not caused by an evil spirit. The discovery that the infection is healed by penicillin may be understood as confirmation that it is not healed by incantations.[31]

Third, the modern universe has been extricated from the premodern cosmos through the process of *demythologizing*. Rudolf Bultmann says that mythology is intended "to explain phenomena and incidents which are strange, curious, surprising, or frightening, by attributing them to supernatural causes,

---

understanding of disenchantment here. A good example of disenchantment can be found in Thomas Hobbes, *Leviathan*, ed. Edwin Curley (Indianapolis: Hackett, 1994), ch. iii, "Of the Consequence or Train of Imaginations," where he attributes visions of ghosts to dreams and poor sleeping habits.

[28]Jenkins, "Disenchantment, Enchantment and Re-Enchantment," 12.

[29]As Bultmann says, the actions of the gods are "incalculable" (Rudolf Bultmann, "Jesus Christ and Mythology," in *Rudolf Bultmann: Interpreting Faith for the Modern Era*, ed. Roger A. Johnson [Minneapolis: Fortress, 1991], 293). In some instances, disenchantment involves the removal of all spiritual beings and powers. In other instances, it involves the removal of the unpredictable spirits and fortunes of superstition, while the God, angels, and demons of orthodoxy remain.

[30]Bernstein, *Against the Gods*, 95.

[31]I am trying to capture here the early modern optimism associated with disenchantment. Taylor, Jenkins, and others rightly criticize straight line, "subtraction" models of disenchantment, where secularism and rationalism are what remain when the religion and magic of earlier ages are steadily and increasingly sloughed off. See Taylor, *A Secular Age*, 22; Jenkins, "Disenchantment, Enchantment and Re-Enchantment," 12.

to gods or to demons." Based on this description of mythology, the process of demythologizing would be similar to disenchantment—the removal of such supernatural powers as causal factors in the world. However, Bultmann says that "there is more than this in mythology."[32] Myths place the "phenomena and incidents" of life into the framework of a larger story. They remind humankind that they are not in ultimate control of the world and ground human existence in a power "beyond all that we can calculate or control."[33] Myths interpret the world and say something about nature that cannot be observed from within it. When Bacon gives his call for the scientific and systematic observation of nature, he equates human senses with the sun. They reveal the terrestrial while concealing the celestial. He advises those who observe the natural world with their senses to exercise restraint in drawing conclusions "so far as the things of God are concerned." Instead, he advocates for "privileged instances," or unique perceptional opportunities, when observing nature. Microscopes and telescopes are examples of such privileged instances. They "open doors or gates" to reveal the hidden parts, structures, and motions of small or far off bodies.[34] This type of observation precludes seeing any mythical qualities in the thing being observed. There may be a myth, for example, that the first man and woman originated from a hole in a particular rock out of which God pulled them.[35] However, a thorough, scientific study of that rock, with the use of the most powerful microscopes and instruments, would never reveal, nor desire to reveal, the mythical or ethical significance of the rock. Such myths may not disappear, but they lose their legitimacy within modernity.[36] Volcanoes do not erupt because a demon is angry. Earthquakes are not caused by God stomping

---

[32] Bultmann, "Jesus Christ and Mythology," 293. Bultmann also describes the process of demythologizing as the removal of nature from the three-tiered cosmos of heaven, earth, and hell, which has overlaps with disembedding as described above (Bultmann, "Jesus Christ and Mythology," 291).

[33] Bultmann, "Jesus Christ and Mythology," 293. When Bultmann speaks of demythologizing the New Testament, he is seeking to remove the first aspect of mythology (supernatural powers and miracles) while retaining a form of the second aspect (belief in a transcendent reality that guides history).

[34] Bacon, *The New Organon*, 12, 170-72.

[35] John S. Mbiti, *African Religions and Philosophy*, 2nd ed. (Portsmouth, NH: Heinemann, 1990), 91-92.

[36] Supernatural myths may lose their place in a demythologized world, but they are replaced by scientifically feasible myths. Modern humanity still seeks to make sense of the events of life by placing them in the framework of a larger story, but the causal factors within that story are limited to the beings, things, and forces of the modern scientific universe. Therefore, the existence of angels as higher spiritual beings may be dismissed out of hand, but the existence of higher level biological or physical beings from other solar systems is earnestly considered.

his feet. The world does not rest on the shell of a turtle. The course of history and humanity's role in a demythologized world are not shaped by the unfolding and mysterious will of a higher power, but by laws of nature and rational motivations.

THE CHARACTERS: A BRACKETED GOD AND BUFFERED HUMANITY

The set of characters in early modern risk is smaller than that of the premodern story. Events that had once been caused by countless beings from other realms are now the lawful processes of nature. Therefore, the role of the gods, along with that of their priests and intermediaries, has greatly, if not completely, diminished. Humans, as the "only minds in the cosmos,"[37] are intended to interact directly with nature and each other in a less hierarchical and more democratic way.

In premodern, Christianized cultures, the gods of superstitions could be repudiated by use of Scripture, which condemns them as idols and false gods (e.g., 1 Cor 8:4). Augustine ridicules frivolous superstitious practices, such as stepping on the threshold when leaving your house, getting back in bed if someone sneezes when you put on your slippers, or viewing your clothes being eaten by mice as an omen of coming misfortune.[38] Although heretical beliefs and superstitious practices were generally more widespread and more difficult to root out than church authorities would have hoped, those beliefs and practices could, at least, be publicly repudiated.[39] The diminishing of the sovereign God's role in the early modern pursuit of safety would require something different.

In early modern times, critiques of superstition came from "religious reformers" and "scientific revolutionaries," both of which are linked to "a profound break with the past" and the advancement of modernity.[40] Because of this connection, the Reformation is sometimes seen as a step toward secularization in the modern world, but the Reformation, with its emphasis

---

[37] Taylor, *A Secular Age*, 32.
[38] Augustine, *On Christian Doctrine*, 2.20 (trans. Shaw, 31). Augustine notes that people are not content to allow their clothes being eaten by mice to be enough of a misfortune in itself.
[39] See, e.g., Bailey, *Fearful Spirits*, and Carlo Ginzburg, *The Cheese and the Worms: The Cosmos of a Sixteenth-Century Miller*, trans. John Tedeschi and Anne C. Tedeschi (Baltimore: Johns Hopkins University Press, 1992).
[40] Bailey, *Fearful Spirits*, 34.

on *sola Scriptura*, was critical of superstitious beliefs, not supernatural powers. Later Protestant theologians made Christian doctrine an inner, psychological matter and held to anti-supernatural convictions that were amenable to secularization. Those later developments are deviations from the teachings of the Reformers.

When Calvin addresses the doctrine of angels, he mentions the Sadducees' disbelief (Acts 23:8) but spends much more time criticizing extra-biblical speculations "concerning the nature, order, and numbers of angels." He expresses caution about the common notion that "each believer has been assigned his own guardian angel." Calvin's hesitancy about guardian angels is not based on anything like the secular notion of disenchantment, but on the weakness of the biblical argument that just one angel has been assigned to protect us: "For if the fact that all the heavenly host are keeping watch for his safety will not satisfy a man, I do not see what benefit he could derive from knowing that one angel has been given to him as his especial guardian."[41]

Three centuries later, Herman Bavinck placed some early modern thinkers alongside the Sadducees in their disbelief in angels, and he criticized early modern theologians who denied or restricted the existence of angels.[42] He said that in modern theology "only little is left of angels." They belong in "folk sagas" but not the modern world. Bavinck warned against old superstitions and the new spiritism that arose in the nineteenth century in opposition to materialism, but he affirmed the existence and ministry of angels, which included, among other things, watching over believers. As this example with angels shows, Reformed theology is a corrective against extra-biblical superstitions and unbiblical materialism, but it is not a step toward secularization.

The Reformation was critical of heresies and superstitions, yet acknowledged God's providential role in humanity's interactions with the dangers of this world.[43] However, the scientific revolution devised means of

---

[41] John Calvin, *Institutes of the Christian Religion*, ed. John T. McNeill, trans. Ford Lewis Battles, LCC 20-21 (Philadelphia: Westminster John Knox, 1960), I.14.4-9, pp. 163-70.

[42] Herman Bavinck, *Reformed Dogmatics*, ed. John Bolt, trans. John Vriend (Grand Rapids, MI: Baker Academic, 2008), 2:444-68. The thinkers and theologians he mentions include Baruch Spinoza, Thomas Hobbes, and Friedreich Schleiermacher.

[43] For example, Calvin contrasts the belief that "men are whirled and twisted about by blindly indiscriminate fortune" with the belief that they are "governed by God's providence" (Calvin, *Institutes*, I.5.11, pp. 63-64).

effectively, if not actually, removing God from the understanding of human engagement with the world. Michael Allen Gillespie describes two ways in which this happened (neither of which can be separated from previous or contemporaneous theological developments)—rationalism and materialism. According to Gillespie, rationalism understands the relationship between God and creation pantheistically. The desire of rationalism is to see the works of God in the events of nature. He explains: "The motion of nature therefore is the motion of God, and nature's laws are the forms and structures of divine will. Rationalist science thus is theologically grounded not in Scripture but in the deduction of the laws of motion from transcendental will or freedom." Materialism, finding such a God extraneous, takes this thinking a step further and understands nature atheistically. As Gillespie says, "The existence or nonexistence of God is irrelevant for the understanding of nature. . . . Science thus does not need to take this God or Scripture into account in its efforts to come to terms with the natural world and can rely instead on experience alone."[44] God therefore has been bracketed off.

This leaves humanity. Unlike premodern humanity, which was porous, open to powers and meanings from others, early modern humanity is buffered, "impervious to the enchanted cosmos."[45] Bacon warns, in his instructions on observing the labyrinth of nature, that the observer must "bid a stern farewell to all superstitious stories" and "experiments of ritual magic."[46] His aim is for humanity to use its knowledge of nature to gain power over it, a power that he believed "could carry humanity to hitherto unimaginable heights."[47] However, "nature is conquered only by obedience."[48] If humanity wishes to master nature, it must first submit to nature with a disposition of humility, patience, and perseverance.

According to Gillespie, this humility is followed by cruelty. He explains: "To come to nature's inner chambers, we must tear it to pieces, constraining, vexing, dissecting, and torturing nature in order to force it to reveal the

---

[44] Michael Allen Gillespie, *The Theological Origins of Modernity* (Chicago: University of Chicago Press, 2009), 36.
[45] Taylor, *A Secular Age*, 146.
[46] Bacon, *The New Organon*, 225.
[47] Gillespie, *The Theological Origins of Modernity*, 38.
[48] Bacon, *The New Organon*, 24.

secret entrances to its treasure chambers."[49] This cruelty can be seen in Bacon's call to cleave nature apart in order to give it "the attention, observation, and scrutiny it deserves."[50] The humble yet cruel extraction of nature's secrets will lead to "human progress and empowerment." Bacon recognizes, though, that this task will be constrained by human frailty and finitude. People are prone to error and limited by death. Therefore, Bacon calls on early modern humanity to avoid past errors and accept that the scientific project will not be finished "in the course of one lifetime." If it is done right, though, he claims that it will eventually be "the end of an unending error."[51] Bodies in nature do not move according to eternal purposes, nor exist according to eternal forms. They can be redirected toward various purposes and reshaped into different forms. According to Gillespie, this foundation laid by Bacon was subsequently built on by René Descartes and Thomas Hobbes.

Descartes and Hobbes had "alternate visions of the modern scientific enterprise," based on differing views of humanity in relation to God and nature.[52] Gillespie says that when Descartes grounds human knowledge in human consciousness, *cogito ergo sum*, a person becomes "an autonomous subject who not only transcends nature but is also able to resist and ultimately challenge (or even replace) God himself."[53] For Descartes, humanity is able to rise above the forces of nature. For Hobbes, though, people "are rather thoroughly natural objects that obey the laws of nature."[54]

---

[49]Gillespie, *The Theological Origins of Modernity*, 38.
[50]Bacon, *The New Organon*, 182.
[51]Bacon, *The New Organon*, 13. Gillespie says, "It is the very democratic character of Bacon's project that makes its success conceivable. It does not depend upon the exercise of great and thus rare genius, but upon the consistent application of ordinary intelligence to a series of small problems that can be easily analyzed" (Gillespie, *The Theological Origins of Modernity*, 39).
[52]Gillespie, *The Theological Origins of Modernity*, 39. He explains: "The differences between Descartes and Hobbes are crucial and central to the bifurcation of modernity. There is one strain of modern thought that begins with Descartes and includes Leibniz, Malebranche, Spinoza, Kant, Fichte, Hegel, Schopenhauer, and most contemporary continental philosophers. There is a second beginning with Hobbes, Locke, Hume, and Mill, and that includes many contemporary Anglo-American thinkers. . . . The differences between them turn on a number of issues, but the question of the nature and relationship of man and God is of central importance."
[53]Gillespie, *The Theological Origins of Modernity*, 40.
[54]Gillespie, *The Theological Origins of Modernity*, 41. By "laws of nature," Gillespie appears to be referring to physical laws or laws of motion (which Hobbes ties to human action). Hobbes himself defines "law of nature" in a "controversial" way, as that which a person is obligated to do for the preservation of life (*Leviathan*, 79, n. 3).

The motions of bodies, human or otherwise, are neither teleological nor arbitrary. Instead, they are mechanical. Humanity is not moved by "intrinsic natural impulses, nor by divine inspiration or free will, but by a succession of causal motions."[55] Bodies in motion tend to stay in motion, unless they collide with another body. For Hobbes, these collisions are limitations on individuals who desire free and unrestrained movement. Yet the world is crowded, so the purpose of science, with obvious political implications, is to orchestrate the movements of these bodies, both human and non-human. People love liberty yet submit to this orchestration because they have in mind "the foresight of their own preservation, and of a more contented life."[56] Hobbes puts a price on this pursuit of safety, though. He eliminates "glory and beatitude as motives for human action."[57] There is no place for heroism, romanticism, or sacrifice in this orchestration of movements. If the eternal can no longer harm us, then it can no longer bless us either.

Gillespie likens the anthropological differences between Descartes and Hobbes to those between Erasmus and Luther. Whether the human will is free from or bound to the laws of nature, early modern humanity pursues safety, not in a conflict with the gods, but with the forces, powers, and laws of the natural world. God, perhaps, could do anything he wanted, but in the modern universe, since it is taken to be so improbable that he would alter the course of nature, humanity should proceed as if he will not.[58] The actions of the gods have been removed and the actions of God are enclosed in the processes of nature. Early modern humanity seeks safety through the mastery of nature, whether the starting point is the disciplined humility of Bacon or the confidence of Descartes.

THE CONFLICT: HUMANITY AGAINST NATURE

The conflict in early modern risk is between humanity and nature. Viruses spread because living beings multiply. Bears attack because they are hungry or protective. Accidents happen because the movements between a hammer

---

[55]Gillespie, *The Theological Origins of Modernity*, 41; Hobbes, *Leviathan*, ch. vi.
[56]Hobbes, *Leviathan*, 106.
[57]Gillespie, *The Theological Origins of Modernity*, 42.
[58]Hobbes, *Leviathan*, 11.

and a thumb, a car and a tree, or a foot and a step are not in harmony. The disharmony between the movements of a hammer and thumb is quite different from the disharmony between good and evil in the premodern world, though. The disharmony of the early modern world is not obviously, or initially, moral. There is not a clear ethical correlation between those who smash their thumbs with hammers and those who do not. Viruses spread to sinners just as easily as to saints, and vaccines seem to work just as well on the unrepentant as on the repentant. However, the modern pursuit of safety eventually redraws the lines of morality. The distinction between those who (inadvertently) smash their thumbs with hammers and those who do not becomes in itself a moral distinction. Those who use a hammer safely are right and those who smash their thumbs are wrong. If viruses spread just as easily to sinners as to saints, then a new standard of righteousness is established in accordance with behaviors that do not tend to spread viruses, or at least in accordance with behaviors perceived not to spread viruses.

The early modern idea of risk developed in relation to this changing relationship between humanity and the dangers of this world. The etymology of the word "risk" is uncertain, though it is usually traced back to the Greek ῥίζα, which means root, as in the root of a plant, but is also used in reference to cliffs, perhaps as the roots of mountains.[59] The old Italian term *risco* or *riscio* began being used in the fifteenth century in reference to the hazards that sailors and merchants faced in the Mediterranean world. It is linked to both the dangers of the sea (sailing around dangerous cliffs) and the economic ventures undertaken. From these beginnings in the interconnectedness of navigation, commerce, and insurance, the term spread to other areas of life and other European languages (e.g., the English *risk*, German *Risiko*, Spanish *riesgo*, and French *risque*). According to Niklas Luhmann, existing language already had words for "danger, venture, chance, luck,

---

[59]Otthein Rammstedt, "Risiko," in *Historisches Wörterbuch der Philosophie*, eds. Joachim Ritter and Karlfried Gründer (Basel: Schwabe, 1992), 8:1045-55. The etymology of risk is sometimes linked to the scene in Homer's *Odyssey* (Book 12), where Odysseus navigates between the Charybdis and Scylla. While the events that take place capture the *concept* of risk quite well, it is a mistake to etymologically link the *term* risk to this text in the *Odyssey*. The term ῥίζα appears in reference to the roots of a fig tree, yet those roots play no significant role. Odysseus is clinging to the trunk of the tree at one point with the branches above and roots below too far from his reach. Odysseus is sailing around dangerous cliffs, but the term used for "cliff" here is σκόπελος.

courage, fear, [and] adventure," so this term came into widespread use out of a need to connote something different or new. Risk has to do with "the realization that certain advantages are to be gained only if something is at stake."[60] Costs can be calculated beforehand, but risk points to the regret or satisfaction that may come if things work out either as feared or hoped.

According to Luhmann, when decisions related to the unknown future are placed in a religious context, something like prudence is the schema by which those decisions are made. Luhmann describes prudence rather crudely as a means of minimizing the need for repentance later. He then characterizes risk calculation as a non-religious type of prudence, "the secular counterpart to a repentance-minimization programme." In the face of a difficult decision, the question changes from, "Is this prudent?" to "Is this risky?" As early modern confidence in humanity's ability to control the world grew, risk calculations became a method for making ethical decisions. Luhmann says: "It is as if, in the face of an increasingly uncertain future, a secure basis for the making of decisions now had to be found." A decision based on compliance with an ethical command is right. A decision based on probabilistic calculations is *probably* right. As with other methods for making ethical decisions, risk analysis is used with intentions to make good decisions, but also, at times, in efforts to avoid blame. According to Charles Perrow, following the rules of navigation in the shipping industry helps avoid fault in the courts more than it helps avoid accidents at sea.[61] A decision could be correct according to risk calculations even if it does not produce the correct results.

Early modern risks are typically characterized, especially in their late-modern descriptions, as isolated and objectified. Sociologist Ulrich Beck portrays them as personal risks that often had "a note of bravery and adventure," like Columbus setting out "to discover new countries and continents." These risks were distinguishable and "perceptible to the senses." Early industrialization brought new "factory-related or occupational hazards," but the machinery was imposing and loud, pollutions were visible and foul.[62]

---

[60]Niklas Luhmann, *Risk: A Sociological Theory*, trans. Rhodes Barrett (New York: Routledge, 2017), 11-13.
[61]Charles Perrow, *Normal Accidents: Living with High-Risk Technologies* (Princeton, NJ: Princeton University Press, 1999), 176.
[62]Ulrich Beck, *Risk Society: Towards a New Modernity*, trans. Mark Ritter (London: Sage, 1992), 13, 21.

While this understanding of risk will be criticized by later thinkers, it is important to remember the advances that it brought. If an endemic disease is spreading, the ability to filter through a host of behaviors, circumstances, stories, and interactions, to trace that risk precisely to a contaminated well can be extremely valuable. I am referring here to the "technico-scientific" approach to risk, "which emerged from and is expressed in such disciplines as science, engineering, psychology, economics, medicine and epidemiology."[63] According to this approach, a risk is seen as a "taken-for-granted objective phenomenon," which can be defeated individually.[64] While safety as the serenity of the sage was a matter of inner tranquility, safety is more commonly conceived of as the absence of dangers. As Gros explains, "There is a second great home for the sense of safety. It is safety as an objective situation characterized by the absence of dangers, the definitive erasure of perils."[65]

Bacon warns that humanity should not seek to dominate nature with a "bare hand."[66] Therefore, aided by technology, probability, and self-control, early modern humanity battles the dangers of this world with the hope, or at least the enticement, of transforming humanity's relationship to risk itself in some sort of cumulative and lasting way.[67]

Early Modern Considerations

In light of contemporary skepticism and critical reflection on early modernity, the temptation may arise to conjure up romantic visions of the Middle Ages, before the machinery of industrialization began grinding away at societies and civilizations, before all that was sacred was bracketed out of the public sphere. If this is done, the joys that came to many from offloading

---

[63] Deborah Lupton, "Introduction: Risk and Sociocultural Theory," in *Risk and Sociocultural Theory: New Directions and Perspectives*, ed. Deborah Lupton (Cambridge: Cambridge University Press, 2000), 1-2.
[64] Lupton, "Introduction," 1-2.
[65] Frédéric Gros, *Le Principe Sécurité* (Paris: Gallimard, 2012), 52, "Il existe un deuxième grand foyer de sens de la sécurité. C'est une sécurité comme situation objective caractérisée par l'absence de dangers, l'effacement définitif des périls." As Gros develops this idea of safety, he rightly notes the difference between attempts to protect against possible dangers and utopian hopes of a perfect world.
[66] Bacon, *The New Organon*, 28.
[67] Thomas Malthus describes this enticement as a fallacy which "infers an unlimited progress from a partial improvement." Thomas Malthus, *An Essay on the Principle of Population* (Mineola, NY: Dover, 2007), 60.

the burdensome and entangling weights of medieval superstitions and fears may not be appreciated. The advancements in knowledge and technology that began with the rise of modernity were truly unthinkable at the time. Freedom, light, and hope accompanied early modern humanity's shift from seeing the gods as the primary source of danger to seeing nature as a disenchanted place that could be studied, explored, and mastered. Bacon believed that humanity's scientific engagement with nature would carry it to unimaginable heights. He says, for example, that the ability to dissect and transform natural bodies "affords vast opportunities to human power, such as human thought (as things are now) can scarcely conceive or imagine."[68] If we consider airplanes and rocket ships, he was quite literally correct. To the ability to fly, we can add penicillin, water treatment facilities, communication technologies, heart transplants, and brain surgery. Modern developments, whatever their limitations, have successfully been the basis for a wide variety of risk management tools, touching on everything from insurance and investments to traffic regulations and occupational safety. Therefore, the optimism of the early modern pursuit of safety should not be derided too easily.

Yet its deficiencies remain, and they stand out all the more as the logic of the secular story of risk pushes forward. Modern risk has made human interactions with other bodies in this universe matters of probability, technology, and procedure. Such a view of our interactions with each other and creation removes existing ethical systems while giving rise to new ones. A universe filled with bodies that tend to stay in motion or stay at rest is not an obviously ethical universe. Instead, ethics are smuggled in with preferences about how the inevitable collisions should be arranged or avoided. The goal is to steer the motions of bodies in desirable ways. This is the foundation of the modern ethic of safety. Bodies, whether human or microscopic, are kept safe by means of nylon straps, latex barriers, and metal railings.

---

[68]Bacon, *The New Organon*, 105.

Humanity Against Itself
Late-Modern Risk

> *He that stands or walks on slippery ground needs nothing but his own weight to throw him down.*
>
> Jonathan Edwards,
> "Sinners in the Hands of an Angry God"

Reflecting on Risk

An unexpected outcome of early modern humanity's conquest of risk has been the production of new risks. Children are given phones to keep them safe, but those devices introduce a new set of dangers into their lives, whether the hazards of having their heads in screens while crossing streets or the content that is now accessible to them. Travel across land used to be dangerous because of steep hills, deep ravines, scorching heat, and violent storms. Now, with cars and highways, people travel quickly and smoothly, slowed only by the most extreme terrains or climates. Yet new risks have arisen out of the ease and proliferation of this high-speed, inexpensive, and accessible mode of transportation. Those who travel on the road are now concerned with high-speed crashes, congestion, and break-downs.

Gregersen highlights the dilemma this presents to late-modern humanity: "If the very preventing of risks creates new risks, we should realize that *safety*, the traditional counterpart to risk, does not exist."[1] He says that there are

---

[1] Niels Henrik Gregersen, "Risk and Religion: Toward a Theology of Risk Taking," *Zygon* 38 (2003): 358, italics his.

first-order risks, the things in the surrounding environment than can cause harm. Then there are second-order risks. These are the risks that arise from efforts to protect against first-order risks. A disease is a first-order risk; the side effects of a vaccination are second-order risks. A key feature of late-modern, or postmodern, thinking about risk is that there is not a linear struggle away from danger and into safety. Encounters with particular dangers have ongoing repercussions that may not be fully understood. In the political realm, the increased security of one nation is often interpreted to come at the expense of the security another nation. Surveillance cameras perched in every corner increase safety in some respects but decrease privacy and security in other respects.

In early modernity the concept of risk emerges as a means of evaluating humanity's relationship to the dangers of this world. Calculative risk deliberations provide not only descriptive, but prescriptive power. They help guide decisions with unknown consequences based on the assumption that "the social and natural worlds follow laws that may be measured, calculated and therefore predicted."[2] So, when faced with an opportunity to lie, moral deliberations might focus on whether it is right or wrong to tell a lie, while risk deliberations might focus on the likelihood of being caught and the amount of trouble the lie could cause. Risk deliberations also involve decisions that are not so obviously moral, such as decisions to carry an umbrella on a cloudy day or to wear a helmet while riding a bike. Such risk deliberations carry their own moral weight, though, because of the harm that may or may not come. Wearing a helmet has become the right thing to do even if a crash never occurs.

In late modernity risk itself has become an object of evaluation and study. The validity and presuppositions of deliberations about risk have come into question. As a result, theories, explanations, and models of risk now abound. It is difficult to categorize all the various understandings of risk, but there are some helpful guides. Gros presents four basic dimensions of safety, looking at each in the context of a specific historical situation. He pairs safety as a tranquil state of mind with ancient philosophy, safety as the

---

[2]Deborah Lupton, "Introduction: Risk and Sociocultural Theory," in *Risk and Sociocultural Theory: New Directions and Perspectives*, ed. Deborah Lupton (Cambridge: Cambridge University Press, 2000), 6.

absence of harm with millennial hopes of the Middle Ages, safety as public order with the modern police state, and safety as process control with the standardizations of specific areas of life (e.g., food safety, energy safety, emotional safety).[3]

The work of identifying dangers and figuring out how to deal with them—that is, risk assessment and management—usually assumes a shared understanding of what is or is not a risk. The study of risk perception takes a step back to understand how risks are understood and decided on in the first place. Sociologist Deborah Lupton provides a helpful overview of current theories of risk perception. She lists seven major categories of risk that are prominent in late-modern Western culture and, as she says, are indicative of cultural perceptions and priorities related to risk. They include environmental risks (harm caused by the world around you), lifestyle risks (harm caused by your behaviors), medical risks, interpersonal risks (harm caused through relationships), economic risks, criminal risks, and political risks.[4] She then discusses five ways that risk perception has been theorized.

The first, mentioned above in connection to the early modern pursuit of safety, is the "technico-scientific" perspective. Scientific means are employed to measure risks and probabilities while technologies are used to manage objective and pre-existing risks. The second way of theorizing risk perception, also connected to the early modern pursuit of safety, is the "cognitive psychological" approach. Based on the assumption that proper risk deliberations are made by the ideal rational agent, it seeks to understand action and thinking related to risk at an individual level, or why some people take greater or lesser risks than others. The third is the "cultural/symbolic" approach, developed by anthropologist Mary Douglas, where risk is a "contemporary Western strategy for dealing with danger" and maintaining boundaries between the self and others.[5] The fourth is the "risk society" perspective, developed by sociologists Ulrich Beck and Anthony Giddens,

---

[3]Frédéric Gros, *Le Principe Sécurité* (Paris: Gallimard, 2012), 9-14. See also Catherine E. Althaus, "A Disciplinary Perspective on the Epistemological Status of Risk," *Risk Analysis* 25 (2005): 567-88, who traces the different ways that risk has been developed within a wide array of disciplines.
[4]Deborah Lupton, *Risk*, 2nd ed. (New York: Routledge, 2013), 22.
[5]Lupton, *Risk*, 52; Mary Douglas, *Purity and Danger: An Analysis of the Concepts of Pollution and Taboo* (New York: Routledge, 2003); Mary Douglas and Aaron Wildavsky, *Risk and Culture: An Essay on the Selection of Technological and Environmental Dangers* (Berkeley: University of California Press, 1983).

where risks are inevitably produced alongside wealth in the processes of modernization. The fifth way of theorizing about risk perception given by Lupton is "governmentality." This perspective is linked to Michel Foucault and seeks to understand risk "in the context of surveillance, discipline and regulation of populations, and how concepts of risk construct particular norms of behaviour."[6]

Lupton says that the "technico-scientific" and "cognitive psychology" theories operate from an epistemological position of "naïve realism," where risks exist objectively and can be perceived clearly. According to these views, if someone's risk perceptions are not congruent with the risks themselves, it is likely that the risk perceptions have been distorted through psychological, social, or cultural frameworks. The "cultural/symbolic" and "risk society" perspectives fall under a weak constructionist epistemological position. This position acknowledges that risk perceptions are related to objective dangers, yet it maintains that those perceptions are mediated through social and cultural frameworks. Finally, Lupton explains, the "governmentality" approach operates from a strong constructionist epistemological position, where risk perceptions and therefore risks themselves are constructed entirely as the products of "historically, socially and culturally contingent 'ways of seeing.'"[7]

Along with their criticisms of early modern perceptions of risk, the last three theories share another commonality. They are all characterized by the late-modern impulse to approach the world in a "highly reflexive" way.[8] They look back on the projects of modernity in order to weigh them up and critically assess their claims of progress. According to Beck, "reflexive modernization" does not merely point to reflection, though, but to self-confrontation.[9] The pursuit of safety has not escaped this critical assessment. Just as early modernity challenged the gods of premodernity, so late modernity challenges the early modern myths of calculability and technology.[10] Dangers can be downplayed or highlighted through things like risk warning signs. The sense

---

[6] Lupton, *Risk*, 37.
[7] Lupton, *Risk*, 50.
[8] Lupton, *Risk*, 23.
[9] Ulrich Beck, *World at Risk*, trans. Ciaran Cronin (Malden, MA: Polity, 2008), 109.
[10] The "myth of calculability" is the myth that everything is calculable because it is predictable (Lupton, *Risk*, 7). The "myth of technology" is the myth that what *can* be done technologically is what *should* be done (Hans Walter Wolff, *Anthropology of the Old Testament*, trans. Margaret Kohl [London: SCM Press, 1981], 164; Jacques Ellul, *The Technological Society*, trans. John

of safety for a society, group, or individual can be raised or lowered even if the circumstances or probabilities do not change. For example, Beck is quite worried about nuclear war. He claims that the threat remains constant, even though related fears rise and fall drastically through time and place.[11]

The general character of late-modern risk has been shaped by critical reflection on humanity itself in relation to the dangers of this world. In its pursuit of safety, late-modern humanity not only faces various kinds of risks, but also disagrees over what should or should not be considered a risk, over which risks should or should not be engaged, and over how the engagement with risks should happen. These disagreements are not new, yet the deliberate and critical reflection of our age has brought them to the forefront of our considerations of risk and safety. Gregersen says safety no longer exists because attempts to conquer first-order risks produce second-order risks, but opinions differ on what can be done about second-order risks. For some, humanity compromises with risks but does not defeat them. Safety is relativized. Risks can be postponed, redistributed, or transformed, but they cannot be eliminated. For others, complex and second-order risks can be dealt with in largely the same way as first-order risks, through a redoubling of our efforts.

THE SETTING: A FINITE AND FRAGILE SPHERE

The setting for the late-modern pursuit of safety, despite the vastness of the universe, is this planet we inhabit. Through its penchant for measurements and quantifications, early modern humanity attempted to give an answer to a question that silenced Job: "Have you comprehended the expanse of the earth?" (Job 38:18). By means of scientific instruments and standardized units of measurement, humanity has taken stock of the storehouses of snow and hail, measured the recesses of the deep, and mapped out the east wind. The late-modern response to this delimiting and quantifying of the earth has been an acute awareness of the world's finitude. Feelings of scarcity, "the mismatch of seemingly unlimited needs and wants in a world of limited resources,"[12] have become a fundamental reality for the late-modern pursuit of safety. The

---

Wilkinson [New York: Vintage, 1964], 191-92). These will be addressed in greater detail in chapters 6 and 7 respectively.

[11]Ulrich Beck, *Risk Society: Towards a New Modernity*, trans. Mark Ritter (London: Sage, 1992), 75.

[12]Noah Toly, "Risk and Responsibility in Global Environmental Governance," *Christian Scholar's Review* 42 (Spring 2013): 265.

movement from early modern calculations to a reflexive awareness of scarcity (with its entailing fears and concerns) can be seen in Thomas Malthus' 1798 study of food production in relation to population growth. He calculated that food production would increase linearly while population increased exponentially.[13] The dangers, if he were correct, are easy to foresee.

Late-modern trepidations about the earth's finitude and the scarcity of its resources can be seen in Beck's concept of a risk society. According to Beck, early modern industrialization produced wealth, along with some unintentional dangers. As industrialization grew and modernized, the production of risks began to outpace the production of wealth. He deduces that a finite planet cannot endlessly absorb the "latent side effects" of modernization. Pollutions and hazards that used to blow away or float downriver have run out of places to go and are now returning home. A finite world, as the setting for late-modern risk, highlights the scarcity of resources on the one hand and the inescapability of risks on the other.

In this finite setting, risks are characterized differently. Unlike the personal, localized, and perceptible risks of early modernity, the risks of late modernity are characterized as societal, globalized, and often imperceptible. They are not limited to certain places or times. They are not the risks of a daring adventure that the individual, to some extent, can choose to take on or not. Instead, they involve entire societies. They are "global dangers" that threaten the "self-destruction of all life on Earth." Beck says a nuclear incident could "outlast generations" and affect those "not yet alive at the time or in the place" where it occurred.[14] These risks are global, yet not immediately obvious to the senses. Hazards like toxins in food or nuclear radioactivity cannot be seen or smelled like the dangers of the past. The concerns of late modernity are not only that trees will be cut down by chainsaws, but also that they may die from far away, invisible pollutants.

The earth is not only the setting for the late-modern story of risk. In this story, the earth itself is subject to risk. The late-modern world is not only finite, but frail. The frailty of the earth does not mean that it will collapse under the slightest pressure, but that there is a conceivable limit to what it can withstand before it is

---

[13]Toly, "Risk and Responsibility"; Thomas Malthus, *An Essay on the Principle of Population* (Mineola, NY: Dover, 2007).
[14]Beck, *Risk Society*, 21-22.

no longer able to support life on a global scale or flourish and function properly at smaller, more localized scales.[15] This late-modern world is vulnerable to the actions of humanity. It seems, then, that it has lost the autonomy of the early modern universe and exists, once again, in something like the premodern hierarchical cosmos, where dangers seem uncontrollable and beyond comprehension. Walking through a crowded city filled with strange faces, powerful machines, and perplexing systems is like walking through a dark forest filled with feuding tribes, wild animals, and malevolent spirits. There are some key differences, though, between the premodern cosmos and the finite and fragile late-modern world. According to the secular story of risk, the late-modern world has no transcendent telos toward which it is spinning. Also, the greatest threats to the late-modern world do not come from without, from supernatural beings, but emerge from within, from beings and powers in the physical world itself.

The Characters: Superhuman Entities, Lay People, and Experts

Late-modern perspectives on risk and humanity's pursuit of safety generally follow early modernity in excluding supernatural beings. Nonetheless, for late-modern humanity the cumulative powers of contemporary institutions, systems, and technologies have some similarities to the gods, spirits, and forces of premodern societies. According to Kamppinen, both the gods and these powers are "difficult to understand, to cope with, and to manipulate." The superior powers of late-modern risk, however, are not supernatural beings but "superhuman (or at least supraindividual)" entities.[16] They include institutions such as modern governments and transnational corporations, systems such as social media and global economics, and technologies such as nuclear power and genetic modification. Although these entities comprise human efforts and ingenuities, they do not always act in ways that humans can predict or manage. They seem to have minds of their own. According to Beck, science is now the source of danger and safety. The threats of these superhuman entities are things like harmful ideologies, catastrophic

---

[15] Beck, *World at Risk*, 27.
[16] Matti Kamppinen, "Playing Against Superior Beings in Religion, Technology and Economy," in *Religion, Economy, and Cooperation*, ed. Ilkka Pyysiainen, Research and Reason 49 (Berlin: De Gruyter, 2010), 95.

system failures, and market collapses. These threats exist in a "shadow kingdom" similar to the premodern "realm of the gods and demons."[17] The complexities of these systems bring about risks that appear chaotic and unpredictable. As Perrow explains, the network of interrelated systems in an airplane, a cargo ship, or a factory might bring together an unforeseeable set of circumstances in which "two failures would interact so as to both start a fire and silence the fire alarm" at the same time.[18] We wonder who looks in on our lives as we look in on the lives of others online.

In this late-modern world, life is at the mercy of such superhuman entities. Risks are global, invisible, and confusing. Therefore, many in the late-modern world relate their experiences of irrationality, amazement, and helplessness to what they think life was like for their premodern ancestors. Kamppinen says the complexities of the contemporary world have "created a milieu for a common citizen that shares many features with the archaic society."[19] According to Beck, there are risks and destructive forces "before which the human imagination stands in awe." This experience of awe changes humanity's relationship to nature and the superhuman entities. A person no longer stands apart as a detached and disciplined observer, but as a living being, interconnected with and caught up by the other beings and things in this world.[20] The complexities and dangers of the late-modern world overtake humanity, not quite in the same way as a magic spell or demonic power, and yet that is the language drawn on when the dangers of the industrialized world are described. We call devices that take on minds of their own possessed, we call the brutalities of urbanization hellish, we have "magical expectations for technology," and we "feel as if we are left at the mercy of fate and experts."[21] This language arises as late-modern humanity interacts with systems and devices that it does not understand. We know that our cell phones work, but not how. We have vague ideas about circuits, processors, and invisible radio signals, but the inner workings between the

---

[17] Beck, *Risk Society*, 155, 72.
[18] Charles Perrow, *Normal Accidents: Living with High-Risk Technologies* (Princeton, NJ: Princeton University Press, 1999), 4.
[19] Kamppinen, "Playing Against Superior Beings," 94.
[20] Beck, *Risk Society*, 20, 72.
[21] See Richard Stivers, *Technology as Magic: The Triumph of the Irrational* (New York: Continuum, 2001), 4; and Kamppinen, "Playing Against Superior Beings," 88, respectively.

hardware, software, and networks are as impenetrable to most of us as the wills of the gods.

These experiences of chaos, confusion, and bewilderment reintroduce the need for mediators in the pursuit of safety. Late-modern humanity does not want priests to mediate between it and the gods, but experts to mediate between it and these "magical" devices and superhuman entities. According to Beck, disagreements within the scientific community lead to conflicting messages about what is safe and what is not. If the side effects of modernization are latent and imperceptible, lay people cannot immediately feel, smell, or see the sources of danger. Beck claims that "the social effect of risk definitions is therefore not dependent on their scientific validity."[22] We cannot always tell if something is a risk through direct personal experience, so guidelines are imposed on us by experts. Beck says that scientists, who were taboo breakers in early modern times, must now become taboo constructors.[23] There are cause and effect relationships that common people cannot see or understand. In order to be safe in the late-modern world, some things, places, and behaviors simply become taboo. During a solar eclipse, school administrators kept children indoors and closed window blinds to protect them from damaging their eyes.[24] As a result, children misunderstood the event. Some thought that the sun burned brighter during an eclipse or that it was dangerous even to be outside while it was happening. For the sake of their safety, the astronomical event was experienced by these children as something dangerous and mysterious even though manageable preparations could have been made. They were treated as if it were beyond their comprehension.

Late-modern humanity has lost the early modern confidence that the rationality and observability of causal relationships can be shared by everyone. This development delivers a severe blow to the idealism of early modernity. According to Bacon, the scientific endeavor was supposed to be a gradual, democratic process founded on rationality and empiricism. The

---

[22]Beck, *Risk Society*, 32. Beck is not critiquing science here, but what he considers to be outdated modes of scientific discovery, consensus, and political influence.
[23]Beck, *Risk Society*, 157; Beck, *World at Risk*, 89.
[24]Greg Toppo, "Solar Eclipse Fears Prompt Schools to Cancel Class, Keep Kids Inside," *USA TODAY*, August 17, 2017, www.usatoday.com/story/news/2017/08/17/teachers-schools-eclipse-fears-drive-kids-inside/578050001.

early modern expert, scientist, or mathematician was an intermediary of sorts, but there was an expectation that the lay person could look into the lens of a microscope or follow the logic of an argument in order to see whatever the expert saw. A crucial development in the late-modern age is that the experts have once again taken on the role of intermediaries, viewed as having access to knowledge that is mysterious and closed off from the lay person.

Kamppinen similarly describes this relationship between the lay person and the expert. Late-modern humanity exists in a world where life's "ultimate boundary conditions ... are known and controlled only by a small group of specialists."[25] Kamppinen appeals to Beck in describing late-modern humanity's experience of risk in premodern terms. According to Kamppinen, Beck is describing not just perceptions of risk in this way, but the reality of people's experiences. For Beck, some experiences are truly unfathomable. Kamppinen is more optimistic, saying that while risks may be experienced in a way that is evocative of premodern times, they "can be assessed on rational grounds."[26]

According to Lupton, expert knowledge also plays an important role for Foucault in guiding society, conforming individuals to expected norms, and maximizing the wealth, welfare, and productivity of the people. Therefore, risk is governed by "a heterogeneous network of interactive actors, institutions, knowledges and practices."[27] Information about risks is collected, analyzed, and acted upon, presumably for the common good, by a cadre of scientific, sociological, and political experts.

The Conflict: Humanity Against Itself

In late-modern risk, the conflict is between humanity and itself. This means, first of all, that late-modern humanity is primarily concerned about the risks that it creates for itself. Some of those risks are the unintentional consequences of modernization. Some, more ironically, are the compounded,

---

[25] Kamppinen, "Playing Against Superior Beings," 94.
[26] Kamppinen, "Playing Against Superior Beings," 95. In light of Beck's later work, though, it seems to me that he and Kamppinen are closer in their views than Kamppinen suggests (Beck, *World at Risk*, 109-14).
[27] Lupton, *Risk*, 116-17.

second-order risks that arise from the pursuit of safety. Other risks emerge out of the unforeseen contradictions of complex systems.

Beck has been criticized for distinguishing between natural hazards as the risks of the past and these human-made hazards as the risks of the present. This historical distinction fails to acknowledge the ongoing risks of natural disasters today, the longstanding history of human-caused catastrophes in the past, and the relationships between the two.[28] It would be a mistake, according to this criticism, to conceive of late-modern risks as only those which humanity creates for itself. However, it seems to me that Beck has at least accurately captured the late-modern imagination as it relates to the story of risk. As he says, the idea that contemporary risks derive from our decisions instead of from the gods or nature is a "historically novel quality of today's risks."[29] Without dismissing other sources of risk (either in reality or perception), we can acknowledge that those who live in industrialized societies are often more concerned with second-order risks than first-order risks—more concerned with genetically modified food supplies than the food supply itself, more concerned with the loss of the forest than being lost in the forest.

The pursuit of safety in this late-modern world has some inherent inconsistencies. Risks are viewed as systemic while solutions are often individualized: "We look for individual salvation from shared troubles."[30] We also look for individual scapegoats for collective failures. Systems fail through their contradictory complexities, yet only the person sitting at the helm is blamed. Another inconsistency can be seen in Perrow's treatment of high-risk technologies. On the one hand, he says that risks seem to appear "faster than the reduction of risks." On the other hand, he is hopeful that through a better understanding of the nature of the risks, "we may be able to reduce or even remove these dangers."[31] If the primary source of dangers in the late-modern world are the dangers humanity brings on itself, it is hard to conceive of a happy, human-based, resolution. The more optimistic resolution is Beck's call for reflexive modernization, where the tools of modernity

---

[28] Lupton, *Risk*, 110.
[29] Beck, *Risk Society*, 155.
[30] Zygmunt Bauman, *Community: Seeking Safety in an Insecure World* (Malden, MA: Blackwell, 2001), 144.
[31] Perrow, *Normal Accidents*, 3.

are employed to overcome the risks of modernity. A more difficult resolution, which may at times drift into despair, is to view late-modern humanity's multiplication of risks as the consequences of guilt, pride, and lust rather than mere inadvertence or inattentiveness. But that would seem to leave late-modern humanity hopeless, stuck in a condition from which it cannot remove itself. Such a conclusion is therefore resisted.[32]

LATE-MODERN CONSIDERATIONS

The transition from one stage in the story of risk to the next is generally understood, not as a mere sequence, but as progress, or movement toward some better condition. Premodern humanity, with some exceptions, is presented as unable or unwilling to overcome risks because of its technological inferiority and beliefs that life is at the mercy of the gods. Early modern humanity frees itself from these beliefs and uses advancements in science, mathematics, and technology to overcome the dangers of nature in a mechanistic universe. Then late-modern humanity, having overcome many first-order dangers of nature, seeks to overcome new dangers it has unintentionally created for itself. Late-modern conceptions of risk, as presented here, are more pessimistic in their outlook than early modern conceptions. Nevertheless, this late-modern stage is considered part of the progression in the secular story of humanity's relationship to risk because its reflections and criticisms are intended to move humanity forward in relation to risk. They are seen as part of a maturing process, whether that means accepting certain limitations or figuring out how to move forward with even greater effectiveness.

It is not surprising that the story of risk is told as a story of progress. After all, in order for it to be a story, there must be a plot, a meaningful explanation of the movement from one state of affairs to the next. As Taylor explains, "our understanding of ourselves and where we stand is partly defined by our sense of having come to where we are, of having overcome a previous condition."[33] There may be other explanations for historical movement from one condition to the next, but the default explanation in

---

[32]Beck is sharply critical of Bauman and others for such views because in his opinion they tend toward hopelessness and inaction (Beck, *World at Risk*, 113-14).
[33]Charles Taylor, *A Secular Age* (Cambridge, MA: Harvard University Press, 2007), 28.

Humanity Against Itself 85

the modern era, even with frequent criticism, has been the inevitability of progress.[34] When the inevitability of progress is applied to humanity's pursuit of safety, the story of risk moves from the microcosm of a train station platform or a congested street, where certain individuals or groups seek to overcome certain dangers, to the macrocosm of human existence, and it makes a claim about humanity collectively progressing in relation to risk itself.

Yet hopes can turn into demands. There is an important difference between overcoming particular risks at particular times and overcoming risk itself. Beck says, "Where everything has become controllable, the product of human efforts, *the age of excuses is over*. There are no longer any dominant objective constraints, unless we allow them and make them dominate."[35] Likewise, Bernstein promotes "systematic probability and its implicit suggestion that the future might be predictable and even controllable to some degree,"[36] and Kamppinen says that late-modern people have transformed the acts of gods into "known and partly manageable lawful forces of nature."[37] Beck admits that not everything "can be arranged exactly as you like,"[38] and Bernstein concedes that probabilities, at their best, will only resemble a likeness to truth. But overall, they make it sound like humanity has a decent handle on this world's sources of danger.

As late modernity continues its critical appraisal of early modernity, there is an opportunity for humility and sober-mindedness with the realization that humanity often endangers itself further in its strivings to be safe. There is an opportunity to heed what Jonathan Edwards pointed out long ago regarding Deuteronomy 32:35 ("Their foot shall slide in due time"), that people are "liable to fall of themselves, without being thrown down by the hand of another."[39] Yet it does not seem that this opportunity will be taken. According to political scientist Christopher Daase, Beck speaks with "epochal" language about the transition from modernization to reflexive modernization

---

[34] Taylor, *A Secular Age*, 301. Taylor is among those who are critical of this explanation.
[35] Beck, *Risk Society*, 234, italics his.
[36] Peter L. Bernstein, *Against the Gods: The Remarkable Story of Risk* (New York: Wiley, 1998), 20.
[37] Kamppinen, "Playing Against Superior Beings," 88.
[38] Beck, *Risk Society*, 234.
[39] Jonathan Edwards, "Sinners in the Hands of an Angry God," in *The Sermons of Jonathan Edwards: A Reader*, ed. Wilson H. Kimnach, Kenneth P. Minkema, and Douglas A. Sweeney (New Haven, CT: Yale University Press, 1999), 49.

(i.e., early modernity to late modernity).[40] Beck says that the foundations of the industrial world are beginning to "crumble and disintegrate" and that there is a need for new ways to conceive of "the new which is rolling over us."[41] He sees a great rupture between early and late modernity, but this rupture is not deep enough to address the shortcomings of humanity's relationship to the dangers of this world. Perhaps this has to do with the underlying continuity that Beck sees between modernity and reflexive modernity. As he says, "Reflexive modernization means not less but more modernity."[42] When all is said and done, reflexive modernization is not the upheaval Beck would have us think. The solutions to the dangers of late modernity are more complex than the solutions to the first-order dangers of early modernity, but they are still modern. They are matters of discipline, self-control, and growth in knowledge of the natural world, but not matters of concern for the hand of God, which is "for good on all who seek him," nor for the power of his wrath, which is "against all who forsake him" (Ezra 8:22).

This is the story that has helped to shape the current form and status of safety. The three epochal antagonists found in this story—the gods, nature, and humanity—helpfully encapsulate the sources of danger in this world, while the historical progression from premodern to early modern to late-modern risk helps us locate ourselves in this story and understand why the pursuit of safety today is shaped by actuary tables, laboratories, and product warning labels, not sacrifices, superstitions, or rain dances. Safety has a high moral status today. This high status is due, in part, to the optimism of early modernity, the removal of the transcendent from the public sphere, and, in a different way, the isolating unsettledness of late modernity.

Nevertheless, there are certain unchangeable things about humanity's standing before God in this world. According to Scripture, humanity lives in a world governed by God, yet influenced by unseen spiritual forces, the processes of nature, and the lives of humans. Therefore, Gregersen's observation regarding late-modern humanity's experience of risk is appropriate: "It seems to me that we today are dealing with the hazards of life in a complex

---

[40]Christopher Daase, "Die Historisierung der Sicherheit. Anmerkungen zur historischen Sicherheitsforschung aus politikwissenschaftlicher Sicht," *Geschichte und Gesellschaft* 38 (2012), 401.
[41]Beck, *Risk Society*, 12-14.
[42]Beck, *Risk Society*, 14.

manner that combines strategies towards the future that have been emphasized in premodernity, modernity, and postmodernity. We live *simultaneously* in a premodern world of fate, in a modernizing attempt to control risk, and in a postmodern awareness of creating risks while trying to prevent them."[43] Late-modern humanity has difficulty conceiving of existence beyond the horizons of death and materiality. Those shared conceptions are shaped by what Charles Taylor calls "social imaginaries," that is, "the ways we are able to think or imagine the whole of society."[44] Put succinctly, an imaginary is a field or realm of possibilities in which imaginations operate. The late-modern imagination has diminished to such an extent that it struggles to think of God, the spiritual realm, the angels and demons that fill it, and their involvement in the affairs of this world. Therefore, I would emphasize that Gregersen's observation is appropriate, not only because it accurately describes late-modern perceptions of risk, but also because humanity in all ages is in danger from itself, nature, and spiritual powers. There are limitations, culpabilities, and vulnerabilities that humanity cannot get out from under no matter how risk or safety are conceived. The resolution of humanity's battle with danger will not take place within the horizons of history.

---

[43] Niels Henrik Gregersen, "Faith in a World of Risks: A Trinitarian Theology of Risk-Taking," in *For All People: Global Theologies in Context*, ed. Else Marie Wiberg Pedersen, Holger Lam, and Peter Lodberg (Grand Rapids, MI: Eerdmans, 2002), 221-22, italics his.
[44] Taylor, *A Secular Age*, 156.

PART THREE

Avoiding Harm in a Fallen World

◆◆◆◆◆◆◆◆◆◆◆◆◆◆◆◆◆◆◆◆◆◆◆

Grasping the Future
Probabilities and the Promises of God

> *My child, become not an omen-watcher, for it leads to idolatry.*
>
> DIDACHE 3:4

CHRISTIANITY AFFIRMS THE GOODNESS of safety—being free of harm, whole. Theological engagement with the world's pursuit of safety is not intended to undermine the desire for safety. Instead, it is meant to raise criticisms about how we satisfy that desire and to place safety in proper relationship to other good things that are, or ought to be, desired. Safety is good, but there are other goods, temporal and eternal, that should not be neglected in its pursuit. The rise of modernity has had tremendous influence on humanity's encounters with the dangers of this world. However, its developments have often been accompanied by a disproportionate rise in humanity's estimation of its abilities to calculate the future, control the world, and therefore be safe. Probabilistic prediction, technological innovation, and procedural guidance have their uses as means of safety within the stability of a world created and upheld by God, but they also have inherent limitations and frequent misappropriations as employed by sinful humanity.

Inevitable tensions arise concerning the extent to which the contemporary pursuit of safety is effective. There is tension within the pursuit of safety itself, where safety is fundamentally approached as the absence of physical harm or material loss. To what extent is the contemporary pursuit of safety able to meet its own standards or live up to its own promises? There is also tension, from a Christian perspective, when the pursuit of physical safety is considered in relation to other aspects of life, other areas in which a person may experience harm or loss, both temporal and eternal. My hope is not to resolve all these tensions, but to understand them as part of humanity's creaturely existence and to consider how a follower of Christ might accept safety's inherent limitations in a way that bears witness to the onlooking world that Jesus is Lord over his church, but also over all of history and creation.

THE CRUMBLING HORIZONS OF TIME

The pursuit of safety concerns humanity's relationship to time. When we look to the past, we remember the pain of various harms, the fright of close calls, and the comfort of stability and protection. The patterns of those memories shape our anticipations of the future, the dangers we will look out for, the provisions we will expect, and the predictabilities we will rely on. All of this entails God's relationship to time. He is in control of the past, present, and future. As the Lord of time, he gives humanity limited access to both the past and the future. He gives us enough access to hold us morally accountable and to command us to have rightly formed memories and anticipations. But he does not give us so much access that we can tame either the past or the future.

God's eternal vision. There are some contemporary doctrines of God in which the future is unknown by him to some degree. If God lacks perfect knowledge of the future, yet has desires and acts in relation to the future, then he is necessarily a risk-taking God.[1] From this perspective, humanity relates to risk by seeing that God himself is not afraid to take risks and is therefore vulnerable to his creation.[2] However, if God truly takes risks then the hope that they will ultimately turn out for good cannot be grounded in

---

[1] See John Sanders, *The God Who Risks: A Theology of Divine Providence*, 2nd ed. (Downers Grove, IL: InterVarsity Press, 2007).
[2] For theological treatments of humanity and risk that are grounded in risk-taking views of divine providence, see Niels Henrik Gregersen, "Faith in a World of Risks: A Trinitarian Theology of Risk-Taking," in *For All People: Global Theologies in Context*, ed. Else Marie Wiberg Pedersen, Holger Lam, and Peter Lodberg (Grand Rapids, MI: Eerdmans, 2002), and Mikkel Gabriel Christoffersen, "Living with Risk and Danger: Studies in Interdisciplinary Systematic Theology" (PhD diss., Copenhagen: University of Copenhagen, 2017).

his being or power. It may be objected that God truly takes risks, but his risks pay off because he is sufficiently intelligent, strong, and wise. However, the very notion of risk involves extending oneself beyond what one can predict or control. If God is always certain about what will happen, or if what actually happens always coincides with what he expects to happen, it is hard to see how his relationship to the world would entail risk in any meaningful way. It may also be objected that God is ultimately able to console himself regarding those things that do not go as he desires.

If God is uncertain about some aspect of what will happen in this world, that uncertainty must arise because some portion of the world behaves in a way that cannot be predicted (randomness, unfettered freewill) or because some portion of the world behaves according to some other power that is unknown or uncontrolled by God. If this is the case, and if God's risks pay off, it is either because of randomness or some other power. If it is because of randomness, then God is lucky. If it is because of some power or principle outside of God—for example, the idea that vulnerable relationships are better than protective isolation—then he is not Lord of heaven and earth. He is no longer the almighty author of "my power is made perfect in weakness" (2 Cor 12:9), but one who needs this axiom somehow to be true. But if it is because of a power or principle that God upholds, or because he is sufficiently wise to bring about good solutions, then he is not actually taking risks. If God has truly taken risks, then when the course of history is over, he will be genuinely and eternally dissatisfied in some way. He will not be "blessed forever" (2 Cor 11:31; cf. 1 Tim 1:11).

In contrast to these approaches, I will be assuming a doctrine of God which affirms divine immutability, eternity, and felicity, along with a view of providence in which the future is fully known by God, as I seek to construct a theology of safety.[3] In this case, humanity relates to risk by entrusting itself to God, who is sovereign over the dangers and vulnerabilities

---

[3] For critiques of the view that God takes risk, as well as defenses of what Paul Helm calls the "no-risk" view of divine providence, see Paul Helm, *The Providence of God* (Downers Grove, IL: IVP Academic, 1994), 39; D. Stephen Long, "Does God Have a Future? Theology and the 'Future' of God," in *Theology and the Future: Evangelical Assertions and Explorations*, ed. Trevor Cairney and David Ian Starling (New York: T&T Clark, 2014); and James S. Spiegel, "Does God Take Risks?," in *God Under Fire: Modern Scholarship Reinvents God*, ed. Douglas S. Huffman and Eric L. Johnson (Grand Rapids, MI: Zondervan, 2002).

of this world. We see Christ do this in the incarnation. He suffered as he walked in obedience to the Father, but his work was not a matter of probabilities or risk calculations. He was neither doubtful about the future nor regretful about the past. Instead, as death came, he committed his spirit into the hands of the Father (Lk 23:46).[4]

Jesus is able to sympathize with our weaknesses. He was tempted like us, but without sin (Heb 4:15). If he is familiar with our weaknesses, we may wonder if he had any false starts or misapprehensions in his ministry. We may wonder if he ever had doubts about who he was or what he was doing. He faced slander, mockery, misunderstandings, and multiple attempted murders. When we face difficulties in our obedience to God, we are quick to compromise or doubt his goodness. But Jesus was without sin, faithful over God's house (Heb 3:6). He went through the depths of suffering, grief, sorrow, and sympathy, but without regret or doubt. He walked forward guided by the Spirit and in obedience to the Father. He is relatable to us

---

[4]Before committing his spirit into the Father's hands, Jesus gives his cry of dereliction, "My God, my God, why have you forsaken me?" (Mt 27:46; Mk 15:34, quoting Ps 22:1). John Yocum says it has become commonplace with modern theologians to understand this cry as "an event that takes place between the Father and the Son, either as an event in the intra-trinitarian life of God, or as an event in the life of the human Jesus of Nazareth" ("A Cry of Dereliction? Reconsidering a Recent Theological Commonplace," *IJST* 7 [January 2005]: 72-73). Moltmann, for example, describes it as an intra-trinitarian event: "The Son suffers in his love being forsaken by the Father as he dies. The Father suffers in his love the grief of the death of the Son" (*The Crucified God*, trans. R. A. Wilson and John Bowden [Minneapolis: Fortress, 2015], 245). Yocum argues that Christ's words indicate neither abandonment of the Son by the Father nor condemnation of the man by God. He says that Christ suffered condemnation at the hands of sinful humanity, not the hands of God. Therefore, Christ's cry "expresses the suffering of the Son and the non-intervention of the Father, a non-intervention fully and freely embraced by the Son" ("A Cry of Dereliction?," 79). Yocum is correct that the cry of dereliction has been increasingly understood in modern theology as an intra-trinitarian event. However, this cry has long been understood as an expression, by Christ, of sinful humanity's realization of its condemnation by God. Augustine says that the triune God forsakes neither Christ nor those who believe in him, but that Christ speaks in that moment on behalf of sinners: "When our Lord said that from the cross, he included us in what he was saying, for we are his body and he is our Head. He was speaking from the cross not with his own voice but with ours, for God never forsook him, nor did he ever leave the Father; it was for our sake that he said, *My God, my God, why have you forsaken me?* . . . God does not forsake you, even when it looks like that" (*Expositions of the Psalms*, ed. John E. Rotelle, trans. Maria Boulding, WSA III/16 [New York: New City, 2001], 2:266, commenting on Ps 44, though tying it to Ps 22:1). Calvin says that Christ spoke these words as he "bore the weight of divine severity" (*Institutes of Christian Religion*, ed. John T. McNeill, trans. Ford Lewis Battles. LCC 20-21 [Philadelphia: Westminster John Knox, 1960], II.16.11, p. 517). As Calvin notes, even at this moment, when Christ takes on himself human weakness and fear, his trust in God's goodness is evident in that "he did not cease to call him his God, by whom he cried out that he had been forsaken" (*Institutes*, II.16.12, p. 520).

because of the difficulties he faced, but he also stands apart, as our example, because he did not doubt or disobey. He expressed grief over Jerusalem, telling what could have been, but at the same time reaffirming that he will "finish [his] course" (Lk 13:32-35). In the Garden of Gethsemane, Jesus was in agony. His soul was "very sorrowful, even to death" (Mt 26:38). The disciples faltered, but an angel strengthened him (Lk 22:43). He bore the full weight of temptation. He asked if the cup could be taken from him. To doubt is to have a double mind. Jesus had his eye on the cross. When he asked if it could be removed, we wonder if he had taken his eye off of it and was now contemplating another path apart from the Father. But he was praying to the Father about the cross, asking if there was any way for the Father to remove it. Jesus dreaded the cross, but he did not doubt God. He prayed that his will would be done.

God sees both the past and the future with equal and unfading clarity. He is the eternal one. A thousand years are like yesterday in his sight (Ps 90:4), yet a thousand years of civilizations rising and falling is only the beginning of his vision of time. His gaze reaches much further, stretching from this world's beginning to its end. He takes in the millennia of history as if they were a few brief and passing moments. The inverse is true as well (2 Pet 3:8). God takes in each day as if it contained a thousand years of history. He sees the significance of every moment without forgetting or conflating any of them. God does not just see the past and the future, though. He holds them in his hand. He rules over them and uses them for his good and wise purposes. Time serves its Creator. It makes no demands on him. God is neither slow nor hasty in bringing about his promises and judgments (2 Pet 3:9-10). He declares beforehand what will be, not merely as an observer of the future, but as its Lord: "Who told this long ago? Who declared it of old? Was it not I, the Lord?" (Is 45:21). His vision and reign over time are free of uncertainties or probabilities. He knows fully. He sees perfectly.

Humanity's constrained vision. God has not given humanity this same access to time. We see the past and the future, but only in dim and fragmentary ways. "All things are always equally instantaneously present" to God, Gregory of Nyssa tells us; the past and future are "firmly held by the power which embraces all," yet for us life is divided "between memory and expectation."⁵ We see the past through memory. That vision is diminished by forgetfulness but reinforced by the testimony of others and the world itself. Natural and cultural conditions, like the twelve stones from the Jordan (Josh 4:5-7), are ongoing signs of past events. God himself has "caused his wondrous works to be remembered" (Ps 111:4). Along with memory, humanity's vision of the past is aided by the fact that it has already happened. It has been "reduced to the sequential order and factual univocity of history"; it is composed of "accomplished facts which can never again be reversed."⁶

Unlike the past, the future is unsettled for humanity. We do not know what will happen, yet we see the future through expectation. God has given humanity the capacity to imagine what tomorrow will be like. Humanity cultivates those expectations, anticipating the future based on the patterns of the past and seeking to shape tomorrow through actions today. Humanity hopes and fears, knowing there will be a tomorrow but not knowing what it will bring. Humanity's access to the divisions of time is limited by its creatureliness, but it is also distorted by sin. Sinful humanity idealizes the past (Eccles 7:10) and presumes about the future (Jas 4:13-15). Humanity worries about tomorrow but forgets God's promises (Mt 6:33-34). As we are warned, "There is no remembrance of former things" (Eccles 1:11), and humanity "does not know what is to be" (Eccles 8:7). Knowledge of the past and future exists to a large degree in the "twilight of uncertainty."⁷ We know what *probably* happened. We anticipate what will *likely* come about.

Augustine observes that "time emerges from some hiding place when it turns from future into present; and retires to some other hiding place when it turns from present into past time."⁸ He then asks what method God uses to teach "our souls what happens in the future," and concludes that God does not teach humanity the future, but "what is in the present yet has a bearing

---

⁵Gregory of Nyssa, *Contra Eunomium I: An English Translation with Supporting Studies*, ed. Miguel Brugarolas (Boston: Brill, 2018), 139-40.

⁶Oliver O'Donovan, *Self, World, and Time: Ethics as Theology, Volume 1, An Induction* (Grand Rapids, MI: Eerdmans, 2013), 121; and Dietrich Bonhoeffer, *Ethics*, ed. Clifford J. Green, trans. Reinhard Krauss, Charles C. West, and Douglas W. Stott (Minneapolis: Fortress, 2005), 77, respectively.

⁷Gerd Gigerenzer, *Calculated Risks: How to Know When Numbers Deceive You* (New York: Simon & Schuster, 2002), 7.

⁸Augustine, *Confessions* 11.17, trans. Carolyn J.-B. Hammond, LCL 27 (Cambridge, MA: Harvard University Press, 2016), 27:225.

on the future."⁹ Using the example of a sunrise, Augustine says there are "present and discernible" phenomena that enable us to predict future events. These include the use of imagination, the ability to see events in our minds that have not yet happened. They also include preceding events, like the changing light of dawn, which are not the event itself, but indications that it is coming. Augustine says, "Future phenomena do not yet exist, and . . . they certainly cannot be seen; but they can still be predicted by means of factors in the present, which do now exist and are visible." According to Augustine, these are the means by which God teaches the human soul to discern what will happen in the future.

When we pursue safety, we are trying to grab hold of the future. Safety implies "the idea of a future in which not everything is possible, in which not everything can happen, but rather a future that is defined and determined."¹⁰ It is the "destruction of the temporality of the future."¹¹ The pursuit of safety seeks to remove discrepancies between anticipations of what might happen and what actually happens. It seeks to overcome the gap between the human "realm of experience" and its "horizon of expectation," so that what is experienced coincides with what is expected.¹² That gap can be overcome in two ways. A person may seek to know the future in order to adjust expectations and make appropriate accommodations, or a person may seek to control the future so that it meets expectations. Either option holds out possible comfort, so both are included in the pursuit of safety.

For the past three centuries, the primary means by which modern humanity has sought to overcome this gap between present expectations and future realities has been the mathematical theory of probability. A basic premise of probabilistic views of the future is that what will likely happen can be calculated based on what has happened. A basic problem with this

---

⁹Augustine, *Confessions* 2:11.18-19 (LCL 27:229).
¹⁰Eckart Conze, "Sicherheit als Kultur. Überlegungen zu einer 'modernen Politikgeschichte' der Bundesrepublik Deutschland," *Vierteljahrshefte für Zeitgeschichte* 53 (2005): 363, "Denn Sicherheit bedeutet die Vorstellung einer Zukunft, in der nicht alles möglich ist, in der nicht alles passieren kann, die Vorstellung einer Zukunft, die vielmehr festgelegt und bestimmt ist."
¹¹Conze, "Sicherheit als Kultur," quoting Franz-Xaver Kaufmann, *Sicherheit als soziologisches und sozialpolitisches Problem*, 2nd ed. (Stuttgart: Enke, 1973), 157, "die 'Vernichtung der Zeitlichkeit von Zukunft.'"
¹²Conze, "Sicherheit als Kultur," 363, "[Das Streben nach Sicherheit] zielt darauf, jenes Auseinandertreten von 'Erfahrungsraum' und 'Erwartungshorizont' zu überwinden."

view of the future is the speed with which the past crumbles behind us. Any particular moment of time begins in the far-off future. It moves toward us and takes its form—perhaps gradually and predictably, perhaps suddenly and shockingly—as the potentialities of the future are sorted and sifted into the definitiveness of the present. The moment surrounds us and shapes us, and then it is gone, moving from the jumbled grayness of the future to the fading rubble of the past. The effectiveness of the theory of probability relates to efforts to rightly see the future, the ability to faithfully remember the past, and the wisdom to discern what, among a host of anticipations and memories, is salient to the needs at hand.

Calculating the Future

Probability as it is known today is *mathematical* probability. Initially, in centuries past, an opinion or judgment was deemed *probable* if it was worthy of approval.[13] Aside from the full certainty of knowledge based on demonstration, a person could also have opinions of varying certainty based on testimony. The *opinion* of medieval epistemology, which was supported by the testimony of tradition or authority, was the basis for *probability* in early modern times, which is supported by the testimony of nature.[14] In early usage, something was described as *probable*, not because it was likely to happen, but because it was approvable by others, especially those with influence or authority. The testimony of tradition, written in books, gave way, however, to the testimony of nature, written in things. Natural objects give signs regarding the past, present, and future. Ashes testify that there was fire, smoke testifies that there is fire, and kindling testifies that there will be fire.

As the testimony of tradition was supplanted by the testimony of nature, the probability (i.e., approvability) of an opinion was no longer based on the probity of the authority from which it came,[15] nor on its conformance to a

---

[13]Ian Hacking, *The Emergence of Probability: A Philosophical Study of Early Ideas About Probability, Induction and Statistical Inference*, 2nd ed. (Cambridge: Cambridge University Press, 2006), 18-23.

[14]Hacking, *The Emergence of Probability*, chaps. 3–5.

[15]As seen, for example, in Aquinas's reply to an objection: "On the contrary, the authority of Bede suffices" (*ST* [London: Eyre & Spottiswoode], 1-2.85.3). Charles Taylor rightly notes that the turn to nature was not an inherently secularizing move, though it is often characterized as such: "That things have a stable nature doesn't prevent them from still being signs pointing us to God. In the words of Hugues of St. Victor, . . . 'The entire sense-perceptible world is like a sort of book

metaphysical principle,[16] but on the frequency with which it turned out to be correct. When there is smoke there is fire, but when there are clouds there is not always rain. Smoke is a more probable sign of fire than clouds are of rain. The union of the testimony of nature with correlative frequency became the theoretical basis for a formalized calculus of probability as a measure of trustworthiness. It is this particular theory of probability, developed in the seventeenth century by Blaise Pascal and Pierre de Fermat, that has had such a transformational influence on modern humanity's relationship to the future and therefore the pursuit of safety.[17]

Classical probability. The rise of calculative probability in Europe began around the turn of the sixteenth century. In 1494, Luca Pacioli, a Franciscan monk, published a book on mathematics that included a longstanding problem from the world of gambling. This problem asks how the prize money from a game should be distributed among the players if they end the game before finishing.[18] He gives an example of a ten-coin wager between three players in a crossbow contest. The first to win six rounds wins the coins, but if the game is ended when the first player has won four rounds, the second player three rounds, and the third player two rounds, "to how much is each entitled?"[19] The premise of the question is that one's portion of prize money should match the likelihood of winning future matches, and that likelihood is based on the scores earned so far. Pacioli's

---

written by the finger of God'" (Charles Taylor, *A Secular Age* [Cambridge, MA: Harvard University Press, 2007], 92-93).

[16]Metaphysical principles included "antipathy," in which a problem was treated by its opposite—using cold to treat a fever—or "similarity," in which a problem was treated by something similar—using kidney shaped herbs to heal kidneys (Hacking, *The Emergence of Probability*, 42-43).

[17]A classic work on the development of the theory of probability is Isaac Todhunter, *A History of Probability from the Time of Pascal to That of Laplace* (Cambridge: Macmillan, 1865). A standard update is F. N. David, *Games, Gods, and Gambling: A History of Probability and Statistical Ideas* (Mineola, NY: Dover, 1998), originally published in 1962. More recent works include Hacking, *The Emergence of Probability*; Peter L. Bernstein, *Against the Gods: The Remarkable Story of Risk* (New York: Wiley, 1998); Leonard Mlodinow, *The Drunkard's Walk: How Randomness Rules Our Lives* (New York: Pantheon, 2008); Anders Hald, *A History of Probability and Statistics and Their Applications Before 1750* (New York: Wiley, 1990); and Matthias Beck and Beth Kewell, *Risk: A Study of Its Origins, History and Politics* (Hackensack, NJ: World Scientific, 2014), chap. 1.

[18]Luca Pacioli, *Summa de Arithmetica, Geometria, Proportioni, et Proportionalita* (Venice, 1494).

[19]Luca Pacioli, "Summa de Arithmetica Geometria Proportioni et Proportionalita: F. 197 R. and 198 V.," trans. Richard J. Pulskamp (Unpublished, 2009), 3, https://citeseerx.ist.psu.edu/pdf/31cb 02840db91b43d719c9cf94f38a328baf2f63. This article provides an English translation of the relevant portion of Pacioli's work.

puzzle may seem trivial, but it came to have enormous significance because of the developments that ignited around it. It asks a predictive question. What would have happened based on what had been happening? It also asks an ethical question. What is a fair way to split the prize money? The puzzle would remain unsolved for another hundred and sixty years, but the surrounding developments "marked the beginning of a systematic analysis of probability—the measure of our confidence that something is going to happen."[20]

According to Galileo, the book of nature stands open before us, but it cannot be read unless we learn the language "in which it is composed."[21] This language is mathematics, and without it, Galileo says, "one wanders about in a dark labyrinth." In the sixteenth century, however, people were not as conversant with this language as many are today. Leonardo da Vinci attempted basic exercises in arithmetic from Pacioli's book. These exercises could be completed by grade school children today, but Leonardo's attempts, preserved in his journals, had "frequent errors and incompletions."[22]

The beginnings of mathematical forecasting were small, but not without significance. One early accomplishment came in the mid-sixteenth century from Girolamo Cardano, a physician from Milan, who developed a simple way to describe chance mathematically—as the ratio between preferred outcomes (e.g., the three odd-numbered sides of a die) and all possible outcomes (e.g., the six total sides).[23] The insight that the chance of rolling an odd number is 3:6 or 50% is commonplace and unremarkable today. However, Cardano successfully squeezed the entire spectrum of certainty and doubt between the integers 0 and 1.

In 1654 Pacioli's puzzle was still unresolved, so, as the story goes, a nobleman and prolific gambler, Antoine Gombaud, commissioned Pascal to

---

[20]Bernstein, *Against the Gods*, 43. Bernstein is correct here, so long as his statement refers to a particular (i.e., calculative) analysis of probability. Byrne is rightly critical of Isaac Todhunter and F. N. David, whom Bernstein follows in overlooking previous, non-calculative, analyses of probability. See Edmund F. Byrne, *Probability and Opinion: A Study in the Medieval Presuppositions of Post-Medieval Theories of Probabilities* (The Hague: Martinus Nijhoff, 1968), 6-7.
[21]Galileo Galilei, *Discoveries and Opinions of Galileo*, trans. Stillman Drake, 24th ed. (New York: Anchor, 1957), 238.
[22]Martin Kemp, *Leonardo da Vinci: The Marvellous Works of Nature and Man*, rev. ed. (Oxford: Oxford University Press, 2006), 241-42.
[23]Hald, *A History of Probability and Statistics*, 38.

solve it. Pascal enlisted Fermat, and through their ensuing correspondence they formulated an inductive "*theory* of probability."[24] They devised a generalized method for calculating what is likely to happen based on what has happened. Pacioli's puzzle entails a decision, though. Therefore, Pascal argued that his calculations determined what is a "just distribution" of the prize.[25] The likelihood of winning future matches is calculated based on past wins. A player who was 70% likely to win the match ought to take 70% of the prize.

These early developments paved the way for later work on probabilities to operate within the parameters of Bacon's seventeenth-century prescription that "natural bodies and natural powers be (as far as possible) numbered, weighed, measured and determined."[26] Bernstein says that the ability to enumerate and calculate probabilities was "a climactic break from making decisions on the basis of degrees of belief."[27] Before that climactic breakthrough, other means were employed to describe gradations of certainty. Socrates's definition of the probable (εἰκός) as that which has a likeness to truth provided a schema for moving from truth, to the probable, to the improbable, to falsehood.[28] Aristotle, followed by Aquinas, classified events in three ways: "(1) certain events that happen necessarily; (2) probable events that happen in most cases; and (3) unpredictable or unknowable events that happen by pure chance."[29] Through the development of the theory of probability, the scale of certainty was externalized and standardized, being determined mathematically and represented numerically.

---

[24]Bernstein, *Against the Gods*, 58, italics his. For the mathematical details of this theory, see A. W. F. Edwards, *Pascal's Arithmetical Triangle: The Story of a Mathematical Idea* (Baltimore: Johns Hopkins University Press, 2002).

[25]Bernstein, *Against the Gods*, 67.

[26]Francis Bacon, *The New Organon*, ed. Lisa Jardine and Michael Silverthorne (Cambridge: Cambridge University Press, 2000), 229.

[27]Bernstein, *Against the Gods*, 58. Bernstein uses the phrase "degree of belief" epistemologically to refer to the level of certainty a person holds regarding a given proposition. This corresponds with subjective probability as defined below. In this passage, however, he appears to be emphasizing premodern, prosaic, expressions of certainty, in contrast to the theory of probability which "provided a measure of probability in terms of hard numbers" and in reference to natural events rather than personal opinions.

[28]Samuel Sambursky, "On the Possible and the Probable in Ancient Greece," in *Studies in the History of Statistics and Probability: A Series of Papers*, ed. Maurice G. Kendall and R. L. Plackett (London: Griffin, 1970), 36-37.

[29]Hald, *A History of Probability and Statistics*, 30; Aquinas, *ST*, 1.57.3, 1.86.4. According to Aquinas, events that appear as chance to us are foreseen by God (*ST*, 1.22.2 ad 1).

The enticement of this development has long held sway in the modern world because numbers provide a consistent means of expression for uncertainty and because numeric representations of states of affairs can bring certain things to light in ways that verbal representations cannot.[30]

Probabilistic calculations were initially developed and applied within the contexts of games. This is known as *classical probability*.[31] The six sides of a die, two sides of a coin, and fifty-two cards in a deck have geometric and quantitative consistencies which allow their behaviors to be calculated as ratios of their symmetries. However, difficulties arose as probabilistic calculations were applied to an ever-widening array of human behaviors, natural phenomena, and historical events. Classical probability, which works neatly with dice, runs into difficulties when used to determine the likelihoods of possible outcomes for events beyond the artificial symmetry of games.

Statistical probability. This difficulty was eased as *classical probability* gave way to *statistical probability*.[32] Another way to determine that a coin has a fifty-fifty chance of landing heads, aside from observing its geometric properties, is to flip it repeatedly, tallying the results. While perhaps superfluous in the case of a coin, this method has a much wider scope of applications than classical probability. According to Newtonian physics, the future outcome of any present state of affairs could be calculated with enough information, knowledge, and computational power. Such causal determinism was epitomized in 1814 by Laplace's demon, that great imaginary intelligence that could comprehend all forces and calculate all movements in the universe. For this mind, "nothing would be uncertain and the future, as the past, would be present to its eyes."[33] According to deterministic models of probability, uncertainty about the future is a matter of ignorance about underlying conditions. In non-deterministic models, uncertainty

---

[30] A good example of this is the way multiple factors, each with high degrees of certainty, quickly decrease in certainty when combined with each other. If multiple factors in a possible event each have 90% certainty, overall certainty reduce by 81%, 73%, 66%, etc., as they are combined.

[31] Peter Olofsson, *Probabilities: The Little Numbers That Rule Our Lives* (Hoboken, NJ: Wiley, 2007), 3.

[32] Olofsson, *Probabilities*, 3.

[33] Pierre-Simon Laplace, *A Philosophical Essay on Probabilities*, trans. Frederick Wilson Truscott and Frederick Lincoln Emory (London: Chapman & Hall, 1902), 4.

may be attributed to ignorance in part, but also to randomness.[34] In either case, statistical probability proves helpful because it does not rely on theories for *how* events happen, but on observations *that* events happen, thus demonstrating correlation even if it does not explain causation.

Girolamo Fracastoro, a sixteenth-century intellectual, says the earth gives signs "as though she knew what is to come."[35] In the premodern era, these signs were frequently superstitious, with no causal mechanism between sign and event. In the modern era, legitimacy is determined statistically, by correlative frequencies between sign and event, but also rationally, by the disembedding, disenchanting, and demythologizing of the modern world. In other words, in the modern world, a black cat is not generally considered a legitimate sign of death, regardless of statistical accuracy.

However, a thousand deaths in your city from the same sickness is taken as a legitimate sign that you might die from it as well. In 1662, John Graunt published a work in which he looked for such signs in the bills of mortality from London churches.[36] Through his study, he founded the modern discipline of statistics and learned, for example, that 82 percent of the deaths in London in 1603 were from the plague and that 36 percent of children born between 1604 and 1624 died before age six.[37] Reflection on his findings led Graunt to wonder "what benefit the knowledge of the same would bring to the World."[38] He did not just want to know the condition of the world, but how to improve it. Still today, societies look for answers to that question from the "watchful Statistician" who keeps a "finger on the pulse of Humanity, and gives the necessary warning when things are not as they should be."[39]

Two centuries after Graunt, the Belgian scientist Adolphe Quetelet became such a statistician. He employed the bell curve to develop the notion of *l'homme moyen* (the average man).[40] Quetelet discovered that while individual lives vary, the composite features of a large population are often quite stable. It is difficult to predict specific crimes, but the overall cost of

---

[34]Mlodinow, *The Drunkard's Walk*, 82, 192-95.
[35]Hacking, *The Emergence of Probability*, 43.
[36]John Graunt, *Natural and Political Observations Made upon the Bills of Mortality*, ed. Walter F. Willcox (Baltimore: Johns Hopkins University Press, 1939).
[37]Bernstein, *Against the Gods*, 80.
[38]Graunt, *Natural and Political Observations*, 18.
[39]George Sarton, "Preface to Volume XXIII of Isis (Quetelet)," *Isis* 23 (1935): 22-23.
[40]Bernstein, *Against the Gods*, 159.

crime in a society is "paid with frightening regularity."[41] In the present day, America pays an annual traffic fatality rate with that same frightening regularity.[42] In order to improve these situations, Quetelet advocated for structural social reforms, arguing that these costs "cannot diminish without the causes that lead to them being changed beforehand."[43] He argued that *l'homme moyen* provides a standard for safety and security. The person who lives under the predictability of the bell curve is "equally removed from all excesses," and represents "all that is great and beautiful and good."[44] This person would be safe by being the rule rather than the statistical exception, avoiding rare and extreme circumstances. For Quetelet, statistics are numerical means of describing social conditions. However, they also have prescriptive and predictive functions, showing people how they ought to live to increase the likelihood that they will be safe.

Subjective probability. A frequent accusation leveled against statisticians is that they see bell curves everywhere, when real life is actually far more complex.[45] Therefore, statistical probability is generally limited to consistent and repeatable events. For some, this is an inherent limitation on probabilistic forecasting. You cannot meaningfully calculate the probabilities of singular events, especially with a post-Newtonian understanding of the universe where uncertainty is a function not just of ignorance, but randomness as well.[46] For others, this limitation is overcome by *subjective*

---

[41]Adolphe Quetelet, *Sur L'Homme et Le Développement de Ses Facultés* (Paris: Bachelier, Imprimeur-Libraire, 1835), 2:249, "qu'on paie avec une régularité effrayante."
[42]See the historical data in "FARS Data Tables," National Highway Traffic Safety Administration, *Fatality Analysis Reporting System (FARS) Encyclopedia*, accessed March 19, 2019, www-fars.nhtsa.dot.gov/Main/index.aspx.
[43]Quetelet, *Sur L'Homme et Le Développement de Ses Facultés*, 2:324, "un résultat nécessaire de notre organisation sociale, et que le nombre n'en peut diminuer sans que les causes qui les amènent ne soient préalablement modifiées."
[44]Quetelet, *Sur L'Homme et Le Développement de Ses Facultés*, 2:275-76, "également éloignée de tous les excès," "tout ce qu'il y a de grand, de beau et de bien." Quetelet usually sought to describe, not a universal *homme moyen*, but *l'homme moyen* for a particular set of people. He was driven, in part, by a curiosity about the differences between various groups of people (Bernstein, *Against the Gods*, 157-59).
[45]See, e.g., Nassim Nicholas Taleb, *The Black Swan: The Impact of the Highly Improbable* (New York: Random House, 2007), 241, for such an accusation.
[46]The literature on probability with which I have interacted has consistently appealed to the indeterminacy of quantum mechanics as support for the claim that there is ontological randomness in the physical world. Vern S. Poythress, for example, says that uncertainty is intrinsic to quantum mechanics (*Chance and the Sovereignty of God: A God-Centered Approach to Probability and Random Events* [Wheaton, IL: Crossway, 2014], 80). However, Thomas F. Tracy notes that

probability, which began in the eighteenth century with the publication of an earlier essay by a Presbyterian minister, Thomas Bayes. Bayes devised a method for calculating probabilities that can be updated as more information is accumulated.[47] The accumulated information changes the subject's understanding of the event. Thus, it is *subjective* probability. It does not measure the likelihood of an event, but a subject's degree of belief about the likelihood of the event.[48]

Subjective probability begins with prior information about an event, and then updates the probability as new information is incorporated. Advocates argue that this allows for a more dynamic interaction with the real world and provides a means of quantifying and tracking degrees of belief about a wide variety of events. The statistical probability of your home being burglarized may be 1 percent. However, on a particular night, you learn that a neighbor was recently burglarized, see a suspicious van, and hear noises outside. Subjective probability allows you to incorporate that information, so that your degree of belief that your house will be burglarized is perhaps 90 percent. If you later hear that the burglar was arrested, see that the van is gone, and realize that it is windy outside, your degree of belief may then drop back to near zero.

Comprehensive knowledge of the world around us is impossible. You could still be burglarized. However, subjective probability in its most technologically sophisticated forms employs assumptions and heuristics that are constantly being tested and refined in order to develop useful models of the world and predictions about the future.[49] Models of the world are not the world, though. They are simplifications of it, and the real world has never had any obligation to conform to these models when the two diverge.

---

this claim is based on the assumption that "quantum theory is complete; there are no hidden variables that, if we knew them, would allow us to assign fully determinate properties" to an entity ("Creation, Providence and Quantum Chance," in *Philosophy, Science and Divine Action*, ed. F. LeRon Shults, Nancey Murphy, and Robert John Russell, Philosophical Studies in Science and Religion 1 [Leiden: Brill, 2009], 252). If Tracy is correct, randomness remains, to some extent, an epistemological issue.

[47]Stephen M. Stigler, *Statistics on the Table: The History of Statistical Concepts and Methods* (Cambridge, MA: Harvard University Press, 2002), 291-301.

[48]As mentioned above, "degree of belief" is used here epistemologically to describe the level of certainty a person holds regarding a given proposition. What is unique (and controversial) about subjective probability is that a subjective degree of belief is expressed with the objectivity of numeric measurements.

[49]Nate Silver, *The Signal and the Noise: Why So Many Predictions Fail—But Some Don't* (New York: Penguin, 2015), 266-67.

Nonetheless, these heuristic models increasingly mediate human interactions with others and the surrounding world. Technologies and industries that seek to function predictively, from weather forecasts and economic predictions to voice recognition, medical diagnostics, and self-driving cars, rely on Bayes' theorem. Bayes died in 1760, "but the basic idea of his fundamental contribution is, two centuries later, the core of the most up-and-coming theory of statistical inference."[50]

The limits of probability. The theory of probability has been relied on heavily in the modern era. The demands made on it highlight its strength, but also reveal its limitations and expose it to criticisms. Laplace's hope of calculating the particularities of the future based on the details of the present was an impossible dream. The future remains unknown. Late-modern humanity relies on probabilistic forecasting because it is often right, yet maintains aversions to it because it is sometimes wrong. If it were always right, it would impinge on human freedom. The world is stable enough that we rely on probabilistic forecasting. Yet there is enough disorder to cast a shadow over probabilistic assumptions. Things might not go as expected. In deterministic models, events can be predicted when the underlying mechanisms are understood. These models are not obviously wrong because they are sometimes right. Halley successfully predicted a comet fifty-three years before it appeared in the night sky. He had other lesser-known and less impressive predictions, though. He surmised that a twenty-five-year-old in Breslau in the late seventeenth century had 80-to-1 odds of living to be twenty-six and that a thirty-year-old had a fifty-fifty chance of living to the age of fifty-eight.[51] These later predictions are less impressive because they are less precise. They merely offer a range of possible outcomes.

One way to relieve the tension between predictive successes and failures is to acknowledge a "predictability horizon."[52] According to this idea, probabilistic predictions have a range of accuracy within which they offer some level of payoff. Beyond that range, returns on predictive investments fall sharply. Weather forecasts are vastly more sophisticated than in the past,

---

[50] Hacking, *The Emergence of Probability*, 15.
[51] Bernstein, *Against the Gods*, 85-87.
[52] Rasmus Dahlberg, "The Roots of Risk: A Brief Conceptual History of Predictability, Uncertainty and Statistics," Copenhagen Center for Disaster Research, Copenhagen, October 7, 2016, 20-22.

yet the number of days and hours out that weather can be reliably predicted has not significantly increased. Societal phenomena are predictable in aggregate and in the short term, but the horizon quickly grows dark when predictions are applied with too much specificity or too far into the future. Opinions differ, of course, on where the predictability horizon lies. Enough predictions are made that someone will be right about something far beyond the usual horizons. It is not always easy to tell the difference between a wild guess that turns out to be correct and a reliable probabilistic forecast. Sometimes contrived predictions succeed; sometimes stable models fail.

Laplace's demon is dead, yet humanity keeps pushing the horizon of predictability because it continues to fall short of the horizon of expectation. Total certainty about the future may be gone, but the desire for more certainty, and the safety that could accompany it, remains. In the pursuit of safety, humanity does not generally want to know the future from a fatalistic perspective, simply to know what harm will or will not occur. Instead, there is a desire to know multiple contingent futures, or all possible outcomes for a sequence of events, so that safety can be pursued either by avoiding courses that would cause harm or by adequately preparing for potentially harmful events. In the film *Back to the Future*, Doc Brown chose the latter. He knew he would be shot on October 26, 1985. He could have chosen another course, avoiding the shopping mall parking lot that night, but instead he used his knowledge of the future to protect himself by wearing a bullet-proof vest.

Without the benefits of time travel, uncertainty remains. Bernstein is optimistic. The future is uncertain because it is open. We are "free souls," he says. "We can change the world," but "whether that change turns out to be for better or worse is up to us."[53] Others are more cautious and seek to balance human freedom with the apparent randomness of the world. Physicist Leonard Mlodinow argues that successes and failures are the combined results of one's decisions, the randomness of the physical world, and the unpredictability of human behavior. Unexpected things will unavoidably happen. He says we should be thankful when randomness does

---

[53]Bernstein, *Against the Gods*, 230.

us good, but not surprised when it does us harm.[54] Some respond to the uncertainty of the world with envy. This can be seen in appeals to "the Matthew effect," based on a (mis)reading of Matthew 13:12 ("to the one who has, more will be given"). According to this argument, those who happen on the right mixture of luck, ingenuity, and popularity are recognized as successful in the past and therefore ushered by others into a successful future, even if their actual past was filled with "accidents, prejudices and plain idiocies."[55] Others respond to uncertainty in the pursuit of safety like the foolish rich man (Lk 12:16-19). They tear down their barns and build bigger ones. They thicken the layer of insulation between themselves and harm. They overcompensate for uncertainty and then overcompensate again.

These criticisms of probabilistic forecasting, along with the various strategies of coping with uncertainty, remind us that humanity's vision of the future is limited and always tentative. We "do not know what tomorrow will bring" (Jas 4:14). However, probabilistic forecasting remains a formative force in the pursuit of safety. The world was duly impressed when Halley predicted the exact year a comet would appear in the sky. Yet the movements of history are rarely so predictable. Probabilities, even if they carry the precision of numbers, are still probabilities, opinions about the future that will turn out to have been more or less approvable. Probabilistic forecasting plays a deeply ethical role in the late-modern era because it serves as a guide for decision and action. It is a lens through which the world is interpreted and a calculative means by which many seek to govern the "passions" that are at war within them (Jas 4:1). A friend whose wife had cancer faced a decision to approve a risky surgery that could give her months to live or forego the surgery, in which case she had weeks to live. Based on the advice of doctors and the desire for more time with her, he approved the surgery. She died on the operating table. Years later he expressed to me his remorse that he gambled for months instead of accepting weeks and ended up with neither. How could he have known?

---

[54]Mlodinow, *The Drunkard's Walk*, 194, 218-19.
[55]Beck and Kewell, *Risk*, 4-5; Robert K. Merton, "The Matthew Effect in Science," *Science* 159 (1968): 57-58.

GUARDING THE WAY

If the dangers of tomorrow came into our lives with the regularity of a comet, the pursuit of safety could be focused and efficient. But dangers are diffuse, like meteor showers. We may know, for example, that the statistical likelihood of a child being injured or killed crossing the street is low, but lots of children cross lots of streets and we do not know how any given instance will turn out.[56] Therefore, children are prohibited from crossing the street.

Pedestrian predictions. A recent study on the matter of children crossing streets claims that five- to fourteen-year-olds suffer the "highest percentage of pedestrian injuries of any age group."[57] Children in this age range who were injured in traffic were injured as pedestrians (instead of in a car, on a bike, etc.) 5 percent of the time, while adults who were injured in traffic were injured as pedestrians 3 percent of the time.[58] This comparison is meaningless. The statistical data could also be interpreted to mean that children have a lower percentage of injuries in cars than adults—which would be understandable since children do not drive. Further, this is a relative comparison that says nothing about the likelihood of being injured as a pedestrian in the first place. Children, it so happens, were overall less likely than adults to be injured as pedestrians.[59] Nonetheless, the statistic was cited to raise concern over the results of the study itself, which used virtual reality technology to determine that the younger children are, the worse they are at crossing a simulated street.

The children who participated in the study improved gradually, from six-year-olds who did the poorest to fourteen-year-olds who did essentially as well as adults. The study did not account for previous training or experience in crossing streets. Did children who had previously crossed streets alone

---

[56] In 2014, the pedestrian fatality rate in America for 5- to 14-year-olds was about 0.315 per 100,000, or 0.000315%. The injury rate for the same was about 15.5 per 100,000, or 0.0155% (National Center for Statistics and Analysis, *Pedestrians: 2014 Data*, Traffic Safety Facts Report No. DOT HS 812 270 [Washington, DC: National Highway Traffic Safety Administration, May 2016], 5).

[57] Elizabeth E. O'Neal et al., "Changes in Perception–Action Tuning over Long Time Scales: How Children and Adults Perceive and Act on Dynamic Affordances when Crossing Roads," *Journal of Experimental Psychology: Human Perception and Performance* 44 (January 2018): 18.

[58] National Center for Statistics and Analysis, *Pedestrians: 2014 Data*, 4.

[59] National Center for Statistics and Analysis, *Pedestrians: 2014 Data*, 5. The 2014 pedestrian injury rate for 5- to 14-year-olds (about 15.5 per 100,000, or 0.0155%) was lower than the rate for 15- to 65-year-olds (about 23.6 per 100,000, or 0.0236%).

perform better? Nor did it account for learning during the trials. Did the children get better through their repeated attempts? Yet we are presented with this information and obligated to respond in some way. The next time a child crosses a street, according to the timings and measurements of this study, there is a probability that the child will not do it as well as an adult.[60]

A parenting article with the societally burdensome title "Science Says Kids Shouldn't Cross a Busy Street Solo Until They're 14," responded to this study by suggesting that children not cross the street alone because they do not do it as well as adults.[61] Even if eight-year-olds do not cross the street as well as adults (however defined), it does not mean that they should be prohibited from doing so. After all, according to the report referenced above, men do not seem to cross the street as well as women.[62] Both children and adults, men and women, must live in our industrialized world filled with cars. All risk injury or death if their movements as pedestrians collide with the movements of vehicles, which are themselves guided by others with their own responsibilities in the matter. Yet Ireland's Road Safety Authority says, "Research shows that children under 12 should not cross roads on their own. They cannot decide how far away a car is or how fast it is going."[63] It concludes with its own societally burdensome admonition that children "should be taken to school by a responsible adult." There is a desire for an expansive safety that encompasses every child, or at least one's own child at every moment. Therefore, adults, along with children, bear present costs in hope of a future that is safe, a future in which not everything can happen. Children are walked to school and escorted across streets. Or, they are driven to school and forbidden from crossing the street. Walking places is a normal part of life, and as with all of life, it has its dangers. Children should not be forbidden from walking places, but trained to do so responsibly.

---

[60]The failure rate ranged from 8% for six-year-olds to 0.3% for 14-year-olds and zero for adults. National Center for Statistics and Analysis, *Pedestrians: 2014 Data*, 5.
[61]Hollee Actman Becker, "Science Says Kids Shouldn't Cross a Busy Street Solo Until They're 14," *Parents*, April 21, 2017. As a concession, Becker recommends training your children, but the primary solution is parental accompaniment.
[62]Men accounted for 54% of pedestrian injuries and 70% of pedestrian fatalities. National Center for Statistics and Analysis, *Pedestrians: 2014 Data*.
[63]Ireland Road Safety Authority, "Going to School: A Parents Guide to Getting Children to School Safely," 2017, www.rsa.ie/docs/default-source/road-safety/r3-education/rsa-going-to-school-guide.pdf.

Over the past twenty-five years, school shootings have also become a part of life in America. The probability of a student being harmed in a school shooting, like the probability of a child being harmed as a pedestrian, is statistically very low. School shootings are not ordinary or normal. They are abnormal, shocking, and tragic. They have become a part of life, though, because they grip our attention and compel us to respond in some way. Each discrete event spills out from the life and actions of the shooter into the suffering and loss of those directly affected and then into the memory, anger, and fear of others. The effects of those discrete events combine and ripple out still further to parents and teachers worrying about what could happen in their schools, to officials and administrators trying to devise safety protocols, and to students wondering how seriously to take all the warnings as they crouch next to each other during active shooter drills.

Experts look back at the perpetrators' patterns of behavior, searching for clues that a shooting was on the horizon. They turn to the future to assess and mitigate threats with surveillance technologies and sterile techniques. Commentators are quick to square these events with their ideological grids as they offer pre-packaged explanations and easy solutions. But we are still stuck with their reality and the possibility of them happening again. The motivations and circumstances under which school shootings happen are varied but they still cohere as a particular category of events that have arisen in a particular time and setting. They are bursts of violence rising up from deeper cultural rot. Those who find themselves strategizing about the possibility of an adolescent shooting fellow students are already deep in an evil situation. It is good and right to protect students and to have prudent, loving policies in place, carried out with courage and dignity. It is good to remember that these events are not sheer randomness and that whoever might do something like this is a specific person with a heart darkened by specific sins, temptations, and evil desires.

In pursuit of safety, people seek to squeeze the life out of school shootings, but often without regard for the deeper cultural rot or what else is gasping for breath in the process. The squeeze is the use of dehumanizing and impersonal methods to control student behaviors. The rot is the godlessness and immorality that is currently the taken-for-granted basis of public life. The gasping is the hopefulness of youth persevering despite being systematically sacrificed to the terrors of the present. Christ's life and ministry was not a matter of probabilities. It was a matter of weakness becoming power in the most improbable way: "For he was crucified in weakness, but lives by the power of God" (2 Cor 13:4). In our results driven world, we should not fall into the trap of manufacturing similitudes of trust, community, or care for the safety of students. But in weakness we should commend ourselves to them by means of such things, along with "purity, knowledge, patience, kindness, the Holy Spirit, [and] genuine love" (2 Cor 6:6). The apostle Paul wielded these "weapons of righteousness" in the midst of "afflictions, hardships, calamities, beatings, imprisonments, [and] riots," among other difficulties (2 Cor 6:4-10). Such a commendation would be a means of comfort to others, as the coming of Titus was for Paul (2 Cor 7:6), and comfort is a great motivator for good. Perhaps God would use his church, as salt in this world, to slow or even reverse the spread of this rottenness: "Sow for yourselves righteousness; reap steadfast love" (Hos 10:12).

It is hard not to pursue a safety that encompasses every child on every street or every student in every classroom. The "acceptable" death rates of transportation bureaucrats sound as harsh as David's words that "the sword devours now one and now another" when rationalizing Uriah's treacherous death (2 Sam 11:25). Yet such an expansive pursuit of safety carries other costs, including the guilt and blame that must be allocated when it fails. A two-year-old was killed by a neighbor backing out of the driveway. After the fact, it was preventable. All accidents appear preventable after the fact. The parents, the neighbor, the child himself could have done any number of things differently. This is the razor's edge of time. The present relentlessly cuts the past off from the future and leaves only its "imprisoning facticity."[64]

Yet memory allows us to recreate sequences of events. We can draw alternative lines, showing what else could have happened. This ability to remember and reimagine the past is good because it provides opportunity to learn from mistakes and successes and to discern the differences between mistakes, malevolence, and tragedies. Sometimes we are safe because we navigated the dangers successfully, and sometimes because we failed but God was merciful—though God's mercy is at work in either situation. Memory,

---

[64]O'Donovan, *Self, World, and Time*, 38.

when it is sufficiently broad, also helps bring the stark severity of rare, grievous events into a right relationship with the cumulative benefits of common, ordinary moments, allowing neither to unduly overshadow the other. The present quickly becomes the past, and children who are not taught to walk the streets of this world soon become adults who had not been taught to walk the streets of this world.

These issues require courage and wisdom because deliberations on the past are also used by people as weapons against each other. In the midst of their grief, the father and mother of the two-year-old were investigated by the authorities concerning their competencies as parents and threatened with the removal of their other children. Nathan rightly rebuked David for guiding the randomness of war toward murderous ends (2 Sam 12:9), but did these parents earn the same rebuke? Is it right to judge the indeterminacy of what was once their future by the solidity of what is now their past? As one investigator into a train accident explains, "There is almost no human action or decision that cannot be made to look more flawed and less sensible in the misleading light of hindsight."[65] When human agency is grounded in desire and fear, we "lay too great a practical weight on anticipation" because desires and fears are speculative.[66] They are not clear guides for moral action. How much greater this weight is when we turn to the past, with the use of hindsight, to say what precisely should have been desired and feared.

Keeping the way pure. The claim that desire and fear are not reliable moral guides does not mean that the capacity to anticipate the future has no legitimate role in moral action or humanity's engagement with the dangers of this world. As we have seen with the theory of probability, human anticipations are intrinsically ethical, shaping the way one walks into the future. Within the horizons of this world's time, we can acknowledge that the capacity God has given humanity to anticipate the future is successfully employed by all people, to some extent or another, in avoiding oncoming dangers. However, inasmuch as human anticipations are entangled with unchastened desires and misplaced fears, those anticipations will be unreliable moral guides,

---

[65] Anthony Hidden, *Investigation into the Clapham Junction Railway Accident* (London: Department of Transport, September 27, 1989), 147.
[66] O'Donovan, *Self, World, and Time*, 122.

regardless of their reliability in pursuing safety. In other words, it is possible to anticipate and avoid certain types of danger, but to do so in an immoral way that exposes you to other types of dangers, a way that is not rightly formed by love of neighbor or love of God, but is based on anticipations that are not rightly formed by Scripture's prophetic testimony regarding the future.

The psalmist asks how a young man may "keep his way pure" (Ps 119:9). Purity here is a moral condition, which primarily concerns his standing before God,[67] whereas safety is a physical condition, which primarily concerns one's standing in the world. In the question of this verse there is a way that must be traveled and a young person who must travel it. Children should be cared for in their vulnerabilities, but they quickly grow and must be taught to move through this world in a way that is pure, godly, and upright. The age of the child addressed by this question is not given,[68] but if a young man is old enough to move through this world, he is old enough to corrupt his way. After all, one of the first things a toddler does with the newfound ability to walk is to walk away from the voice of his mother. According to Bonhoeffer, anyone who takes absolute responsibility for the wellbeing of another person does so at the expense of the other person's dignity and moral agency. Therefore, a parent's responsibility to a child is not absolute. It is limited by the responsibilities of the child. The parent is called to help the child "become conscious of his own responsibility," but the parent cannot directly keep the child's way pure.[69] Children who are old enough to corrupt their way in this world are old enough to be the audience of this verse.

When the psalmist asks how a young man may keep his way pure, it is an ethical question, likely concerned more with the snare of the seductress than oncoming traffic. However, "wisdom helps one to succeed," in avoiding both moral and physical dangers (Eccles 10:8-10).[70] Patience, discipline, and self-control could be of great benefit to children, and adults, as they navigate the dangers of this world. According to the ethics of probabilistic forecasting and the logic of our world's pursuit of safety, the way forward

---

[67] BDB, 269.
[68] The term נַעַר, translated "young man" in Ps 119:9, is used to refer to children from infancy (Ex 2:6) to seventeen years of age (Gen 37:2) and possibly beyond (e.g., Gen 34:19; 2 Sam 18:5).
[69] Bonhoeffer, *Ethics*, 231.
[70] This theme will be discussed further in chapter 8.

Grasping the Future

into the future for a young man, or for a mother with a small child, could not be simultaneously pure and injurious. Much less could it be pure and fatal. But this is where such ethics and logic fail. For this world is injurious. Death may come to those who are "old and full of days" (Gen 35:29), but it may also come unexpectedly, to those who still have life and vigor within them: "He has broken my strength midcourse; he has shortened my days" (Ps 102:23). Probabilistic forecasting does not always fail. Hindsight gives assurance that the probabilistic pursuit of safety could have worked, almost worked. Therefore, humanity often doubles down on its probabilistic forecasts, giving them even more authority and squeezing them for a resoluteness of action that they cannot produce. Yet, not all injuries and fatalities come predictably.

The inescapable reality that the future is uncertain produces various responses. There are the vigilant, who, for the sake of getting children to walk to school, march them down guarded routes.[71] There is the one who abandons all prudence in the face of danger, the wrongdoer who "arrogantly hasten[s] to death."[72] This is the "madman who throws firebrands, arrows, and death" (Prov 26:18).[73] He does so out of recklessness and folly, not courage, allowing the impulses of the present to consume the concerns of the future. Finally, there are the fearful who are driven to inaction. "There is a lion outside! I shall be killed in the streets!" says the sluggard (Prov 22:13). But this is no path forward. The sound of the door being shut to the street is the sound of death. It is the sound of youthfulness fleeing, fears rising, and desires failing (Eccles 12:1-8). Inaction is the option of the sluggard, the fearful, and the dying, but not of the young, nor of any for whom the future still holds hope.

A biblical view onto the street. The prophet Zechariah saw a day when "old men and old women shall again sit in the streets of Jerusalem," and when "the streets of the city shall be full of boys and girls playing in its streets" (Zech 8:4-5). This is the future that Oliver O'Donovan calls the

---

[71]See, e.g., the Safe Routes to School National Partnership (http://saferoutespartnership.org/) and the Center for Cities and Schools (http://citiesandschools.berkeley.edu).
[72]Calvin, *Institutes*, II.16.12, p. 519.
[73]I am using the figure of the madman on his own, recognizing that in context he is the vehicle of a simile (Prov 26:19).

"absolute future" of God's promises.[74] It is the future that comes with "the appearing of Christ and the judgment of God on history."[75] It is the believer's in hope, but as with all that is hoped for in faith, it is a thing "not seen" (Heb 11:1). It is not given to be grabbed hold of today. Instead, humanity is called to live within the horizons of time.[76] Aside from this absolute future of the age to come, O'Donovan differentiates three futures within this age. (1) There is the actual future, known only to God. This future is certain, "high in ontic density," yet cannot be seen.[77] According to O'Donovan, if we knew the actual future, we could not make meaningful choices. God limits humanity's vision of the future so that people may legitimately exercise their agency and walk by faith in the goodness of God. (2) There are the futures of anticipation. These include predictive futures that are based on "observed regularities" in nature,[78] as well as the imaginary futures of fear and desire that become enmeshed with the predictive futures. These futures are tempting because they hold out the possibility of "peeping round the edges of the actual," but they are ontically "shallow."[79] (3) There is the immediate future. This is the future that God has given humanity to act into, the future that is not yet realized but offered as a perpetually present gift.

Actions into the immediate future may be done in light of more distant futures, like planting in anticipation of a harvest, but tomorrow's deeds cannot be performed today. You cannot reap before you have sown. God has not yet given tomorrow. He may not. He may give a tomorrow different from what is expected. But it will be that tomorrow, not the tomorrow of expectations, for which we will be responsible when it arrives. For now, we are

---

[74] O'Donovan, *Self, World, and Time*, 121. The proximate fulfillment of Zechariah's word from the Lord would be the return of the exiles and rebuilding of Jerusalem. However, as George Klein notes, it "remains a promise that the Lord has not completely fulfilled" (*Zechariah*, NAC 21B [Nashville: B&H Academic, 2008], 236).

[75] O'Donovan, *Self, World, and Time*, 16-17.

[76] O'Donovan notes that the present is "constituted and contained by what Heidegger has taught us to call its 'horizons' of past and future" (O'Donovan, *Self, World, and Time*, 121). See Martin Heidegger, *Being and Time*, trans. Joan Stambaugh, rev. ed. (New York: Suny, 2010), 227, 321-23.

[77] O'Donovan, *Self, World, and Time*, 16. O'Donovan gives the exception of prophetic revelation.

[78] O'Donovan describes these predictions as "lazy presumptions of regularity," but later he treats them less harshly, saying that "on the basis of such perception we reasonably, though without certainty, anticipate outcomes" (O'Donovan, *Self, World, and Time*, 121-22).

[79] O'Donovan, *Self, World, and Time*, 121, 16.

responsible for present action, even as it is done in anticipation of the future. Christ does not call his followers to predict or worry themselves into that future moment. He calls them to trust him as the good shepherd, who leads and restores them even as they stumble and lose their way. He calls his disciples to walk in obedience to him, using the future that opens before them to do something that will "endure before the throne of judgment."[80]

Those who hope in the future fulfillment of God's promises wait for the day Zechariah saw, when boys and girls play in the streets with no worry or possibility of harm. In the meantime, they are called by Christ to live meaningful lives in this world full of dangers. The streets of this age are not paved with gold, but with gravel and asphalt. They are stained with blood. When we look out onto these streets through the lens of Scripture, we see many dangers, not just those of traffic or violence. We also see many good things. The street is where the prostitute sets her trap and where lovers meet. The street is where cries of mourning are heard and where good news is announced. It is where hypocrites seek the approval of others and God's judgment is proclaimed. The streets are where travelers are robbed and foreigners show kindness, where the sick are healed, sinners meet their Savior, and Christ's disciples are given understanding. In short, the street is where life happens with all of its joys and pleasures, sorrows and pains.[81]

The godly life is described in Scripture as a particular road through this world—the "way of the good" and the "paths of the righteous" (Prov 2:20). It is also described as a particular way of traveling through this world—in a manner worthy of Christ's calling (Eph 4:1; Col 1:10). Wisdom cries out in the street because that is where she is most needed. It is where people move through this world, interacting and colliding with each other. Streets are noisy, though, filled with dangers, distractions, and temptations, so wisdom raises her voice and cries loudly (Prov 1:20-21). She calls out, inviting those who hear to travel her ways of pleasantness and paths of peace (Prov 3:17). She gives assurance that those who heed her voice will walk securely; their "foot will not stumble" (Prov 3:21-23).

---

[80]O'Donovan, *Self, World, and Time*, 17.

[81]For this description of streets, see 2 Sam 1:20; Prov 7:8, 12; Song 3:2; Is 5:25; 10:6; 15:3; 24:11; Jer 11:6; Mt 6:2; Lk 10:30-35; 24:32; Acts 5:15.

The question still stands, then, of how God calls humanity to navigate through this world and into the future. By bringing the question to Scripture, we find that it has changed. The emphasis is no longer on how to keep the way safe, but how to keep it pure. This is the more important question, the one God most directly addresses. God does not call us to abandon hope or prudence. He calls us to keep our way pure by guarding it according to his Word (Ps 119:9). This entails acting rightly in relation to anticipations of the future, but those anticipations themselves must be submitted to the lordship of Christ and the authority of Scripture.

Considering the Signs

As we look to God's Word for guidance, we find affirmation that nature does indeed give signs concerning the future. In Proverbs 6:6-11 Solomon points to the hard-working ant, who gathers food at harvest time, as a deterrent to oncoming poverty, and in Luke 12:22-31 (//Mt 6:25-34) Christ points to the worry-free ravens and lilies, who are fed and clothed by God, as deterrents to anxiety about the practical needs of life. We also find exhortations to interpret these signs correctly. Both passages give commands to "consider" creation,[82] but this is not license to leave Scripture behind and look at these signs through some other lens. Galileo's admonition to interpret the book of nature through the language of mathematics is therefore inadequate.

According to Calvin, God's creatures are "burning lamps [that] shine for us in the workmanship of the universe." But because of sin, they alone cannot "lead us into the right path." Humanity's contemplation of nature may "strike some sparks," but those sparks are soon smothered, failing to provide true knowledge either of God or of nature as that which Christ upholds "by the word of his power" (Heb 1:3).[83] Creation's signs must be considered through the lens of Scripture, allowing God, through his Word, to guide the observer to the appropriate conclusions. The command to consider the ant in Proverbs 6:6 conveys the idea of looking willfully, "with

---

[82]Multiple English translations (ESV, NRSV, KJV, and NIV) translate the respective verbs, רָאָה and κατανοέω, as "consider."

[83]Calvin, *Institutes*, I.5.14, p. 68. In describing the theology of Proverbs, Tremper Longman says, "Pagans may well stumble on some interesting and helpful truth that provides insight on how to avoid a problem or achieve a desired goal." However, "there is no wisdom apart from a relationship with Yahweh" (Tremper Longman, *Proverbs* [Grand Rapids, MI: Baker Academic, 2006], 58).

moral discernment."[84] It is "an appeal to the cosmos as a source of moral knowledge," given with the expectation that the ant will be observed correctly and the appropriate theological and ethical lessons will be learned.[85] Likewise, in Luke 12:24, 27, when Jesus commands his disciples to consider God's care for ravens and lilies, he is engaging them "in reading the signs of God's gracious presence all around them," with the expectation that they will then rightly consider God's care for them as his children.[86] Scripture's expectation that the signs of the ant, ravens, and lilies will be interpreted correctly does not happen automatically. Instead, it carries with it the additional need to first read Scripture rightly, through eyes of faith. Only then can its admonition to consider nature properly be followed.[87]

Dangers of tomorrow and eternity. The first thing we see in considering the lilies, ravens, and ants, especially as presented in their broader scriptural contexts, is that the dangers of tomorrow, and anticipations of them, are relativized in light of Christ's coming judgment. Through the course of history, people will rise and fall with successes and failures in relation to the dangers of this world, but Jesus keeps those relative successes and failures distinct from a person's standing or falling before the final judgment of God. In relation to that final standing or falling, Bonhoeffer says that God has displayed, in the cross, the nature of this judgment—"the total condemnation and invalidation" of all the various routes humanity pursues in its efforts to stand before God apart from Christ.[88]

When Christ acknowledges humanity's ability to predict the weather, to properly interpret "the appearance of earth and sky" (Lk 12:54-56), he says that those predictive capacities are used in hypocritical ways. People employ

---

[84] Bruce K. Waltke, *The Book of Proverbs, Chapters 1–15*, NICOT (Grand Rapids, MI: Eerdmans, 2004), 337.

[85] Daniel J. Treier, *Proverbs & Ecclesiastes*, Brazos Theological Commentary on the Bible (Grand Rapids, MI: Brazos, 2011), 37. In regard to this expectation, Longman says that after the teacher instructs his pupils to observe the ant, he "feels confident that the hearer will draw the lesson that follows in the text" (Longman, *Proverbs*, 75).

[86] Joel B. Green, *The Gospel of Luke*, NICNT (Grand Rapids, MI: Eerdmans, 1997), 493.

[87] "The death of Christ shows us the outcome of the encounter between the true human life and the misshapen human life, between the order of creation as God gave it to be lived and known and the distorted and fantastic image of it in which mankind has lived." Oliver O'Donovan, *Resurrection and Moral Order: An Outline for Evangelical Ethics*, 2nd ed. (Grand Rapids, MI: Eerdmans, 1986), 94.

[88] Bonhoeffer, *Ethics*, 123.

their anticipative capacities selectively. They look at the sky and know rain is coming. They watch the wind and know it will be hot. But Jesus asks how it is that those same people "do not know how to interpret the present time" (Lk 12:56). When anticipations of the future are limited to the sphere of this world, it is a false limitation in which guilt and the need to settle with the divine accuser are willfully ignored (Lk 12:57-59). The most sophisticated human anticipations of the future are woefully inadequate when they overlook this coming judgment.

When the pursuit of safety, and human judgments of it, exist within the boundaries of history, there are necessarily winners and losers, those who read the signs correctly and those who do not, those who are safe and those who die under collapsing towers (Lk 13:4). However, God does not maintain his rewards for righteousness and retributions for wickedness in perfect balance, moment by moment, throughout the course of history. Instead, he allows the wicked to store up wrath (Rom 2:5), while nonetheless giving opportunities for repentance. He allows the righteous to store up treasures (Mt 6:20), even while they suffer loss. Inequities within the course of history should not therefore cause doubt regarding the faithfulness of God. Instead, as Calvin says, today's imbalances and the desire to see them balanced are signs that there will be "another life in which iniquity is to have its punishment, and righteousness is to be given its reward."[89]

If every deed promptly received its just retribution throughout the course of history, then we could happily follow the example of Job's friends. They thought that their present safety and Job's present misery were predictable outcomes of past behaviors (Job 11:13–12:6). From this mistaken perspective, those who are "at ease" look at danger with prideful contempt, as something they have mastered, while they view misfortune as something for the careless, for "those whose feet slip" (Job 12:5). Job challenges this self-assurance. Sometimes the righteous stumble, while "those who provoke God are secure" (Job 12:6). He then exhorts his counselors to ask God's creatures, the beasts, birds, bushes, and fish, about the unassailable movements of the hand of God (Job 12:7-8). These creatures know that "the hand of the LORD has done this" and that life and breath are in his hands (Job 12:9-10). Therefore,

---

[89]Calvin, *Institutes*, I.5.10, pp. 62-63.

Scripture's lessons about the ant, ravens, and lilies need to be considered within a theological framework that recognizes humanity's guilt and need for mercy before a sovereign God who is weaving the tangled threads of history together in accordance with his good and wise purposes. These lessons also need to be considered within a timeframe that extends beyond earthly lifespans to include resurrection and judgment, when the inequities of history will be resolved.

This theological and eschatological framework is not immediately apparent in Proverbs' lesson of the ant. Proverbs 6:6-11 makes no explicit reference to God, much less the return of Christ or his coming judgment. It seems to be more worldly wisdom than redemptive revelation, a reminder that the lazy need to work to eat. If this were the totality of the proverb's lesson, the preparations of the ant would be categorically similar to humanity's preparations for the dangers of tomorrow. And indeed, there is a large degree of similarity. The proverb's impact comes from the fact that the lowly ant prepares for the future better than the sluggard even though the sluggard's capacity as a human to anticipate the future is, I assume, much greater than the ant's. However, the book of Proverbs grounds its entire curriculum in the fear of the Lord (Prov 1:7), the one who has power over life and death (Prov 10:27, 14:27). The lesson of the ant, that we too should labor today in preparation for tomorrow, has to do with the relationship between the reader, the world, and God, not just between the reader and the world.

When wisdom claims to be "a tree of life to those who lay hold of her" (Prov 3:18), it would be a mistake to conclude that such wisdom pertains to practical matters of life in a theologically neutral way that can be separated from humanity's standing before God. To be sure, the tree of life symbolizes "the quality of earthly life" within the book of Proverbs.[90] Diligence, like that of the ant, brings food—an obvious benefit to earthly vitality. It adds quality to earthly life in other ways as well, reducing strife among households and neighbors and enabling generosity and care for those in need.[91] However, this proverbial lesson, as with others, has its exceptions. Sometimes those who gather do not eat and those who eat did not gather (Eccles 2:21). The

---

[90]Treier, *Proverbs & Ecclesiastes*, 27. Treier explains, though, that "ultimate ends are pertinent, since relationship with God is so crucial to eating from the tree."
[91]Leo G. Perdue, *Proverbs* (Louisville, KY: John Knox, 2012), 123.

typical explanation for these exceptions is to say that the proverb is usually, though not always, true. Within this age, that is the case, but if anticipation of this proverb's fulfillment is extended into the age to come, then the hope arises that all who labor and gather in this world according to wisdom will ultimately be filled (Col 3:23-24). The invitation to life that is extended throughout the book of Proverbs (e.g., Prov 8:35; 9:6) is partially fulfilled in this age, but remains to be completely fulfilled in the age to come, when God will "smooth out the inevitable inequities of how the wise and the foolish experience life in the here and now." Wisdom is a tree of life, both practically and eschatologically, even though the full implications of its future hope "remain undefined" in the book of Proverbs.[92]

The dangers of tomorrow are real, but they are not humanity's most significant dangers. Therefore, the fear of the Lord must remain central. This becomes clearer with Jesus' teachings in Luke 12. Like Solomon, Jesus gives instruction concerning the practical matters of life, but as he addresses matters of daily provision and physical safety, he puts them in sharp contrast with the dangers and rewards of eternity.[93] He warns not to fear those who kill the body but to fear God, who "has authority to cast into hell" (Lk 12:4-5). He tells the parable of the rich man, who outdid the ant in gathering for the future, yet was a fool in the end because he was "not rich toward God" (Lk 12:15-21). Against the backdrop of these warnings about the dangers of eternity, Christ tells his disciples not to worry about their lives, what they will eat or wear (Lk 12:22). The dangers of eternity are far more significant than the dangers of tomorrow; the treasures of heaven far outweigh the riches of this world (Lk 12:31-33).

When Christ puts the dangers of tomorrow in their proper place in relation to his coming judgment, he does not nullify the safety of everyday life. He maintains its legitimacy, but he does so in light of the care of the Father. The pursuit of safety is subjected to Christ's command to seek first the kingdom of God. Otherwise, it becomes idolatrous, the strivings of the nations, or it becomes legalistic, a pharisaical attempt to leverage one's

---

[92]Treier, *Proverbs & Ecclesiastes*, 78-79.
[93]John N. Jones argues that Solomon's splendor is compared to that of the lilies in Lk 12:27 because the saying in Lk 12 is "meant to echo and invert" Prov 6:6-11 ("'Think of the Lilies' and Prov 6:6-11," *HTR* 88 [January 1995]: 176). I agree that the saying in Lk 12 echoes Prov 6, though, as I will argue below, it does not invert but rather complements it.

supposed purity in the pursuit of safety against the power and freedom of God. In either case those who do so are vainly obligating the future to conform to their wills, not his. There is a particular foolishness in seeking for safety apart from the fear of God. Adam and Eve's desire for the knowledge of good and evil exceeded their fear of disobeying the command of God. All are guilty of this foolishness. The hope of standing amid the dangers of tomorrow in a way that is pure and endures to eternity is to be found in what God has done on our behalf through Christ: "The Lord will be your confidence and will keep your foot from being caught" (Prov 3:26).

Lilies, ravens, and ants. Christ's command not to worry about tomorrow is an affirmation of the Father's love. Likewise, the question, "How long will you lie there, O sluggard?" (Prov 6:9), is an irritation in the ear of the foolish and a burden in the mind of the doubtful, but for those who trust in the Lord, it is freedom and life, bringing healing to the flesh and refreshment to the bones (Prov 3:5-8). When the needs of tomorrow are approached, not simply in light of one's relationship to this world and its goods, but in light of one's relationship to God and his goodness, anticipations do not have to be burdensome worries and preparations do not have to be "vain graspings of soul for what is beyond reach."[94]

The lesson of the ant not to waste opportunities to gather for the needs of tomorrow, as well as Christ's command not to seek or worry about food and clothing, can both be expanded to include sluggishness, worry, and striving related to the pursuit of safety as well. The search for food and clothing is representative of humanity's overall "quest for security," whatever is needed to be safe.[95] In the late-modern world, there is a sense in which food and clothing can be separated from matters of safety. I am speaking here of the way in which safety is often an added, reflexive, component of more primary pursuits. The safety industry proclaims "safety first," but that slogan is an indication that safety has been attached to some other endeavor after the fact. There is a meaningful distinction today between transportation and transportation safety, food and food safety, construction and construction safety, and so on. In other settings, these distinctions are less meaningful. For those who are isolated, hungry, or in need of shelter, transportation,

---

[94]"Robert S. Payne," *The Weekly Nashville Union* (Nashville, January 6, 1847), sec. Obituary.
[95]Green, *The Gospel of Luke*, 494.

food, and construction are themselves matters of safety, not activities to which safety may or may not be attached. It makes little difference, for the purposes of these passages, whether safety is considered in a primary sense as provision for the basic needs of life or in a reflexive sense as auxiliary efforts to reduce the probability of unexpected harms. When Christ gives his command not to worry about your body, what you will wear, both normal attire and safety equipment can be included. The command not to be anxious equally applies to food scarcity as a first-order risk and food contamination as a second-order risk.

Christ's instruction related to the ravens and lilies follows his warning against covetousness and the parable of the rich man who sought to secure his future by means of wealth and material goods (Lk 12:15-21). The rich man was prepared for the future materially. However, Christ tells the parable to emphasize an error of the human heart. The rich man thought he could sow worry today and reap ease tomorrow, but worry only begets more worry. His question to himself, "What shall I do, for I have nowhere to store my crops?" (Lk 12:17), does not seem to epitomize worry, but worry appears when earthly goods, whether by their plentitude or scarcity, "deceive the human heart into believing that they give it security and freedom from worry."[96] Christ then gives his command not to be anxious about your life, what you will eat or wear (Lk 12:22). Later, he gives his command not to seek what you are to eat or drink (Lk 12:29). The prohibition against worry applies to both thought and action.

As Jesus calls his disciples to consider the ravens, he points out that they do not sow or reap (Lk 12:24-26). Unlike the rich man, they do not have storehouses or barns. Yet God feeds them. They fly around and find food as is fitting for birds, but the food is there to find, "not due to their own labor, but to God's goodness."[97] Christ then reminds his disciples that they are more valuable than these birds. They should not worry because they have a heavenly Father who rules over creation and cares for them. Anxiety does not accomplish anything anyway. It cannot extend one's life. This is true of worry as an internal dialogue, which may be easy enough to concede, but it

---

[96] Dietrich Bonhoeffer, *Discipleship*, ed. Geffrey B. Kelly and John D. Godsey, trans. Barbara Green and Reinhard Krauss, Dietrich Bonhoeffer Works 4 (Minneapolis: Fortress, 2003), 171.

[97] Martin Luther, "Exposition of Psalm 127, for Christians at Riga in Livonia (1524)," in *The Christian in Society II*, ed. Walther I. Brandt, LW 45 (Philadelphia: Muhlenberg, 1962), 326-27.

is also true of worry as action, as a perpetual quest to shore up the vulnerabilities of life, ever tearing down barns and building bigger, safer, ones.

Christ then directs his disciples to the lilies, in relation to what they will wear (Lk 12:27-28). Unlike ravens, lilies are immobile. They draw their nutrients and life from the soil, rain, and sunlight as is fitting for flowers. They are not able to toil or spin, but they do not need to. God arrays them in splendor. Humanity has different and greater capacities than birds and flowers, able to sow and reap, toil and spin. All people make use of those capacities as they feed and clothe themselves, as they prepare for the dangers and needs of tomorrow. But humanity also misjudges and misuses these God-given capacities. Overextended strivings to predict and secure the future are as misdirected as a lily trying to thread a needle with its petals or a raven trying to plow a field with its beak. God cares for humans in a way that is fitting for humans, and this care includes the capacities he has bestowed on humanity to remember the past, anticipate the future, and interact in diverse ways with the created world. Jesus does not say that God will feed and clothe those who have a large enough amount of faith or a small enough amount of anxiety. If that were the case, we would all be hungry and naked. Instead, God provides for all people. The sign of faith in a person's life is not the presence or absence of material goods, but the presence or absence of worry.

In Luke 12, Jesus contrasts the strivings and worries of the nations with their absence in the case of the ravens and lilies. It would be a misinterpretation of these signs to conclude that Christ's disciples do not, therefore, need to give their hands to the labors that God sets before them. Instead, in order to properly consider the signs of the lilies and ravens, a distinction needs to be made between the strivings of the nations for their daily needs and the labor of God's children who know he will provide for them.[98] The labor of today is closely linked to the needs of tomorrow—harvesting food that will be eaten, earning money that will be spent, even installing airbags that will be deployed. But the cause-and-effect links here that seem so obvious and straight are always tenuous and often unreliable. Moneybags fall apart, moths eat, rust destroys, and thieves steal (Mt 6:19-20; Lk 12:33).

---

[98]"Security comes from the realization that God actively cares for his children" (Darrell L. Bock, *Luke 9:51–24:53*, BECNT [Grand Rapids, MI: Baker Academic, 1994], 1164; see also Green, *The Gospel of Luke*, 494).

God uses both anxious striving and faithful labor as secondary causes, as the means by which he provides for his creatures. But there is not a straight line between labor and provision, between humanity and creation. God and his angels are always involved. He gives the rain. He causes the earth to yield its fruit. He sends his mighty ones to accomplish his word and his ministering spirits to serve his elect. In order to emphasize God's role in providing for daily needs, Martin Luther uses strong language to weaken the connection that is naturally made between labor and provision: "Man must necessarily work and busy himself at something. At the same time, however, he must know that it is something other than his labor which furnishes him sustenance; it is the divine blessing." Luther then gives a warning: "Because God gives him nothing unless he works, it may seem as if it is his labor which sustains him."[99] Certainly, God provides for us by means of our labors. Yet if the words of Jesus are true, then a person may sow the seed, harvest the grain, grind the flour, bake the dough, and eat the bread, but is nevertheless fed by God. The connection between human labor and provision for the future is weakened, not to lessen the dignity of labor but to magnify it as worship and to reestablish God's rightful place in the human heart as the one who always has and always will provide for his creatures in accord with his purposes.

The sign of the ant, which points to the need to work today in order to be prepared for the needs of tomorrow, is therefore complementary, not contradictory, to the signs of the lilies and ravens.[100] Jesus forbids his disciples from seeking after food and clothing in order to secure their lives apart from God, but he does not forbid them from reaping, sowing, harvesting, or spinning. He forbids them from worrying about tomorrow, but he does not forbid them from rightly anticipating the future. Anticipating the future rightly is not simply a matter of predictive accuracy though. It involves an overall awareness of God's faithfulness to his creatures, both to "give them their food in due season" and to hide his face when he "take[s]

---

[99]Luther, "Exposition of Psalm 127," 326-27.
[100]Contra Jones, who says the lessons drawn from these two passages "are quite antithetical . . . ; the ant's success results from industry; the ravens', from God's natural beneficence" ("Think of the Lilies," 176), and Richard J. Dillon, who says Prov 6:6-11 "is a reproach of those who fail to cultivate self-sufficiency," while Lk 12:22-31 is an "admonition" to give it up ("Ravens, Lilies, and the Kingdom of God [Matthew 6:25-33/Luke 12:22-31]," *CBQ* 53 [October 1991]: 606).

away their breath" (Ps 104:27-29). Humanity may, at times, rightly calculate what tomorrow will bring, but it will never know for sure until tomorrow comes. Further, right calculations about tomorrow do not ensure right conduct today.

There is a contrast in Proverbs 6:6-11 between the ant, who rightly prepares for the future by gathering food at harvest time, and the sluggard, who repeatedly miscalculates his days, thinking he can rest just a bit more when God is calling him to action today. The ant prepared for tomorrow through fruitful labor today. God calls us to participate in such fruitful labor as well, looking not only to the coming seasons but to the coming age (Gal 6:9). The signs of the ant, ravens, and lilies, as presented in Scripture, show therefore that we can engage in fruitful preparations apart from fruitless predictions or faithless worries.

Calculative probabilities arose in the early modern era as a unique and influential expression of humanity's enduring capacity to anticipate the future. Anticipating the future serves useful purposes, but those anticipations have limitations that are frustratingly difficult to pin down, especially by those who are unwilling to recognize their dependence on God. When people chase after probabilistic certainty in relation to things like children crossing streets, school shootings, or any number of other dangers, the results have often been to neglect other moral responsibilities or to forfeit other good things for the sake of safety. Those other moral responsibilities include things like training children to make trustworthy decisions, being open and caring to others, turning from immorality, and exhibiting patience, kindness, love, and truthfulness in the midst of danger or harm. Those other good things include freedom, contentment, and a life that is fresh and invigorating, open to what tomorrow may bring.

The Christian teaching not to worry about the future, epitomized in Christ's words about lilies and ravens, seems to run against the grain of human capacities to anticipate and prepare for the future. The lesson of the ant in Proverbs 6 seems to present a more reasonable, prudent, view, with its instruction to labor today in order to have provision for tomorrow. Prudence and faith do not contradict each other. Prudence is not worry, and faith is not laziness. With these distinctions clarified, practical questions still remain about what faithful prudence looks like. Should I let my kid walk to school or not? Should I stop taking this medicine that increases my risk for cancer? Should we spend the money on a new car since this one is probably going to need a major repair soon?

I read a story years ago about a small panic induced by a headline saying that the new version of a pharmaceutical drug doubled the risk of cancer in women. Women using the drug were concerned. Some stopped using it. But a closer look at the numbers revealed that the risk doubled from next to nothing to next to next to nothing, from a one-in-a-million chance to two-in-a-million chance, or something like that, well within an acceptable level of risk for most women. Probabilities are often used in sensational ways to prove points and stifle discussion, but it is worthwhile to understand what they are actually saying about the possible futures of this world before making decisions based on them. When doing something good, something that has benefits, there may also be risks. The possibility of those risks happening, of fears becoming a reality, should be acknowledged and accepted, but that should not stop someone from doing what is good and right.

Exercising faith and prudence often feels like walking a tightrope, with pits of worry and anxiety on one side and laziness and foolishness on the other. This is especially so when we worry about what others think of us, but if our hearts are pure, God gives much freedom and latitude to do what seems best to us as we serve him. He sets our feet in wide places (Ps 18:36). If he provides the means, buy the new car and enjoy it. If he does not, enjoy seeing how long the old one will last and how God will care for you, often in unexpected ways. In many situations, we are free to make a decision one way or another. If a medical procedure is not necessary but might be of help, we are free to decline it and deal with things as they are, and we are free to accept it and see if it helps. Whether things get better or worse in either direction, we are called by Christ to learn "godliness with contentment," which is "great gain" (1 Tim 6:6). God's promises are a safer guide into the future than probabilistic predictions. Our vision of the future, even with the most powerful probabilistic predictions, is limited and faulty. His vision is perfect. He knows what tomorrow will bring. He will keep his children safe both in life and in death.

SEVEN

Ordering Creation

Technology, Idols, and the Cross of Christ

> *To supply heat, the mighty sun is ready, and the invention of fire makes life more secure.*
>
> VITRUVIUS, *ON ARCHITECTURE*

TECHNOLOGY'S ADVANTAGES AND DISADVANTAGES

The pursuit of safety concerns humanity's relationship to the future. But the future takes its shape by means of the world we inhabit. Therefore, the pursuit of safety also concerns humanity's relationship with creation as brought forth, ordered, and governed by God. Inasmuch as God is sovereign over time, he is also sovereign over the movements and welfare of those things he has created. When a sparrow falls to the ground, it is not enough, in seeking to understand the significance of its descent, to say that it did so because of gravity. That would be sheer redundancy. Nor is it enough to say that it fell because God upholds the world in such a way that gravity remains consistent, though that is so. Instead, when a sparrow falls to the ground, the church is called to confess with Christ that it did not do so apart from our Father who loves us and cares for us (Mt 10:29). The things of this world, whether microscopic or astronomic, natural or artificial, simple or complex, move in accordance with the knowledge and purpose of him who numbers our hairs, commands the waves, and raises up impetuous armies to exact his will (Mt 10:30; Jer 5:22; Hab 1:5-10). God speaks and angels obey. He guides his creation through the perfect efficacy of his word.

God has given humanity the capacity to move and shape the things of this world as well. This capacity is not in competition with God's government of creation but is established by it. God has given humanity dominion over the works of his hands (Ps 8:6), "yet without in any way diminishing his own sovereign being and power."[1] People haul and plow, cut and sew, push and pull, to guide their movements and arrange their surroundings in ways that are conducive to life, or whatever else they may be pursuing. Technology aids this work. It helps people see clearer, listen closer, and calculate better. It helps them move faster, lift more, and stand stronger. It enhances powers to dig pits, break through walls, quarry stones, and split logs. Like humanity's capacity to anticipate the future, though, its capacity to move and shape the world is limited and faulty, fraught with errors, inefficiencies, and evils. Accidents happen despite perpetual resolves to be accident free. We rely on technology to move, shape, and interact with the world around us, but also to protect us from the dangers inherent in such activities. In the pursuit of safety, probabilistic anticipations lead to technological interventions.[2] We might fall into pits, so we put fences around them. Children might get lost, so they are equipped with tracking devices. Homes might be intruded on, so surveillance systems are installed. Our technological world is filled with supplementary technological restraints to keep ourselves and our surroundings safe.

The modern rise of technology is closely related to the historical development and current influence of the concept of risk and the theory of probability. Modern technology arose out of the medieval period with the transition from the premodern view of the world as a porous and enchanted

---

[1]Oliver O'Donovan, *Resurrection and Moral Order: An Outline for Evangelical Ethics*, 2nd ed. (Grand Rapids, MI: Eerdmans, 1986), 124. God's sovereignty over the movements of creation is not "a zero sum situation" in which "a decision by me is one less for [God] to make or vice versa" (Robert W. Jenson, *Systematic Theology* [New York: Oxford University Press, 1999], 2:22). Instead, "if there is the biblical God, there can be free creaturely choices only and precisely because God's will is so entirely of another sort than ours that he not only can will us to choose this rather than that, but that our choice be in itself uncoerced by his. But just so—and that is the present point—neither then do our choice and responsibility obviate his; precisely when we freely choose, we fulfill his choosing" (Jenson, *Systematic Theology*, 2:22-23).

[2]This relationship can be seen, for example, in Nikolas Rose, "The Politics of Life Itself," *Theory, Culture & Society* 18, no. 6 (2001): 7, and Claudia Aradau and Rens Van Munster, "Governing Terrorism Through Risk: Taking Precautions, (un)Knowing the Future," *European Journal of International Relations* 13 (March 2007): 98.

cosmos to the early modern view of the world as a constant and neutral universe. It has been further shaped by the late-modern view of the world as a finite and fragile sphere. Technology, like risk and probability, contains within itself a way of thinking about the world. It also frequently takes a physical form that lends a certain obviousness to its use and usefulness in the pursuit of safety. The pervasiveness of safety devices gives ample testimony to its use, and images like those of the flailing limbs of crash test dummies provide potent testimony of its usefulness. The advantage of the physical form and visible movements of technology in the pursuit of safety is that its presence and influence are self-evident. The disadvantage is that the way of thinking about the world that is contained within humanity's technological endeavors is more difficult to perceive and evaluate. Much that could be said about the development of technology or the effectiveness of particular technological devices in the pursuit of safety will be taken as given here. Instead, we will focus on the more fundamental issue of how technological activity fits in the relationship between humanity and the world, between God's vice-regents and his creation.

There are costs involved in the technological pursuit of safety, costs that are often overlooked when humanity enthralls itself with the promises of technology. Someone may say, for instance, that the change coming with the latest technological revolution is "all very exciting, for this revolution promises the opportunity for a more tailored, longer and safer life."[3] Such a life will be tailored by *someone*, though, cut and stretched toward some idealized shape. In this vision of the future, life is tailored, partly in the "absence of tradition," partly by "big data prediction." With whatever losses to cultural identity, historical situatedness, or interpersonal freedom these methods will entail, the petty hope is extended that this longer, safer life will have "even more personal choice in entertainment and shopping." Apparently, those are two areas of life in which human freedom most deeply wishes to express itself, and there is little worry that big data predictions will become big data prescriptions. Yet, "predicting what is useful, however value-neutral this may sound, can shade into

---

[3]Gerard Clancy, "Foreword to Our Strategic Plan," in *Strategic Plan 2017–2022: Building the Foundation for a Great Story and a Greater Commitment at the University of Tulsa*, accessed January 11, 2020, https://utulsa.edu/about/strategic-plan/.

deciding what is useful."[4] I do not raise these concerns about humanity's over-enthrallment with technology to advocate for over-suspicion, but a proper level of godly sober-mindedness.

My purpose is to confront the obvious effectiveness of technology with its frustrating inability to remain faithful to its makers, so that we may sharpen the distinction in our hearts and minds between God, who is the source and goal of our safety in Christ, and the things of this world, which are the means by which God sustains life, but also the means by which he brings death.

The Meaning of Technology

Technology is the human endeavor to transform the natural world by means of the natural world toward practical ends. The term refers to the knowledge of *techne* (craftsmanship or the practical arts), but it also refers to the practical arts themselves, including their devices, systems, and applications.[5] At a basic level, practical arts take place through the interaction of human hands with material creation—the potter's hand forming the clay, the farmer's hand scattering the seed, the reaper's hand gathering the grain, and the shepherd's hand guiding the sheep. However, such practical tasks are usually considered technological when they involve the use of tools.[6] Humanity reshapes the stuff of this world into tools and systems that enable it to better reshape the stuff of this world. Wood and iron are reshaped into saws, axes, and picks to better reshape dirt, wood, and stone. These efforts have cumulative effects as devices (things devised by human minds and hands) grow in complexity, yet they all serve to transform the natural world toward practical ends.

A sharp line is sometimes drawn between that which is non-technological and that which is technological, between *natural*—the world as it exists and

---

[4] Jon Askonas, "How Tech Utopia Fostered Tyranny," *The New Atlantis* 57 (Winter 2019): 6, italics his.
[5] Frederick Ferré, *Philosophy of Technology* (Englewood Cliffs, NJ: Prentice Hall, 1988), 14. Technology and art are often divided between utility and aesthetics, but they are closely related in that both involve the reordering of nature by human hands and in that some things are made to be both useful and beautiful. My focus, however, is on the practical uses of technology in the pursuit of safety. On the usefulness of art, see Nicholas Wolterstorff, *Art in Action: Towards a Christian Aesthetic* (Grand Rapids, MI: Eerdmans, 1980).
[6] In this chapter, I will use *technology* in reference to the practical tasks and *technological devices* in reference to the tools.

moves apart from human intervention—and *artificial*—the world as shaped and directed by human intervention. It is perhaps more helpful to understand this distinction in relation to human activity in a comparative sense, or as varying points across a spectrum. Some foods, medicines, or materials are *more* natural than others because they have undergone *less* refinement, because they are *less* artificial. In the same way, some activities or devices are *more* technological than others. Looking at the stars, a compass, or a GPS screen are all part of the practical art of navigation, but engage in a spectrum of technological sophistication.

Technology as control. In the late-modern era, technology has become more than the knowledge of the practical arts. It is the sustained and systematic union of practice (*techne*) and knowledge (*logos*), where the goal of science is no longer primarily to develop theoretical explanations of the world as it is, but, as "the servant of *techne*," to apply those theories in practical ways to the reordering of the world.[7] This technological reordering includes both the physical and social dimensions of the world. It involves "ordered systems of people and machines," manipulations of "material creation and social relations."[8] The practical arts are similar to the magical arts in that both desire to manipulate the physical and social conditions of the world, but the magical arts seek to do so by means of spiritual powers that reside in or preside over the natural world, whereas the practical arts seek to do so by means of the natural world alone.[9]

With this basic understanding of technology in place, we can now observe what technology is supposed to mean—that is, what its significance is—in the modern world.[10] Under the influence of a widespread "*world-perfecting postulate*," the modern rise of technology is supposed to mean that humanity is creating "an ever better world in which ever more evil and

---

[7] O'Donovan, *Resurrection and Moral Order*, 52; see also Brian Brock, *Christian Ethics in a Technological Age* (Grand Rapids, MI: Eerdmans, 2010), 74-75.

[8] Ian Barbour, *Ethics in an Age of Technology* (San Francisco: Harper, 1993), 3 and Brock, *Christian Ethics*, 169, respectively.

[9] See Jacques Ellul, *The Technological Society*, trans. John Wilkinson (New York: Vintage, 1964), 24-28 and Richard Stivers, *Technology as Magic: The Triumph of the Irrational* (New York: Continuum, 2001).

[10] The authors cited in this paragraph are describing but not endorsing contemporary understandings of technology, with the exception of Verkerk et al., who are describing their own viewpoint.

suffering disappear from it."[11] Technology is supposed to mean that the world is becoming "more predictable, more controllable, safer or more comfortable."[12] It is meant to give humanity the power to change its standing "with the world as well as with society, culture, and the environment."[13] Technology is "a curtain of objects" or an "artificial envelope" with which humanity protects itself from harm.[14] It is meant to eliminate "uncertainties from the future."[15] Technology, therefore, means control. It is "an instrument whose principal aim is the control of the material world."[16]

The enticement of technology. Technology is also meant to be rational. It is supposed to be the "practical implementations of intelligence."[17] Yet, humanity is consistently unable to maintain the rationality of its technological endeavors. Technology exerts power over humanity, whether people are using the technology themselves or others are using it on them. Encounters with technology, especially advanced technology, evoke strong emotional reactions—perhaps mixtures of hope and derision, eagerness and apprehension. Technology is powerful yet constantly changing, developing along an unpredictable path. The latest, most technological devices can do things the old ones could not. They present new possibilities. A young mother once said that her anxiety about her children's safety in the car was not being fueled by news of traffic accidents but by the sight of ever-newer, ever-safer car seats. These new devices proclaimed safety and protection with their use but suggested danger and violence in their absence. She needed to have the latest models. New technological devices make demands on us, whether implicitly or explicitly, with which we have

---

[11]Holm Tetens, "Der Glaube an die Wissenschaften und der methodische Atheismus: Zur religiösen Dialektik der wissenschaftlich-technischen Zivilisation," *NZSTR* 55 (2013): 273, italics his, "*Postulat der Weltperfektionierung*," "schaffen wir eine immer bessere Welt, in der immer mehr Übel und Leiden aus ihr verschwinden."

[12]Maarten J. Verkerk et al., *Philosophy of Technology: An Introduction for Technology and Business Students* (New York: Routledge, 2016), 21.

[13]Ludwig Jaskolla, "Der Mensch als 'homo faber'?: Überlegungen zur Philosophie der Technik," *Stimmen der Zeit* 233 (June 2015): 388.

[14]André Leroi-Gourhan, *Milieu et Techniques* (Paris: Albin Michel, 1973), 332, "un rideau d'objets," "enveloppe artificielle."

[15]Charles Mabee, "Biblical Hermeneutics and the Critique of Technology," in *Theology and Technology: Essays in Christian Analysis and Exegesis*, ed. Carl Mitcham and Jim Grote (Lanham, MD: University Press of America, 1984), 161.

[16]Jacques Ellul, *The Presence of the Kingdom*, trans. Olive Wyon (New York: Seabury, 1967), 111.

[17]Ferré, *Philosophy of Technology*, 26.

not yet negotiated. The devices have not yet become ordinary. As their life cycles continue, these once strange and alluring devices are incorporated into our lives. We learn to rely on them, and they shape our pursuit of safety. When even newer technologies come along, we are once again unsettled because we are again offered new ways of relating to creation and navigating the dangers of this world. We are also confronted with new dangers in need of navigation. Technological devices are conceived by human minds and built by human hands yet hold this enchantment over the human soul.

This disordered relationship, in which a maker sits under the power and authority of the thing made, is most explicit with idolatry, where the power and authority are given the ontological status of a god and submitted to willfully. However, the disorder can be found, to varying degrees, in humanity's relationships with all that its hands have formed. As C. S. Lewis says, "Man's conquest of Nature turns out, in the moment of its consummation, to be Nature's conquest of Man."[18] Technology is ever new, yet its enticements are quite old. The disordered relationship between humanity and technology is not merely a modern phenomenon. Throughout the history of ancient Israel, the iron chariot, as an instrument of war, was a notorious recipient of misplaced hopes and fears (e.g., Is 31:1, Ex 14:9-10); the queen of Sheba was breathless when she saw the splendor of all that Solomon had built (1 Kings 10:5); and King Uzziah was destructively proud of his success in making machinery "to shoot arrows and great stones" (2 Chron 26:15-16).

The reversal of technology. The concern that technology "threatens to slip from human control"[19] did not appear with the explosive growth of technological devices in the late-modern era. It certainly intensified, though, and has been furthered by a reversal in humanity's understanding of its relationship to creation. In the premodern era, humanity had a degree of technological power over its surroundings, but the powers of technology were largely overshadowed by the powers of nature. As demonstrated by Jürgen Moltmann, premodern humanity, in the eyes of modern humanity, was

---

[18]C. S. Lewis, *The Abolition of Man* (New York: HarperCollins, 2001), 80.
[19]Martin Heidegger, "The Question Concerning Technology," in *The Question Concerning Technology and Other Essays*, trans. William Lovitt (New York: Garland, 1977), 5.

"dependent upon uncomprehended forces in nature and history, recognizing in this dependence [its] total reliance on the gods or on God."[20]

Today, the powers of technology overshadow the powers of nature—in imaginations, if not in actuality. It is not that technology as a whole is more powerful than nature as a whole, but that this reversal of power is conceivable, supposedly, for the first time in human history. As the tower of Babel, the campaigns of Alexander the Great, and the Roman Empire attest, civilizations have long been able to conceptualize the conquest of the world, even if they did not do so in modern technological or cosmological terms. Their visions of the scope and power of the world may have been incomplete, but that does not mean that late-modern humanity's visions are complete. God's challenge to Job, "Where were you when . . . ?" (Job 38:4), still stands.

Nonetheless, it is historically accurate to observe, as Moltmann and others have, that humanity's interactions with nature have become dramatically more technological in the last two or three hundred years and that this increase has had a profound effect on late-modern humanity's conceptualizations of its relationship to nature. Jacques Ellul says, "The world had to wait for the eighteenth century to see technical progress suddenly explode in every country and in every area of human endeavor," and Giddens says that modern industry, "shaped by the alliance of science and technology, transforms the world of nature in ways unimaginable to earlier generations."[21] Both built and natural environments are "subject to human coordination and control."[22] In line with the late-modern conception of risk, Moltmann goes on to say that humanity is now less concerned with how to survive the forces of nature, as ruled by "gods and demons," than with how to survive its own "destruction of the balance of nature."[23]

Modern humanity's technological endeavor is precisely an attempt to destroy the balance of nature, to disassemble creation and reassemble it in conformity with the desires of humanity—safety being preeminent among those desires. In this reversal, the call for humanity to conform to the order of nature diminishes while the call for nature to conform to the desires of

---

[20]Jürgen Moltmann, *The Crucified God*, trans. R. A. Wilson and John Bowden (Minneapolis: Fortress, 2015), 130.
[21]Ellul, *The Technological Society*, 42; Anthony Giddens, *The Consequences of Modernity* (Standford, CA: Standford Univeristy Press: 1991), 60.
[22]Giddens, *The Consequences of Modernity*, 60.
[23]Moltmann, *The Crucified God*, 130.

humanity increases. Martin Heidegger captures this well when he compares the presence of a hydroelectric powerplant on a river with that of a wooden bridge. The bridge is built into the river and its banks, conforming in large measure to the shapes and forces of nature. The powerplant, though, has the river built into itself, conforming nature to the shapes and forces of technology. Concerns about this reversal may arise on traditional or aesthetic grounds, as matters of sentimentality or proportion, but also because it indicates that nature is no longer looked to as a cosmos, whose order and beauty humanity's technological endeavors ought to honor and enhance. Nature is now "standing-reserve," called on to yield its energies and resources to humanity's task of technologically reordering the world.[24]

The nineteenth-century author John Ruskin observes another possibility, present in Greek thought, in which nature does not need to be reordered because it already lends itself to human comfort and safety. Ruskin explains, "as far as I recollect, without a single exception, every Homeric landscape, intended to be beautiful, is composed of a fountain, a meadow, and a shady grove." In these idyllic settings, there is "the evident subservience of the whole landscape to human comfort," the "quiet subjection of their every feature to human service." Such settings are indeed mythical, though, and on the rare occasions when they occur naturally, they usually need human cultivation in order to retain their pleasurable qualities. Ruskin concludes, "The god's admiration is excited by the free fountains, wild violets, and wandering vine; but the mortal's, by the vines in rows, the leeks in beds, and the fountains in pipes."[25] Respite in the wilderness is a fortunate find. However, humanity looks to the cultivated world, "nature under human hands and ingenuity,"[26] for consistent and collective safety, despite the worries that technology threatens to slip out of control.

Order and history. In considering humanity's technological endeavors, it will be helpful to understand the theological distinction between the *order* and *history* of creation.[27] The *order* of creation refers to its enduring

---

[24]Heidegger, "The Question Concerning Technology," 15-17.
[25]John Ruskin, *Modern Painters* (London: Routledge, 1856), 3:197-98.
[26]Katherine Sonderegger, "Creation," in *Mapping Modern Theology: A Thematic and Historical Introduction*, ed. Kelly M. Kapic and Bruce L. McCormack (Grand Rapids, MI: Baker, 2012), 117.
[27]O'Donovan, *Resurrection and Moral Order*, 60-62. Alternatively, the terms *structure* and *direction* may be used. See Albert M. Wolters, *Creation Regained: Biblical Basics for a Reformational Worldview* (Grand Rapids, MI: Eerdmans, 1985), 49.

structure, its completeness and ongoing consistency as brought forth and maintained by God. This order refers to the integrity of individual creatures, their various kinds, and their proper interrelations with each other. The order of creation is part of its original goodness, and remains even though it now upholds a fallen creation with rebel forces at work within it. God gives assurance, as he did with Noah after the flood, that this world, as long as it remains, will not fall into chaos (Gen 8:22; 9:11). The order of creation refers to "that which is not negotiable within the course of history, that which neither the terrors of chance nor the ingenuity of art can overthrow."[28]

The *history* of creation refers to the direction of the world, that which is negotiable and contingent, the sequences of events that it goes through with all the accompanying movements and changes. In view of the providence of God, creation will move through history to the final destination for which it was originally intended, but in the meantime it is pushed and pulled in different directions, whether in rebellion or submission to God. Albert Wolters describes these two possible directions: "Anything in creation can be directed either toward or away from God—that is, directed either in obedience or disobedience to his law." Similarly, Bavinck says, "The stuff (*materia*) of all things is and remains the same. However, the form (*forma*), given in creation, was *de*formed by sin in order to be entirely *re*formed again in the sphere of grace."[29] Throughout history, the world is constantly being shaped and reshaped. Civilizations rise and fall. Things are built up and torn down. However, the *history* of creation, including sinful disorderings and various reorderings, all happens within the bounds of creation's primal and eschatological orderings by God.

The thought that humanity could undo God's ordering of creation in an enduring way is suggested by the idea of the destruction of the balance of nature. However, destroying the balance of nature, whether the thought brings dread or hope, means either that humanity is able to undo the order of creation as established by God or that such an enduring order does not exist.[30] Therefore, it seems better to say that humanity is able to disrupt the

---

[28] O'Donovan, *Resurrection and Moral Order*, 60-61.
[29] Wolters, *Creation Regained*, 49; Herman Bavinck, *Reformed Dogmatics*, ed. John Bolt, trans. John Vriend (Grand Rapids, MI: Baker Academic, 2008), 2:576, italics his.
[30] For a helpful critique of this latter claim, see O'Donovan, *Resurrection and Moral Order*, 58-75.

balance of nature, to tilt it in one direction or the other during the course of history. This disruption may be positive or negative. It may be done as a means of healing, to impede the spread of a disease, or as a means of harm, perhaps to develop and spread an artificial disease. Either way, it is a disruption of the balance of nature, not its destruction, because both efforts degenerate apart from constant human attention. There is "a time to be born, and a time to die," "a time to break down, and a time to build up" (Eccles 3:1-8). Regardless of technological protestations, the repetition of these times and seasons will not cease until the coming of the Lord. The transformation of the created order is an eschatological event brought about by God, not a historical event brought about by humanity. Therefore, human reordering takes place within creation's *history*, where it has significance, yet is constrained by creation's *order*. This distinction accommodates both the consistencies of nature and the vagaries of history, while circumscribing "the scope of our freedom and the limits of our fears."[31] It reminds us of the importance of our actions in history, but also that there is a God in heaven.

With the distinction between creation's *order* and *history* in mind, two further distinctions can be made. First, a distinction can be made between possible and impossible reorderings of creation. This created world can be pulled apart and put back together in an astonishing variety of ways. Some of those ways, such as those that allow human flight, were declared "unnatural" when they first appeared, just as others, such as those that manipulate human genetics, might presently be declared "unnatural." But all of these, and others not yet conceived by human imagination, are possible within the created order, while others are simply contradictory to the underlying fabric of creation and therefore impossible. Immortality and genuine love come to mind as impossible to devise technologically. I would venture that instantaneous travel through time or space are also impossible technological reorderings of creation. Second, a distinction can be made among possible reorderings of creation between those that ought to be done and those that ought not be done. In the late-modern world, answers to technological questions about what *can* be done have far outpaced answers to ethical questions about what *should* be done.

---

[31]O'Donovan, *Resurrection and Moral Order*, 61.

Technological compulsions. The starting point for theological reflection on humanity's technological endeavors—and their role in the pursuit of safety—is the givenness of the world as the handiwork of God, not the givenness of technology as the handiwork of humanity.[32] According to O'Donovan, the world exists as God's creation "and in no other way." This world is not only "an ordered totality," but one that is "ordered to its Creator."[33] Humanity re-forms the world through technological endeavors, but the world was formed first by the hand of another. Therefore, what place is there for the handiwork of another alongside God's? What right does humanity have to reorder what God has ordered, to disrupt the processes by which nature runs its course through history? Was it God's intention, within his original purposes and ordering of creation, to allow, accommodate, or even encourage human efforts to reorder it technologically?

This is an ethical question regarding what ought to be, not a historical question regarding what actually happens. As Augustine says regarding a different matter, "We are not now asking whether this was done but whether it should have been done."[34] Historically, humanity reorders creation technologically to whatever extent it is able and willing. We live in a world where antibiotics, radio waves, nuclear fusion, and genetic engineering are known and available, for good or for ill. However, the modern world has long been held captive by a "myth of technology" that says the technologically possible must be done simply because it can be done.[35] When someone sends me a message, I do not know why my laptop, my tablet, and my phone all need to ding at the same time, but I know they can. Some people have watches

---

[32]This follows a similar line as one taken by Karl Barth, who argues that the Christian doctrine of creation should begin, not by asking whether there is a God who exists alongside creation, but how it is that creation exists alongside God. He asks, "What place is there for another when God is there? How can there be another being side by side with his being?" (Karl Barth, *Church Dogmatics: The Doctrine of Creation*, vol. III/1, ed. G. W. Bromiley and T. F. Torrance, trans. J. W. Edwards, O. Bussey, and Harold Knight [Edinburgh: T&T Clark, 1958], 6). Barth comes to this perspective through his insistence that theology begin where the Apostles' Creed begins, "I believe in God the Father Almighty, Maker of heaven and earth." Then the affirmation that heaven and earth exist as God's creation is no less a matter of faith than the affirmation of God as their Creator.

[33]O'Donovan, *Resurrection and Moral Order*, 31.

[34]Augustine, *City of God* 1.22, trans. George E. McCracken, LCL 411 (Cambridge, MA: Harvard University Press, 1957), 1:99.

[35]Hans Walter Wolff, *Anthropology of the Old Testament*, trans. Margaret Kohl (London: SCM Press, 1981), 164.

that also ding. Francis Bacon's program of extracting nature's secrets and finding ways to employ them has become a compulsion. Asking and answering the question of what right humanity has to reorder creation, even though this right will eventually be affirmed, gives an opportunity to reflect critically on the prevailing technological ethic of our time—that humanity ought, or even must, increasingly reorder creation in the hope of gaining ever more control and ever more safety.

The Work of Our Hands

In order to address the question of technology's theological validity, I will lay biblical groundwork through a canonical study of the phrase "work of one's hands" and closely related terminology. The phrase brings humanity's handiwork, including its technological handiwork, into relief against God's creative and redemptive handiwork. It also draws attention to the disparity between those who put their hope in the works of their own hands and those who put their hope in God's faithfulness to the works of his hands.

The biblical phrase. The phrase "work(s) of one's hand(s)" occurs fifty-eight times in the Bible. It occurs fifty-five times in the Old Testament, where מַעֲשֶׂה (deed/work) is used in conjunction with יָד (hand), e.g., מַעֲשֵׂה יָדֶךָ (work of your hands).[36] Most of these occurrences are spread throughout Deuteronomy, Psalms, Isaiah, and Jeremiah. It is used three times in the New Testament, where ἔργον (work) is used in conjunction with χείρ (hand), e.g., ἔργα τῶν χειρῶν σού (work of your hands).[37] Various works are ascribed to the hands of angels, but the specific phrase "work of one's hands" is used only in reference to God and humanity.[38] Because of the frequency with which the phrase "work of one's hands" occurs in Scripture, along with its variety of locations, it serves as a suitable biblical anchor for my present aims regarding Scripture's evaluation of humanity's technological endeavors.

---

[36]According to a study on this same phrase by Winfried Thiel, there are fifty-four occurrences in the Old Testament. See Winfried Thiel, "Das 'Werk der Hände,'" in *Houses Full of All Good Things: Essays in Memory of Timo Veijola*, ed. Juha Pakkala and Martti Nissinen (Göttingen: Vandenhoeck & Ruprecht, 2008), 205. Perhaps the difference can be accounted for by the dual occurrence of the phrase in Ps 90:17.

[37]The three New Testament occurrences are found in Acts 7:41; Heb 1:10; Rev 9:20.

[38]The hands of angels execute judgment (2 Sam 24:16-17); bear swords (Num 22:23; 1 Chron 21:16), a staff (Judg 6:21), and the key to the bottomless pit (Rev 20:1); offer incense and prayers to God (Rev 8:4); and bear up those who are in danger (Ps 91:11-12).

First, this phrase serves as a suitable biblical anchor because of its conceptual consistency. As I explain below, this phrase is sometimes used in reference to an action performed and sometimes in reference to the result of an action. Also, there are obvious differences between God's and humanity's modes of working in this world. "Hand" is used anthropomorphically of God, while it is used literally or as a synecdoche in reference to humanity. With that distinction and those differences in mind, though, this phrase is consistently used in Scripture to denote action taken by persons in relation to creation toward various ends.

Second, this phrase serves as a suitable anchor because of the consistency with which the biblical authors describe, evaluate, and offer admonitions related to the works of hands, both human and divine. This consistency is grounded in Deuteronomy, where the phrase first appears canonically and is used solely in reference to the works of human hands, which are either blessed by God because they are done in obedience to the law (e.g., Deut 30:9) or cursed because they are done in disobedience—with particular mention of the carving of idols (Deut 4:28; 27:15; 31:29). The division between works of human hands that are blessed or cursed continues through the Old Testament, with an emphasis in the prophets on the condemnation of idols (e.g., Is 2:8; Jer 1:16; see also Acts 7:41; Rev 9:20).[39] Yet petitions and promises regarding Israel's hope that God would again bless the works of their hands can be found as well (e.g., Ps 90:17; Is 65:22; Hos 14:3). In contrast to this divided evaluation of human handiwork, Psalms and Isaiah apply the phrase to God, presenting the works of his hands as faithful and praiseworthy (Ps 111:7; Is 60:21).

Third, this phrase serves as a suitable anchor because it gives a fair representation of Scripture's overall evaluation of humanity's technological handiwork. Scripture has much to say about human action in relation to creation, the human fashioning of devices, and the human use of those devices. The passages that use the phrase "work of one's hands" do not exhaust Scripture's teachings on these subjects. There is the possibility that these passages do not reflect Scripture's overall tenor. This concern is most

---

[39]Deuteronomy 30:1-10 "was to influence in many ways the preaching of the prophets in subsequent generations" (Peter C. Craigie, *The Book of Deuteronomy*, NICOT [Grand Rapids, MI: Eerdmans, 1976], 363).

apparent with the heavy use of the phrase in reference to the making and worshiping of idols. Perhaps the emphasis on idols leads to an overly negative evaluation of the works of human hands. However, Deuteronomy started off in a balanced way, with both encouragements and warnings. The later emphasis in the Old Testament, especially in the prophets, on the idolatrous works of human hands came as a response to the inclination of Israel and surrounding nations to look to the works of their own hands, apart from the blessings of God, for prosperity and security. Therefore, this phrase offers a limited, but fitting, representation of Scripture's evaluation of human handiwork, especially with the inclusion of rare but hopeful prophetic promises: "You shall bow down no more to the work of your hands" (Mic 5:13).

In some instances, this phrase signifies the activity that one engages in to be productive or to accomplish meaningful tasks (e.g., Deut 2:7; Ps 90:17). In other instances, it is used to denote the results of this activity, the artifact or condition produced, such as "earthen pots, the work of a potter's hands" (Lam 4:2). The "work of one's hands" may "denote the work process, but also the results of the proceeds of this activity."[40] Both of these aspects are brought together in Deuteronomy 30:9, where Israel's work and the fruit of its work will both be blessed: "The LORD your God will make you abundantly prosperous in all the work of your hand, in the fruit of your womb and in the fruit of your cattle and in the fruit of your ground."

Further, while this phrase is used in Scripture to denote both deeds that are done and things that are produced, the biblical authors consistently do so with an eye toward the motivations, purposes, and ends for which these works are done or produced. In other words, the works of one's hands are moral, being either good or evil (Ps 111:7; Jer 1:16). In the case of human handiwork, it is approved and blessed by God or condemned and cursed by him (Deut 24:19; 27:15; Ps 28:4). Finally, there are several instances in which the works of one's hands are treated as revelatory, disclosing the character and power of the one whose hands perform them. The heavens are the handiwork of God. They "declare his glory" (Ps 19:1). Things that are beautiful are "the work of a master hand" (Song 7:1).

---

[40] Thiel, "Das 'Werk der Hände,'" 209, "den Arbeitsprozeß, bezeichnen, aber auch resultativ den Ertrag dieser Tätigkeit."

Alongside "work of one's hands" are some closely related phrases and terms that are also helpful in understanding Scripture's evaluation of humanity's technological endeavors. Parallel verbal phrases are found in the Old and New Testaments. In the Old Testament עשׂה (to make/do) is used in conjunction with יָד (hand), e.g., "whatever your hand finds to do" (Eccles 9:10) or "the hand of the LORD has done this" (Job 12:9). In the New Testament ἐργάζομαι (to work) is used in conjunction with χειρ (hand), e.g., "to work with your hands" (ἐργάζεσθαι ταῖς χερσὶν ὑμῶν).[41] Another related term in the New Testament is χειροποίητος (made by hands). It is used to contrast that which is made by human hands with that which is made, not by hands (ἀχειροποίητος or οὐ χειροποίητος), but by God.[42] This term is used in the New Testament only in reference to dwelling places and circumcision.

The work of God's hands. When used in reference to God, the phrase "work of one's hands" has several notable features. All that God does is described as the work of his hands. This includes his work of creation (Ps 8:6) and the redemptive works he does on behalf of his people (Ps 92:4; 111:5-7; 143:5). However, the language of handiwork is used most directly in reference to two of God's works in particular—the heavens and humanity. The "sky above proclaims his handiwork" (Ps 19:1); "the heavens are the work of [his] hands," even his fingers (Ps 102:25; 8:3). In regard to humanity, Isaiah calls both Assyria and Israel the work of God's hands (Is 19:25; 29:23; 60:21). Later, with an allusion to Genesis 2:7, Isaiah says that all people are the work of God's hands: "We are the clay, and you are the potter; we are all the work of your hand" (Is 64:8). Prayers to God, that he would intervene on humanity's behalf, are grounded in this claim. After the psalmist professes confidence that God will preserve his life, he ends with a petition to God not to "forsake the work of your hands" (Ps 138:7-8; see also Job 14:15; Is 64:8-9). God's faithfulness to the work of his hands is the basis for the prophetic hope that he will establish Israel forever (Is 29:23; 60:21). Additionally, the works of God's hands are morally upright; they are "faithful and just" (Ps 111:7).

---

[41]This phrase occurs in 1 Cor 4:12; Eph 4:28; 1 Thess 4:11.
[42]Χειροποίητος and its negations appear nine times in the New Testament (Mk 14:58; Acts 7:48; 17:24; 2 Cor 5:1; Eph 2:11; Col 2:11; Heb 9:11; 9:24). Χειροποίητος is used a number of times in the Septuagint as a translation of אֱלִיל, which refers to that which is worthless, i.e., idols (BDB, 47). For example, see Isaiah 2:18.

The works of God's hands display his glory. His ongoing faithfulness to those works further displays his glory, mercy, and goodness. Creation does not stand alone as something to be observed apart from God. Accordingly, when we look at the world around us through the lens of Scripture and with eyes of faith, we cannot learn about creation without also learning about the Creator. The moon and stars have been set in place by the majestic one (Ps 8:1-3). Our hearts have been fashioned by the one enthroned in heaven (Ps 33:13-15). All things are upheld by the Son through whom the Father created the world (Heb 1:1-5). God brought forth this world with goodness, order, and beauty. He delights in the perfection of what he has made (Gen 1:31). As Calvin explains, God "revealed himself and daily discloses himself in the whole workmanship of the universe." The "skillful ordering of the universe is for us a sort of mirror in which we can contemplate God, who is otherwise invisible."[43]

The term χειροποίητος (made by hands) presents the works of God in a slightly different light. As I said above, this term is used in the New Testament in reference to human hands while its negation is used in reference to God. Those who are in Christ are circumcised "with a circumcision made without hands"; that is, the putting off of sinful flesh and the rising to life (Col 2:11-12). As high priest, Christ enters the presence of God through "the greater and more perfect tent (not made with hands, that is, not of this creation)" (Heb 9:11). Christ's work as high priest is superior because of the "uniqueness of the sacrifice that he presented," but also because of "the uniqueness of the sanctuary he entered," one that is not made by hands.[44] The present body, "the tent that is our earthly home," is contrasted with the resurrection body, "a house not made with hands, eternal in the heavens" (2 Cor 5:1). So, while "work of one's hands" is used anthropomorphically of God throughout Scripture, "not made by hands" (ἀχειροποίητος or οὐ χειροποίητος) is used of certain of his works—the circumcision of the heart, the resurrection of the body, and the heavenly temple—to highlight that

---

[43] John Calvin, *Institutes of the Christian Religion*, ed. John T. McNeill, trans. Ford Lewis Battles (Philadelphia: Westminster John Knox: 1960) I.5.1, pp. 52-53. Despite the clarity of God's revelation in creation, Calvin tells us that fallen humanity looks at creation as an independent object, contemplating the sign while ignoring the one to whom the sign points. Therefore, God has revealed himself through "another and better help," i.e., Scripture, as "a more direct and more certain mark whereby he is to be recognized" (Calvin, *Institutes* I.6.1, p. 70).

[44] William L. Lane, *Hebrews 9–13*, WBC 47B (Grand Rapids, MI: Zondervan, 2015), 237.

they are not the work of (human) hands. They are of a higher quality. They are eternal, complete, perfect. They are the "true things," while those made by hands are at best "copies" (Heb 9:24).

The work of human hands. Along with the work of God's hands, Scripture also speaks of the work of human hands. When Israel was wandering in the wilderness, God blessed the work of their hands, so that they "lacked nothing" (Deut 2:7). When they renewed their covenant with God, he told them repeatedly that he would bless the work of their hands—their families, labors, livestock, and harvests—if they were faithful. If Israel obeyed God's commandments, cared for those in need, and kept the appointed feasts, he would open "his good treasury, the heavens" to give them rain and make them prosperous in all the work of their hands (Deut 28:12). Israel is warned, though, that they will "serve gods of wood and stone, the work of human hands" (Deut 4:28) and that they will provoke God to anger when they do what is evil with their hands (Deut 31:29).

In a few passages, the works of human hands that provoke God to anger are unspecified or depicted generally as sin, turning aside from what is commanded or doing evil in the sight of the Lord (e.g., 1 Kings 16:7; Jer 32:30). In one passage, dishonest words are linked directly to God's destruction of the works of human hands (Eccles 5:6). However, the single most common use of the phrase "work of one's hands" is in reference to the fashioning and worshiping of idols. In fact, with two exceptions, the idol is the only human artifact to which this phrase is applied. Those two exceptions are jewels in Song of Solomon 7:1 and earthen pots in Lamentations 4:2, both of which occur in poetic passages and are used as similes.[45] Idols of wood and stone are "the work of men's hands" (2 Kings 19:18). Those who make them are cursed (Deut 27:15) and those who worship them provoke God to anger (2 Chron 34:25; Jer 25:6).

Just as God's handiwork displays his glory, mercy, and goodness, so humanity's handiwork displays its glory, ingenuity, and creativity (Ex 35:10-35), but also its shame, cunning, and foolishness (Eccles 4:4; Jer 10:8-9; Hos 13:2).

---

[45]This is not meant to discount the various goods and artifacts, such as baked goods (Gen 40:17), needlework (Ex 26:1), and metalwork (Ex 27:4), that are made by human hands and often used in worship of God, nor the various wordings used to describe them, but to highlight that when the phrase "work of one's hands" is used in reference to human-made objects, it almost exclusively refers to idols. For an exhaustive survey of human-made objects in Scripture, see Ray Pritz, *The Works of Their Hands: Man-made Things in the Bible* (New York: United Bible Societies, 2009).

Scripture exhibits a certain ambivalence toward the work of human hands that is not present regarding the work of God's hands. On the one hand, the work of human hands is "normal, vital, and beneficial to life," but on the other, it often leads away from God to worship of foreign gods.[46] The works of human hands and the artifacts produced by them are intertwined with the morality of their makers, but are not themselves imbued with moral agency. Evil is not a substance that resides in an idol, but a state of affairs that accompanies the making and worshiping of the idol.[47] Therefore, when God commands that idols or other artifacts be destroyed, it is not to destroy the evil but to remove the circumstances in which the evil occurs, the evil to which those artifacts gave opportunity.

Those works in the New Testament that are said to be "made by hands" (χειροποίητος) are circumcision and temples. Circumcision is "made in the flesh by hands" (Eph 2:11). It was commanded by God to Abraham and his descendants as a covenantal sign. Yet, it was inadequate on its own. Israel was commanded also to circumcise "the foreskin of your heart, and be no longer stubborn" (Deut 10:16). Circumcision with flint knives, as important as it is, is overshadowed by a circumcision that human hands are incapable of performing, regardless of the precision of the tool, the circumcision of the heart (Deut 30:6; Rom 2:29). Temples are "houses made by hands" (Acts 7:48; see also Mk 14:58; Acts 17:24). In Acts 7, Stephen points this out to a Jewish audience regarding the temple in Jerusalem. Solomon built a house for God in accordance with the prescriptions of the Law and God's promises to David (Acts 7:47; 1 Chron 22:10). But the Most High does not dwell in such houses, no matter how magnificently built. Heaven is his throne. The earth is his footstool (Acts 7:49). At the Areopagus, Paul makes a similar point to a pagan audience. God made all things. He does not need a house or anything from us (Acts 17:24-25).

According to commentators, χειροποίητος is a "pejorative term," used in the New Testament "in a deprecating way."[48] Yet, our understanding of

---

[46]Thiel, "Das 'Werk der Hände,'" 204, "normal, lebensnotwendig und lebensförderlich."
[47]The Old Testament "attends to evil as event (rather than as substance)." O'Donovan, *Resurrection and Moral Order*, 84.
[48]See Lane, *Hebrews 9–13*, 219, and Darrell L. Bock, *Acts*, BECNT (Grand Rapids, MI: Baker Academic, 2007), 302, respectively. Lane explains, "As an earthly sanctuary, the tabernacle is not only transitory but participates in the imperfection of the present world" (Lane, *Hebrews 9–13*, 219).

Scripture's evaluation of that which is "made by hands" requires nuance. Both circumcision and the temple were ordained by God. This term does not indicate a wholesale denunciation of either. Rather, it points to their inherent limitations as made by sinful humanity and the erroneous, arrogant, prideful views that often accompanied them. Circumcision of the flesh does not remove the flesh's sinful desires. God is transcendent "over the temple," even as he made himself present to Israel through the temple.[49] Other nations may build a temple for God to dwell in, but that does not mean he needs such a house or that he is obligated to dwell in it. Such works of human hands, even when done in accordance with the provisions of the old covenant, have "validity only in reference to the eschatological reality associated with Christ's definitive sacrifice and exaltation."[50] They are passing shadows and imperfect copies.

Establish the works of our hands. There is a division in Scripture, related to the works of hands, between true and false worship. True worship is directed to God on account of the works of his hands (Ps 92:4), but false worship is directed to idols, the works of human hands. An idol, like all artifacts, is creation reordered by human hands. The tree is cut down from the forest, worked with the ax, and decorated with silver and gold (Jer 10:3-4). Humanity is chastised for its refusal to turn away from these blind, deaf, and lame idols (Rev 9:20). Yet, the prophets express a twofold hope regarding the works of human hands. First, they foretell of a day when God's people will no longer worship them (Is 17:7-8; Hos 14:3; Mic 5:13). Second, Isaiah speaks of a time when God's "chosen shall long enjoy the work of their hands" (Is 65:22).

That prophetic hope, grounded in God's covenant promises, is fulfilled in Christ, who sets his people free to enjoy the works of their hands without worshiping them. I noted earlier that technology and art are frequently separated from each other in the modern era, with utility in one hand and beauty in the other. Beauty is often seen as excessive or extravagant. Aesthetic desires are more quickly condemned as unrealistic or idolatrous than

---

[49]Dennis D. Sylva, "The Meaning and Function of Acts 7:46-50," *JBL* 106, no. 2 (1987): 270-71. Elements of Sylva's argument related to the temple can be applied to circumcision. See also Bock, *Acts*, 302-3.

[50]Lane, *Hebrews 9-13*, 248.

pragmatic desires. One way the church can enjoy this freedom is by bringing usefulness and beauty back together in its buildings, furnishings, meals, and worship. Another way that Christians can enjoy this freedom is through diligence and excellence in their vocations. The command is given: "Whatever your hand finds to do, do it with your might, for there is no work or thought or knowledge or wisdom in Sheol, to which you are going" (Eccles 9:10). As Christians with the hope of resurrection, this verse is striking because it looks to death, but not through death to the other side. It is helpful, though, as a reminder that these are the days God has given you to live in his creation, this is the strength he has put in your hands, these are the tasks he has given them to do. Not other days, other strength, other hands, other tasks; these ones. You will rest from your labors someday (Rev 14:13), so build what God has called you to build today. Enjoy using his creation for his glory.

Moses prays that God would "establish the work of our hands" (Ps 90:17), that we would enjoy the prolonged benefit of their completion in this life and that their effects would endure into the age to come.[51] In contrast to the vanity and pride of those who literally or figuratively lift up the works of their hands as gods, Scripture calls us to work with our hands modestly, performing the tasks that God sets before us with diligence so that we may not be a burden to others, but instead provide for ourselves and those who may be in need (Eph 4:28). It is good to give our hands to such work.

The (Re)ordering of Creation

The question raised earlier, of what right humanity has to reorder what God has ordered, carries with it the assumption that creation already has an inherent and enduring logic, a rationality by which God has ordered it. That rationality, to use such a term in reference to a person, is the Son of God, the divine *Logos*.

Christ orders creation. Christ orders creation in its origin, as the one "through whom [God] created the world," and he orders it in its consummation, as the one whom God appointed "the heir of all things" (Heb 1:2;

---

[51]See John Calvin, *Commentary on the Book of the Prophet Isaiah*, trans. William Pringle (Edinburgh: Calvin Translation Society, 1850), 4:402. Calvin notes both the temporal and eternal benefits while commenting on Isaiah 65:22.

cf. 1 Cor 8:6). As Wolfhart Pannenberg explains, "The final ordering of creatures to the manifestation of Jesus Christ presupposes that creatures already have the origin of their existence and nature in the Son."[52] The coherence of existence we find in created beings, their unique identities and distinctions, their abilities to relate and interact, their various abilities to move, grow, and change, are given to them by the Father through Christ, in whom "all things hold together" (Col 1:17). According to the teachings of Maximus the Confessor, the *logoi* of created beings, "the fundamental meaning in accordance with which they have been created," are derived from and contained in the *Logos*.[53] The logic and ordering of creation are bestowed on it by the Son.

Christ orders creation, but more than that, he orders it toward himself, and through himself to the Father. The Father sent the Son into this world on a redemptive mission. The Son freely came. In so doing he accepted creaturely finitude, becoming wholly reliant on the goodness of his heavenly Father. Such a life of childlike reliance on God as Father is precisely what creaturely existence ought to be; it is the properly ordered life of the lilies, ravens, and ants. "These all look to you, to give them their food in due season" (Ps 104:27). Adam, and all who are in him, succumbed to the temptation of pride, though, and rejected this way of life, this ordering of creaturely existence, conforming instead to the patterns of this age (Rom 12:2) and seeking in vain to establish some other order of existence. Outside of Christ, humanity is disordered and disorderly, refusing to humble itself before the Father or entrust itself to his lovingkindness. This does not always mean that the world is disordered in the sense of being chaotic, but in the sense of trying to order itself in the wrong way, by the wrong means, and toward the wrong ends. The world was made through the *Logos*, but when he came to that which is his own, "the world did not know him" (John 1:10-11). Therefore, again according to the teachings of Maximus, the "*logoi* of creation," or the

---

[52] Pannenberg continues, "Otherwise the final summing up of all things in the Son (Eph. 1:10) would be external to the things themselves, so that it would not be the definitive fulfillment of their own distinctive beings" (Wolfhart Pannenberg, *Systematic Theology*, trans. Geoffrey W. Bromiley, vol. 2. [Grand Rapids, MI: Eerdmans, 1994], 2:25). I find Pannenberg's explanation of Christ's role in creation helpful on several points, though I agree with O'Donovan's criticisms of his historical teleology (O'Donovan, *Resurrection and Moral Order*, 59-60).

[53] Andrew Louth, *Maximus the Confessor* (New York: Routledge, 1996), 68; see also Pannenberg, *Systematic Theology*, 2:25. Louth is describing Maximus's teaching.

various parts of creation, are obscure to those who have been "cut off from the *Logos*."[54]

Yet people get by in this world without Christ. Peter Lombard says that humanity has the knowledge "of disposing of and providing for things" and "of providing for the necessities of the flesh." He says that this knowledge was given by God at creation and that humanity "did not lose this knowledge by sinning." As evidence that humanity retains this practical knowledge, he says, "Man is not instructed in Scripture about these sorts of things, but about the knowledge of the soul, which he lost by sinning."[55] Although there are passages in Scripture that appear to give instruction on such practical matters, Lombard references 1 Corinthians 9:9, regarding God's lack of concern for the muzzling of oxen, as an interpretive key to such passages, indicating God's general lack of concern in instructing humanity on these practical matters. The difficulty with Lombard's use of 1 Corinthians 9:9 is that "the necessities of the flesh" are the subject matter at hand. Paul and Barnabas are defending their right to secure the means by which to eat and drink (1 Cor 9:4). Lombard's comments are important because they draw attention to the fact that sinful humanity is often capable of providing for the physical necessities of earthly life apart from any redemptive revelation or acknowledgment of Jesus as Lord. However, Maximus's observation that a lack of understanding of the Creator obscures one's understanding of his creatures is a corrective reminder that efforts to provide for the physical necessities of life may be crudely effectual while nonetheless burdensome and evil, producing unnecessary costs of worry, strife, and sorrow.

Humanity looks to nature to extract its secrets and powers, but not to God to receive good things from him. This posture, of looking up to God for provision, is in accordance with the logic of creaturely existence that God brought forth through his Son in the original work of creation and to which he called Israel through the giving of the Law. It is also in accordance with the ordering of life to which Christ calls his disciples. This mode of creaturely existence—the full awareness and acceptance of one's reliance on the Creator—was established by the eternal Son of God and accomplished in his

---

[54] Louth, *Maximus the Confessor*, 68.
[55] Peter Lombard, *The Sentences, Book 2: On Creation*, trans. Giulio Silano, Mediaeval Sources in Translation 43 (Toronto: Pontifical Institute of Mediaeval Studies, 2008), 105-6.

incarnate life. All creatures exist in reliance on Christ, and through him in reliance on the Father, who sends forth the Spirit as the giver of life. This is the order of creation and remains so whether those creatures are aware and accepting of it or not.

Therefore, the question of what place there is for the handiwork of another alongside God's must reckon with the scope of the work of the triune God, who brought every feature of this world into existence for his own glory and is now bringing retribution and redemption to this world for the magnification of that glory. The center of this work is the cross, where Christ fulfills his creaturely reliance to the utmost by committing his spirit into the Father's hands (Lk 23:46). In so doing he proclaims God's judgment on all who rebel against their own creatureliness. At the cross, the Son's creaturely existence is most clearly seen, as is the totality of his dependence on the Father and the totality of human depravity. Those who crucified Christ were indeed ordered toward him, and therefore they were also ordered through him to the Father. But it was disorder on their parts because they were ordered toward him in opposition, in rejection of him as their brother and God as their Father. It was "the destructive dialectic of unrighteous order and disordered anger."[56] In crucifying Christ, the world sought to orphan itself. Yet he is on the cross for those who mock, reject, and accuse him. He is reordering what has been disordered through sin. Even in the darkness of Golgotha, this world is ordered through the Son to the glory of the Father.

Humanity reorders creation. Yet there is still more to the logic of creation, and at this point an answer to the question of what place there is for the handiwork of another alongside God's begins to emerge. Creation is the means by which God displays his goodness, kindness, and generosity toward humanity. He created the world and then shared it with us. God quite literally made time for us.[57] He made space for us as well, room to "live and move and have our being" (Acts 17:28). Moreover, in giving humanity a place in this world, he has given it the capacity and occasion to reorder creation to some degree. In themselves, though, the capacity and occasion to reorder creation do not entail an imperative, nor even a right, to do so. As

---

[56]O'Donovan, *Resurrection and Moral Order*, 74.
[57]See Augustine, *Confessions* 11, trans. Carolyn J.B. Hammond, vol. 2, LCL 27 (Cambridge, MA: Harvard University Press, 2016), 27:190-259; and Jenson, *Systematic Theology*, 2:25.

the Reformer Wolfgang Musculus explains, "We should not claim [the earth's] use for ourselves just because we can or because we are people endowed with reason, wisdom and what not." Instead, he says that we have a right to make use of creation "because that authority was conceded to us at the very outset of our race."[58] God told the animals to be fruitful and multiply; he gave them "every green plant for food" (Gen 1:22, 30). He did the same with Adam and Eve, giving them the earth's grains and fruits as food (Gen 1:29, 2:16). However, humanity's right to the earth's produce as food is accompanied by the commands to Adam and Eve to subdue the earth and have dominion over the animals (Gen 1:26, 28, cf. Ps 8:6) and by the placing of Adam in the Garden of Eden to work and keep the land and trees that will provide him his food (Gen 2:15). The man and woman are God's image bearers, vessels through whom he manifests his presence in creation. They are therefore given authority to reign over the rest of creation.[59] The language of having dominion (רדה) and subduing (כבשׁ) denote humanity's royal position and right to rule over creation.

Technology as a creational mandate. Among biblical scholars, the creational mandate in Genesis 1–2—to rule over the earth and subdue it, to tend and keep the garden—is usually understood to include a technological mandate. God presents creation to Adam and Eve as "very good" (Gen 1:31), but he also calls them to work it. Accordingly, work is "an essential part of human existence," and without it life would not "have meaning or fulfillment."[60] Paradise is not conceived statically "as absolute perfection, but only as a wonderful place of sojourning."[61] There are hidden potentialities to be uncovered and betterments to be formed in creation. Humanity's God-given dominion involves "not only preservation and care, but also active transformation with

---

[58]Wolfgang Musculus, *In Mosis Genesim plenissimi Commentarii, in quibus veterum & recentiorum sententiae diligenter expenduntur* (Basil: Johann Herwagen, 1554), 46; translated and quoted in John L. Thompson, *Genesis 1-11*, Reformation Commentary on Scripture (Downers Grove, IL: IVP Academic, 2014), 61.

[59]For an account of the image of God as "divine presence" in which dominion is a "closely associated" human function, see Marc Cortez, *ReSourcing Theological Anthropology: A Constructive Account of Humanity in the Light of Christ* (Grand Rapids, MI: Zondervan, 2018), 107-13.

[60]Claus Westermann, *Genesis 1-11: A Commentary*, trans. John J. Scullion (London: SPCK, 1984), 220; see also Kenneth Mathews, *Genesis 1-11:26*, NAC 1A (Nashville: B&H Academic, 1996), 209.

[61]Hermann Gunkel, *Genesis: übersetzt und erklärt* (Göttingen: Vandenhoeck & Ruprecht, 1922), 10, "das Paradies sich nicht als absolut vollkommenen Ort, sondern nur als wunderschönen Aufenthalt vorstellt."

the help of technology."⁶² Humanity is called by God not only to oversee the flourishing of the world according to its created order and natural processes, but also to reorder and adapt it in ways that bring glory to God, help all creatures flourish, and serve human interests and desires. In the context of the Pentateuch, the transformation of nature revolves primarily around agriculture and civilization (food and shelter). However, the working and keeping of Genesis 2:15 are normally expanded to include every human occupation, "all that a person is capable of" apart from sin.⁶³ According to this view, humanity's technological endeavors are "fundamentally affirmed" as part of the created order and as an expression of human creativity.⁶⁴ "Man [is called by God] to complete the work of creation, to gradually take possession of all its goods and to make them useful to himself and his neighbors."⁶⁵ Bavinck says, "Man's dominion over the earth through science and art, and so forth—while all these things have undoubtedly been modified by sin and changed in appearance, they nevertheless have their active principle and foundation in creation, in the ordinances of God, and not in sin."⁶⁶

Technology as a post-fall concession. Jacques Ellul disagrees with this interpretation of the creation mandate. Many assume that Adam and Eve were to exercise their dominion over creation through technological means, but Ellul argues that God's command to rule does not entail the development of technology. He says that technology arises later, out of *technique*. For Ellul, *technique* is an all-encompassing methodology, a way of getting things done

---

⁶²Hans J. Munk, "Technik, Technologie," in *Lexikon für Theologie und Kirche*, eds. Walter Kasper, et al. (Freiburg: Herder, 2000), 9:1310, "Der in Gen 1,26.28; 2,15 ergehende Grundauftrag intendiert nicht nur Bewahrung u. Pflege, sondern auch aktive Umgestaltung mit Hilfe der T[echnik]."

⁶³Westermann, *Genesis 1–11*, 221-22. See also Victor P. Hamilton, *The Book of Genesis: Chapters 1–17*, NICOT (Grand Rapids, MI: Eerdmans, 1990), 140, and R. R. Reno, *Genesis*, Brazos Theological Commentary on the Bible (Grand Rapids, MI: Brazos, 2010), 69.

⁶⁴Münk, "Technik, Technologie," 1310, "Technisches Handeln wird somit grundsätzlich bejaht, zugleich aber auf die gottgesetzten Grenzen verpflichtet."

⁶⁵Henri Rondet, "Arbeit II, Theologisch," *Lexikon für Theologie und Kirche* 1, eds. Josef Höfer and Karl Rahner (Freiburg: Herders, 1957), 1:803-5, quoted in Jacques Ellul, "Technique and the Opening Chapters of Genesis," in *Theology and Technology: Essays in Christian Analysis and Exegesis*, ed. Carl Mitcham and Jim Grote (Lanham, MD: University Press of America, 1984), 124. Rondet's entry is from 1957. The more recent 1993 entry says that the purpose of the creation mandate is to pass on to the rest of creation the "Segenskraft Gottes" (blessing-power of God) and warns that Gen 1:26-28 should not be misinterpreted as giving legitimization for forced rule or exploitation (Friedrich V. Reiterer, "Arbeit I, Biblisch-theologisch," *Lexikon für Theologie und Kirche* 1:917).

⁶⁶Bavinck, *Reformed Dogmatics*, 2:576.

in this world, based in rationality, efficiency, and procedure. As he explains, "The term *technique*, as I use it, does not mean machines, technology, or this or that procedure for attaining an end. In our technological society, *technique* is the *totality of methods rationally arrived at and having absolute efficiency . . . in every* field of human activity."[67] In other words, *technique* is a fundamental way of relating to the world in which humanity seeks to find freedom and ease by arranging the world and performing tasks in the best possible way (where "best" is usually defined in terms of efficiency for the sake of security, in order to have more of whatever is needed). Ellul argues that *technique* ends up enslaving humanity to its inhuman demands. He argues that *technique* has been a part of human history since the time of Cain but was "impossible in Eden."[68]

The beginning of humanity's technological endeavors and the accompanying appearance of technological devices in history are linked to a set of circumstances that did not exist until after the fall. According to Ellul, creation was "*perfect and finished*" when it left God's hands. There was "no imaginable progress" in this perfect world, no way to improve on what God had given. Adam and Eve were not called to serve a demiurgic function in the ongoing creation of the world, but to receive it as a gift. The food that God gave was immediately available and useful. Adam exercised his dominion over the animals by naming them, using only his voice. Adam and Eve were called to cultivate and watch over the land, not out of necessity, as if their lives depended on it, but out of "freely given love," by which they would reflect back to God his "royal image" and reign over creation.[69]

Ellul contrasts this Edenic work with work as experienced today: "In Eden, it was not useful to have a tool, because everything was a whole. But now Adam is in a world which does not give him anything freely." The land that yielded its abundance is bridled because of the curse. Nature's fruit, that which is conducive to life, must now be drawn out, while its thorns and thistles, that which inhibits life, must be suppressed. Humanity employs *technique* as a means of increasing power and efficiency. According to Ellul, humanity's technological endeavors have arisen, not as

---

[67]Ellul, *The Technological Society*, xxv, italics his.
[68]Ellul, "Technique and the Opening Chapters of Genesis," 132.
[69]Ellul, "Technique and the Opening Chapters of Genesis," 125-27, italics his.

an integral part of the creation mandate, but because of the fall. He clarifies that *technique* is neither "a fruit of sin," nor "contrary to the will of God," but rather a necessity of a fallen world, "the product of the situation in which sin has put man."[70] In other words, Ellul is saying that participation in *technique* is neither a return to Eden nor a path to hell, but a necessary aspect of life in a world where fellowship with God and each other has been broken.

Ellul says that humanity's technological reordering of creation began in earnest when Cain built a city (Gen 4:17).[71] As Brock explains, Ellul distinguishes between Adam and Eve's fall and response to God, in which they received the garments of skin as God's provision, and Cain's fall and response to God, in which he refused to accept his mark as God's provision. This refusal birthed *technique*.[72] Cain's city was not built as an exercise in human dominion, but as a revolt, an attempt to "satisfy his desire for security" apart from God. Ellul says that Cain "creates the art of craftsmanship" in order to build a city that will remedy his problems, but each new remedy is "a new disobedience."[73] Ellul nevertheless maintains that technology is not contrary to the will of God through his view that "the only relationship for God is one of love, which means running the risk of not being loved in return." God, "because he loves, is vulnerable."[74] For Ellul, God's love has no element of violence or compulsion, which means that God accepts humanity even in its rejection of him. He "assumes to himself even man's revolts and transforms them, remakes them."[75] Ellul says that God incorporates Cain's technological rebellion into redemption as he gives humanity the dwelling place it wants, a city, the new Jerusalem.

---

[70]Ellul, "Technique and the Opening Chapters of Genesis," 133-35.

[71]Jacques Ellul, *The Meaning of the City*, trans. Dennis Pardee (Grand Rapids, MI: Eerdmans, 1970), 1-9. Brock says that Ellul sees multiple fall narratives that start with Adam, then move out to Cain, Nimrod, and others with the ramifications of the first fall spreading out further and further. The consequent falls are "reverberations" of Adam's. See Brian Brock, "Culture as Flight from God: Jacques Ellul on the Fall," in *Fall Narratives: An Interdisciplinary Perspective*, ed. Zohar Hadromi-Allouche and Áine Larkin (New York: Routledge, 2017), 37-39.

[72]Brock, "Culture as Flight from God," 45.

[73]Ellul, *The Meaning of the City*, 5-6.

[74]Jacques Ellul, *On Freedom, Love, and Power*, trans. Willem H. Vanderburg, expanded (Toronto: University of Toronto Press, 2015), 71. See my comments at the beginning of chapter 6 regarding the problems of attributing risk to God.

[75]Ellul, *The Meaning of the City*, 175.

Ellul concludes from his insistence that "there could not have been technique" in Eden that there was no place for technology (i.e., tools) in Eden.[76] His argument is dependent on efficiency and necessity being the only conditions in which technology would arise. Yet, it seems to me that technological activities and their accompanying devices could have arisen in Eden because there are other conditions, related to sociality, pleasure, worship, and artistry, in which human handiwork could be rightly developed, not as a *post facto* concession by God, but as a legitimate expression of human vice-regency over the earth. Instead of viewing humanity's technological endeavor as a post-fall concession by God to human rebellion, it should instead be understood as part of God's creational purposes for humanity that is in need of redemption, a redemption rooted in the love of God that indeed does violence to the idolatrous desires that cause us to languish, like Cain, in the pit of destruction. But for those who trust in God, he brings them up out of the mire, sets their feet upon a rock, and makes their steps secure (Ps 40:2-4).

Ellul is unconvincing in his argument that the right to technologically reorder creation was given as a post-fall concession. However, his depiction of the original goodness of creation is helpful because it highlights humanity's current unwillingness to live by grace. When Adam was sent out of the garden to work the land, the conditions for survival were suddenly harsh. It takes work to stay alive in this fallen world. Yet Christ confronts humanity's unwillingness to live by grace east of Eden, where the dangers are real, where the fight to survive takes place amid pain, desire, sweat, and toil. Humanity has grown accustomed to its contention with thorns and thistles. It longs to have victory, to overcome danger and deprivation. But it lacks the imaginative capacity to comprehend Eden as a place where there is work but no such contention. Humanity's image of a paradise without this contention is usually a paradise without work. Humanity is "summoned to a destiny," even in its origin, but that destiny is not immediately given in creation.[77] There is a *telos* for human life and work that is not yet fully defined in Eden. Ellul's concern, with which I sympathize, is that we read our own technological and ideological *teloi* back into the creation narrative. Eden, a world with

---

[76]Ellul, "Technique and the Opening Chapters of Genesis," 128-29.
[77]O'Donovan, *Resurrection and Moral Order*, 56.

nothing to strive against, at least until the serpent appears, seems to have nothing to strive toward. Existence by grace, like salvation by grace, is a scandalous thought. It bestows on its recipients the freedom to perform the work that God has given them with hope, not exasperation or despair.

The power of technology in the pursuit of safety has an empirical obviousness. The thud of a helmet's outer shell as your head is cushioned within, the image of a crash test dummy being absorbed into an airbag, the arrows on a screen directing you out of an unfamiliar place—these interactions with technological safety devices declare their usefulness. However strong and clear such evidence may be, though, the point that I have been driving at here is that humanity's technological reorderings occur within the scope of Christ's creational and redemptive ordering of the world. Humanity's use of technology in the pursuit of safety takes place in accordance with a logic that runs deeper than the logic of the technological devices themselves. Ellul attempts to put his finger on this deeper logic through his development of the concept of *technique*. At a practical level, this does little to change our understanding of the physics of brains, skulls, helmets, and impacts or of the design and production of helmets. It does, however, force us to place these isolated movements and events back into the complex web of reality out of which they were extracted, a web of reality given and governed by God.

Technology's Redemptive Hope

Although Cain and his descendants are the ancient forebears of technology (Gen 4:17-22), humanity's technological project does not begin out of a desire for efficiency, in response to the ground being cursed. It begins before the curse, with fig leaves (Gen 3:7). It begins as an attempt by Adam and Eve to cover themselves.[78] They had been naked and unashamed, but after their disobedience, they stood alone, alienated from each other and God, alienated from the vast world in which they stood, and, importantly, aware of that alienation. They transgressed the limit that God had placed on them, and now, through the sewing of fig leaves, they are seeking to establish their own protective limits.[79] The desire for safety comes to include protection from

---

[78]Ellul pays greater attention to this in his later work, *On Freedom, Love, and Power*, 77.
[79]Dietrich Bonhoeffer, *Creation and Fall*, ed. John W. De Gruchy, trans. Douglas Stephen Bax, Dietrich Bonhoeffer Works 3 (Minneapolis: Fortress, 2004), 124.

the hazards of nature, with its wind, rain, snow, and heat, but initially, the loincloths, as the first human artifacts, are devised to cover their shame before each other and to hide from the presence of God.

Technology's limited usefulness after the fall. After God pronounces his curses (Gen 3:14-19), he does not re-expose Adam and Eve's nakedness. Instead, he fashions garments for them from the skins of animals (Gen 3:21), and here, where God mercifully affirms fallen humanity's need for covering and protection, is an important part of the answer to the question of what right humanity has—not only as creatures, but now as sinful creatures—to reorder what God has ordered. If God had stripped them of their fig leaves and left them naked, even in their shame, he would have invalidated humanity's post-fall technological endeavors. All attempts to reorder creation toward humanity's own comfort and safety would be done in rebellion against God, with him allowing us to remain in the pit into which we had cast ourselves. But he does not do this. He is kind. He allows Adam and Eve to be clothed, confirming the ongoing validity of humanity's technological project and its usefulness as a means of limited protection in a fallen world.

This kindness should not lead to excessive technological optimism, though. The development of humanity's technological endeavors is presented bleakly in Scripture. Adam and Eve fashion loincloths from fig leaves, but they are removed by God. Cain builds a city and his descendants develop various technologies, but their achievements are destroyed by the flood. Nimrod builds Nineveh (Gen 10:11), but in a later age "that great city" falls into idolatry, repents, and then falls again (Jon 1:2, 3:5; Nahum 3:5). The people gather at Shinar to build the tower of Babel and make a name for themselves, but God confuses their language, the tower is abandoned, and Shinar is later depicted as a gathering place of Israel's wickedness (Gen 11:2-8; Zech 5:5-11).[80] Solomon builds a temple, but it is later taken apart piece by piece (2 Chron 5:1; 2 Kings 25:13-17). These are dark beginnings for the human task of making.

However, there is more to this pattern that prohibits excessive technological pessimism. God replaces the loincloths that he removed, at the cost of blood. Against the darkness of the tower of Babel shines another

---

[80]Brock, "Culture as Flight from God," 40.

primitive technological feat, the ark, as a means of God's salvation. After Babel, God enters into a covenant with Abraham to bring those scattered nations back together (Gen 12:3). God gave Bezalel, Oholiab, and others the knowledge, skill, and craftsmanship to construct the tabernacle and its implements (Ex 31:2-6). Later, God will establish Jerusalem, an earthly city, as a type of the heavenly city that is to come (1 Kings 15:4; Ps 87:5; Heb 12:22). The temple was destroyed but rebuilt again. It was also destroyed again, but both the first and second temples were built at God's command by human hands according to the patterns of "heavenly things," the true temple, where Christ himself entered on our behalf to put away sin "once for all" (Heb 9:23-26).

Humanity has the right to reorder what God has ordered because in his grace he has shared what is his with us. He has generously given humanity dominion over the works of his hands (Ps 8:6). However, this dominion is properly Christ's because God has put all things, even death, in subjection "under his feet" (1 Cor 15:25-27; see also Heb 2:5-9). In its technological endeavors, humanity ought to reorder creation toward Christ, submitting to his authority and obeying his teachings, in reliance on God. Humanity ought to rule over and subdue creation in the nobility of the position in which it was first placed by God as stewards of his creation. Humanity ought to reorder creation in participation with Christ in his reign over all things. But what ought to be is corrupted by sin. In its technological endeavors, humanity reorders creation, but this reordering has an underlying disorder inasmuch as it is done in opposition to Christ and his kingdom. Whatever safety is to be found in such technological endeavors will not endure.

God, in his kindness and wisdom, allows all people, even those in rebellion against him, to benefit from the goodness, order, and beauty of creation, to perceive some of its mysteries and reorder it toward their own comfort and safety. When God replaced the clothing fashioned by human hands with clothing that he himself provided, he exposed the limitations of technology and its inadequacy to meet the idolatrous expectations that are placed on it. However, he simultaneously extends the hope that the desire for safety, the desire to be "further clothed" (2 Cor 5:4), will ultimately be fulfilled. The work of human hands is insufficient for such a hope. God allows humanity to make use of creation, to find comfort in the safety that technology affords. He gives us, in creation, the time, space, and means to "live and move and have our being." He does this so that we "should seek God" (Acts 17:26-28).

However, he has not given creation fully into humanity's hands. He remains at work in history, restraining efforts to reorder creation away from himself. The people said, "Come, let us build ourselves a city and a tower," but "the LORD dispersed them from there over the face of all the earth" (Gen 11:4-8). Edom says, "We will rebuild the ruins," but God replies, "They may build, but I will tear down" (Mal 1:4). Israel forms an idol, but Moses smashes it to dust and compels them to ingest it (Ex 32:20). Those who build towers, walls, and ships with a false hope will tear them down in despair (Is 2:12-21). Technology is a legitimate part of life. It ought to be engaged with in ways that "respect the natural structures of life in the world,"[81] but also with humility, recognizing that God limits its power.

Technology's endurance. The prayer remains, though, that God would establish the works of our hands (Ps 90:17). This prayer reflects a desire to see the works of one's hands endure for some extension of time in history. It reflects a desire for those works to be of benefit to the one who performs them, to bless others, and to be "useful to the master" (2 Tim 2:21). This prayer also reflects the hope that one's works would endure the coming fire that will "test what sort of work each one has done" (1 Cor 3:13). Christ is the foundation for any work that hopes to endure this testing (1 Cor 3:11), and his church, "God's building," is the enduring artifice being built (1 Cor 3:9; cf. 1 Pet 2:5). Regarding the manner in which human handiwork might endure this testing, O'Donovan is correct in saying that we "cannot speculate on what 'redemption' will imply for the non-human creation."[82] It seems best to understand any endurance of one's technological endeavors into the new creation to be related to the ends for which they are devised and used—perhaps to bear witness to Christ, demonstrate love to others, or reflect the glory of God in his work of creation—rather than their material forms.

This world and the works done in it will be baptized by fire (2 Pet 3:7, 10; 1 Pet 3:20-21). As a pattern for this coming judgment, Peter points to the

---

[81]O'Donovan, *Resurrection and Moral Order*, 58.
[82]O'Donovan, *Resurrection and Moral Order*, 55.

flood, in which many people perished, and all their works, except the righteous work of Noah, were destroyed (2 Pet 3:5-6; 1 Pet 3:20). On the coming day of judgment, the heavens, the earth, and the works done on it—"all these things"—will be dissolved (2 Pet 3:11). Through this baptism, the works done on earth will be "exposed" (v. 10), a term which "suggests a judicial inquiry through which God will discover the deeds of humanity and will execute his judgment on the basis of what he finds." Our works will be laid bare. As strong as the language is in 2 Peter 3, though, regarding this divine judgment, "the Christian hope is the renovation of creation and not its annihilation."[83] Just as the flood ushered in the present world, so this second baptism will bring about a new creation. First, the works done here will be purified, in order to remove all that is ungodly. Then, there will be a "new heavens and a new earth in which righteousness dwells" (2 Pet 3:13). Peter's emphasis is not on the material form of this new creation, but its moral order, an order that shapes the present lives of those who await this new creation (2 Pet 3:14). As Irenaeus says, "Neither the substance nor the essence of the created order vanishes away, for he is true and faithful who established it, but the pattern of this world passes away, that is, the things in which the transgression took place." He then explains that "when this pattern has passed away, and man is made new, and flourishes in incorruption, so that he can no longer grow old, then there will be new heavens and a new earth."[84]

Christians look forward to eternal life in the new creation. Today, the church is a community of "sojourners and exiles" (1 Pet 2:11), called to be mindful of this world's coming dissolution in a way that chastens affections for the things of this age and the temporal safety that they afford. Chastening affections is not the same as killing them, though. In fact, Peter goes on to address these exiles as those who desire "to love life and to see good days" (1 Pet 3:10, quoting Ps 34:12). He gives instruction on how Christians are to conduct themselves within the present order of creation, commanding them to use their freedom as servants of God (1 Pet 2:16). The exilic character of the Christian life captures well the challenges faced in rightly ordering it in response to the possibilities and demands of technology. Christian ethics

---

[83]Gene Green, *Jude and 2 Peter*, BECNT (Grand Rapids, MI: Baker Academic, 2008), 330-34.
[84]Irenaeus, "Selections from the Work *Against Heresies*" 5.36.1, in *Early Christian Fathers*, ed. Cyril C. Richardson, trans. Edward Rochie Hardy, LCC 1 (Westminster: n.p., 1953), 396-97.

"looks both backwards and forwards, to the origin and to the end of the created order."[85] Theological and ethical considerations about how one ought, or ought not, to use technology in the pursuit of safety must simultaneously account for the goodness of life in this age, the suffering and death that nevertheless accompany it, the "futile ways" of those who walk in disobedience (1 Pet 1:18; 2:8), and the all-surpassing goodness of life with God in the age to come.

The Rightly Ordered Life

God has given humanity the ability to (re)order creation technologically. It is a gift with limitations imposed on it by its Giver and a gift that is frequently misused by its recipients, those who "worshiped and served the creature rather than the Creator" (Rom 1:25). For some people, the world appears controllable. They want total power over creation, the ability to order it to their every desire and be completely safe. There are some who cling onto life, who will do all in their power to remain alive and healthy. There are others who despair of life, those for whom the world appears out of control. There are some—because of guilt, grief, shame, hopelessness, or pain—who use what strength and control they have over this world against their own bodies, whether through neglect, harm, or suicide.

Between those two poles is an array of practical and ethical questions about the extents to which people go in order to avoid harm. The government of Canada, for example, implemented numerous restrictions and mandates in relation to Covid-19 in the name of safety and, since 2016, the government of Canada has also opened and systematically expanded its "Medical Assistance in Dying" (MAID) program, in which medical practitioners either take the lives of Canadian citizens or provide the means for them to do so themselves. The reasons for doing so were originally restricted to terminally ill situations with unbearable pain and the imminence of death. The illness can now be serious instead of terminal, the imminence of death has been removed as a criterion, and mental illness will soon be an acceptable reason to receive this assistance.[86]

---

[85] O'Donovan, *Resurrection and Moral Order*, 58.
[86] "Canada's medical assistance in dying (MAID) law," *Department of Justice Canada*, June 19, 2023, www.justice.gc.ca/eng/cj-jp/ad-am/bk-di.html.

Two of the factors considered in discourse about these sorts of public issues are the personal agency and desires of the individual and the effects of the individual's actions on others. In the case of Covid-19 restrictions, there were numerous instances in which the government overrode the agency and desires of individuals because of the harm they may have caused themselves and others. In the case of suicide, government officials and medical practitioners are ordinarily obligated morally, and in some instances legally, to intervene and prevent individuals from exercising personal agency in such a way because it is a great harm to themselves and to so many others around them. With suicide assistance, the desires of the individual are exalted, while the deep and widespread harm to others is ignored or rationalized away—the sorrow, the regret, the numbness, or, for those assisting, the guilt, the hardening of heart and conscience.[87]

Life and whatever is directed thereto. Within Roman Catholic moral theology a distinction was developed between ordinary and extraordinary means of conserving life. According to this distinction, ordinary means are readily available and can be used with relative ease—things like food and basic medicine. It was determined that a person is morally obligated to use such means. Extraordinary means are not readily available and can only be used with difficulty—things like expensive safeguards or complicated medical procedures. According to Roman Catholic moral theology, a person is not morally obligated to use such means.

The distinction between ordinary and extraordinary means of conserving life arose out of teachings from Aquinas on humanity's love of earthly life. Despite doctrinal differences between Protestant and Catholic theology, it will be helpful to engage with this distinction because it is a well-developed attempt to establish moral guidelines regarding the extent to which a person may, should, or must pursue health and safety.[88] Decisions about the use of technology in the pursuit of safety are considered in light of affections for

---

[87]For a treatment of some of the widespread cultural harm of medically assisted suicide, see David Michael Elliot, "Institutionalizing Inequality: The Physical Criterion of Assisted Suicide," *Christian Bioethics* 24, no. 1 (April 2018): 17-37. For biblical, ethical, and pastoral arguments in opposition to medically assisted suicide, see John F. Kilner, ed., *Why the Church Needs Bioethics: A Guide to Wise Engagement with Life's Challenges* (Grand Rapids, MI: Zondervan, 2011), chapters 9–12.

[88]Those doctrinal differences arise in relation to the Roman Catholic teaching on the *donum superadditum* and the doctrine of justification, which I address in footnote 108. For a Reformed response to the *donum superadditum*, see Bavinck, *Reformed Dogmatics*, 2:539-53.

earthly life on the one hand and the desire of the Christian to reach the final end in Christ on the other. That final end, according to Aquinas, is eternal happiness found in "the vision of the Divine Essence."[89]

Humanity's final end is the joy that comes from beholding God, being in the presence of his steadfast love that is better than life (Ps 63:3).[90] Earthly life, including efforts to technologically reorder creation toward its good, is rightly ordered when it is directed to that end. Since Christians have this hope, Aquinas says that the mind cannot be set on the preservation of the body for its own sake, nor on those things that preserve the body—what you will eat and wear (Lk 12:22)—for their own sakes. He says that doing so is like the captain of a ship thinking that the supreme goal is to keep the ship afloat, forgetting that it is kept afloat for the greater purposes of navigating its course and arriving at its destination.[91] Aquinas argues that affections for the temporal goods that sustain and protect one's body are rightly ordered when they are grounded in the love of life and that the love of life is rightly ordered when it is grounded in the love and fear of God.

He says that every person "has it instilled in him by nature to love his own life and whatever is directed thereto"—things like food, drink, clothing, and shelter. Such things, and the technological capacity to develop them, are given by God to sustain life. The desire for these goods is rooted in the desire for life. Affections for locked doors, buckled seatbelts, and fully-charged phones—the technological devices that assist in the pursuit of safety—are rooted in an affection for life. This love of life, according to Aquinas, is matched by a proper fear of, or antipathy toward, those things that destroy life. Both the love of life and fear of that which hinders it must be "in due measure," though. Those who take their own lives, maim their own bodies, or fear nothing at all have a disordered love of life. It is too small. Aquinas says that the love of life is also disordered when it is too large, when the love of this world with its passing pleasures and the fear of death, pain, or loss exceed the love and fear of God. Instead of following these disordered loves and fears, Aquinas says that temporal goods should be loved or despised to

---

[89] Thomas Aquinas, *ST* (London: Eyre & Spottiswoode), 1-2.3.8 co.
[90] As the first question of the Westminster Shorter Catechism teaches, this enjoyment of God is paralleled with his glorification.
[91] Aquinas, *ST*, 1-2.2.5 co.

the extent that they help or hinder life and that life should be loved inasmuch as it is given by God to love, fear, and enjoy him.[92]

Ordinary and extraordinary safety. Based on these teachings of Aquinas, the distinction between ordinary and extraordinary means of conserving life was developed and has been used to determine the lengths to which people ought to go when trying to conserve their earthly lives. If you are in danger, whether from certain harm or improbable risk, how hard should you fight to remain alive and whole? How much money should you spend? What inconveniences should be endured? What costs should others bear? Of all the technological devices that could potentially provide protection, which ones should be used? Or to turn the question around—since Aquinas also says that we err when loving this life too much—at what point have efforts to conserve life become excessive? How much is too much in the pursuit of safety? Are there situations in which you should not, or need not, avail yourself of technological means of conserving life? Should a person ever hasten death technologically? How should Christians simultaneously affirm the goodness of life and the destruction of death's sting?

The distinction between ordinary and extraordinary means of conserving life offers a program for answering these types of questions. This program involves the pursuit of safety when probable harm is encountered and the pursuit of healing when actual harm has occurred, but it begins with the affirmation that life is worth conserving. Archbishop Daniel A. Cronin, in his account of this teaching, says that it takes as its starting point Christianity's opposition to suicide, which is simultaneously a confirmation of the goodness of life.[93] We are not our own masters. Life is a gift from God. We are "bound to take proper care of it," Cronin says, "until such time as is indicated by the rightful owner," and Aquinas says, "A man has the obligation

---

[92] Aquinas, *ST*, 2-2.65.5, 65.1, 125-26.

[93] Daniel A. Cronin, *Ordinary and Extraordinary Means of Conserving Life* (Philadelphia: The National Catholic Bioethics Center, 2011), 3-4. Similar teachings regarding suicide are found in Protestant theology as well. Calvin says, "It is against nature that a man kills himself regardless of the method. We have this natural sense to flee from death, we have a certain horror of death, which God has instilled in us" (John Calvin, *Supplementa Calviniana*, ed. Hanns Ruckert [Neukirchen, Germany, 1961], 512-13; translated and quoted in Jeffrey R. Watt, "Calvin on Suicide," *Church History* 66, no. 3 [1997]: 469). Watt explains, "The central argument that Calvin made against suicide is that in taking one's life, one is being disobedient by refusing to submit to the will of God. God has given life to humans, God alone has the right to take it away" (Watt, "Calvin on Suicide," 465).

to sustain his body, otherwise he would be a killer of himself." And so this teaching moves from the desire for life as a proper affection to the conservation of life as a moral obligation. The "same precept which prohibits suicide also prescribes by that very fact, the conservation of one's life, since not to conserve one's life and to commit suicide are virtually the same."[94]

With the goodness of life and the obligation to conserve it in place, this teaching must account for occasions when the obligation to conserve life is superseded by other obligations or circumstances. For example, Aquinas cites Augustine, who says that Samson, although he took his own life when bringing down the Philistine house (Judg 16:30), is numbered among the saints because the Holy Spirit "had secretly ordered this," and that young Christian women who threw themselves into rivers to avoid being violated by their pursuers did so, perhaps, "by divine command."[95] Along with these divine permissions, Cronin says that a person is released from the moral obligation to conserve life if it is impossible or extremely difficult to do so. In other words, conserving one's life by ordinary means is a moral obligation, but conserving one's life by extraordinary means—those that are extremely difficult for one reason or another—is not. The problem with this last exception comes in determining "how grave this difficulty has to be" before the person is released from the obligation.[96]

Francisco de Vitoria, a sixteenth-century theologian, "had tremendous influence" in establishing the obligation to use ordinary means and in determining where the line between ordinary and extraordinary should be drawn.[97] He says that a person is morally obligated, aside from divine

---

[94]Cronin, *Ordinary and Extraordinary Means*, 18. Thomas Aquinas, *Super epistolas S. Pauli* (Turin: Marietti, 1953), II Thess., lec. 11, n. 77; translated and quoted in Cronin, *Ordinary and Extraordinary Means*, 48. H. Noldin and A. Schmitt, *Summa Theologiæ Moralis*, 27th ed. (Innsbruck: Rauch, 1940), II:309; translated and quoted in Cronin, *Ordinary and Extraordinary Means*, 19.

[95]Augustine, *City of God*, 1:1.21, 26 (LCL 411:97, 111); Aquinas, *ST*, 2-2.64.5 ad 4. See Cronin, *Ordinary and Extraordinary Means*, 18. The case of these women is given by Augustine and Aquinas as a possible exception to their teachings (and that of Calvin) that "it is wrong to commit one evil [suicide] in order to avoid another" (Watt, "Calvin on Suicide," 468). According to Watt, Calvin does not acknowledge such exceptions. Calvin says, "If I am in some sort of danger, I must see if God will provide some means of escape. But if God does not provide a way out and I try to kill myself by jumping from atop the walls or from a high window, then it is as if I wanted to have more foresight than God" (*Supplementa Calviniana*, 515; translated and quoted in Watt, "Calvin on Suicide," 468-69).

[96]Cronin, *Ordinary and Extraordinary Means*, 42-44.

[97]Cronin, *Ordinary and Extraordinary Means*, 55.

permission, to conserve life through *natural* means, those provided by God in nature, such as food, sunshine, air, and rest.[98] However, a person is only obligated to use natural means that are affordable and accessible. You might be able to extend your life by eating "the most delicate and most expensive" food, but you are only obligated to eat common food, even if your life is shortened as a result. Vitoria also seeks to account for pain, discouragement, and likelihood of benefit in determining whether a means of conserving life is obligatory. So, in the case of a sick person for whom it is extremely difficult to eat, he says the person should eat if "there exists some hope of life," unless it is too difficult or painful.[99]

There are also *artificial* means of conserving life. This category has vastly expanded since Vitoria's day, but it includes things like drugs and medical care. These too are provided by nature to conserve life, though usually through technological development, and in a supplementary way, aiding a person in conserving life when "he is sick or in pain or unable to sustain himself by natural means."[100] In the modern world, these supplementary means of conservation are not only used when natural means are insufficient, but as a regular part of life. Vaccinations and dietary supplements are artificial means of conserving life that have become ordinary for many people. These artificial means, according to Vitoria, are only obligatory if they are affordable and offer a sure hope of benefit.[101] So, a sick person does not have to take a drug unless there is certainty that it would bring healing. Then, "the use of the drug would be obligatory," unless it is too expensive.[102]

Vitoria and others sometimes describe artificial means of conserving life as extraordinary means. According to Cronin, this was not because they were artificial, but because in those times almost all artificial means of conserving life were extraordinary. As artificial means became more prevalent, reliable, and affordable, the distinction between natural and artificial became

---

[98]Cronin, *Ordinary and Extraordinary Means*, 49, 110-13.
[99]Francisco de Vitoria, "De temperantia," in *Relectiones theologicae* (Lyon, 1587), 9; translated and quoted in Cronin, *Ordinary and Extraordinary Means*, 49-51.
[100]Cronin, *Ordinary and Extraordinary Means*, 112.
[101]Vitoria, "De temperantia," n. 1; translated and quoted in Cronin, *Ordinary and Extraordinary Means*, 49.
[102]Gary M. Atkinson, "Theological History of Catholic Teaching on Prolonging Life," in *Moral Responsibility in Prolonging Life Decisions*, ed. Donald G. McCarthy and Albert S. Moraczewski (St. Louis: Pope John Center, 1981), 98-99.

less important, while the other factors Vitoria discussed—such as affordability, accessibility, hope of benefit, and level of pain—became decisive in distinguishing between ordinary and extraordinary means.[103]

Based on the writings of Vitoria and subsequent theologians into the twentieth century, Cronin offers a summary of these factors, identifying five distinguishing marks of both ordinary and extraordinary means. An ordinary means of conserving life, one which a person is morally obligated to use, (1) offers some hope of benefit, (2) is in common use, (3) is in keeping with one's social or financial status, (4) is not too difficult, and (5) is reasonably simple. A means of conserving life is extraordinary if it meets any of the following criteria: (1) it is impossible to obtain or use, (2) it requires great effort or excessive hardship, (3) it involves excruciating pain, (4) it is extremely expensive, or (5) it causes intense fear or repugnance.[104]

Further clarifications are needed. Something could offer a small hope of a small benefit, a sure hope of a big benefit, or anything in between. Therefore, an ordinary means needs to be "proportionately useful and beneficial before it can be called obligatory."[105] Juan de Lugo, a seventeenth-century cardinal, imagines a situation in which a man trapped in a fire has enough water to slow the fire but not extinguish it. De Lugo says the man is not morally obligated to use the water because this brief extension of life is "morally considered nothing at all."[106] In a more recent real life example, controversies over Covid-19 vaccinations, which were taken by many to be morally obligatory, had to do with uncertainty about the size of the risk and the hope of benefit, both of which diminished with hindsight. The distinction between ordinary and extraordinary also has to do with the availability and costs of such means in relation to a person's place in society. The ordinary means for an impoverished monk differ from those of a wealthy magistrate, just as ordinary means in the sixteenth century differ from those in the twenty-first century.

---

[103]"When these moralists were living, artificial means of conserving life were extraordinary means because they were too costly or did not offer any hope of benefit. When, however, medicines became useful and offered some hope of success, these means became ordinary means, and the moralists then called them obligatory" (Cronin, *Ordinary and Extraordinary Means*, 116).
[104]Cronin, *Ordinary and Extraordinary Means*, 122-58.
[105]Cronin, *Ordinary and Extraordinary Means*, 124.
[106]Juan de Lugo, "De iustitia a iure," in *Disputationes scholasticae et morales*, vol. VI (Paris, 1868), VI: disp. X, sect. I, n. 30; translated and quoted in Cronin, *Ordinary and Extraordinary Means*, 75.

A person may use extraordinary means if desired, but in most cases there is no moral requirement to do so. However, according to Cronin, there are exceptions, cases in which a person is morally obligated to use extraordinary means of conserving life. There are two primary examples. The first involves a person who is "especially necessary" to a particular family or society. This may be "the father of a large family," whose death would be an extreme hardship on others. In this case, he would be required to endure excessive costs or excruciating pain for the sake of his family. The second example involves people who ought to use extraordinary means to conserve their lives for the sake of their own "spiritual welfare." Cronin gives the example of a dying person who has been "away from the Sacraments for twenty years," but could take an expensive medicine and live long enough to make peace with God and be administered the Last Sacraments. Cronin says that in this case the person would be bound to "use the drug in question" because of the spiritual obligation to care for one's soul.[107]

These teachings on ordinary and extraordinary means of conserving life are helpful insofar as they are grounded in a vision of life that extends into the age to come. In the late-modern world, safety is often calculated and pursued solely within the diminished horizon of the present age. It becomes an end in itself, one whose demands can never be fully satisfied. When efforts to conserve life are viewed in light of God's commands to love, obey, and behold him, they have a rightful place in a life ordered in and through Christ. It is a life lived in light of Christ's return and coming judgment. These teachings also acknowledge the complexities of life, the various cultural, financial, personal, and spiritual circumstances that affect the means by which a person or group of people can and should pursue safety. Further, regarding the use of extraordinary means of conserving life, the importance of serving others is apparent in the first example given above, and the importance of making peace with God "today" (Heb 3:12-14) is apparent in the second.

The extension of life beyond the present age, the particular circumstances in which God has placed each individual, and the calling to serve others each set helpful limits on the pursuit of safety and establish a

---

[107]Cronin, *Ordinary and Extraordinary Means*, 163-64.

framework within which to consider related technological obligations and freedoms. Life is a gift from God that is worth conserving, but safety should not be pursued at all costs. As Christians, we want lives of significance, we want to navigate faithfully the course that Christ sets before us, and we want to arrive at the destination that he has for us, even at the cost of our safety. There are limits to the demands that safety may make on us. There are limits to the demands that technological devices may make on us as well. With the recognition that some means of conserving life are extraordinary, we are reminded of these limits and that we are not obligated, nor should we be compelled, to use every technological means of conserving life that is at our disposal.

The use of technology is a negotiation between its ability to bring good to one's life and its demands that life be conformed to its logic and ordering to reap those benefits. Whether those negotiations enhance or hinder life, and at what costs, should be at the forefront of our minds, especially for those who have answered the call of another, to order their lives, as he did his, around the wisdom of the cross. Therefore, the love of life and whatever is directed thereto is properly ordered when it is rooted in the love and fear of God, the one in whom everlasting joy is found.

The opposite of taking your life is not conserving it, but giving it, laying it down for the sake of others. Conserving life needs to be framed, therefore, in relation to suicide, but also in view of Christ's call to serve God and others. The theologians who develop this teaching on ordinary and extraordinary means of conserving life, as represented by Cronin, acknowledge such a calling by Christ, but their central concern seems to be determining, in an often formulaic manner, the difference between ordinary and extraordinary. As a result, the greater purposes for which the ship is kept afloat become obscured at times, as does Aquinas' teaching that the love of life is disordered not only when it is too small, but also when it is too great.

A life ordered by the gospel. The distinction between ordinary and extraordinary means of conserving life draws attention to some of the complexities involved in the use of technology in the pursuit of safety. But it has significant theological shortcomings. Cronin says that life is a gift from God, but that it is given as an opportunity to "merit heaven." He says that humanity, through the proper use of the "natural gifts" given by God, may "merit eternal salvation."[108] The proper use of natural gifts entails the proper conservation of one's life. According to this teaching, properly distinguishing between ordinary and extraordinary means of conserving life may be of salvific importance. As a result, the attempt to distinguish between the two becomes an ethical tight rope walk, and the conservation of life, which should be an affirmation of its goodness and the means by which one loves and serves God, runs the danger of contradicting Aquinas' advice "that it is better to concentrate on pursuing particular goods rather than on avoiding particular evils,"[109] where the particular evils are the miscalculations and misapplications that could be made when conserving life. In 1942, one author was bold enough to suggest that no one was morally obligated to spend more than two thousand dollars in seeking to conserve their life, while another author exemplifies well the teeter-totter effect of evaluating the factors involved when he says, "A remedy which includes rather great difficulty, though not moral impossibility, is hardly obligatory unless the hope of success is more probable, whereas a remedy which is easily obtained and used seems obligatory as long as it offers any solid probability of success."[110]

Christ does not call his disciples to conserve their lives as opportunities to merit heaven. He calls them to lay down their lives as those who have already been given heaven. It seems to me, therefore, that the Catholic moral teaching on ordinary and extraordinary means of conserving life, as it has been developed, needs to be turned on its head. There are some people who fear life. There are some who are too timid, fearful, or discouraged to conserve their lives, those who forget to eat because their hearts are "struck down like grass" (Ps 102:4) or whose "life loathes bread" because of great pain (Job 33:19-20). The lack of strength or motivation to conserve life may

---

[108]Cronin, *Ordinary and Extraordinary Means*, 20. Richard Muller, describing the teachings of Franciscan theology on the *donum superadditum*, says, "Since Adam could, by doing a minimal or finite act, merit the initial gift of God's grace, fallen man might, by doing a minimal act, also merit the gift of first grace" (Richard Muller, *Dictionary of Latin and Greek Theological Terms: Drawn Principally from Protestant Scholastic Theology* [Grand Rapids, MI: Baker, 2006], 97).
[109]Aquinas, *ST*, 2-2.125.1 co.
[110]Edwin F. Healy, *Moral Guidance* (Chicago: Loyola University Press, 1942), 162; referenced in Cronin, *Ordinary and Extraordinary Means*, 126; Gerald Kelly, "The Duty of Using Artificial Means of Preserving Life," *Theological Studies* 11 (June 1950): 214-15; quoted by Cronin, *Ordinary and Extraordinary Means*, 128-29.

come from the immediate shock of tragic news—the death of a loved one, the loss of a job, the news of betrayal. It may come from the accumulation of pain through the years—chronic sickness, repeated sins, ongoing mistreatment. It may also come from past disappointments—looking back at missed opportunities, unmet expectations, or unanswered questions.

Such people need to be encouraged and reminded that life is worth preserving. They should be reminded that whether in life or death, peace with God is theirs through faith in Christ. These situations, while more common than we may be aware, are the exceptions. Most people hold on to their lives too tightly. The error of most people is to cling to their lives and fight for them as if they were all that they had. In a world saturated with technological attempts to attain safety, are there means of safety that are not obligatory? Are there situations in which one is obligated to not make use of a means of safety because of Christ's call to lay down your life for the sake of the gospel and in service of others? Great freedom comes from just asking these questions. Those who do so recognize that life does not have to be lived under the late-modern world's technological imperative, nor the age-old irony of having life slip through their fingers the tighter they squeeze.

Humanity, through the work of its hands, is able to manipulate the world in powerful ways. This power is enticing and holds out the hope of success in the pursuit of safety. Yet technology also causes fear because it is itself a source of danger and cannot be perfectly controlled. It is often difficult to determine what, exactly, is a "solid probability of success" when using technology in pursuit of safety. Technology is meant to enhance and conserve life, yet it often impedes it. People often trust in the work of their own hands for provision and safety instead of trusting God to bless that work. In either case, humanity's earthly needs are to be met through the work of hands. However, there is a difference between those who seek, like Cain, to establish themselves apart from God and those who work with their hands but do so trusting God to bless those works. God knows the heart. He can see the difference between those who trust in chariots and those who use chariots but trust in God. The difference is significant. Those who trust in chariots (Ps 20:7-8), like those who trust in idols (Is 42:17), are put to shame. Those who trust in God are rescued (Ps 22:5).

EIGHT

Guiding Action
*Procedures, Forgiveness,
and the Advantage of Wisdom*

> Science Finds, Industry Applies, Man Conforms.
>
> Motto, 1933 World's Fair,
> Chicago

THE BEST LAID SCHEMES of mice and men often go askew, but not always. Therefore, we plan and act, and despite the regularity with which creaturely life proves that "foresight may be vain," the actions of mice have remained quite stable over the past couple of centuries and more since Robert Burns's memorialized encounter with one of their kind.[1] They scurry around in their mousy ways as they always have, gathering food to fend off hunger and building nests to fend off winter, whatever successes and failures may accompany those simple but ceaseless actions. Over that same period of time, though, humanity has subjected its own actions to much scrutiny and revision as it has sought to lessen, if not eliminate, the vanities of foresight.

Within the late-modern world, efforts to gain mastery over human action have been characterized by what Alan Jacobs calls "a commitment to certain fixed *procedures* applied to all," in which any given task is best accomplished by determining and prescribing *in advance* the right way to do it—however

---

[1] Robert Burns, "To a Mouse: On turning her up in her Nest with the Plough, November 1785," in *The Complete Poems and Songs of Robert Burns* (Glasgow: Gresham, 2015), 83-84.

that right way may be defined.² Thus, along with a probabilistic approach to the future and a technological approach to creation, the contemporary pursuit of safety is also shaped by a procedural approach to human action.³

The Unavoidability of Death

God knows the future completely. He is sovereign over creation, the work of his hands. Likewise, when God acts in this world, he accomplishes what he intends: "I have purposed, and I will do it" (Is 46:11). But to say that God knows the future, that he is sovereign over creation, and that he accomplishes his purposes is just to acknowledge in three different ways that God is perfect in his being and work. He is eternal, changeless, and faithful. As we sing, "Unresting, unhasting, and silent as light; Nor wanting, nor wasting, Thou rulest in might."⁴

Humanity's relationships to the future, creation, and action, like God's, are also necessarily united. Yet this unity is not characterized by eternality and perfection, but by the enigmatic condition of humanity itself. God's action, that of governing all things toward his purposes in Christ, may be "silent as light," but human action is often "tumult" and "clamor" (Ps 65:7; 74:23). Sometimes humanity's God-given capacities fly free, giving success. A person may be swift as a gazelle (1 Chron 12:8) or strong as a lion (2 Sam 1:23). At other times, though, people stutter and start, trip and fall (2 Sam 4:4; 2 Kings 1:2). Humanity's vision of the future is often a matter of shifting probabilities and overextended anticipations; its technological control of creation, a matter of continual compromises and frequent idolatries. Unsurprisingly,

---

²Alan Jacobs, "After Technopoly," *The New Atlantis* 58 (Spring 2019): 5, italics his.
³"Action," whether divine or human, is a topic of much philosophical and theological discussion. See William J. Abraham, *Divine Agency and Divine Action: Exploring and Evaluating the Debate* (New York: Oxford University Press, 2018), 1:1. For the purposes of this chapter, it will suffice to affirm minimally that action seems "to involve the basic idea of 'bringing about something'" (Abraham, *Divine Agency and Divine Action*, 1:5) and that an "action" is "a causing of an event by an agent" (Maria Alvarez and John Hyman, "Agents and their Actions," *Philosophy* 73 [April 1998]: 233). An "action" is typically distinguished from an "event" by the "criterion of intentionality," and although this criterion may not hold up as a necessary condition for action (Abraham, *Divine Agency and Divine Action*, 1:3), the line from intentions to actions, and then beyond to immediate results and further consequences, is, as we will see, important to the procedural aspect of safety, especially in relation to accidents, in the everyday use of the term, where there are harmful discrepancies between intentions, actions, results, and consequences.
⁴Walter Chalmers Smith, "Immortal, Invisible," in *The Hymnal for Worship and Celebration*, ed. Tom Fettke and Ken Barker (Waco, TX: Word Music, 1986), 25.

then, humanity's procedural oversight of action is susceptible to similar inaccuracies, constraints, and shortcomings.

The limits of human action. To be sure, human actions produce effects. God has endowed us with such power. People regularly accomplish what they intend, and even improve their actions through training and practice. But human actions are not perfectly effective. The "posture of control" that humanity so often assumes regarding its actions is "marked in its finitude by certain unavoidable constraints" and is deformed by the corruptions of sin.[5] People, whether as individuals or groups, do not always accomplish what they intend. Sometimes, they accomplish what they intend but their intentions are flawed. At other times, unintended consequences accompany actions. People misjudge and miscalculate. They lose focus and grow weary. Their bodies do not always behave as expected. Nor do the other people, creatures, devices, and systems with which they interact. Because of humanity's alienation from God, there is disharmony within each individual, between individuals, and between humanity and the rest of creation.

Human action, even when guided by the best probabilistic predictions and enhanced by the most powerful technologies, is nevertheless "limited in many ways" and always ruled over by "divine providence."[6] The pursuit of physical safety in this fallen world is not futile. It is frustrating. But herein lies the irony. It is frustrating just because it is occasionally futile, and something that is occasionally futile turns out to be frequently useful. Safety is actually present in many situations but potentially absent from any situation. We do not know with certainty whether our efforts to keep ourselves safe will succeed or fail until after the fact.[7]

Safety's potential absence. Safety's actual presence is a testimony to God's goodness. Its absence, whether actual or potential, is a witness to his coming judgment (Heb 9:27). God reserves the right to call any given individual at any given time to an account before him (Eccles 12:14; Mt 12:36). The occasion

---

[5]Ian A. McFarland, "Original Sin," in *T&T Clark Companion to the Doctrine of Sin*, ed. Keith L. Johnson and David Lauber (New York: T&T Clark, 2016), 316.
[6]Wolfhart Pannenberg, *Systematic Theology*, trans. Geoffrey W. Bromiley, vol. 2. (Grand Rapids, MI: Eerdmans, 1994), 2:202.
[7]As Martin Honecker explains, the pursuit of safety (*Sicherheitsstreben*) takes place under conditions of epistemological uncertainty (*Ungewissheit*). Martin Honecker, "Sicherheit, Gewissheit, Geborgenheit: Suche nach Verlässlichem in einer verunsicherten Welt," *ZTK* 112 (2015): 238-39.

of this summoning is death, and while not all dangers can kill, humanity's frailty, or general susceptibility to harm, is inseparably linked in Scripture to human mortality. As Brevard Childs explains regarding the Psalms: "The dominant anthropological note struck in the Psalter is that of human frailty and vulnerability."[8] This frailty is grounded in humanity's creaturely reliance on things like food, water, and shelter as the means by which God sustains life. But there is an ease and frequency with which this openness to creation becomes disordered, threatening, and harmful as a result of the hostility between God, humanity, and creation brought about by sin. Frailty and vulnerability are also important political notes in the Psalms. God is securely on his throne (Ps 47:8), but kingdoms totter and nations rage (Ps 2:1; 46:6). They sink into pits, perish, and have their counsel brought to nothing (Ps 9:15; 10:16; 33:10). At one moment they appear firm and fixed, safe and secure, but at the next they are driven out, wiped out, and struck down (Ps 80:8; 83:4; 135:10). God establishes nations and destroys them (Job 12:23).

This world is a source of many harms, but it is also the means by which we live. Without food, water, shelter, and protection, hunger, sickness, exposure, and threats confront humanity as "different aspects of encroaching death."[9] Life "oozes slowly away"[10] under these dangers and deprivations in such a way that the one who suffers, though still alive, is "like the slain that lie in the grave" and "close to death from my youth up" (Ps 88:5, 15). Exile from one's land or nation is like death.[11] Any imposition on human frailty is also an imposition on human mortality. It signals and hastens death. Danger threatens one's flourishing in the life that God has given today. Safety's potential absence from any situation, even if it would not be fatal,

---

[8] Brevard S. Childs, *Biblical Theology of the Old and New Testaments: Theological Reflection on the Christian Bible* (Minneapolis: Fortress, 1992), 573. See, e.g., Psalm 6:4-5, 55:4-5, 118:17-18; and Job 33:29-30.

[9] Childs, *Biblical Theology of the Old and New Testaments*, 573. Hans Walter Wolff says that "the dangerously ill, the accused who face the court without any support, the persecuted who are helplessly delivered over to their enemies—all these already belong to the world of the dead" (Hans Walter Wolff, *Anthropology of the Old Testament*, trans. Margaret Kohl [London: SCM Press, 1981], 111).

[10] Brevard S. Childs, *Old Testament Theology in a Canonical Context* (Philadelphia: Fortress, 1989), 231.

[11] Christopher Wright notes: "Life without the land was scarcely life as God's people at all. In fact, it might as well be death." Christopher J. H. Wright, *Old Testament Ethics for the People of God* (Downers Grove, IL: InterVarsity Press, 2013), 82.

would still be an encroachment on life, a reminder that "all flesh is grass" (Is 40:6), and a signal of the coming judgment.

One way or another, death comes to all, and there is always a sequence of events that leads up to death, a particular set of circumstances that, historically speaking, could have gone differently. The historical contingency of events that lead to death, or to harm that encroaches on life, is especially palpable in the realm of safety, where particular attention is given to accidents, anomalies, coincidences, and catastrophes—those events that often seem to come about by nothing more than the "conjunction of the stars and other natural causes."[12] But since our lives are not helplessly driven by the stars, nor any other "irresistible blind force having neither consciousness nor will," it is apparent that these things could have gone differently.[13] While all things may be "ordained by God's plan," "hidden in God's purpose," and "foreseen by God's eye," Calvin says that many things nevertheless seem to happen by chance because we cannot apprehend their "order, reason, end, and necessity," that is, how they line up with God's eternal purposes in Christ.[14] Yet God accomplishes his will, giving life and taking it away (Deut 32:39; Job 1:21; 1 Sam 2:6), through such seemingly fortuitous, fateful, and random events.

Death and its attendant harms come "to the righteous and the wicked, to the good and the evil" (Eccles 9:2). However, it comes to the righteous differently than to the wicked. Apart from Christ, humanity, "through fear of death," is "subject to lifelong slavery" (Heb 2:15). Death "makes itself felt in the experience of anxiety."[15] Anxiety, in turn, reveals itself in the striving after food, drink, and clothing—whatever things one relies on to keep death's encroachments at bay. But Christ brings freedom from these strivings

---

[12]John Calvin, *Institutes of the Christian Religion*, ed. John T. McNeill, trans. Ford Lewis Battles, LCC 20-21 (Philadelphia: Westminster John Knox, 1960), I.16.5, p. 204.
[13]Herman Bavinck, *Reformed Dogmatics*, ed. John Bolt, trans. John Vriend (Grand Rapids, MI: Baker Academic, 2008), 2:600. As Bavinck explains, the Christian doctrine of providence differs from such pagan doctrines of fate, teaching that "in the world of creatures there is a nexus of causes and consequences" and that in that natural order all things happen according to the "wise, omnipotent, loving will of God."
[14]Calvin follows Augustine in emphasizing that although many things *seem* to happen as a result of fortune or chance, such concepts are pagan and foreign to the Christian belief in a sovereign God (Calvin, *Institutes*, I.16.8-9, pp. 207-10; Augustine, *The Retractations*, trans. M. Inez Bogan, FC 60 [Washington, DC: Catholic University of America Press, 1968], 6-7).
[15]William L. Lane, *Hebrews 1–8*, WBC 47A (Grand Rapids, MI: Zondervan, 2015), 60-61. Lane references Sir 40:1-5, which speaks of people's "anxious thought of the day of their death."

and anxieties by bringing freedom from the power of death. He does so by reconciling us to our heavenly Father, divesting "the devil of his ability to intimidate [us] with death," and helping those who are tempted to turn away from God in the midst of suffering (Heb 2:14-18).[16] Those who eagerly await his return do not need to avoid the reality of death.

The Preventability of Accidents

Within the pursuit of safety, some are concerned that the acceptance of safety's potential absence, especially as an abiding theological reality, encourages passivity, fatalism, or superstition. In response, they emphasize that the pain, suffering, and costs involved with accidents are unnecessary. They also argue that all accidents can be prevented because human efforts effectively prevent many individual accidents.

Accidents need not happen. Ida Tarbell, an early twentieth-century journalist, speaks of "ignorant communities" where diseases and epidemics are accepted as inevitable and interpreted "as the visitation of an angry God."[17] But because humanity recently learned some things about the material causes and preventions of diseases, Tarbell dismisses the concurrence of theological purposes in such sufferings, as if the discovery of bacteria meant the wicked were no longer shepherded by death (Ps 49:14). Instead, she insists, "We need not be sick. We need not suffer epidemics."

What is said of diseases is said of accidents as well.[18] In contrast to those who think accidents are caused by "fate," part of "God's will," or an

---

[16]Gareth Lee Cockerill, *The Epistle to the Hebrews*, NICNT (Grand Rapids, MI: Eerdmans, 2012), 148.

[17]Ida M. Tarbell, "Effects of Safety on the Community," *Proceedings of the NSC Third Annual Safety Congress* (Chicago: NSC, 1914), 120-21.

[18]Unless otherwise noted, I am using the term "accident" in this chapter to denote such instances in which our actions, whether directly or indirectly, produce "unintended injury, death, or property damage" (Philip E. Hagan, John F. Montgomery, and James T. O'Reilly, eds., *Accident Prevention Manual for Business & Industry: Administration & Programs*, 14th ed. [Itasca, IL: NSC, 2009], vi). This excludes unharmful and happy accidents. This also excludes malevolent actions that intentionally cause harm. According to Boholm, Möller, and Hansson, the prevention of "intentional harm (i.e., malicious acts)" is more closely associated with "security," and the prevention of "unintentional harm (i.e., accidents)," with "safety" (Max Boholm, Niklas Möller, and Sven Ove Hansson, "The Concepts of Risk, Safety, and Security: Applications in Everyday Language," *Risk Analysis: An International Journal* 36 [February 2016]: 322, 330). In line with this distinction, yet acknowledging overlap, my focus is on safety and therefore on accidents and unintentional harm.

unavoidable price "we pay for progress," Tarbell says we need not have them either. For when accidents are investigated, someone invariably finds "some controllable cause or element," and whether it is a "material cause," such as mechanical failure, or a "psychological" cause, such as carelessness, something always could have been done differently to prevent any given accident.

Therefore, in line with the modern conception of risk, in which "human beings are not totally helpless in the hands of fate, nor is their worldly destiny always determined by God,"[19] the conviction has arisen that all accidents are preventable. This conviction can be seen clearly in the safety movement that arose in America's mining, manufacturing, and transportation industries at the turn of the twentieth century.[20] This safety movement emerged in response to the sharp increase in illnesses, injuries, and deaths that accompanied modern industrialization. As new production methods developed, there was a "lag between the emergence of new working methods and the creation of health and safety standards."[21] As that discrepancy was addressed, the safety movement quickly grew to become an industry itself, a specialized profession and field of study that seeks to prevent accidents by ensuring that the tasks of late-modern, industrialized humanity are performed according to appropriately safe procedures.[22]

Lucian Chaney, an early leader within the safety movement, opened the first annual conference of the National Safety Council by stating that the organization's work is "distinctly a phase of applied Christianity."[23] Its work was to be done for the well-being of others and the progress of society. Within the safety movement, the conviction that all accidents are preventable has consistently led to the conclusion that something should be done to prevent accidents and to direct involvement in the prevention of accidents in industrial, public, and domestic activities.[24] According to the

---

[19] Peter L. Bernstein, *Against the Gods: The Remarkable Story of Risk* (New York: Wiley, 1998), 20.
[20] Mark Aldrich, *Safety First: Technology, Labor, and Business in the Building of American Work Safety, 1870–1939* (Baltimore: Johns Hopkins University Press, 1997), 6.
[21] Hagan, Montgomery, and O'Reilly, *Accident Prevention Manual*, 5.
[22] Mark Aldrich, *Safety First*, 117-20.
[23] Lucian W. Chaney, "Federal Session," *Proceedings of the First Co-operative Safety Congress* (Princeton, NJ: Princeton University Press, 1912), 7.
[24] Robert W. Campbell, "President's Address," *Proceedings of the NSC Third Annual Safety Congress* (Chicago: NSC, 1914), 9.

NSC today, which is no longer distinctly Christian, people should be "working hard" to prevent accidents because, among other reasons, there is a moral responsibility both to avoid "needless destruction of life and health" and to take "necessary precautions against predictable accidents and occupational illnesses."[25] This moral responsibility is applicable in some degree to all people, not just those in charge of or participating in dangerous industrial activities. Safety "is the business of everybody," and "one of the great aims of society" is "to get us all looking out for the other fellow, so that the whole thing will work smoothly."[26]

Accidents are harmful and inefficient. In 1913, Robert W. Campbell, the first president of the NSC, described the burgeoning industrial safety profession as "the study of the right way to do things." Safety is "one of the greatest aids to shop efficiency and economy," he said, but above all it is "a humanitarian work."[27] During the same decade, the trade journal *Safety Engineering* promoted this dual work of economic efficiency and humanitarianism through various appeals to empirical evidence, images of technological innovations, statistical analyses, poetic mockeries, and more:

> If a hand is worth a fortune
> And an eye is worth a few,
> Why take a chance of losing 'em
> When you know just what to do?
> A little care, a little thought
> Preserve the lives of men;
> So buck up, "Bill," and take a think
> Of safety now and then.[28]

For those who think "Safety First" is "all bunk," one column offers a satirical enumeration of the benefits of "Safety Last," such as the "nice artificial limbs" developed since World War I began and the fun to be had pretending your wheelchair is a car.[29] There are in-depth reports on major catastrophes and brief notices regarding smaller-scale tragedies: "December 3, 1918.

---

[25]Hagan, Montgomery, and O'Reilly, *Accident Prevention Manual*, 4.
[26]Tarbell, "Effects of Safety on the Community," 124.
[27]Campbell, "President's Address," 14.
[28]Charles M. Seuft, "Take a Think of Safety," *Safety Engineering* 37 (March 1919): 136.
[29]P. O. Rispalje, "The Fourteen Points of the League of 'Safety Last,'" *Safety Engineering* 37 (April 1919): 192.

Newark, N. J. . . . Two children killed, playing with matches;" "February 8, 1919. Platteville, Wis. . . . Occupants safely out of building but caught by falling walls. Eight killed, 20 injured."[30]

These various informative and persuasive techniques were employed to break down passivity within a culture that accepted the increase in accidents as inescapable and to push against the short-sighted greediness of those who balked at the costs of accident prevention. On the one hand, safety is the right way to do things because of obvious humanitarian concerns for loss of life and limb. On the other hand, it is the right way to do things because accidents are costly and inefficient.[31] Many were drawn to the safety movement out of compassion, but "there are countless others that would never be drawn into the movement because of its humanitarianism."[32] They were drawn by economic motivations. It was not the inherent efficiency of safety that drew such attention though. Instead, lawmakers "aroused companies' interest in accident prevention as never before" by shifting the financial burden of accidents from employees to employers.[33]

When accidents happened, the hardships that workers experienced, the strains on communities, and the economic losses of corporations were linked to each other. As one safety official explains, "every lost-time accident costs the corporation $100," and "no overseer cares to see his department lose a hundred very often." He then adds, "Our nurses and doctors are impressed with the cost of lost-time accidents, not only to the corporation but to the injured." In a factory where multiple workers lost fingers, a safety professional comments, in reference to the solution, "Knowledge of this remedy a little earlier would have saved $750 in cost and three of the workmen would not have been permanently disabled at a time when man power was exceedingly scarce." A safety inspector confesses, "We believe we are saving human life and limb, and that we are saving dollars and cents." Today, the NSC continues this dual focus, affirming both the economic and

---

[30]"Recent Fires and Their Lessons: Compiled from Special Reports to *Safety Engineering,*" *Safety Engineering* 37 (January 1919): 49; "Recent Fires and Their Lessons: Compiled from Special Reports to Safety Engineering," *Safety Engineering* 37 (March 1919): 152.
[31]D. R. Kennedy, "Efficiency in Safety Work," *Proceedings of the NSC Third Annual Safety Congress* (Chicago: NSC, 1914), 129-30.
[32]George T. Fonda, "Response to 'Efficiency in Safety Work,'" *Proceedings of the NSC Third Annual Safety Congress* (Chicago: NSC, 1914), 135.
[33]Aldrich, *Safety First*, 104.

humanitarian benefits of safety, saying that it is effective "in reducing accident rates and promoting efficiency."[34]

The humanitarian observation that accidents are harmful and the economic observation that they are costly, whatever their relative importance, are neither profound nor novel in themselves. However, over the past century, these observations have been quantified and highlighted with much precision and intensity in order to draw attention to the dangers of the industrial world and make its societies more receptive to the idea that accidents, rather than being "bound to happen," or their numbers depending "only upon the whims of the goddess of chance," can, and therefore should, be prevented.[35] Beginning in the early twentieth century, attitudes about the preventability of accidents shifted from the view that accidents are an unavoidable part of life to the view that many accidents are preventable to the now widespread view that all accidents are preventable.[36] As a director of safety education declares, echoing Laplace, "No accident ever happened, nor are they a visitation from God. Every accident has behind it a train of logical, connected circumstances to account for its occurrence, and 'Safety First' means the elimination of these causal circumstances."[37]

It may seem confusing that this safety professional first says that no accident ever happened and then says something about the nature of every accident that has ever happened. But this linguistic move reflects a long-standing effort within the safety industry to block people from thinking of accidents as unexpected events that happen outside of human control, whether as random coincidences, strokes of bad luck, or the results of inexplicable divine action. Instead, the claim is made that "so-called *accidents* are not random events but rather preventable events."[38] There is even an insistence by some that the word "accident" not be used because it "promotes a false narrative that workplace deaths and injuries could not have

---

[34]See, respectively, William S. Ide, "Safety Education in Textile Industry," *Safety Engineering* 38 (November 1919): 284; "Time for 'Human Engineering,'" *Safety Engineering* 37 (May 1919): 255; William H. Doolittle, "Condition of Factories of Our Members," *Proceedings of the First Co-operative Safety Congress* (Princeton, NJ: Princeton University Press, 1912), 276; and Hagan, Montgomery, and O'Reilly, *Accident Prevention Manual*, 4.
[35]Kennedy, "Efficiency in Safety Work," 130-31.
[36]Aldrich, *Safety First*, 114-15.
[37]"Accidents are Logical," *Safety Engineering* 37 (March 1919): 143.
[38]Hagan, Montgomery, and O'Reilly, *Accident Prevention Manual*, vi, italics theirs.

been prevented."[39] The concern is that those who claim that an accident could not have been prevented often do so in order to avoid moral responsibility. The claim that "all these deaths and injuries were preventable" leads to the conclusion: "There are no accidents," not in the sense that there are no events in which unintended harm occurs, but in the sense that someone could have, and should have, sufficiently foreseen, intended, and acted so that there was no harm. In other words, "We can do much better; we can do much more."[40]

In everyday language, an accident is an unforeseen and unintended harmful event. In a more technical sense, something is accidental if it could have been otherwise, as opposed to those things that are essential or necessary, which could not have been otherwise.[41] In my opinion, if we bring out this more technical sense, which is implicit in the everyday sense, then an accident can be understood as a harmful event that, humanly speaking, was unintended and could have been otherwise. But to say it could have been otherwise, in the views represented above, is to say it was preventable, just as to say it should have been otherwise is to say it should have been prevented.

Therefore, it is worth asking why the term *accident* should be removed from our vocabulary instead of having its meaning clarified. The motivation, at least in part, appears to be a desire to delegitimize the category of unintentionality in relation to human action, like someone responding to a child's insistent, "I didn't mean to," with, "Well, you didn't mean not to," for careless children can learn to be more careful. By insisting that accidents be called preventable events, the safety industry magnifies the fact that something could have been done differently to possibly avoid an accident and minimizes the fact that what actually happened in the case of a true accident was unintended by those involved.

Certainly, those involved in dangerous activities can learn to be careful, to look out for the needs of others. Scripture commands us to do so. The

---

[39]Jonathan D. Karmel, *Dying to Work: Death and Injury in the American Workplace* (Ithaca, NY: Cornell University Press, 2017), 210.
[40]Karmel, *Dying to Work*, 210-16.
[41]Teresa Robertson Ishii and Philip Atkins, "Essential vs. Accidental Properties," in *The Stanford Encyclopedia of Philosophy*, ed. Edward N. Zalta, October 26, 2020, https://plato.stanford.edu/archives/win2020/entries/essential-accidental/.

sixth commandment is a simple prohibition against murder (Ex 20:13; Deut 5:17). However, beyond not taking another person's life, this commandment has a "wider sphere" of fulfillment that includes love toward fellow humanity.[42] Positively, this commandment promotes life, doing good for others (Lk 6:9), and rescuing those who are perishing (Prov 24:11-12). Calvin says that "unless you endeavor to look out for [your neighbor's] safety according to your ability and opportunity," you violate the commandment. Likewise, Luther says, "If you see anyone who is condemned to death or in similar peril and do not save him although you have means and ways to do so, you have killed him."[43] Within the safety industry, the conviction that all accidents are preventable often brings with it the moral imperative to prevent all accidents, an imperative always easier to fulfill hypothetically and in hindsight than actually and by means of foresight.[44] Unlike Calvin's and Luther's applications of the commandment not to murder, this moral imperative sets no limits on ability and opportunity, or better, it assumes that it can be perfectly fulfilled within the limits of human ability and opportunity.

Yet little room is left to respond compassionately when accidents are not prevented.[45] And this is where we are confronted once again by the elusiveness of safety. To be sure, the safety industry is correct that the label "accident" is frequently misapplied to events that would be better described as corruption, laziness, sabotage, or greed. If the human actions that led up to any given accident could be analyzed, surely something would be seen that could have been done differently. Surely, with enough foresight and fortitude, what ought to be done could be done. So, the argument goes. Any of us could prevent our accidental drowning by not getting on the

---

[42]Peter C. Craigie, *The Book of Deuteronomy*, NICOT (Grand Rapids, MI: Eerdmans, 1976), 160.
[43]Calvin, *Institutes*, II.8.40, p. 405. Martin Luther, "Larger Catechism," in *The Book of Concord: The Confessions of the Evangelical Lutheran Church*, ed. Robert Kolb and Timothy J. Wengert, trans. Charles P. Arand, 2nd ed. (Minneapolis: Fortress, 2000), 412.
[44]For example, Karmel says it was "foreseen, expected, and inevitable" that a worker would be electrocuted "because he was not properly trained and was not supplied with inexpensive thermal gloves" (*Dying to Work*, 212), but Karmel can make that claim only after the fact. Those conditions may have increased the likelihood of that tragic death, but they did not make it inevitable. Further, the removal of those dangerous conditions would reduce, but not eliminate, the possibility of death.
[45]Sidney Dekker, Robert Long, and Jean-Luc Wybo, "Zero Vision and a Western Salvation Narrative," *Safety Science* 88 (October 2016): 219-23.

boat—especially if we foresaw that it would sink—but real life is not so clear cut, and despite uncertainty, people must live and work. They must move through this world in some way.

It is worthwhile at this point simply to acknowledge the inevitability of accidents in this fallen world. This acknowledgment is not an endorsement of accidents, nor is it meant to disregard the moral ideal laid forth by God's law in which neighbor does no harm to neighbor. It is meant as a reminder of Christ's example of sympathizing with others in their weaknesses. The potential ability to prevent any given accident does not lead to the conclusion that all accidents, cumulatively, can be prevented. Nor does it lead to the conclusion that humanity, as finite creatures, should compel each other to devote all possible efforts to the prevention of accidents to the neglect of other good things. Certain people may know how to prevent certain accidents, and they may have the ability to do so. However, human knowledge and power is limited by God, by the freedom he has given to others to act in this world, and by the corruptions of sin. Sometimes, those who have the knowledge and ability to prevent an accident lack the will. The fulfillment of the sixth commandment includes watching out for the safety of others and being careful not to cause accidental harm. However, Luther also says that those who do not forgive their enemies, who do not pray for them and are not "kindly disposed" toward those who cause them harm, also break this commandment because they are not seeking the life and welfare of the other.[46]

Jesus tells us to love our enemies and pray for those who persecute us (Mt 5:44). Enemies and persecutors are violent, hateful, and derisive. They intentionally seek to cause harm, like the Babylonian officials setting a trap for Daniel, Nero burning early Christians, or soldiers dragging others away to prison to mock and beat them. Forgiving those who intentionally cause harm is difficult to do, even in less severe cases where someone steals from us, lies about us, hits us, or manipulates us. Forgiving those who unintentionally cause harm is also difficult to do. Someone may cause harm unintentionally by accidentally damaging our property, being forgetful about

---

[46]Martin Luther, "A Brief Explanation of the Ten Commandments, the Creed, and the Lord's Prayer," in *Works of Martin Luther: With Introductions and Notes*, ed. Lane Hall (Philadelphia: A.J. Holman Company, 1915), 2:361.

something important we told them, speaking careless words within earshot of us, or being inattentive to something that injures us. We get upset when a careless driver almost causes an accident, when someone is a little too rough in a game, when we are overlooked for an opportunity. Both the harm and the unforgiveness are destructive.

Zero accidents? The early days of modern industrialization provided much to motivate the human spirit regarding the preventability of accidents. The tragedies that the industrial safety movement addressed were horrendous; the working conditions it sought to improve, abysmal. A young woman was crushed boarding an elevator; "nine women, one man and one boy" died in a button factory; black powder detonated on a train, killing ninety-three coal miners on board.[47] In such conditions, safety advocates rightly drew attention to accidents that were easily preventable and working conditions that were readily improvable. The "realization of the ease with which a large percentage of the ordinary accidents can be prevented"[48] gave the industrial safety movement early success and optimism. Accidents that previously seemed inevitable were no longer viewed as such: "We are no longer going to permit babies and workmen to have all the evils in the calendar in their bodies."[49] As a result of these efforts, American industrial activities have seen significant declines in fatality and injury rates over the past century.[50]

While these reductions are significant, the ongoing insistence that all accidents are preventable has created a tension within the safety industry. If the awareness of the preventability of accidents entails the moral responsibility to prevent them, then, as accident rates decrease, more and more knowledge must be gained and more and more effort must be exerted to prevent fewer and fewer accidents. One perspective on this situation is that "work was generally as safe in the late 1980s as it is now. Yet the amount of safety bureaucracy has doubled over the same period." Another perspective

---

[47]See, respectively, "Elevator Accidents in Detroit," *Safety Engineering* 38 (August 1919): 96; "Lacquers, Shellacs, Enamels and Japans," *Safety Engineering* 38 (July 1919): 15; and "Delaware and Hudson Coal Mine Disaster," *Safety Engineering* 37 (June 1919): 286.
[48]H. W. Forster, "Practical Results Obtained in Safety," *Proceedings of the NSC Third Annual Safety Congress* (Chicago: NSC, 1914), 138.
[49]Tarbell, "Effects of Safety on the Community," 120.
[50]Aldrich, *Safety First*, 5.

is that even if the workplace is arguably "safer than it has ever been," this is "beside the point" because we are not "doing everything that we can to make the workplace as safe as it can be."[51] In line with this second perspective, many in the safety industry today have been compelled to set zero as the only acceptable number of accidents that should occur. In response to favorable trends in traffic accident rates, the traffic safety industry began "asking a bolder question—not 'How else can traffic crashes be reduced?' but 'Is it possible to eliminate roadway deaths altogether?'" This leads to the ethical question, "What level of death on the roads should we as a society accept?"[52] Assuming that it is possible to eliminate accidental deaths, anything more than zero is "ethically unacceptable" and "a consent of failure."[53]

There is debate on whether these demands for and visions of such perfection are motivational ambitions, attainable goals, or utopic nonsense. However, the future-oriented claim that an accident *can be* prevented becomes the past-oriented claim that it *could have been* prevented and the ethically oriented retroactive claim that it *should have been* prevented. Advocates of zero-based safety programs recognize that their messages foster this sort of thinking. They are intended to, as important weapons "in the battle against common fatalism." Zero-based safety programs promote the dual belief "that all accidents can and should be prevented."[54] The claim that there *should* be no accidents is no more disputable than the claim that there *should* be no sin. Jesus tells us to go to radical lengths to avoid sin (Mt 5:29-30). However, a vision of zero suggests that there *could* be no accidents, and this is as unrealistic as the claim that there *could* be no sin. These advocates propose various ways of handling the guilt and blame that inevitably follow, whether using them to insist that participants try harder or minimizing them by treating mistakes as learning opportunities.

---

[51] Sidney Dekker, *The Safety Anarchist* (New York: Routledge, 2018), 6; and Karmel, *Dying to Work*, 4, respectively.

[52] Liisa Ecola, Steven W. Popper, Richard Silberglitt, and Laura Fraade-Blanar, *The Road to Zero: A Vision for Achieving Zero Roadway Deaths by 2050* (Santa Monica, CA: NSC and the RAND Corporation, 2018), 6, xi.

[53] Simon F. M. Twaalfhoven and Willem J. Kortleven, "The Corporate Quest for Zero Accidents: A Case Study into the Response to Safety Transgressions in the Industrial Sector," *Safety Science* 86 (July 2016): 65; Gerard I. J. M. Zwetsloot et al., "Zero Accident Vision Based Strategies in Organisations: Innovative perspectives," *Safety Science* 91 (January 2017): 266.

[54] Gerard I. J. M. Zwetsloot et al., "The Case for Research into the Zero Accident Vision," *Safety Science* 58 (October 2013): 44-45.

Yet the critics of zero-based safety programs seem to be correct that this approach to safety is at a fundamental disadvantage in humanely handling the inevitability of unintentional, human-caused suffering. This disadvantage is present in industrial safety programs, as well as individual hearts and interpersonal relationships, whenever moral indignation for any number of accidents greater than zero is flaunted, and whenever perfection is demanded yet the reality of human fallibility is ignored and paths of forgiveness and redemption are barricaded. Instead of clinging to the false hope of "an eradication of the incidents that cause suffering," these same critics propose "a commitment to alleviate the suffering that remains inevitable" even after safety has been diligently pursued.[55] That is a wise proposal, as far as it goes.

There is no activity of mortals from which they can banish their mortality. When tens of thousands of people accidentally die, humankind should humble itself and repent of its foolishness before God, but even if no one accidentally dies, humankind should still humble itself and repent, thanking God for his mercy. Then, if there are some who wish to proceed with the question of how many accidental deaths are acceptable, they should recognize that they are asking a numerical question that they assume will be answered within the constraints of a calculative rationality. Remembering that all are sinners subject to death and that death, especially untimely death, is always grievous, they could consider answers other than zero: the level of deaths commensurate with the freedom, dignity, and responsibility each person has been given by God; the level of deaths commensurate with the pursuit of love, peace, and righteousness; the level of deaths commensurate with the humble recognition that we are finite creatures in need of God's merciful care; the level of deaths commensurate with the recognition that there are "reckless and careless" fools in this world (Prov 14:16) who bring harm—but not irredeemable harm—to others; or perhaps the level of deaths commensurate with obedience to Christ's command to make disciples of all nations.

It would be impossible to assign a meaningful numerical value to any of these options. It is not as if quantifiable measures of freedom or sacrificial love disseminate into this world in correspondence with accidental death

---

[55]Dekker, Long, and Wybo, "Zero Vision and a Western Salvation Narrative," 222.

rates. Calculative rationality, like humanity's ability to prevent accidents, has its limitations. Thankfully, when God responds to such calculating questions, he demonstrates that whatever equation or metric or formula he may be using is heavily biased toward compassion, longsuffering, and mercy. In his response to Abraham's inquiry about Sodom, God says, "For the sake of ten I will not destroy it" (Gen 18:32). Christ teaches about the shepherd who leaves the ninety-nine to find the one that went astray (Mt 18:12). Whatever the level of accidental deaths in this world, it is not in excess of the goodness of God.

The Forgivability of Accidents

When there are discrepancies between the way things should be and the way they actually are, the conviction that all accidents are preventable, whether individually or cumulatively, is enticing because it appears that people could have acted differently. They could have slowed down before entering the turn. They could have thought before speaking. They could have replaced the worn component before operating the machinery. This is not a new train of thought regarding human failures and the unwanted results they produce. We could also look back on all the sin and misery that have come upon the human race and conclude with Pelagius and his followers that if sin can be avoided—and we have all successfully avoided certain sinful acts—then surely humanity can "be without that which can be avoided."[56] However, the conclusion that humanity *could* act the way that it *should* act disregards or underestimates the corrupting power of sin and the weakness of the flesh.

Accidents are inevitable. According to Pelagianism, the fall of Adam did not result in the fall of the entire human race. His disobedience in the Garden of Eden did not have "any residual corrupting impact on the affections and volition" of their offspring.[57] It did not enslave humanity or compel others to sin. Instead, Pelagianism teaches, humanity is free and able

---

[56]Augustine, *A Treatise Concerning Man's Perfection in Righteousness* II.3, in *St. Augustine: Anti-Pelagian Writings*, trans. Peter Holmes and Robert Ernest Wallis, NPNF¹ 5 (Buffalo: Christian Literature, 1891; reprint, Grand Rapids, MI: Eerdmans, 1975), 160. Augustine is quoting the Pelagian author Celestius.

[57]Thomas H. McCall, *Against God and Nature: The Doctrine of Sin* (Wheaton, IL: Crossway, 2019), 304, 281-82.

to prevent unwanted sins. Adam and Eve need not have eaten the forbidden fruit, but their sin imposed no necessity on their offspring. Israel need not have fallen into idolatry, and we need not have transgressed the law of God in whatever way we most recently did. We could have acted differently. We could do what is right next time.

However, both Scripture and human history testify to the contrary. Augustine is Pelagianism's most famous opponent, and while my argument here does not require a full affirmation of Augustine's doctrine of original sin, the church has historically agreed with him, against Pelagius, that the fall has had a universally deleterious effect that renders humanity unable not to sin and that this deleterious effect is inherited by each person through birth.[58] As Augustine explains, the original sin of Adam, which came about by the prelapsarian "freedom of choice," has now "produced necessity" for the human race in the sense that all are bound by sin and in need of deliverance.[59]

It is not necessary, historically speaking, for a given person to commit a given sin, yet sin inevitably manifests itself through the actions of humanity. This does not mean that it is necessary to sin in order to be truly human. Jesus himself "reveals what it means to be truly human in the midst of a fallen world."[60] However, apart from God's grace, humanity is enslaved to sin and its destructive consequences. In this corrupt state, Augustine says, humanity has "too little determination of will to avoid sin."[61] Through blindness and weakness, humanity either fails to see or fails to accomplish what ought to be done. Augustine says that because of the corruption that sin has brought, humanity lacks the power and will to avoid it. Paul describes this weakness when he says he does not understand his own actions, "For I do not do what I want, but I do the very thing I hate" (Rom 7:15). Augustine says that by God's grace, "sin can be avoided," but only insofar as the sinful corruption of one's nature has been made "sound" by Christ. This

---

[58] In AD 431, in Canon 1 of the Council of Ephesus, the Pelagian "doctrines of Celestius" were condemned. See Henry R. Percival, ed., *The Seven Ecumenical Councils*, NPNF² 14 (New York: Christian Literature, 1900), 225.
[59] Augustine, *Concerning Man's Perfection* IV.9, 5:161.
[60] Marc Cortez, *ReSourcing Theological Anthropology: A Constructive Account of Humanity in the Light of Christ* (Grand Rapids, MI: Zondervan, 2018), 187-89.
[61] Augustine, *Concerning Man's Perfection* II.3, 5:160-61.

healing work "takes place in believers who are being renewed day by day," and will be completed when the "fulness of health" comes, when there will be "fulness of love, when 'we shall see Him even as He is.'"

In humanity's efforts to prevent unwanted diseases, epidemics, and accidents, there are some people who lazily attribute their ignorance to mystery, deceptively obscure their guilt with skepticism, and fatalistically blame their negligence on the providence of God. However, others err when they assert that sinful humanity can somehow attain and sustain the foresight, strength, and resolution of will necessary to prevent all accidents.

We do not know beforehand whether any given action will successfully accomplish what was intended. In fact, the more presumptuous people are about their success, the stronger the warning to take heed lest they fall (1 Cor 10:12). Even if creation were somehow freed from the reign of God and the sustaining power of his Spirit, even if the cosmos somehow existed apart from him as nothing more than a great, manipulable machine, even if death were not a summoning by our Creator to give account for our actions and words, humanity is simply not up to the task of ensuring its own safety. The "hearts of the children of man are full of evil, and madness is in their hearts while they live" (Eccles 9:3). As Daniel Treier explains, people "are so sinful as to misunderstand their own best interests, falling into folly—out of step with the created order, even to the point of craziness."[62] The inability to perfectly fulfill the commandment to do nothing but what promotes the life of others, as well as the ever-present possibility of suffering and death, should drive us to Christ, who keeps our frailty and mortality ever before us so that we would look to him for life.

Accidents are forgivable. We need forgiveness. We need to receive it, and, when others encroach on our lives, we need to extend it. It does not matter if the encroachment was intentional or accidental. Forgiveness is the very means by which Christ himself promotes life and infuses our actions with hope (Lk 7:47). Even when people know what ought to be done, they still "stumble in many ways" (Jas 3:2), whether according to the standard of God's law (Jas 2:9-12) or their own standards of safe behavior. Within the teachings of Scripture, under the category of unintentional sin, there is a sober

---

[62]Daniel J. Treier, *Proverbs & Ecclesiastes*, Brazos Theological Commentary on the Bible (Grand Rapids MI: Brazos, 2011), 205.

acknowledgment of the reality of accidents and instruction on dealing justly and mercifully with their tragic consequences.

Oliver O'Donovan makes a distinction between dogmatic and moral theology in relation to sin. Dogmatic theology tells us of sin's necessity. It tells us that sin is an unavoidable aspect of humanity's "historical actuality." Moral theology tells us of sin's possibility. It presents sin "not as a necessity but as a danger. It 'crouches at the door,' as God said to Cain (Gen 4:7), warning him of the sin that lies *ahead*, which he may either succumb to or escape from."[63] The dogmatic claim that sin and accidents are a necessary part of human existence in a fallen world does not preclude moral theology's reflection on what could have happened, its deliberation on what ought to happen, or appropriate responses to what actually happens.

According to the Mosaic law, preventive measures should be taken to avoid accidents (Deut 22:8). These requirements specified for Israel one of the ways in which they were to fulfill the sixth commandment, by ensuring the safety of others. However, the passages regarding unintentional sins (e.g., Lev 4–5; Num 15; 35) do not give instruction on preventing them, but on how to respond after they happened. Later, in the Wisdom literature, the possibility of avoiding unintentional harm in the first place is reflected on more fully.

The first thing to observe about the person or assembly of people who sin unintentionally is that they sin (Lev 4:2, 22). To sin, as depicted by the term used here (חטא), is to miss the mark.[64] The mark is the law of God. As Bavinck explains, "The essential character of sin consists in lawlessness (ἀνομια, 1 John 3:4), in violating the law that God has revealed in his Word." Bavinck then disagrees with Friedrich Schleiermacher, who says that "sin exists only insofar as a consciousness of sin also exists." Bavinck rightly insists that "the standard of sin is not the consciousness of guilt but the law of God."[65] If a person misses the mark or, to change biblical metaphors, transgresses the boundary of the law of God, that person sins.

---

[63]Oliver O'Donovan, *Finding and Seeking: Ethics as Theology, Volume 2* (Grand Rapids, MI: Eerdmans, 2014), 18, italics his.
[64]BDB, 306.
[65]Bavinck, *Reformed Dogmatics*, 3:136, 150. The same point is made by McCall, *Against God and Nature*, 248; and Jay Sklar, "Sin and Atonement: Lessons from the Pentateuch," *BBR* 22 (2012): 468. See Friedrich Schleiermacher, *Christian Faith*, ed. Catherine L. Kelsey and Terrence N. Tice, trans. Terrence N. Tice, Catherine L. Kelsey, and Edwina Lawler (Louisville, KY: Westminster John Knox, 2016), 68.2.

Neither ignorance, in not knowing where the boundary lies, nor inattentiveness, in not intending to cross it, exempt a transgression from also being a sin.

The next thing to observe about those who sin unintentionally is that they do so unintentionally (שְׁגָגָה). They miss the mark, but do not intend to, whether because of carelessness or ignorance.[66] The target and their failure to hit it are hidden from their eyes. They are guilty of sin but do not realize they are until it is made known to them (Lev 4:13-14). Such sinners are "unaware of doing wrong (and thus obviously had no intention to do so)."[67] When an Israelite or the whole congregation sinned unintentionally, God provided means of atonement. In most cases, it was a sacrificial offering. God provided these means of atonement so that the guilty party could be forgiven and restored to fellowship (e.g., Lev 4:3-12; Num 15:24).

Unintentional sin is at the other end of the spectrum from high-handed sin (Num 15:27-30), in which the person misses the mark by willfully shooting in the opposite direction. High-handed sins are acts of apostasy, blasphemy, rebellion, and defiance. No sacrificial provision was offered, only banishment or death (Num 15:30-31). However, God did offer mercy to high-handed sinners like David who repented. Between unintentional and high-handed sin is intentional, but not high-handed, sin, in which someone misses the mark by aiming at a lesser target.[68] Atoning sacrificial provision was also offered for these sins (e.g., Lev 5:1; 6:1-7). This spectrum of intentionality should not lead to the minimization of unintentional sin or its exclusion from the category of sin. Instead, the utter sinfulness of all sin should be acknowledged (Rom 7:13), with thankfulness that God deals with varying levels of intentionality in variously fitting ways. Unintentional sins, though they are done inadvertently, ignorantly, mistakenly, or involuntarily, are still sins that need atonement.

---

[66]Victor P. Hamilton, "שְׁגָגָה," *TWOT* 2:904. Unintentional sins are described as "rash promises, unfulfilled duties" (Gordon J. Wenham, *The Book of Leviticus*, NICOT [Grand Rapids, MI: Eerdmans, 1979], 103). They may occur because "one was ignorant of the rules" or "one knew them and nonetheless inadvertently violated them" (Lloyd R. Bailey, *Leviticus-Numbers*, Smyth & Helwys Bible Commentary [Macon, GA: Smyth & Helwys, 2005], 68). They carry "the connotation of sin by accident or inadvertence" (Mark F. Rooker, *Leviticus*, NAC 3A [Nashville: Broadman and Holman, 2000], 108).

[67]Sklar, "Sin and Atonement," 469.

[68]Sklar, "Sin and Atonement," 471-82.

Along with sacrificial provisions, cities of refuge were another means of such saving purposes in Israel and signs of a future refuge in the "city that is to come" (Heb 13:14). The Mosaic law makes no sacrificial provision for the taking of another's life, even if it happens unintentionally. This testifies to the value of human life. The penalty for intentional murder was death (Num 35:16-21). However, if a person killed another unintentionally, he could flee to a city of refuge to escape the death penalty (Num 35:11). This included accidental deaths, such as when one person "used a stone that could cause death, and without seeing [the other person] dropped it on him" (Num 35:23) or when someone's "hand swings the axe to cut down a tree, and the head slips from the handle and strikes his neighbor so that he dies" (Deut 19:5). Such killings are unintentional, but they are still transgressions, violations of the law and "an intrinsic offense" against God.[69]

All lawlessness is sin, whether intentional or unintentional. Accidents—such as dropping a rock, using a malfunctioning ax, or forgetting a boiling pot of water—may not, in themselves, be sins if they cause no harm. But they are frequently the result of other sins such as impatience, pride, or worry, and they may become sins if they lead to harm. O'Donovan says that an elderly person who forgets boiling water is as "close as possible to an imperfection that was not a sin." Yet, that forgetfulness might start a fire or cause a burn, endangering others. The forgetful person, and others involved, must take responsibility, if not by remembering to turn the stove off, then by somehow accommodating the forgetfulness.[70]

When accidents happen and we cause harm to others, we violate the command to love our neighbor. When accidents happen and we cause harm to ourselves, we fall short of the wisdom of the one who "is cautious and turns away from evil" (Prov 14:16). We neglect to watch over our lives "in due measure."[71] Furthermore, apart from faith, actions flow out of prideful and selfish hearts that are prone to misjudge themselves and the world. Any given accident cannot be isolated from the larger setting in which it happened, nor from the actions, dispositions, desires, and decisions that come before and after it. It is one drop in a stream of action and agency.

---

[69]Bailey, *Leviticus-Numbers*, 607.
[70]O'Donovan, *Finding and Seeking*, 17.
[71]Aquinas, *ST* (London: Eyre & Spottiswolde), 2.2.126.

Sometimes a person's actions set in motion a sequence of events that result in harm to others, but the person never knows. When the Covid virus first began to spread, efforts were made, with minimal success, to trace the web of its transmission. The actions of many, knowingly or unknowingly, intentionally or unintentionally, were part of that web with its sometimes harmful and occasionally fatal consequences. While a spotlight was put on the spread of this particular virus, human interactions and movements contribute to the spread of viruses constantly. The common flu is transmitted through seemingly innocuous movements and gestures, yet it is the cause of death for tens of thousands of people in America every year.[72]

Responding to unintentional sin. We live in a world governed by a good and holy God. Thankfully, he has not burdened us with a system of morality based on fate or chance in which people are responsible either for their part in an endless chain of unchangeable events or for the random and unknowable results of their actions. Within the overall course of history, he calls all people to follow a path of righteousness in which their actions are given by him a certain sphere of influence and moral liability. It may seem that we are trying to choose the right path through a labyrinth of uncertainties and potentialities, but God has revealed in his Word what is good and what he requires of us—"to do justice, and to love kindness, and to walk humbly with your God" (Mic 6:8). He sets the path firmly before us, as obedience to his commands.

Knowledge of Scripture thus plays a crucial role in discerning one's path forward through this world. Scripture reveals the manner in which one should walk, the manner in which the people of God should live in fellowship with each other. When a person or group becomes aware of unintentional sin, they know that they have strayed. The question is not yet how to reduce this unintentional harm, but what one's posture should be toward others in light of its inextricable presence in this world. The instruction in the Mosaic law is revelatory of God's posture toward accidents and paradigmatic of how those in the church should treat each other today. These laws are helpful in understanding and responding to the accidental harm that we cause each other.

---

[72]See "Past Seasons Estimated Influenza Disease Burden," Centers for Disease Control and Prevention, November 22, 2023, www.cdc.gov/flu/about/burden/past-seasons.html.

First, they show that accidents are tragic, often deeply so. This is just as true of industrial accidents and car crashes as of slipping ax-heads and falling rocks. If a person in ancient Israel inadvertently killed a neighbor, the neighbor's family would suffer terrible grief, while the person would suffer shame and the loss of a neighbor. He could flee to a city of refuge, but would have to abandon or uproot family to do so. Likewise, in our world today, regardless of the systems of restitution in place, fatal accidents cause genuine harm and loss. They tear families, churches, and communities apart.

Second, God offers forgiveness for the accidental harm that people cause for each other. Since accidental harm is sin, God treats it with all the seriousness that he treats any sin, in both his condemnation of it and merciful provision for it. When Israel unintentionally transgressed the law, God did not ignore it. Instead, he provided instruction on how sacrificial atonement could be made. Any human fault serious enough to need atonement is also serious enough to "be forgiven" (Num 15:28). Although "it is impossible for the blood of bulls and goats to take away sins" (Heb 10:4), those sacrifices testified to Christ, who has "offered for all time a single sacrifice for sins" (Heb 10:12). God extends forgiveness, in Christ, for accidental harm, just as he does for all sin.

Third, neighbor ought to extend forgiveness to neighbor for accidental harm. Inasmuch as an Israelite who accidentally caused harm was forgiven and welcomed back by God, he was to be forgiven and welcomed back by others. If "the whole population was involved in the mistake" (Num 15:26), they were all called to repent and be forgiven. And if "one person sins unintentionally," he was also to be forgiven (Num 15:27-29). Even the person who unintentionally killed someone could return home after the death of the high priest (Num 35:28) and would once again be a neighbor whom the victim's family was commanded to love. When accidents happen, God commands forgiveness, just as he, in Christ, forgives (Mt 6:12; Eph 4:32).

Finally, God calls for redemptive accountability regarding accidents. When an Israelite erred, he could only make atonement when his sin "becomes known" (Lev 4:14). It was the responsibility of priests, leaders, parents, and neighbors to inform others of their errors and instruct them about their ignorance or carelessness. Then they could make amends for unintentional sins and learn to avoid them in the future (Deut 6:7; Prov 22:6; Mt 18:15).

In light of Christ's atoning work, the proper response to the forgivability of accidents is not to throw caution to the wind so that "grace may abound" (Rom 6:1). Rather, it is to not let sin "reign in your mortal body" (Rom 6:12), a body "severed from its servitude to sin," but "nevertheless a body that still participates in the weakness, suffering, and dissolution of this age."[73] The hope for those who receive forgiveness and grow in grace is that they would also grow in doing good, not harm, to others. With this last conclusion, that by God's grace those who are in Christ might cause less accidental harm, there is a transition from the need for forgiveness in light of the reality of accidents to the possibility of avoiding accidents in the first place.

THE PREVENTION OF ACCIDENTS

The safety industry's conviction that all accidents can be prevented leads to its commitment to prevent all accidents. The prevention of accidents is meant to be accomplished by "techniques [that] are effective in reducing accident rates and promoting efficiency."[74] Secular visions of a world without accidents are indeed utopic nonsense. Nevertheless, things tend to go better when done in some ways rather than others. The concession that accidents are inevitable features of this world has not been welcomed within the contemporary pursuit of safety. Instead, there has been a concerted effort to establish an ever-growing set of procedures for "doing things the right way." We are told that "unwanted events can be prevented," with the help of "preventive and corrective procedures, monitoring, evaluation, and training."[75]

The rise of proceduralism. According to Brock, a "procedural grammar," or "formalist decision-making logic," has penetrated into "every region of modern society."[76] This includes the pursuit of safety. Proceduralism has become prevalent in the late-modern world, but it is important to maintain a distinction between the *use of procedures* and *proceduralism* that is akin to the distinction between the *use of money* and the *love of money* (Mt 6:24;

---

[73]Douglas J. Moo, *The Letter to the Romans*, 2nd ed., NICNT (Grand Rapids, MI: Eerdmans, 2018), 406.
[74]Hagan, Montgomery, and O'Reilly, *Accident Prevention Manual*, 4.
[75]Hagan, Montgomery, and O'Reilly, *Accident Prevention Manual*, vi.
[76]Brian Brock, *Christian Ethics in a Technological Age* (Grand Rapids, MI: Eerdmans, 2010), 377-78. While making the claim that this procedural grammar is present in wider society, Brock is specifically showing its presence in "technology assessment," the process of analyzing the viability, impact, and usefulness of technological developments.

1 Tim 6:10). On the one hand, procedures may be used in service of a higher ethic, namely obedience to Christ, inasmuch as they help one do good and not harm to others. On the other hand, proceduralism is a thoroughgoing commitment to procedures as the right way to do things. Under proceduralism, following procedures, like the acquisition of money, may be a shortsighted end in itself, or it may be elevated as the only possible means of attaining some other end, such as safety or efficiency. In such cases, proceduralism requires that other aspects of life serve its demands instead of it being in service to one's life.

Human action is a matter of ethics, but the proceduralism under consideration here approaches it first as a matter of mechanics. When people act, they ought to accomplish what is right, in a proper way, and in proper relation to God and others. One's actions are part of an entire life that ought to be lived in worship and service of God. They are the means by which we respond to and interact with both creation and the Creator. Actions are therefore encounters with the living God and oneself "in which what is good and true is proved."[77] Within proceduralism, though, the mechanics of human action—the size and shape of the human body, the space it occupies, the way it moves and bends, the forces it exerts, and its reactions to forces exerted on it—are of primary importance. The good person and the evil person may produce good and evil out of the treasures of their hearts (Lk 6:45), but proceduralism locates the rightness of an action in the movements of the body and their conformity to a procedure, whether or not it acknowledges some sort of relationship between the inner person and outward actions.[78]

The development and prevalence of proceduralism in the late-modern world are connected to the secular understanding of risk, as well as probability and technology as means of controlling the future and creation. Proceduralism is a means of controlling human action in the pursuit of safety. Of course, probabilities themselves make demands on human action, just as

---

[77]Brock, *Christian Ethics*, 4-5.
[78]B. F. Skinner's behaviorism, in which the "root causes of unsafe behavior" are not internal but external and environmental, has been influential in the safety industry (Hagan, Montgomery, and O'Reilly, *Accident Prevention Manual*, 43). However, for criticism of the use of behaviorism in the safety industry, see Clive Lloyd, *Next Generation Safety Leadership: From Compliance to Care* (Boca Raton, FL: CRC Press, 2020), 23-27.

technology is a means of controlling it. To continue C. S. Lewis's comments from the previous chapter, "What we call Man's power over Nature turns out to be a power exercised by some men over other men with Nature as its instrument."[79] This is true of technology as a way of thinking about the world, in which humanity is one more source of standing-reserve, whose energies are to be extracted. It is also true of technological devices, whose designs compel their users to interact with them in predetermined ways. Thus, proceduralism "arises from the technological core of culture," being guided by a probabilistic approach to the future.[80]

A number of authors looking back on the early modern period have observed various manifestations of proceduralism as a means of ensuring that people act the right way. These manifestations have been seen in relation to social, governmental, technological, and even religious matters. Michel Foucault speaks of eighteenth-century techniques developed to exercise "a subtle coercion" upon *l'homme-machine*, to obtain "holds upon it at the level of the mechanism itself—movements, gestures, attitudes, rapidity: an infinitesimal power over the active body."[81] Through such holds, there was a desire to increase the "utility" of the human body by exerting control over "the processes of the activity rather than its result." For example, the goal for the military was not simply to have obedient soldiers, who fired their guns when commanded, but soldiers who carried, cleaned, loaded, aimed, and fired their guns in a certain way so that the whole army would be more powerful and effective.

According to Taylor, though, the coercions by which human actions were controlled and manipulated were not always subtle. He says that people in early modern Europe were "badgered, bullied, pushed, preached at, drilled and organized to abandon their lax and disordered folkways and conform to one or another feature of civil behaviour."[82] Brock, summarizing Foucault, speaks of a rising expectation in early modernity that the bodily movements

---

[79] C. S. Lewis, *The Abolition of Man* (New York: HarperCollins, 2001), 69.

[80] Jacobs, "After Technopoly," 5. As the title of this article suggests, Jacobs describes technological proceduralism, but also speaks of current trends in which it seems to be losing its authoritative status.

[81] Michel Foucault, *Discipline and Punish: The Birth of the Prison*, trans. Alan Sheridan, 2nd ed. (New York: Vintage, 1995), 137, 143-55. Foucault references Julien Offray de La Mettrie, *L'Homme Machine* (Paris: Galerie D'Orléans, 1865).

[82] Charles Taylor, *A Secular Age* (Cambridge, MA: Harvard University Press, 2007), 102.

of soldiers, workers, and students be perfectly efficient, "free of defects" in relation to both time and performance. Brock explains: "Acts are broken into elements, and each element, or body part, is assigned a task whose order of succession is prescribed."[83] Finally, Ellul describes the proceduralism of the twentieth century, saying, "every operation [is] carried out in accordance with a certain method in order to attain a particular end." The twofold assumption is that every "procedure implies a single, specific result" and that any specific result has its own "one best means" by which it should be achieved.[84]

Attempts to gain power over human action, to harness and direct it, are nothing new. But with the modern rise of proceduralism, human action that was "previously tentative, unconscious, and spontaneous" has been brought into "the realm of clear, voluntary, and reasoned concepts," where it is analyzed, measured, evaluated, and adjusted with a new level of thoroughness.[85] According to Ellul, human action is brought under such scrutiny principally out of a desire to increase efficiency. Similarly, Foucault says that this "new type of control" was implemented in factories in order "to derive the maximum advantages and to neutralize the inconveniences," including accidents.[86] As Brock explains, the "idea that workers are most productive when treated as standardized biological machines is the hallmark of modern industrial processes."[87]

Proceduralism, then, seeks to guide human action toward particular outcomes by analyzing and prescribing the movements of the human body. It emphasizes the mechanical aspect of human action in order to make people move their bodies reliably, in accordance with predetermined patterns.

---

[83]Brock, *Christian Ethics*, 120.

[84]Jacques Ellul, *The Technological Society*, trans. John Wilkinson (New York: Vintage, 1964), 19, 21, 75. As discussed in the previous chapter, technology and procedure are united for Ellul under *technique*, which he describes as the fundamental way in which humanity seeks to accomplish things in this world apart from God through efficiency and control (p. xxv). For Ellul, *technique* is equally a means of controlling nature and human action. I am treating the technological control of creation and procedural control of human action separately in order to draw out more aspects of the pursuit of safety. However, in line with Ellul, I think there is fundamental continuity between them.

[85]Ellul, *The Technological Society*, 20. Foucault ties this thoroughness to the development of surveillance (*Discipline and Punish*, 170-77).

[86]Foucault, *Discipline and Punish*, 142.

[87]Brock, *Christian Ethics*, 128.

Predetermined movements are expected to produce predetermined results, and this is where the mechanics of human action tie back to the ethics of human action. As a means of control, proceduralism is intended to increase efficiency, predictability, and safety—thereby signifying that these are the proper outcomes of right behavior. Those who submit to the demands of proceduralism do so with the hope of contributing to and benefiting from "a safe, well-ordered society."[88]

However, as Gros observes, the dangers that accompany these new methods of procuring safety are "commensurate with the progress: formidable."[89] One of those dangers is proceduralism's dehumanizing tendencies. It is dehumanizing when it places such a strong emphasis on the mechanics of human action that people are viewed as machines. At times, the idea of *l'homme-machine* has been unapologetically embraced in the pursuit of safety. The early industrial safety movement sought to help make "the human machine work more efficiently and with less harm to itself."[90] But, whatever the similarities between an embodied person and a machine, the metaphor is of very limited usefulness in understanding how people should relate to each other as creatures whose actions flow out of hearts and minds full of desires, fears, ambitions, and hopes. In response to proceduralism, Ellul protests that humanity "is not a mere package to be moved about, an object to be molded and applied wherever there is need."[91]

Proceduralism is also dehumanizing when it impinges on the freedom of responsible individuals to do what God sets before them. One of the more interesting themes of the safety movement is the constant need to motivate those closest to danger to put safety first. Early safety advocates were amazed that workers "bearing the brunt" of suffering often objected to efforts made on their behalf and refused to cooperate with accident prevention protocols.[92] This response was frequently attributed to stubborn workers unwilling to change or foolish workers unwilling to learn. Certainly, pride and

---

[88]Taylor, *A Secular Age*, 106.
[89]Frédéric Gros, *Le Principe Sécurité* (Paris: Gallimard, 2012), 202, "Parce que, ici comme toujours, les dangers sont à la mesure des progrès: formidables." Gros is speaking here of the tension between convenience and intrusions of privacy that come with technological surveillance.
[90]Chester C. Rausch, "The Safety Engineer—His Qualifications and Duties," *Safety Engineering* 38 (November 1919): 298.
[91]Ellul, *The Technological Society*, 104.
[92]Forster, "Practical Results Obtained in Safety," 138.

ignorance play their parts in accidents. However, when the safety industry says that "dangerous places must be rendered absolutely *foolproof*,"[93] perhaps the workers' hesitations in putting safety first—as prescribed by others—can also be attributed to an aversion to being treated like a fool. After all, the fruits of foolproofing, whatever its benefits may be, have included such foolish things as requirements to wear hardhats under blue skies and steel-toed boots on tennis courts.[94] How is a railroad employee supposed to feel when handed the keys to a company car with loud "pinchpoint" stickers on every door, hatch, and window?

Procedural prudence. Such dehumanizing effects are not the fault of procedures as such, but of a desire, in the name of safety, to perfectly align intention, action, and result. A procedure is a way forward, a method for accomplishing something, a path on which to proceed.[95] All deeds are accomplished in some way—perhaps as adventures, reactions, habits, or improvisations—but a procedure is a way forward that has been decided on and formalized in advance. It is "the established or prescribed way of doing something."[96] Procedures provide obvious benefits in the pursuit of safety. Those who develop procedures afford themselves opportunities to anticipate dangers and decide beforehand how to navigate them. Good procedures represent "the codification of accumulated wisdom," refined through lessons of the past.[97] Those who follow procedures are being guided by others who have gone before them. Procedures lay out what is expected. They provide clear paths forward for all, including the simple who have not learned prudence, the young who have not learned discretion, and the foolish who have not learned sense (Prov 1:4; 8:5). A factory marked by "high labor turnover, unintelligent labor supply, night work and rush work" is able to reduce accident rates through diligent "safety work" and the application of basic procedures.[98]

---

[93]"Roundtable Discussion," *Proceedings of the NSC Third Annual Safety Congress* (Chicago: NSC, 1914), 150, italics theirs.
[94]Dekker, *The Safety Anarchist*, 3-4.
[95]The word *proceed* is a combination of the Latin *pro* (forward, toward) and *cedere* (to go, move, walk). *Method* (μέθοδος) is a combination of the Greek μετα (with, after) and ὁδός (way). See "proceed, verb," in the *Oxford English Dictionary*, www.oed.com/dictionary/proceed_v; "method, noun," in the *Oxford English Dictionary*, www.oed.com/dictionary/method_n.
[96]"procedure, noun," in the *Oxford English Dictionary*, www.oed.com/dictionary/procedure_n.
[97]Michael Power, *The Risk Management of Everything* (London: Demos, 2004), 61.
[98]"Safety News and Comment," *Safety Engineering* 38 (September 1919): 164.

Procedures have their benefits, but they also have limitations. They are only as good as the foresight of those who develop them, and no one has perfect foresight. Someone who relies on a procedure, but faces circumstances it did not anticipate, can quickly become lost. Sometimes, procedures are developed not based on how things will actually go, but on how someone wishes they would go. In a desire to "control and managerialise the future," people often exert a "pretence of knowledge" as a "defence against anxiety."[99] In other words, the initial certainty of procedures provides comfort even when their eventual outcomes are uncertain. Furthermore, procedures are limited because they are unable, in themselves, to instill wisdom. The simple, the young, and the foolish are not admonished to just do as told, but to acquire prudence, discretion, and sense so that they may determine themselves how to proceed (Prov 1:4; 8:5).

Procedures provide distilled wisdom, but it takes further wisdom to apply them successfully. Instead of enabling people to "imagine *alternative futures*," procedures often seek to merely "predict *the* future" and then prescribe an appropriate course of action.[100] There are times when it is wise to simply follow a procedure, perhaps in an emergency where you are relying on the expertise of another person. But the broader goal of godly wisdom is not merely to learn to follow directions, but to develop the character and skill needed to navigate this world according to the complexities with which it confronts human life, to be faithful stewards of the treasures one has been entrusted with by God (Mt 25:14-30).

In fact, Scripture's sapiential instruction presents apparent contradictions and occasional ambiguities, at least in part, to guard against such proceduralizing.[101] The acquisition of wisdom cannot be proceduralized, but procedures require wisdom. Even with the divinely ordained procedures of the Mosaic law, legitimate participation involved more than mere

---

[99] Power, *The Risk Management of Everything*, 59.
[100] Power, *The Risk Management of Everything*, 61, italics his.
[101] An example of apparently contradictory aphorisms, whose unity requires wisdom to perceive, is found in Proverbs 26:4-5. An example of verbal ambiguity is found in Ecclesiastes 10:4, which, "through its ambiguity," "provokes the readers to multiple readings that stimulate them to reflect critically on the advice of the text, instead of following it without question" (Thomas Krüger, *Qoheleth*, ed. Klaus Baltzer, trans. O. C. Dean Jr., Hermeneia [Minneapolis: Fortress, 2004], 183; quoted in Daniel J. Treier, *Proverbs & Ecclesiastes*, 212).

compliance.[102] Moses told Israel that if they kept the commands, their obedience would display wisdom and understanding to the nations (Deut 4:6). Israel later learned that formally enacting those procedures did not in itself exhibit wisdom and understanding. Instead, as the prophets proclaimed and Jesus clarified, the form must be matched with substance. The inside of the cup must be clean for wisdom to manifest itself (Lk 11:39-41). The actions prescribed in the law were to be done with sincerity regarding the higher aims toward which they were directed and sensitivity to the particular circumstances in which they took place.[103] Jesus condemns those who tithe "mint and rue and cumin," but neglect "the weightier matters of the law: justice and mercy and faithfulness" (Mt 23:23). James says that those who are "wise and understanding" conduct themselves in the "meekness of wisdom" (Jas 3:13). In other words, as Bavinck explains, "the value of ethical conduct far surpasses that of cultic and ceremonial acts."[104]

Procedures must be paired with prudence. They should be followed in ways that fit the particular circumstances of one's life. In Israel, this meant that the law, including its more procedural portions, would be legitimately performed, manifesting a right relationship with God's created order, harmony among God's people, and uprightness within the godly individual.[105] "The prudent sees danger and hides himself, but the simple go on and suffer for it" (Prov 22:3). Israel would display wisdom and understanding to the nations when this sort of prudence was fulfilled in its midst. Jesus did just that, evading death before his hour had come and then offering to God, at the prescribed time and in the prescribed manner, the sacrifice of his own body. When the hour approached, Athanasius tells us, Christ "no longer hid himself from those who sought him but stood willing to be taken by them."[106] But even as Jesus hung on the cross—like a fool with nowhere to hide—he acted with prudence in light of his accomplishment of the work God had given him to do and his subsequent petition to the Father to "glorify me in

---

[102]I have in mind passages such as Ex 25–30, where specifications are given for the ark of the covenant, the tabernacle, its various furnishings, the priestly garments, and the consecration of the priests, and Lev 1–6, where detailed instructions are given regarding various types of offerings.

[103]See, e.g., Hos 6:6; Mic 6:8; Mt 12:1-14; Mk 7:1-13; 10:2-9.

[104]Bavinck, *Reformed Dogmatics*, 3:149.

[105]These three levels of right relationships are noted in Treier, *Proverbs & Ecclesiastes*, xx.

[106]Athanasius, *Defense of His Flight*, in *St. Athanasius: Select Works and Letters*, ed. Archibald Robertson, trans. Archibald Robertson, NPNF² (New York: Christian Literature, 1892), 4:260.

your own presence with the glory that I had with you before the world existed" (John 17:4-5). He entrusted himself to the Father, who would not let his "Holy One see corruption" (Acts 13:34-37).

Unlike Christ, we "do not know the day of [our] death" (Gen 27:2), nor should we expect to miraculously evade it. There are, of course, notable examples of those who did so—Shadrach, Meshach, and Abednego in the fiery furnace (Dan 3:27), Daniel in the lion's den (Dan 6:22), and Paul with the viper (Acts 28:3-5). These occurrences remind us that God may grant miraculous deliverance, but in the normal course of his governance, such encounters are fatal. In the face of danger, the Christian is called to proceed with neither carelessness nor cowardice but a Christlike prudence that properly accounts for God's power to raise the dead and his call to present our bodies "as a living sacrifice" (Rom 12:1).

When approaching procedures with prudence, we should also be cautious of efforts to control human action that simultaneously demand and promise that safety will be achieved through reliance on "a dense network of procedures and routines." The sheer abundance of procedures in the late-modern world "reinforces myths of controllability" and creates the "appearance of manageability."[107] In the end, though, procedures are unable to remove uncertainties about the future. This caution regarding the allure of proceduralism is especially warranted when such proceduralism purposefully neglects or actively suppresses the development of prudence, discretion, and sense, as if humankind were not sinful creatures existing in this world before a sovereign God. Humanity cannot determine ahead of time the details of its path through this world. We live toward the future, but the actual path forward will have unforeseen dangers and opportunities for which procedures, no matter how thorough, have not accounted.

Procedures for fixing procedures. Yet the safety industry has consistently looked to proceduralism, on grand social scales and in the minutiae of every conceivable task, to gain an advantage in its commitment to the prevention of accidents. Over the past century, this commitment has provoked questions about who, exactly, is able to prevent any given accident, who ought to prevent it, and how, precisely, it is to be prevented. Within the American industrial

---

[107]Power, *The Risk Management of Everything*, 31, 59.

setting, three overlapping yet sequential responses to those questions can be traced that help show the influence proceduralism has had on the contemporary pursuit of safety.[108] These three phases have to do with differing views on who has the *power* to keep workers safe and who is held *responsible* for their safety, as the setting for work transitioned from privately owned farms and workshops to corporately owned mines, factories, and warehouses. Roughly speaking, in the first phase, the worker has both the power and responsibility; in the second phase, the worker has the power and the company has the responsibility; and in the third phase, the company has the power and responsibility.

Through these three phases, answers to questions of accident prevention move from the individual to corporate level. The early accomplishments of the safety movement coincide historically with an emphasis on the individual pursuit of safety, just as the later diminishing returns of safety efforts coincide with an emphasis on the corporate pursuit of safety. In my mind, neither the initial successes nor diminishing returns are linked directly to the respective emphases on individual or corporate safety. The early efforts were successful because there was so much low-hanging fruit. At a time when sawblades, belts, and gears spun openly and the use of vehicles, machinery, and explosives was in its infancy, even small efforts produced noticeable results. Efforts at both individual and corporate levels have reduced accident rates and rightly drawn attention to various levels of interconnected responsibilities. It is not my purpose, therefore, to commend the individual pursuit of safety over the corporate pursuit of safety or vice versa. Instead, I hope, once again, to draw attention to the inherent limitations of the pursuit of safety, showing that those limitations cannot be overcome and are indeed exacerbated by proceduralism, whether that proceduralism is applied at the individual or corporate level.

The first phase of answers to the questions about the prevention of accidents places the *power* and *responsibility* for preventing accidents on the individual directly engaged in the dangerous activity. This phase is centered on the transition in the American workforce from craftsman to employee.

---

[108]This follows the arguments of Aldrich, *Safety First*, especially chaps 2–3.

Stereotypically, a craftsman was an independent worker who "marched to his own drum. He set his own standards for quality, worked at his own pace, and looked out for his own safety."[109] As workers moved from the "family-owned shop" to corporately owned factories, plants, or mines, the expectation that they should look out for their own safety, as well as that of fellow workers, remained in place. This moral responsibility fell to the workers because of commonly held notions that they ought to watch out for their own welfare and the welfare of others as they work, and that workers engaged in dangerous activities do so "with full knowledge of the risks and hazards involved."[110]

In 1898, when a coal miner blew up himself and his fellow worker opening a keg of black powder with a pick-ax, the commonly held opinion—which did not preclude sympathy—was that such deaths were "individual tragedies for which the company bore little if any responsibility." "Carelessness, thoughtlessness and lack of knowledge all conspire to cause him injury," yet the individual is responsible to navigate the larger setting in which these injuries take place.[111] The consistency of a situation in which individuals were responsible for their own safety in their own shops gave way to the inconsistency of a situation in which employees were responsible for their own safety in settings that they did not design nor were able to control. The first phase ended as worker compensation laws began holding companies financially responsible for injuries and fatalities.

This gave rise to the second phase of answers in which the individual was still believed to have the *power* to prevent accidents, but the financial and ethical *responsibility* was placed on those who oversaw the systems in which they worked. Here we see proceduralism rise in American industrial safety. If accidents occur because individuals are careless or ignorant, then "the proper solution was to modify worker behavior through selection, education, training, and enforcement of rules." The individual is told what to do within the existing system. Safety devices and re-designs may prevent some injuries, but the "posting of reasonable rules and reasonable enforcement will do more to prevent accidents than most any other form of

---

[109] Aldrich, *Safety First*, 4.
[110] Hagan, Montgomery, and O'Reilly, *Accident Prevention Manual*, 5-6.
[111] Aldrich, *Safety First*, 2, 115.

safeguarding."[112] This approach to safety might focus more, for example, on prohibiting workers from touching live electrical lines than on developing systems to isolate and insulate the wires.[113] As a result, workers experienced a surge in the number of procedures with which they were expected to comply. Workers were resistant to this influx of procedures because they had "far less freedom to determine their own work practices."[114] However, the expectation was that as their behaviors became more controlled and predictable, injuries and fatalities would decrease, justifying the losses of freedom.

Prescribing employee behavior is only so effective, though, in the prevention of accidents. Therefore, the third phase of answers to the questions of who can and should prevent accidents, and how they should prevent them, shifts focus from the actions of the individual to the physical systems and cultural environments in which those actions occur. Accidents had long been labeled "a result of careless employee behavior." However, investigations revealed that oftentimes "management—not the injured worker—was responsible for behavior that led to accidents." The safety industry emphasized that workers were not properly trained, machines were inadequately designed, and jobsites were poorly laid out. This led to the conclusion that causes of accidents were less worker behaviors that needed to be controlled and more design problems that needed to be engineered. According to this view, "even injuries that stemmed from workers' errors reflected imperfect supervision." Lucian Chaney represents this changed perspective. His "faith in the progress of science and its applications far exceeded his faith in the malleability of worker behavior." He said that the reduction of serious accidents, if it "is to be dependent principally upon the perfecting of human nature," is "an iridescent dream." However, he believed that engineering revisions could "result in the entire elimination of fatalities."[115] In this third phase, then, the *power* and *responsibility* to prevent accidents are located in

---

[112] Aldrich, *Safety First*, 115, with quotations from the proceedings of the 1915 NSC Safety Congress.
[113] On the novelty of preventing electrocution by protecting bare wires, see J. C. Roberts, "Safety Measures in the Rocky Mountain Mining District," *Proceedings of the First Co-operative Safety Congress* (Princeton, NJ: Princeton University Press, 1912), 99.
[114] Aldrich, *Safety First*, 7.
[115] Aldrich, *Safety First*, 116, 167.

the system in which the dangerous activity is performed and are in the hands of both those who design and those who oversee those systems.

Since the beginning of the industrial safety movement, workers have been expected to be vigilant regarding dangers and dutiful regarding procedures. Along the way, corporations, institutions, and agencies were increasingly expected to anticipate "unforeseen risks" (an inherently difficult task) and maintain "a continuous desire to improve safety."[116] Another layer of procedures has arisen at the system level that sometimes replaces, but mostly adds to, the procedures that prescribe action at the individual level. These system-level procedures have a different flavor. Instead of "Eye Protection Required," or "Use Handrail at All Times," they prescribe the "prioritization of proven safety strategies," "multi-departmental collaboration," and "data-driven decision-making." This approach rightly acknowledges that "people will make mistakes" at the individual level and is intended to design systems that can accommodate human error.[117] A roadway system intent on eliminating fatalities "needs to be arranged such that the consequences of human error do not exceed the resilience of the human body."[118] Safety becomes primarily "the responsibility of system designers and policymakers."[119]

Clearly, designing systems and developing policies are human activities—like mining for coal and operating machines—in which people ought to watch out for the welfare of others, just as they are human activities in which people will make mistakes. But Chaney was able to ignore that simple fact a century ago, just as others do today. The perfecting of human culture through the design and management of societal systems is as much an iridescent dream as the perfecting of human nature in those who live and move within those systems.

Nevertheless, despite the impossibility of perfection on any level of human action, the hope remains that if the steps could just be laid out clearly enough, if everyone would just pay enough attention to what they are doing, humanity could prevent itself from stumbling. The pursuit of safety is a total pursuit, one that places ethical obligations on the entire society. The attention

---

[116]Zwetsloot et al., "The Case for Research into the Zero Accident Vision," 45.
[117]Kathleen Ferrier et al., *Vision, Strategies, Action: Guidelines for an Effective Vision Zero Action Plan* (Vision Zero Network, December 2017), 3.
[118]Twaalfhoven and Kortleven, "The Corporate Quest for Zero Accidents," 58.
[119]*Core Elements for Vision Zero Communities* (Vision Zero Network, November 2018), 4.

given over the past century to human action, whether to the mechanics of the most basic bodily movements or to the design and operation of complex systems, has brought significant reductions to injury and fatality rates in the workplace, as well as in American society as a whole. The same is true of other industrialized nations. The prevention of accidents is held out as a means of attaining other goods—financial and relational stability, physical well-being, and other improvements in the material aspects of life. It is important to remember, though, that the state of affairs in which these improvements come is narrowly conceived not as an increase in freedom or love, nor as growth in wisdom or prudence, nor as repentance or humility before God, but as a decrease in accident rates and an increase in procedural conformity. As Brock says, "Method offers itself as the only proper heuristic for perceiving all that is valuable for human life."[120]

THE ADVANTAGE OF WISDOM

Within the contemporary pursuit of safety, procedures are intended to prevent people from accidentally dying like fools before their time (Eccles 7:17). However, the danger of proceduralism, with its ever-expanding claim on human action, is that people would destroy themselves anyway through overly righteous ambitions (Eccles 7:16). Therefore, another heuristic is needed for understanding what is valuable for human life: the teachings in Ecclesiastes on the vanity of earthly pursuits. The Mosaic laws on unintentional sin give instruction on how to respond after an accident happens. Ecclesiastes gives instruction on the prevention of accidents for those who dwell "under the sun" (Eccles 9:11).

The hazards of labor in an uncertain world. Ecclesiastes 10:8-11 is a "small, self-contained unit" on the occupational hazards of everyday life.[121] The first half of the passage makes four assertions about the dangers of various occupations. Chopping trees and handling large rocks, which appeared earlier in relation to accidental death (Deut 19:5; Num 35:23), reappear here, along with digging pits and breaking through walls:

---

[120]Brock, *Christian Ethics*, 168.
[121]Jean-Jacques Lavoie, "Ironie et ambiguïtés en Qohélet 10:8-11," *Studies in Religion* 41 (September 2012): 472; see also C. L. Seow, *Ecclesiastes: A New Translation with Introduction and Commentary*, Anchor Bible Commentary (New York: Doubleday, 1997), 326.

> He who digs a pit will fall into it,
>> and a serpent will bite him who breaks through a wall.
> He who quarries stones is hurt by them,
>> and he who splits logs is endangered by them. (Eccles 10:8-9)

The second half of the passage offers commentary on two of the hazards—log splitting and the serpent:[122]

> If the iron is blunt, and one does not sharpen the edge,
>> he must use more strength,
>> but wisdom helps one to succeed.
> If the serpent bites before it is charmed,
>> there is no advantage to the charmer. (Eccles 10:10-11)

The unit is framed by the repetition of serpent (נָחָשׁ) and bite (יִשֹּׁךְ) in Ecclesiastes 10:8, 11.

Some commentators argue that the descriptions of these dangerous activities are not to be taken literally, as advice on manual labor, but figuratively, as advice for "the court staff who should not be careless in their conduct before an unwise king."[123] However, the pattern of these verses, in which the inherent dangers of various activities are highlighted, can be expanded to include all human occupations without excluding the primary reference to physical activities, or suggesting a separation between "wisdom and work done by hand" that would be entirely foreign to Scripture.[124]

Images of people falling into their own pits or having large stones roll back on them appear frequently in the Old Testament and are typically symbols of trouble (e.g., Ps 7:15; 9:15; Prov 26:27; 28:10). These passages often carry retributive implications, where those who get caught in their own trap do so because they were causing trouble.[125] But that does not seem

---

[122] Lavoie, "Ironie et ambiguïtés," 460-61.
[123] Daniel C. Fredericks and Daniel J. Estes, *Ecclesiastes and the Song of Songs*, Apollos Old Testament Commentary (Downers Grove, IL: IVP Academic, 2010), 219. Fredericks and Estes say that these images are "more than instruction for common labourers," so they do not exclude the literal meaning but seem to highlight the metaphorical.
[124] Krüger, *Qoheleth*, 186.
[125] Haman's death is a famous biblical example (Esther 8:7). Retribution has a "reciprocal structure of action," according to which "the act returns to the actor as 'wage' or 'result'" (Nach Maßgabe dieser zirkulären oder besser: reziproken Struktur des Handelns kehrt die Tat als »Lohn« oder

Guiding Action

to be the emphasis here.[126] In fact, the potency of this passage stands out when we resist the urge to read it retributively.

This unit is set in a larger literary section (Eccles 9:11–10:15) that "paints a picture of a world fraught with uncertainties and risks."[127] It undoes all that seems secure in this world, all that is sensible, stable, and predictable. The swift do not win races, nor the strong battles (Eccles 9:11); humankind, which had been crowned with glory and honor (Ps 8:5), is as vulnerable as a fish or bird (Eccles 9:12); a lowly wise man defeats a great king (Eccles 9:14-15), but a little folly sabotages much wisdom (Eccles 9:18–10:1).

Principles of retribution give comfort in the knowledge that the world is morally upright. They motivate people to act in accordance with that moral order, even in the face of conflicting experiences, trusting that it will eventually regain balance. Nevertheless, while Scripture affirms that every wrong will eventually be made right (e.g., Heb 2:2-3), such formal retribution is just a bit too sensible in the context of this passage. Care should be taken therefore in attaching the qualifier "careless" to the deeds that occasion the dangers of Ecclesiastes 10:8-11.[128] Doing so may lead to the unwarranted comfort of concluding with certainty that those who fall into pits or suffocate in bins of cement were not being as safe as those who did not suffer such ends. Sometimes the wise suffer accidental harm, while the foolish go unscathed. This portion of Ecclesiastes emphasizes such exceptions to the normal patterns of the cosmos that bring stability and comfort.

Advantages and promises. There is an appeal to a world in which nothing inscrutable ever happens, one in which causes and effects are always equitable and predictable. There is also a desire for explanations as to why that person, splitting that log, was injured. Some interpret the central motif of Ecclesiastes, that all is "vanity" (Eccles 1:2, 12:8), to mean

---

»Erfolg« zum Täter zurück). Bernd Janowski, "Die Tat kehrt zum Täter zurück: Offene Fragen im Umkreis des 'Tun-Ergehen-Zusammenhangs,'" *ZTK* 91 (1994): 248.

[126]See Lavoie, "Ironie et ambiguïtés," 464 and Francesco Bianchi, "Qohelet 10,8-11 or The Misfortunes of Wisdom," *Bibbia e Oriente* 40 (Spring 1998): 111, who exclude any retributive meaning in this passage, and Treier, *Proverbs & Ecclesiastes*, 212-13, who accommodates both a retributive and non-retributive reading.

[127]Seow, *Ecclesiastes*, 52.

[128]Contra Fredericks and Estes, *Ecclesiastes and the Song of Songs*, 219. Krüger says that Ecclesiastes 10:8 "seems at first to reinforce" retribution, but by Eccles 10:9 it becomes clear that we are not dealing with "repercussions of a bad action on the actor but with dangers that immediately threaten him in the carrying out of his action" (*Qoheleth*, 185).

that all is utterly absurd, meaningless, or futile.[129] If that were the case, there would be no coherent explanation for why any given accident, or anything at all, happens. However, Ecclesiastes' teaching that all is vanity serves as a heuristic for all that is important, not by stripping life of its coherence or meaningfulness, but by stripping us of delusions that this world will conform to the patterns we impose on it and by forcing us to reckon with the present incoherence and apparent meaninglessness of life. The claim that all is vanity indicates that life "cannot be grasped or controlled."[130] Humankind is called to be vice-regents over creation, but there is a Regent to whom we ultimately answer.

Ecclesiastes 10 does not deny that coherent explanations exist, nor does it contradict teachings on retribution elsewhere. It just does not offer definitive explanations. Instead of highlighting the cause-and-effect relationships within the physical or moral structures of this world, it highlights the "time and chance" that happen to all people (Eccles 9:11). It emphasizes the "apparent absurdity" of life and the "effects of the cosmos on misshapen, idolatrous human lives."[131] The absurdity is only apparent, though. The futility need only be temporary. In the center of the second half of this passage (Eccles 10:10c), there is a reminder of the life-giving advantages (or help) of wisdom. Much could be said about the multifaceted and nuanced advantages of wisdom, but they are presented here with subtle simplicity: a sharp ax eases the life of the person splitting logs. The work can be done more accurately and effectively. The worker is less prone to overexertion, distraction, or frustration. This "little precautionary measure in the routine helps one reduce the danger of accidents."[132] The advantages of wisdom can be multiplied out from there.

---

[129]For a helpful discussion on the meaning and theological importance of "vanity" (הֶבֶל) as well as a criticism of these "strongly negative translations," see Treier, *Proverbs & Ecclesiastes*, 122-26. Treier concludes his discussion by suggesting "ungraspable" as a good candidate to convey the meaning of this term: "The theological thrust of the Sage is that sometimes earthly life remains outside intellectual grasp; at other times it challenges our emotional hold on ourselves; and always it thwarts any full sense of spiritual accomplishment or predictive control" (126). Tremper Longman argues that הֶבֶל means "meaninglessness," though he concludes that the epilogue (Eccles 12:8-14) ultimately invalidates this teaching as unorthodox (Tremper Longman, *The Book of Ecclesiastes*, NICOT [Grand Rapids, MI: Eerdmans, 1998], 61-65, 37-39).

[130]Seow, *Ecclesiastes*, 47.

[131]Treier, *Proverbs & Ecclesiastes*, 125.

[132]Seow, *Ecclesiastes*, 326.

The outcomes of efforts to be safe are never certain, though, because the advantages of wisdom in this age cannot be multiplied infinitely. After presenting an advantage, this passage then confronts us with a lack of advantage. The juxtaposition between the advantage and lack of advantage in Ecclesiastes 10:10, 11 follows a pattern found throughout Ecclesiastes. On the one hand, wisdom has an advantage over folly, "as stark as the advantage of light over darkness (Eccles 2:13)."[133] Further, wisdom offers advantages superior to those of strength and money in the preservation of life (Eccles 7:12; 10:10). On the other hand, there is no advantage, "nothing to be gained under the sun" (Eccles 2:11; see also Eccles 1:3; 3:9; 5:16). The relative advantages of wisdom in this life have their limitations and will ultimately be cut short by death: "How the wise dies just like the fool!" (Eccles 2:16).

Excluding notions of magic that are sometimes associated with snake charming, the person breaking through a wall encounters a dangerous animal and wisely looks to the charmer, the expert, for help. But sometimes there is no advantage. Sometimes not even the experts can help. Wisdom offers advantages in the practical tasks of life, but it is not so foolish as to make unfounded promises. For those who have been forgiven through Christ, this means that they should sharpen their ax, so to speak, and give their hands to whatever tasks God sets before them, with the attention that those tasks and other people who may be nearby deserve. I imagine that many accidents, many unintentional sins, occur because of an inability to give oneself fully to the tasks that God has given one's hands to do, an inability to let the troubles of the day be sufficient fodder for anxious minds. But there is wisdom to be found in Scripture. Those who look to it for guidance "will not (and can not) glibly excuse themselves by saying, 'I didn't know.' Thereby, one learns to be more diligent in the study of Scripture, more thoughtful and less spontaneous about actions before they are taken, and more responsible after-the-fact."[134]

Wisdom offers advantages, but death looms. Efforts to keep safe will at best be successful usually or most of the time. The various commentators on Ecclesiastes, like our very lives, shout at times that practical wisdom usually works, while whispering that it sometimes does not. Or they shout

---

[133] Seow, *Ecclesiastes*, 67.
[134] Bailey, *Leviticus-Numbers*, 476.

that it does not always succeed, while whispering that it usually does. However controllable life seems, humanity cannot demand a guarantee—the prevention of any given accident—that God has not offered in this world. Yet the advantages that he gives to act in this world in meaningful ways—advantages that extend beyond the bounds of proceduralism—should be received with thankfulness. According to the contemporary pursuit of safety, "we must progress not by the sacrifice of human life,"[135] and that is certainly true in the sense that love prohibits carelessly expending others' lives. However, the only path by which humanity may truly progress was indeed opened by the self-sacrifice of human life—Christ laying down his life so that by the foolishness of the cross he might take it up again. He calls us to do the same. God does not offer lasting success against the vanities of life apart from participation in the death and resurrection of Christ (Rom 8:35-37).

For those called by God to walk in obedience to him, it is good to understand what can be understood about the consequences of actions within the order of creation, so that the life given by God may be stewarded well. According to Calvin, it would be incorrect to conclude that if God is sovereign over all things, then "it is vain for anyone to busy himself in taking precautions." Instead, God's creation is the setting in which we live in obedience to him. For "he who has set the limits to our life has at the same time entrusted to us its care; he has provided means and helps to preserve it; he has also made us able to foresee dangers; that they may not overwhelm us unaware, he has offered precautions and remedies."[136] Christ calls his followers to do good. As we navigate the dangers of this world, we hope to avoid accidents. But more than that, the church is given the hope that there would be forgiveness when they nevertheless happen and the hope that through its actions it could bear witness to Christ and bear each other's burdens in love. Prudent obedience to God's commands involves more than the avoidance of sin. Calvin says that we fulfill the sixth commandment by concerning ourselves "with the safety of all," using whatever is at our disposal "in saving our neighbors' lives," and lending a helping hand "if they are in any danger."[137]

---

[135] Tarbell, "Effects of Safety on the Community," 125.
[136] Calvin, *Institutes*, I.17.3-4, pp. 215-16.
[137] Calvin, *Institutes*, II.8.39, p. 404.

The proceduralism of the contemporary pursuit of safety inhibits wisdom and prudence inasmuch as it tries to make tasks foolproof. It restricts creativity and adaptability. It allows people to shift moral responsibility for their actions away from themselves and onto the procedures. Christ gives forgiveness for the past and hope for the future. He sets us free to live and move and act in this world, to begin a task like Noah gathering gopher wood, Abram setting out from Ur, or Simon and Andrew dropping their nets. There may be procedures, some instruction regarding inner chambers and exterior doors, some information about the destination, some clues about the one you are following, but the exact course, the challenges that will be faced along the way, and the details of how things will ultimately turn out are unknown. Life compels us to move, to take action, and so we do, grateful for the forgiveness, instruction, and wisdom that God gives.

PART FOUR

Living and Dying Under the Lordship of Christ

◆◆◆◆◆◆◆◆◆◆◆◆◆◆◆◆◆◆◆◆◆◆◆

NINE

Discipleship and the Demands of Safety

The world is beautiful, but much fairer is the One by whom the world was made.

CAESARIUS OF ARLES, SERMON 159

AVOIDING HARM AND PURSUING LIFE

Safety, according to its contemporary pursuit, is the absence of harm. This is a negative definition, which says what safety is not. It is not hurt, damage, or harm. Expressed positively, safety is wholeness, soundness, and health.[1] To a large extent, these negative and positive definitions are simply two sides of the same coin. There is little difference between saying a person is unharmed and saying a person is well. There is, however, some difference between the two, and the priority given to the negative definition is significant inasmuch as it reflects a contemporary emphasis on safety as the absence of something bad rather than the presence of something good.[2] The tokens of safety in the late-modern world—with their demands to anticipate dangers,

---

[1] The primary entry in the *Oxford English Dictionary* says that to be "safe" is to be "free from hurt or damage; unharmed." The second entry gives a positive definition, saying that to be "safe" is to be "in sound health, well." This positive definition reflects the word's origin, traced back to the Latin *salvus* and connected to the Greek ὅλος, which carries the basic idea of being whole ("Safe," *Oxford English Dictionary*, www.oed.com/dictionary/safe_adj).

[2] This emphasis can be seen in the shift regarding the meaning of risk from the early modern idea of a venture that could turn out either good or bad to the one-sided, late-modern understanding of risk as synonymous with danger or threat. Deborah Lupton explains, "Risk is now generally used to relate only to negative or undesirable outcomes, not positive outcomes" (Deborah Lupton, *Risk*, 2nd ed. [New York: Routledge, 2013], 9). The emphasis can also be seen in the safety

avoid hazards, and prevent accidents—warn of harm far more than they beckon toward wholeness.

Accordingly, the contemporary pursuit of safety might be more accurately called a retreat from danger, and for those whose lives are enslaved by the "fear of death" (Heb 2:15), it is just that, a perpetual flight away from harm and toward nothing. Retreat from danger has a legitimate place in our lives. Again, as the proverb says, the "prudent sees danger and hides himself" (Prov 22:3). But hiding from danger is an occasional strategy to be used in service of the pursuit of life, neither an end in itself, nor a sustainable pattern for honorable living. Therefore, in line with wisdom's call to pursue the path of life (Prov 3:18-26; 8:35-36), and in contrast to a one-sided emphasis on the avoidance of harm, Proverbs 22 immediately complements the prudence of retreating from danger with a beckoning toward "riches and honor and life," blessings to be received as the "reward for humility and fear of the LORD" (Prov 22:4).[3] Throughout Proverbs, as well as the rest of Scripture, warnings are given against those who desire riches, honor, and life for idolatrous purposes and who seek to gain them through unrighteous means.[4] But there is no condemnation for those who look to their heavenly Father to receive such things from his hand. As Christ tells his disciples, "all these things"—what you will eat, drink, and wear—will be added to those who "seek first the kingdom of God and his righteousness" (Mt 6:33).

The probabilistic, technological, and procedural avoidance of harm has inadequacies and limitations. Christ calls all people to find wholeness and life in him. Therefore, I will conclude this theological engagement with the contemporary pursuit of safety by considering safety in subjection to Christ's call of discipleship. Several key topics from within the curriculum of discipleship have already been employed. I have addressed holiness, with the priority of keeping one's way pure over keeping it safe; trust in God's fatherly care, with the distinction between anxious toil and faithful labor; the

---

industry to the extent that it focuses on the prevention of accidents more than the skilled completion of work.

[3]See also Prov 3:16, where these same three blessings are found in wisdom's hands. Proverbs 27:12 repeats Prov 22:3 but does not have a similar beckoning toward life in close vicinity. However, it should still be understood in light of Proverbs' overall call to pursue life.

[4]Regarding riches, see Prov 11:4, 28; 18:11-12; Jer 17:11; 1 Tim 6:17. Regarding honor, see Prov 26:1, 8, 29:23; Mt 6:1; 23:5-12; Jas 4:10. Regarding life, see Prov 5:3-6; 14:30; Mt 6:27.

freedom of a life ordered by the gospel; and forgiveness as foundational to relationships with God and each other. Christ's call of discipleship meets us in this world and addresses us concerning matters of life and death, both in the here and now and in the then and there—that is, in the age to come. The theme of discipleship uniquely draws attention to the connections between those different times and places by uniting the life of the disciple to the cross of Christ—that central event of history.

THE NATURE OF DISCIPLESHIP

Discipleship, following after Christ, has to do with the Christian life, what John Webster describes as "that form of human existence which is brought into being and upheld by the saving work of God." According to Webster, Protestant theology has most commonly structured its conceptualization of the Christian life, not around the theme of discipleship, but "around the Pauline and Johannine theology of union with and life in Christ."[5] Entrance into the Christian life is conversion, marked soteriologically by justification and ecclesiologically by baptism. Movement through the Christian life is sanctification, marked soteriologically by perseverance and ecclesiologically by worship and mission. Completion of the Christian life is glorification, marked soteriologically by resurrection and ecclesiologically by eschatological matrimonial celebration (Rev 19:6-9). These doctrines are deep and wonderful, and the theology of the Christian life itself is tied to broader themes of theological anthropology regarding the nature and purpose of humankind within God's creative and redemptive works.[6] But they do not exhaust the scope of the New Testament's teaching on the Christian life.

There is also "the Synoptic theme of following Jesus."[7] This theme, discipleship, encompasses much of what usually fits under several of these other doctrines, but does so with a different "semantic range," presenting the Christian life in a slightly different light, emphasizing different basic metaphors—hearing, turning, and following.[8] Webster says that this theme, discipleship, "has traditionally enjoyed little profile" within Protestant

---

[5]John Webster, "Discipleship and Calling," *SBET* 23 (Autumn 2005): 133-34.
[6]See Philip Ziegler, "Discipleship," in *Sanctified by Grace: A Theology of the Christian Life*, ed. Kent Eilers and Kyle C. Strobel (New York: T&T Clark, 2014), 175-76.
[7]Webster, "Discipleship and Calling," 134.
[8]Ziegler, "Discipleship," 173.

theology's description of the Christian life, playing at best "an informal or illustrative role."[9] Ernst Wolf says that discipleship's role in the understanding of Christian ethics "retreated sharply" after the Reformation, confined to the "narrow, pietistically understood realm of individual sanctification."[10] Philip Ziegler acknowledges that Protestant works on the Christian life have addressed "motifs like self-denial, neighbour love, cross-bearing and submission to Christ" but, he says, "they rarely spoke of 'discipleship.'"[11] The point is not that discipleship should replace these other themes that are so central to Protestant theology, nor that the Christian life is understood in its totality under the heading of discipleship. Rather, the point is that discipleship has a rightful place in the theology of the Christian life. Under the theological *loci* of discipleship, the shape and direction of that life "may be illuminated by specific reflection on the patterned relations between Jesus and those he gathered to himself during his ministry."[12] Discipleship reveals the structure of the community of Christ. It reveals its internal structure, showing how the members of the church relate to Christ and each other. It reveals its external structure also, showing how the church relates to the world.

Present suffering and future glory. One of the challenges in subjecting the pursuit of *physical* and *temporal* safety to the call of Christ is that the life to which he calls his disciples, as presented in the New Testament and understood within the Christian faith, is distinctly *spiritual* and *eternal*. How are physical and temporal matters to be kept in proper relation to spiritual

---

[9]Webster, "Discipleship and Calling," 134. Webster notes two exceptions: the prominent role of discipleship in contemporary Anabaptist ecclesiologies and the wide influence of Dietrich Bonhoeffer's *Discipleship*. Michael Mawson takes these exceptions as indications that theological interest in discipleship is growing and adds two further factors: New Testament studies focused on the historical Jesus and, on a more popular level, a desire to balance evangelicalism's emphasis on conversion with attention to post-conversion sustenance and growth ("Suffering Christ's Call: Discipleship and the Cross," *The Bonhoeffer Legacy* 3, no. 2 [2015]: 1-2). Assuming Webster's comment is made in relation to the academy or formal theological works, it seems to have validity. The *loci* for systematic treatments on the Christian life are generally based on Pauline and Johannine categories, rather than the Synoptic categories of discipleship. In Protestant ecclesial life, though, discipleship's place is well-established.
[10]Ernst Wolf, *Sozialethik: Theologische Grundfragen* (Göttingen: Vandenhoeck & Ruprecht, 1975), 149, "bald wieder stark zurücktrat," "in dem engen, pietistisch verstandenen Bereich individueller Heiligung."
[11]Ziegler, "Discipleship," 175-76.
[12]Ziegler, "Discipleship," 173.

and eternal matters? How are the killing of one's body and the numbering of one's hairs to be kept in proper relation to the destruction of "both soul and body in hell" (Mt 10:28)? How is the wasting away of the outer self to be kept in proper relation to the renewal of the inner self (2 Cor 4:16) or the "light momentary affliction" of the present age in proper relation to the "eternal weight of glory" (2 Cor 4:17)? These relations become imbalanced when the desire for the comforts of bodily safety outweighs the desire for the comforts of Christ and the blessings of eternal life. The peace of Christ and the hope of glory that lies beyond the grave often appear transient, insignificant, and distant in comparison to the weightiness, persistence, and nearness of present dangers.

These relations also become imbalanced when the bodily experiences of this life, whether good or harmful, are so denigrated that they are afforded no spiritual or eternal significance.[13] Clearly, the benefits of Christ's presence far outweigh any burden or pleasure of this life. His glories are "beyond all comparison" (2 Cor 4:17). Yet in God's wisdom, the glory of the age to come is inextricably linked to the trials and vicissitudes of this age. For those called by Christ, present suffering is "preparing" future glory (2 Cor 4:17; cf. Rom 5:3-4; Jas 1:3-4). We must enter the kingdom of God "through many tribulations" (Acts 14:22). Calvin says that the children of God are "predestined to be conformed to Christ in enduring the cross, and in this way they are made ready to enjoy the heavenly inheritance."[14] As Webster explains, "Those foreordained by God are appointed to a particular end, and to a history which moves toward that end."[15] This work of

---

[13]This error is often associated with the "dualism of Hellenistic anthropology" (Raymond F. Collins, *Second Corinthians*, Paideia [Grand Rapids, MI: Baker Academic, 2013], 104). In light of a future, bodily resurrection, Collins rightly notes that "Paul's thought does not abide" such dualism (104). Nevertheless, the Hellenistic idea that the body and its earthly experiences are "dispensable" or "a matter of indifference" in relation to the soul's journey to heaven has had lasting influence (Craig S. Keener, *1–2 Corinthians*, New Cambridge Bible Commentary [Cambridge: Cambridge University Press, 2005], 177-78).

[14]John Calvin, *2 Corinthians and Timothy, Titus & Philemon*, ed. David W. Torrance and Thomas F. Torrance, trans. T. A. Smail, Calvin's Commentaries (Grand Rapids, MI: Eerdmans, 1996), 64. Calvin clarifies, contrary to papists and the later Council of Trent, that this preparation is not meritorious. He says, "We do not deny that afflictions are the means by which we reach the heavenly kingdom, but we do deny that by afflictions we can merit the inheritance that comes to us only by the gracious adoption of God" (64; see also Paul Barnett, *The Second Epistle to the Corinthians*, NICNT [Grand Rapids, MI: Eerdmans, 1997], 252).

[15]Webster, "Discipleship and Calling," 144.

preparation encompasses the entire Christian life. It is the process by which Christ brings about his purposes in his disciples, and in such a way that lasting joy is the fitting consummation of transient sorrow. All of this means that temporal safety and eternal salvation are properly related to each other within the context of discipleship, where Christ's lordship and the eschatological character of the Christian life are both clearly seen.

Christ's lordship. Discipleship draws attention to Christ's lordship. There is a Lord who calls, and a disciple who follows; a master who commands, and a servant who obeys. Christ is a loving and gentle Lord. He calls disciples to gather servants and subjects but, ultimately, to gather friends and siblings (John 15:13-15; 20:17; Rom 8:29). He calls them so that they may share in the fellowship that he has with the Father and Spirit by virtue of his divine nature. His disciples participate in this unity through his work of salvation, by virtue of adoption and grace. All this is accomplished by the power and authority of Christ and begins, for the disciples, with submission to his lordship. As Philip Ziegler says, "The life of discipleship is an answer to the question, 'Who is lord of the world?'"[16] This question is answered in both word and deed. The church confesses that Jesus is Lord through its words and proclamations. It also confesses that Jesus is Lord through obedience to him. If Christ's followers are unwilling to take up their crosses, then they are actually denying his lordship before each other and the world. When Jesus calls a person to follow him, it is a call to fulfill the commandment, "You shall have no other gods before me" (Ex 20:3). "None but Christ, and no other God," says Luther.[17]

In the Gospel of Mark, when the disciples were unable to follow Christ to the end, their failure is tied to their inability to comprehend his true identity: "And he said to them, 'Do you not yet understand?'" (Mk 8:21). Jesus is the one on whom the Spirit descended, the beloved Son in whom the Father is well pleased (Mk 1:10-11). He is the "definitively new and unsurpassable revelation of God." His coming shatters history: "As he appears, the old passes away and the new comes."[18] Discipleship is the outworking

---

[16]Ziegler, "Discipleship," 184.
[17]Martin Luther, "On the Councils and the Church," in *Church and Ministry III*, ed. Eric W. Gritsch and Helmut T. Lehmann, *LW* 41 (Philadelphia: Fortress, 1966), 165.
[18]Webster, "Discipleship and Calling," 136.

of a true understanding of Christ's identity as Lord. When he calls his disciples to lay aside their nets and follow him, it is the quickening voice of the Son of God that they hear.

As Lord, Christ sets boundaries on all that the human heart is prone to reify and deify. He exposes the limitations and ultimate failure of all that humanity pursues apart from participation in his cross: "For what does it profit a man to gain the whole world and forfeit his soul?" (Mk 8:36). Throughout this work, I have sought to affirm consistently the goodness of the condition of safety, even as I have criticized the form and status of its pursuit and argued that the goodness of safety needs to be considered in relation to other goods, both creational and redemptive. But a Christian theology of safety would not be complete if it stopped short of following Christ all the way to this stark comparison. Stark is not strong enough of a word, though, because Jesus' question of what a man can give in return for his soul (Mk 8:37) "looks to an exchange rate and here points to no amount being worth real life."[19]

What is gained in holding the future course of this world perfectly in one's mind? What is gained with total technological mastery over creation? What is gained in acting with complete procedural proficiency? Answers come to mind: power, control, wealth, safety; maybe even happy people or peaceful communities. Even if the whole world could be gained by such means, it would be of no benefit to those who have forfeited their lives. Christ calls disciples to follow him today. Then he connects the gaining or losing of life to his coming judgment (Mk 8:38). The benefits of life that are gained in following him begin now with the advent of his kingdom and extend into its consummation. In discipleship, the goodness of safety, as with all other goods, is subjected to the lordship of Christ. In the words of the early medieval theologian Caesarius of Arles, "The world is loved, but let the One who made the world be preferred to it. The world is beautiful, but much fairer is the One by whom the world was made. The world is flattering, but more delightful is He by whom the world was created."[20] And as Bonhoeffer

---

[19]Darrell L. Bock, *Mark*, New Cambridge Bible Commentary (New York: Cambridge University Press, 2015), 246.

[20]Caesarius of Arles, *Sermons*, trans. Mary Magdaleine Mueller, FC 47 (Washington, DC: Catholic University of America Press, 1964), 2:369.

says, "Other gods and the world want to tear away from Christ what he deprived them of, namely, the ability to relate immediately to human persons,"[21] but Christ's boundaries are immovable. He does not negotiate with idols nor share his lordship (Lk 9:57-62). In discipleship, all matters of life are mediated through him.

The eschatological character of the Christian life. Along with the lordship of the one who calls, discipleship also draws attention to the eschatological character of the Christian life. In fact, the eschatological character of the Christian life flows from the identity of Christ as the Lord who will return to bring the history of this world to its rightful conclusion. As I said earlier, the theme of discipleship presents the Christian life in a particular light. According to Webster, discipleship is "uniquely qualified to draw our attention to one feature of that life, namely its eschatological character."[22] Jesus established the pattern, a life shaped by the cross. He calls others to follow: "If anyone would come after me, let him deny himself and take up his cross and follow me. For whoever would save his life will lose it, but whoever loses his life for my sake and the gospel's will save it" (Mk 8:34-35). Similarly, Jesus says that those who give up house, family, or land for his sake will receive back all those things a hundredfold in this age and eternal life in the age to come (Mk 10:29-30). He adds that persecutions will be included in this age, though, showing both the superiority of life in the age to come and the goodness of companionship, home, and material safety in this age.

In discipleship, Christ sets the trajectory of life toward the cross. It is a trajectory of separation from the world, separation from what is passing and toward what is coming. It is a trajectory without the "prior guarantees" and supposed predictabilities that lesser masters are quick to promise in the course of life.[23] As Bonhoeffer says, "The disciple is thrown out of the relative security of life into complete insecurity (which in truth is absolute security and protection in community with Jesus)."[24] The call of Christ does not just set the trajectory of life toward the cross, but beyond it, "not around

---

[21]Dietrich Bonhoeffer, *Discipleship*, ed. Geffrey B. Kelly and John D. Godsey, trans. Barbara Green and Reinhard Krauss, Dietrich Bonhoeffer Works 4 (Minneapolis: Fortress, 2003), 94.
[22]Webster, "Discipleship and Calling," 134.
[23]Craig Hovey, *To Share in the Body: A Theology of Martyrdom for Today's Church* (Grand Rapids, MI: Brazos, 2008), 45-46.
[24]Bonhoeffer, *Discipleship*, 58.

death but through it,"[25] to resurrection and the coming of the Son of Man "in the glory of his Father with the holy angels" (Mk 8:38). Webster explains: "Obedient discipleship entails cross-bearing, the loss of self. But cost is not all: to lose one's life is indeed to save it; mortification is the obverse of vivification; obediently to follow Jesus is to come alive."[26] "Just as a man is lost through loving himself, so he is found by denying himself," says Caesarius. He continues, "Learn, then, to love yourself by not loving yourself."[27]

Discipleship brings together life in this age with eternal life in the age to come. The details of how the two should overlap are notoriously difficult to work out. As a result, Ziegler says that discipleship is "potentially one of the most 'seductive' and 'dangerous' dogmatic *loci*."[28] A distinction is often made between the ordinary Christian life of this age, and the life of discipleship, which is more focused on the age to come. That distinction can be seen in the monastic orders of Christendom, where the members strictly followed the teachings of Jesus on things like going the extra mile or giving away an extra tunic, while the broader Christian culture was not expected to do so. In Protestantism, the distinction between the members of religious orders and other Christians was largely removed. Instead, there was a greater emphasis on the distinction between the church—in which all members are disciples—and the world. There are further differences within Protestantism on how to bring together the teachings on discipleship and the kingdom of heaven with the prudential ethics of life in this world. Ziegler says, "The alternatives—either 'homeless discipleship or a home without discipleship'— were adjudged unthinkable and unworkable, overzealous or impious"[29]

Many struggle with these difficulties in the church today. If all Christians are disciples, should we all live monastic lives and take vows of poverty, or whatever the current equivalents would be? Should we all sell what we

---

[25]Hovey, *To Share in the Body*, 119.
[26]John Webster, "Discipleship and Obedience," *SBET* 24 (Spring 2006): 8. Webster makes this point while registering concern that Bonhoeffer so emphasizes the cross-bearing aspect of discipleship that there is "a certain loss of teleology" (8). However, the passage from Bonhoeffer just cited is at least one example where he balances the cross-bearing and life-giving components of discipleship.
[27]Caesarius of Arles, *Sermons*, 2:366-7.
[28]Ziegler, "Discipleship," 177; see also Wolf, *Sozialethik*, 148-67, who argues for a more robust role for discipleship in Christian ethics.
[29]Ziegler, "Discipleship," 176.

have and give it to the poor? Should we all be missionaries, abandoning prudent conventions of safety and risking our lives for the sake of the gospel? When God put Adam in the garden and gave Eve as his wife, he set the pattern for life in this world—caring for the land, building a family, enjoying the fruits of productive labor, walking with God, receiving good things from his hand. That life was pointed in a direction—eternal life and union with God. When Jesus called disciples to follow him and was given the church as his bride, he set a pattern for life in the kingdom of God that is contrary to the sinful patterns of this world but not to the patterns he established in creation.

When Jesus promised that those who give things up in this life will receive back good things in this age and the age to come, he had just watched the rich young ruler walk away sad. Jesus told him to "go, sell all that you have and give to the poor, and you will have treasure in heaven; and come, follow me" (Mk 10:21). Jesus revealed the greed in his heart. Mary Magdalene, Joanna, and Susanna had means to provide for Jesus and his disciples (Lk 8:2-3), but he did not tell them to sell all that they had. They were being generous with their wealth. Jesus calls all of his disciples to lay down their lives. We should all be generous, selfless, and compassionate. The specific shapes that our lives take are given by our master based on who he created us to be and the purposes he has for us. Being crucified with Christ may come through martyrdom or a selfless marriage; it may come in plenty or in want. Jesus knows which of our saddle bags have idols hidden in them. We can be both comforted and unsettled, knowing that whatever path he sets us on, he has made accommodations for their destruction.

The living Christ has ushered in the kingdom of God. He calls disciples to follow him today, in the particularities of life, as the true king, reigning over this world. Yet disciples are called to follow one who is beyond following. On the seashore in Galilee, when Jesus walked past, saying "Follow me," he was already immeasurably out of reach, having just been victorious in the face of temptation where Adam and all who are in him have failed (Mk 1:13-16). Jesus calls disciples to follow him to the cross. When the moment came, "they all left him and fled" (Mk 14:50). But Christ's call is an effectual, life-giving call. He called disciples at the beginning of his ministry (Mk 1:17). He called them to follow him to the cross (Mk 8:34). When they scattered, they failed, but Christ succeeded. His journey to the cross is redemptive. He had to go alone. At the empty tomb, the women learn from the young man dressed in white that Jesus "is going before" the disciples to Galilee. There they would see him (Mk 16:6-7). After the cross and resurrection, the church "is given another chance to lose its life. The end of Mark's Gospel is the beginning again."[30] Neither the striking of the shepherd nor the scattering of the sheep was final (Zech 13:7; Mk 14:27). Christ calls and gathers his sheep that are "scattered through the labyrinth of the world."[31] Through the coming of the Spirit, the disciples "walk in the wake of Jesus, pulled along by his movement, set in motion by him but always *unlike* him and so *behind* him."[32]

Discipleship draws attention to the eschatological character of the Christian life, but Webster describes that eschatological character specifically as "drastic separation."[33] Indeed, a life of discipleship is a life of separation from the world, "life in alienation."[34] Christ calls his disciples away from the wide, easy, and populous way that leads to destruction and onto the narrow, difficult, and sparse way that leads to life (Mt 7:13-14). This directional separation entails affective and ethical separation as well. The disciples leave nets and family behind (Mk 1:18-20). Christ's disciples live in various times and places, but their lives are ordered and interpreted by the cross, "that central moment of history." Therefore, his disciples' loyalties are not given entirely to the time and place where they live. As O'Donovan explains, the disciple "identifies with more than one time and place: a time and place to inhabit, another time and place to be centered upon."[35] Christ draws the histories of his disciples into his own history, and it is there that they find significance. Discipleship then shares in the cross, bringing its significance and power back into the present, "in as much as it takes shape in lives of service, lives of humble self-giving for others, and as such, lives marked by suffering."[36] Christ "confronts us and co-opts us into his service

---

[30]Hovey, *To Share in the Body*, 121.
[31]John Calvin, *Institutes of Christian Religion*, ed. John T. McNeill, trans. Ford Lewis Battles, LCC 20-21 (Philadelphia: Westminster John Knox, 1960), III.6.2, pp. 685-86.
[32]Webster, "Discipleship and Calling," 141, italics his.
[33]Webster, "Discipleship and Calling," 134.
[34]Wolf, *Sozialethik*, 154, "das Leben in der Fremdlingsschaft."
[35]Oliver O'Donovan, *Finding and Seeking: Ethics as Theology, Volume 2* (Grand Rapids, MI: Eerdmans, 2014), 117-18.
[36]Ziegler, "Discipleship," 182.

to the world."[37] He calls disciples to live under his lordship today, even as they await the coming manifestation of his reign.

SAFETY AND THE PECULIARITIES OF DISCIPLESHIP

Christ is Lord, yet safety retains its elevated moral status in human society and human hearts. It constantly pushes to become an end in itself, a pursuit to which all others must be subjected. Apart from any regard for the lordship of Christ, late-modern technological societies are aware of the totalitarian tendencies of activities such as the pursuit of safety and have well-established procedures in place to determine and implement appropriate moral limitations. However, the influence of these procedures is diminishing, and, as Brock says, such ethical procedures and the deliberations that accompany them are often shaped by the "prototypical moral question of the juvenile: 'How far can I go?'"[38] Exactly how persistently can humanity pursue safety before being crushed by the weight of its demands, before crossing over into the destructive realms of fear, selfishness, and pride? The scribe who asked Jesus, "And who is my neighbor?" (Lk 10:29) was not content with the simplicity of the command to love. He did not want to embody it. As Bonhoeffer says, he wanted to retreat "into ethical conflict."[39] He wanted to evade the central thrust of the command by exploring its outer limits, ever ready to convince himself and others that he had not transgressed it.

Likewise, when the moral shape of humanity's engagement with danger is formed by some version of the question "How safe shall we be?," the whole matter is being driven away from the center of goodness, light, freedom, and life to the edges of evil, darkness, enslavement, and death. For the question "How safe shall we be?" assumes human autonomy rather than divine rule. As Brock says, it has no meaningful place for "the claim that human life finds wholeness by dwelling in God's new temple, Jesus Christ."[40] It is motivated by an interest in what humanity can do for itself, not in what Christ has done for humanity, and it indicates "the eclipse of delight in the good pleasure of God by the desire for self-determination and self-protection."

---

[37]Brian Brock, *Christian Ethics in a Technological Age* (Grand Rapids, MI: Eerdmans, 2010), 169.
[38]Brock, *Christian Ethics*, 187-88. Brock notes, "This question hides a fatal narrowing of moral vision because it in fact assumes the further clause 'before I get into trouble?'"
[39]Bonhoeffer, *Discipleship*, 75.
[40]Brock, *Christian Ethics*, 169.

Humanity may set boundaries for itself. It may say that only so much safety is realistic, that it is willing to give up only so much of other goods for the prospect of more safety, or that the desire for safety can impinge only so much on other ethical responsibilities. But when safety has been idolatrized, humanity will always renegotiate with itself, for "there is no boundary for autonomous humanity."[41]

Radical discipleship. Discussions of Christian discipleship often involve the modifier "radical."[42] When missionaries quit well-paying jobs, trust God to provide the means, and head off to a strange city or new land in order to tell others about Jesus, it seems radical, out of the ordinary, to other people. Christians and non-Christians alike told my wife, Kaci, and I as much when we went and lived in Kazakhstan many years ago. One of the draws of doing something "radical" like that with your life is that it demonstrates your devotion to Christ. It is disruptive and clarifying. Our decision to go to Kazakhstan was certainly disruptive to our lives, but it rippled out into the lives of others in encouraging ways. The status quo was challenged. The decision to go gave focus to our lives. It helped us see who we wanted to be and ignore distractions. We learned to trust God and saw him work in powerful ways.

For many in the church today, questions loom about the place that something "out of the ordinary" like that should have in the Christian life. Some observations may be helpful in thinking through those questions. The first observation is that people do radical and disruptive things for many reasons, not just for Jesus. If Christians think that being radical—in the sense of doing something out of the ordinary, or counter-cultural—is what distinguishes them from the world, they may be surprised, when they buck societal norms, go to a remote corner of the world, head into the aftermath of an earthquake, or serve in an impoverished area, to find others there doing the same things. Someone may object that the distinguishing mark of Christians is our radical love and if we exhibit love, then we will stand out. I agree. Love is a necessary mark of Christianity that can exhibit itself in many ways, including what is stereotypically labeled "radical" discipleship. But love may exhibit itself in other ways as well.

---

[41]Brock, *Christian Ethics*, 188.
[42]See, for example, Bonhoeffer, *Discipleship*, 50; Wolf, *Sozialethik*, 150; Webster, "Discipleship and Calling," 134; Ziegler, "Discipleship," 179.

The second observation is that life can be disrupted in innumerable ways. Jesus has many ways of getting the attention of his sheep and calling them to trust more fully in him, to go against the flow of godlessness in the world. In the process of leaving for Kazakhstan, I emptied my keychain. I gave up the key to my apartment, my truck, and my bike lock in a short period of time. I also gave up all that they represented. It was unexpectedly hard, but cathartic. The empty key chain was a small symbol of the cost of following Christ. It revealed that my heart clings to material possessions. But I have had friends whose belongings burned up in house fires. They were seeking to serve Jesus while staying put, but they also had earthly possessions taken from them. I imagine that they also found it hard, but ultimately cathartic. I imagine that they too discovered the materialism of their hearts.

The third observation is that a life of "radical" discipleship is often ordinary. It either already is or quickly becomes so. God prepares his children in advance for whatever is coming next. A step that once seemed radical and too far out becomes the logical next move when the time comes. Or, it seems to come out of nowhere, but after the fact the person is able to see how all the pieces had been coming together for a long time. Once that step is taken, there are still the ordinary responsibilities of life—work to accomplish, meals to cook, and sin to mortify; a wife to listen to, a husband to give companionship to, and children to raise. These observations are not meant to take away from the high standard to which Christ calls his disciples, nor the fact that we each must take up our cross to follow him. They are meant to expand our understanding of the many ways that Christ's call of discipleship takes shape in the life of the church.

The modifier "radical" is unfamiliar to the Gospel writers. Sometimes it is used in the church descriptively or exhortatively to draw attention to the fundamental differences between the manner of life to which Christ calls his disciples and the manner of life that is generally expected within this fallen world. Turning the other cheek and going the extra mile instead of retaliating against those who mistreat you are radical behaviors. Loving enemies, not being anxious about your life, not striving after food, drink, and clothing—all these actions are radical because they are shaped by a fundamentally different understanding of life as lived in this world under the care of a Father who gives "good things to those who ask him" (Mt 7:11).

Sometimes, though, the modifier "radical" is used pejoratively because a life of discipleship comes across as unnecessarily extreme. It violates the boundaries of culturally acceptable behavior in the world, and sometimes in the church. In his *Apology* of the Christian faith, Tertullian says that his opponents should not condemn the doctrines of eternal punishment and reward because, "even if they are false and silly, they are harmful to no one." Tertullian himself does not think that the Christian belief in resurrection and judgment is false. He defends its veracity. But then he argues for its ethical utility. Even if it is a silly belief, it is a useful one, "since those who believe in it are driven to be better." Indeed, anyone who desires peace, virtue, justice, and safety, whether in the Roman Empire of the third century or the late-modern world of the twenty-first century, should find much in the teachings of Christianity that commend it to the fulfillment of those desires. Christians are taught to put the needs of others above their own (Phil 2:3) and to exhibit love like the good Samaritan, who went out of his way to rescue someone from danger (Lk 10:25-37). Even if opponents of Christianity find some of its teachings ridiculous, Tertullian says that they should not find them threatening or dangerous: "If there is to be sentence passed, the fit sentence is laughter—not sword and fire, not cross and beast!" He highlights areas of compatibility between the Christian life and Roman life more broadly to argue that the persecution of Christians is unnecessary.[43]

However, as Tertullian concludes his *Apology*, he reveals that practical compatibilities between the world and church are constrained by fundamental conflicts. "There is a rivalry between God's ways and man's,"[44] between life according to the pattern of this age and life under the lordship of Christ. Tertullian's earlier argument that others should not be threatened by Christianity's doctrines nor its adherents' manner of life, while making valid points, perhaps belies the subversive power of Christ's call of discipleship and the community that he establishes. For the world may want safety, but not by way of the cross. It may want fellowship, but not at the foot of the cross. When the church follows Christ—and in so doing violates the

---

[43]Tertullian, *Apology* 47-50, trans. T. R. Glover and Gerald H. Rendall, LCL 250 (Cambridge, MA: Harvard University Press, 1931), 211-27.
[44]Tertullian, *Apology* 50 (LCL 250:227).

boundaries within which safety is supposed to be pursued—it exposes the weaknesses, limitations, contradictions, and hypocrisies of the world's pursuit of safety. Bonhoeffer says that opponents of the church can "see in all of our words and all of our actions that their own words and deeds are condemned," even though those same opponents sense "that we are indifferent to their condemnation of us."[45] When the church is "able to adopt a rather free and sometimes unimpressed attitude to the other voices which clamour for its attention,"[46] the authority of those voices is necessarily threatened and weakened. The disciple is "'for the world as God's creation' and 'against the world as a power of self-assertion.'"[47] That is where the radical nature of discipleship lies, however it is lived out.

Reasonable discipleship. In actuality, it is those other voices that carry their listeners to dangerous, radical extremes, not Christ's. The thief's is a voice of theft, death, and destruction. The shepherd's is the voice of wholeness and life (Jn 10:10-11). In contrast to the various forms of "self-fulfillment and self-preservation" in our culture that have "no deep sense of human nature or the ends of human life," Christ's call of discipleship "protects, vivifies and dignifies, by directing us to the perfection of our nature."[48] Undoubtedly, he sounds extreme to faithless ears and hard hearts, but he is prudent and wise, gentle and lowly. He understands our created form, that we are made of dust and in need of shelter and sustenance. He sympathizes with our weaknesses as sinners. He knows that we are neither beasts nor gods, neither angels nor machines, but men and women made to bear the image of God.

When Jesus calls his disciples to love their enemies and pray for their persecutors, he asks, "And if you only greet your brothers, what more (περισσός) are you doing than others?" (Mt 5:47). They would not be doing anything extraordinary, peculiar, or remarkable, as the word expresses.[49] Bonhoeffer is right to point out that love for enemies is peculiar (περισσός) in comparison to the "natural love" that people have for their friends.[50]

---

[45]Bonhoeffer, *Discipleship*, 142.
[46]Webster, "Discipleship and Calling," 146.
[47]Wolf, *Sozialethik*, 158, "'In der Welt', heißt dabei stets, 'für die Welt als Schöpfung Gottes' und 'gegen die Welt als Macht der Selbstbehauptung.'"
[48]Webster, "Discipleship and Obedience," 17.
[49]See BDAG, 805.
[50]Bonhoeffer, *Discipleship*, 143-44.

However, when Christ calls his disciples to do something as radical as loving their enemies, he is simply calling them to display the likeness of God in their lives, to be children of their "Father who is in heaven. For he makes his sun rise on the evil and on the good, and sends rain on the just and on the unjust" (Mt 5:44-45). The peculiarities of discipleship appear radical to a sinful world and doubtful minds, but they are quite reasonable to those whose lives are held secure by the love of God.

Subjecting safety to the call of Christ puts it under his authority so that it may find its proper place in one's life. When this happens, it becomes immediately clear that safety ranks below Christ and loyalty to him. Those who do not take up their crosses and follow him are not worthy of him (Mt 10:38). Eternal life, obedience to Christ, the proclamation of the gospel, and love for others all rank above physical safety.[51] In Christ's earthly ministry, he drew many to himself by healing them, affirming the goodness of physical wholeness. But he then promised those whom he healed that they would suffer for his sake, and they gladly accepted his offer. Bartimaeus "recovered his sight and followed him on the way" (Mk 10:52). Scripture presents a clear picture: Christ's disciples are called to give up physical well-being, even to the point of death, for his sake. When the call of Christ conflicts with the pursuit of safety, the call of Christ prevails. Shadrach, Meshach, and Abednego faced a simple choice: "If you do not worship [the golden image], you shall immediately be cast into a burning fiery furnace" (Dan 3:15). They responded with matching simplicity: "We will not serve your gods or worship the golden image that you have set up" (Dan 3:18).

Sometimes idols, or, more accurately, the demonic powers that lie behind them, make bold demands, insisting that we bow before them. Often, though, they just insist that we wink at them in a thousand small ways as they slowly draw us in the wrong direction. Shadrach, Meshach, and Abednego faced such a stark choice because they were unwilling to make smaller compromises (Dan 1:7-16). The desire for safety and the efforts made to procure it are not necessarily idolatrous. But as with all desires for the temporal goods of creation, the desire for safety becomes idolatrous when it exceeds the desire for God, when it is sought outside the lordship of Christ. From a

---

[51]See, e.g., Mt 10:16-42; 18:8-9; Mk 8:38; 10:29-30; Lk 9:57-62; 12:4-12; 13:1-5.

practical standpoint, this means that it is impossible to delineate an external set of guidelines or expectations concerning what the subjection of safety to Christ's call of discipleship will look like. After Peter learned that his path of discipleship would be marked by humiliation, suffering, and crucifixion, he inquired about John's, but Jesus corrected the impulse to compare: "If it is my will that he remain until I come, what is that to you? You follow me!" (Jn 21:22). That correction in turn led to another error, the rumor that "this disciple was not to die" (Jn 21:23). John was to die. Nevertheless, whatever dangers he would or would not face, Christ's point still stands: "What is that to you? You follow me!"

Delivering Up Your Life

In the first missionary journey of Paul and Barnabas, these two men repeatedly demonstrated that following Christ was of greater importance than physical safety. The Word of the Lord spread as persecutions were stirred up against them (Acts 13:49-50). They narrowly escaped an attempt "to mistreat them and to stone them" (Acts 14:5-6). The threat of harm became actual harm when Paul was stoned and left for dead (Acts 14:19). But he was miraculously healed, and they went back through the cities where these things had happened in order to strengthen the disciples. It was at this time that Paul and Barnabas told the disciples that they would enter the kingdom of God "through many tribulations" (Acts 14:20-22). Whether Paul and Barnabas faced the threat of harm or actual harm, they continued forward in their ministry to the Gentiles, and when they returned to Antioch in Syria (Acts 14:27-28), they were "now able to look back over what had happened and recognize the hand of God at work," even in the midst of great hostility.[52]

Risking lives for the name of Jesus. After Paul and Barnabas were exposed to these dangers, the church in Jerusalem commended them as "men who have risked their lives for the name of our Lord Jesus Christ" (Acts 15:26).[53] If this verse is read with modern eyes, with modern conceptions of risk in mind, it may come across as a calculative assessment of the dangerous

---

[52] I. Howard Marshall, *Acts: An Introduction and Commentary*, TNTC 5 (Downers Grove, IL: IVP Academic, 1980), 240.
[53] Most modern English translations say they "risked" their lives. The King James Version says they "hazarded" their lives.

situations Paul and Barnabas entered into for the cause of Christ, as if risking their lives had to do primarily with calculating and navigating probable responses to their proclamation of the gospel. If we consider the dangers that they encountered through the lens of historical contingency and risk assessment, then we can easily conclude that they faced great risk, that they almost died, that they were safer in some cities than others, and that Paul's rapid recovery was highly improbable, statistically speaking. We could even survey the entire book of Acts and calculate the probability of Paul being harmed upon the proclamation of the gospel in any given city. However, these conceptions of risk keep the entire relationship between action, possible outcomes, and actual outcome, as well as the relative values of various possible outcomes, entirely within a causal stream of history. The success—if we want to call it that—of Paul and Barnabas in the face of great risk must then be attributed to something like their predictive skills or the development of proper missionary procedures.

The outcome of a life of discipleship is then viewed as a matter of achievement or "forecast" rather than "promise." But when disciples lay down their lives and take up their crosses in response to the call of Christ, there is "no measurement for calculating the consequences of such a risky action."[54] The scriptural account of Barnabas and Paul's journey certainly highlights the various dangers they faced. But it also highlights that the entire journey and everything that resulted from it was "directed by God who had opened up the way to the Gentiles."[55] By means of danger and persecution, God "opened a door" so that the nations might enter the kingdom of God (Acts 14:27).[56] How could that have been calculated or proceduralized in advance? The point of Acts 15:26 is not that Paul and Barnabas navigated dangers successfully in order to produce positive results for the cause of Christ, nor is the point that they had wagered their lives in the hope that their venture would yield a highly desirable but highly improbable gain.

When Paul and Barnabas "risked their lives" (παραδεδωκόσι τὰς ψυχὰς αὐτῶν; Acts 15:26), they gave them over or delivered them up for the sake of

---

[54]Hovey, *To Share in the Body*, 139-47.
[55]Marshall, *Acts*, 240.
[56]Mikeal C. Parsons, *Acts*, Paideia (Grand Rapids, MI: Baker Academic, 2008), 204.

Christ.[57] According to commentators, this giving over (παραδίδωμι) should be understood at a basic level as an act of "devotion" or "dedication."[58] Paul and Barnabas are commended by the church in Jerusalem as "those willing to lose their lives or dedicate their lives for the sake of the Lord Jesus Christ."[59] I. Howard Marshall agrees that they "devoted themselves," but he pushes back on rendering the phrase as "risked their lives" because it is "perhaps too strong."[60] According to John Polhill, though, the phrase "can mean either *to devote* or *to risk*, and the distinction between the two in this context would be slim. It was in their wholehearted devotion to Christ that the two missionaries had incurred so many dangers."[61] When the church in Antioch heeded the Holy Spirit's word, "Set apart for me Barnabas and Saul for the work to which I have called them," it "sent them off" into the midst of dangers (Acts 13:2-3). Paul and Barnabas went, willing to suffer and die. They handed over their lives *coram Deo* before their lives were ever at risk *coram mundo*.

The emphasis is not on whether they took this risk or that risk, much less on whether this risk or that risk materialized. The emphasis is on the initial and ongoing act of giving up their lives for the sake of Christ. Discipleship "is a movement which has a beginning and a continuation." It begins with "the abandonment of a ruined way of life and setting out on a new way." It continues as the repetition and outworking of that initial movement "away from self-will and self-direction toward glad embrace of the divine will and direction which is set forth in Christ."[62] Calculative language about discipleship can be found in the words of Jesus: "Whoever does not bear his own cross and come after me cannot be my disciple. For which of you, desiring to build a tower, does not first sit down and count the cost, whether he has enough to complete it?" (Lk 14:27-28). But calculating costs is not the same as calculating risks. Costs are certain. Risks are probable, unknown. Jesus makes the cost of discipleship clear. He states it

---

[57]See BDAG, 761.
[58]See Marshall, *Acts*, 255; John B. Polhill, *Acts*, NAC 26 (Nashville: B&H Academic, 1992), 334; and Darrell L. Bock, *Acts*, BECNT (Grand Rapids, MI: Baker Academic, 2007), 512.
[59]Bock, *Acts*, 512.
[60]Marshall, *Acts*, 255.
[61]Polhill, *Acts*, 334, italics his.
[62]Webster, "Discipleship and Obedience," 8-9.

plainly at the start. It is not a matter for predictive capacities. Jesus would go to the cross. He would suffer and be rejected. When he calls others to follow, he makes it "clear and unmistakable to his disciples that the need to suffer now applies to them, too."[63]

The disciples must respond to this call. They must "stride out toward their coming blessedness."[64] There may be a desire to anticipate beforehand what one's life of discipleship will look like, what specific risks will be encountered, even how to navigate them successfully. But to be a disciple, to share in the body of Christ, "is not to assess risk and safety on the basis of reason but to hope for presence on the basis of faithfulness."[65] The appropriate response to Christ is self-denial (Mk 8:34), and that includes the renunciation of such self-interested questions, as well as the disavowal of "obedience to that intense impulse to survive."[66] Calvin says, "We are not our own: let not our reason nor our will, therefore, sway our plans and deeds. We are not our own: let us therefore not set it as our goal to seek what is expedient for us according to the flesh."[67] When Jesus says that "the Son of Man has nowhere to lay his head" (Lk 9:57-58), he offers himself and fellowship in his sufferings to those who will follow, but not predictive certainty regarding the shape and means of God's providential care.

If self-interested questions should be renounced, if the intense impulse to survive should be disavowed, if what is expedient for the flesh should not be sought, how does a life of discipleship fit with the love that Aquinas says we have been given for "life and whatever is directed thereto"? First, Aquinas says we err when this love is too strong and when it is too weak. Bonhoeffer, Webster, and Calvin are speaking of instances when the love of life is too strong and faith in God is absent, when remaining alive has become the goal instead of seeing and knowing God. Second, those who lose their lives for

---

[63]Bonhoeffer, *Discipleship*, 85.
[64]Webster, "Discipleship and Obedience," 5.
[65]Hovey, *To Share in the Body*, 23.
[66]Webster, "Discipleship and Obedience," 15. According to Wolf, *Sozialethik*, 155-56, Calvin understands the Christian life primarily as the denial of ourselves, "the resignation of all our personal desires and wishes to what we owe to God and humanity" ("das Zurücktreten all unseres persönlichen Begehrens und Wünschens hinter dem, was wir Gott und dem Menschen schuldig sind"). See Calvin, *Institutes*, III.7, pp. 689-701. On self-denial, see also Bonhoeffer, *Discipleship*, 86.
[67]Calvin, *Institutes*, III.7.1, p. 690.

the sake of Christ do not have too little a love of life. He is the source of life. They lose their lives in order to gain more life, abundant life, both in this age and the age to come.

A continuity of language. As we saw with the example of Barnabas and Paul, Christ's disciples deliver up their lives for his sake. However, Christ first delivered up his own life. In relation to the delivering up of Christ, Augustine observes an intriguing continuity of language within the New Testament.[68] The Father "did not spare his own Son but *gave* him *up* for us all" (Rom 8:32).[69] Likewise, the Son "loved me and *gave* himself for me," he "loved us and *gave* himself *up* for us," he "loved the church and *gave* himself *up* for her" (Gal 2:20; Eph 5:2, 25). But Augustine notes that Judas also "*delivered* him *up*."[70] Jesus asks: "Judas, would you *betray* the Son of Man with a kiss?" (Lk 22:48).[71] There was "a '*traditio*' (delivering up) by the Father; there was a '*traditio*' by the Son; there was a '*traditio*' by Judas."[72]

The continuity of vocabulary extends further than these three instances. To begin, although Satan is never said to deliver up Christ, Judas "conferred with the chief priests and officers" on how to *betray* Jesus immediately after Satan entered into him (Lk 22:3-4; Jn 13:27).[73] Before his arrest, Jesus said he would be *delivered* "into the hands of men," "over to the chief priests and scribes," "over to the Gentiles," "up to be crucified," and "into the hands of sinners" (Mt 17:22; 20:18-19; 26:2; 26:45). And so it happened. Judas *betrayed* Jesus to the chief priests and elders (Mk 14:10; Lk 22:4). The chief priests and elders *delivered* Jesus *up* to Pilate (Mt 27:2). Then Pilate *delivered* Jesus *up* to Roman soldiers to be crucified (Mt 27:26), and in so doing he *delivered* Jesus *over* to the will of the crowd (Lk 23:25). In the Gospels, aside from John

---

[68] Augustine, *Homily VII on the First Epistle of John*, in *St. Augustine: Homilies on the Gospel of John; Homilies on the First Epistle of John; Soliloquies*, ed. Joseph H. Myers, trans. H. Brown, NPNF¹ 7 (Buffalo: Christian Literature, 1888; reprint, Grand Rapids, MI: Eerdmans, 1978), 503-4; and Augustine, *Saint Augustine Letters*, trans. Wilfrid Parsons, FC 18 (New York: Fathers of the Church, Inc., 1953), 2:63.

[69] The verb παραδίδωμι (to give up, offer up, deliver up) is used here and throughout the following verses. I have italicized the English translation of the Greek verb throughout this section.

[70] Augustine says that Judas is a traitor, a "'*traditor*,' one that delivered up" (Augustine, *Homily VII on the First Epistle of John*, 504). See, e.g., Mt 27:3, where Judas is "the betrayer" (ὁ παραδιδοὺς).

[71] The verb παραδίδωμι is used consistently throughout all four Gospels in reference to Judas' betrayal. It is most commonly translated as "betray" (e.g., Mt 26:21-25), but occasionally also as "deliver" (e.g., Mt 26:15).

[72] Augustine, *Homily VII on the First Epistle of John*, 504.

[73] Augustine, *Saint Augustine Letters*, 2:63.

19:30, where Jesus *"gave up* his spirit" (cf. Mt 27:50; Lk 23:46), this verb (παραδίδωμι) is used passively of him. Others *deliver* him *up*. Peter continues this pattern in his sermon at Pentecost, proclaiming Jesus as the one "whom you *delivered over* and denied in the presence of Pilate" (Acts 3:13). Humanity *delivered up* Christ to death, and did so out of greed, envy, and political expediency (Mt 26:15; 27:18; 27:24-26).

Christ also *gave up* himself, but he did so out of love (Eph 5:2). Likewise, the Father *handed* him *over* to this fallen and sinful world for its redemption, in order to fulfill what he had "foretold by the mouth of all the prophets, that his Christ would suffer" (Acts 3:18). As Augustine says, "Judas had in his thoughts the price for which he sold the Lord," but "God had in his thoughts our salvation."[74] The continuity of language regarding the *delivering up* of Christ extends a step further, into his relationship with the Father. When Christ was suffering and being reviled, he did not "revile in return" or "threaten, but continued *entrusting* himself to him who judges justly" (1 Pet 2:23).[75] As Jesus was being *delivered up* unjustly by others to be crucified, he *delivered* himself *over* to the Father, the one who judges justly, to be vindicated.

A unity of meaning? So far, I have followed Augustine in observing a continuity of language in the New Testament regarding the arrest and crucifixion of Christ. Augustine then seeks for a unity of meaning that encompasses all the various instances of Christ being *delivered up*: "When the Father delivered up the Son, and Christ Himself delivered up His Body, and Judas delivered up His Master, why, in that delivering up, is God good and man guilty, except that though they all did the same thing, they did not do it for the same reason?"[76] But did the Father, the Son, and Judas, as well as the crowds, the soldiers, and the rulers, really all do the same thing? The same word is used (παραδίδωμι). That which is *delivered up* in each case is the same—Christ. The actions of those involved, from Jesus to Judas, all

---

[74] Augustine, *Homily VII on the First Epistle of John*, 504.
[75] There is no object attached to the verb παραδίδωμι. "The absence of an object for the verb leaves unclear what it is that Jesus delivered over to God, whether his person, in which case this could well be a rather clear reference to the passion, or his cause, which could have broader implications" (Paul J. Achtemeier, *1 Peter*, ed. Eldon Jay Epp, Hermeneia [Minneapolis: Fortress, 1996], 201). In light of the references to his suffering, most English translations seem to be correct in saying he delivered up himself.
[76] Augustine, *Saint Augustine Letters*, 2:63.

came together under God's sovereign hand to result in one great salvific event. But were the actions of all those involved the same kind of action? Clearly not. There are meaningful differences in what these various actors are doing. Judas *delivered* Jesus *up* as an act of betrayal. Pilate *delivered* Jesus *up* as an act of execution. Jesus *delivered* himself *up* as an act of self-sacrificial love (Gal 2:20). Judas' betrayal was not an act of self-sacrificial love, and Pilate's delivering of him up for execution was not, technically, an act of betrayal.

Further, those who *delivered up* Jesus did so for different reasons. Augustine says that the likeness of these deeds joins them together, though the unlikeness of their causes distinguish them from each other. Perhaps it would be better to say, as Calvin comes closer to doing, that these are various deeds performed for various reasons but are nonetheless united in the will of God and result in a singular event.[77] When Jesus was being betrayed into the hands of sinners, he was, in that very moment, offering himself up for the sake of others and entrusting himself into the hands of the Father. The Evangelists proclaim Christ being *delivered up* to death at the hands of sinners. The apostle explains the significance of that event, teaching that Christ, in union with the Father, *delivered* himself *up* "for our trespasses" (Rom 4:25; cf. Rom 8:32). And it is the task of the church, as it reads Scripture, to hear its unified witness to Christ's self-sacrificial love for a rebellious world. God has spoken. "Attending to what is said," O'Donovan reminds us, "is our first concrete moral undertaking."[78] Therefore, the continuity of language to which Augustine was rightly attuned, points to a theological unity in Scripture regarding God's work of salvation—that Christ would be *delivered up*. The beauty and intricacy of that theological unity is enhanced, not threatened, by the variety of meanings that παραδίδωμι carries in the New Testament.

A pattern to follow. The task of attending to what is said in Scripture is especially important when Christ's self-sacrificial love is set before the church as a pattern to follow in the world today. When Christ delivered himself up to the Father, instead of pushing back against violent impositions on his life, he left an example. The church is to "follow in his steps"

---

[77]Calvin, *Institutes*, I.18.4, pp. 236-37.
[78]O'Donovan, *Finding and Seeking*, 132.

(1 Pet 2:21).[79] Likewise, Jesus' delivering up of himself for us establishes a pattern of love to be followed. Paul says that the life he now lives, he lives "by faith in the Son of God, who loved me and *gave* himself for me" (Gal 2:20). Christ's disciples are called to "walk in love, as Christ loved us and *gave* himself *up* for us" (Eph 5:2). Husbands are called to love their wives, "as Christ loved the church and *gave* himself *up* for her" (Eph 5:25). In all of these passages, Christ's delivering up of himself has ethical significance for the church, demonstrating how to walk and how to love.

Christians are called to deliver up their lives for the sake of others, putting others' needs ahead of their own, seeking to secure the safety of others even at the cost of their own. We ask God to give us our daily bread, but Luther says that caring for one's body is a "Christian work," not only for its own sake, but for the sake of others (Eph 4:28): "If the body is healthy and fit, we are able to work and save money that can be used to help those in need." In showing such love, Luther says, we demonstrate "that we are children of God, caring and working for the well-being of others and fulfilling the law of Christ by bearing one another's burdens."[80] We are to walk as Christ walked, whether that means entrusting ourselves to God in the face of unjust treatment or loving others sacrificially.

Christ calls his disciples to follow him in delivering themselves up. He also says that his disciples will follow him in being delivered up by the hands of others to suffering and death. And so there is another arm in this continuity of language, especially in the Synoptic Gospels, that extends to Christ's disciples. Again, allowing for the various connotations of παραδίδωμι in its various usages, the use of this verb in relation to Christ's disciples provides a further window into the unity of God's work of salvation. First, Jesus says that his disciples will be *delivered over* to councils and courts. Then, he says that this will be an opportunity to be a witness, a martyr. They are not to worry about what they will say. Whatever words are to be spoken will be a gift from the Holy Spirit: "If martyrdom is itself a gift, the words spoken or withheld in the trial are likewise a gift. The lack of anxiety over what to say is also a

---

[79] The language of following, common to the teachings of Jesus, is used here as a "call to discipleship" (Achtemeier, *1 Peter*, 199).
[80] Martin Luther, *The Freedom of a Christian*, trans. Mark D. Tranvik (Minneapolis: Fortress, 2008), 80.

gift."[81] Finally, Jesus says that his disciples will be *delivered up* by those closest to them—family and friends (see Mt 10:17-22; Mk 13:9-12; Lk 21:12-16).

This pattern unfolds with the birth of the church. Saul ravaged the early Christians, *delivering up* men and women to prison (Acts 8:3; 22:4). James was killed by violent hands while Peter was *delivered over* to squads of soldiers (Acts 12:1-4). Paul himself was later *delivered* by his own people "into the hands of the Gentiles" (Acts 21:11; 28:17). Through all of this, the church bore witness to Christ. All the various ways in which Christ was *delivered up* are united in the eternal purposes of God, just as they are united by the consistent witness of the Holy Spirit in Scripture.[82] The first disciples recognized this unity and confessed that Herod, Pilate, the Gentiles, and the people of Israel all did whatever God's hand and his plan "had predestined to take place" (Acts 4:27-28). Based on this confession, they prayed that God would watch over them and give them boldness (Acts 4:29-31), trusting that if the various ways that Christ was *delivered up* are united in the eternal purposes of God, then the various ways his disciples are *delivered up* will also be united in those eternal purposes.

Returning to Paul and Barnabas, this instance of disciples being *delivered up* (Acts 15:26) is unique within the context of the Gospels and Acts because it says that the disciples *delivered* themselves *up*, not that they were *delivered up* by others.[83] In fulfillment of Christ's words, Paul and Barnabas are certainly *delivered over* by others (Mk 13:9). They are opposed, contradicted, reviled, persecuted, and driven out. They face all the normal dangers of this world as well: sicknesses, snakes, and stormy seas (2 Tim 4:20; Acts 28:3; 27:14). Paul and Barnabas were apostles who "*risked* their lives" in particular ways and in accordance with Christ's specific calling on their lives. Yet, as Paul makes clear, all Christians are called to *deliver up* their lives for the sake of Christ, walking in love, "as Christ loved us and *gave* himself *up* for us" (Eph 5:2). The act of devotion for which Paul and Barnabas were so highly commended by the church in Jerusalem is an act that all Christians are called to perform *coram Deo*, whatever form it may take *coram mundo*.

---

[81]Hovey, *To Share in the Body*, 143.
[82]On the unity of God's will in all things, see Calvin, *Institutes*, I.18.3-4, pp. 232-37.
[83]The other instances in the New Testament that speak of people delivering up themselves are 1 Cor 13:3, "If I deliver up my body to be burned, but have not love, I gain nothing," and Eph 4:19, "They have . . . given themselves up to sensuality" (cf. Rom 1:24-28).

When Christ's disciples *deliver up* their lives for the sake of his name, that *delivering up* is realized by means of all the turbulences of history, with its natural disasters, seemingly random events, political upheavals, processes of creation, and accidents. When risks become reality, the life of discipleship is therefore not diminished but advanced. Discipleship "takes form as human history with shape and duration."[84] Whatever the sharp edges may be in the shape that it takes, however long it drags on or abruptly it finishes, when disciples *deliver up* their lives for the name of Christ, they are uniting their wills with the unified will of God, and that is exactly God's will for them in Christ (Jn 17:21).

Therefore, Webster is correct in describing discipleship as the "enactment of that which is decreed by God." It is first enacted by Christ, who has "once for all replaced our corruption and disobedience by his pure embrace of the Father's will; as substitute, representative and head of the human race, he has achieved our rescue and done what our ruined humanity cannot do: he has rendered obedience to God." Christ's call of obedience, his call for us to follow him, is a life-giving call. It gives life at the beginning, in order to start on the road of discipleship, and it gives life along the way, in order to continue on that road. Webster explains: "The human venture of obedient discipleship, both in its beginning and in its continuation, is wholly enclosed by one fact: Jesus Christ is in our place." Ziegler makes a similar point, saying that "the form and substance of discipleship is entirely derivative of the identity and saving work of the living Lord Jesus Christ." When Christ calls disciples, he does so presently, as the living Lord, "eloquent in the power of the Spirit to announce with effect the forgiveness and sovereign claim of God."[85] He does not call them to reenact what he has done in their own strength, as if he were dead and gone and his legacy lives on only through the endeavors of others. He is with them.

LIFE, DEATH, AND THE PURSUIT OF SAFETY

Discipleship is not a retreat from danger but a pursuit of life, an answer to a call toward eternal life. There is an aspect of discipleship that could be called a retreat from danger, but only if we move away from the categories

---

[84]Webster, "Discipleship and Obedience," 11.
[85]Webster, "Discipleship and Obedience," 5-11; Ziegler, "Discipleship," 178.

of danger and harm as understood within the contemporary pursuit of safety and toward the theological category of mortification, "the abandonment of what has already been disqualified, judged and set aside by the call of Jesus to new life."[86] Discipleship is a sustained movement toward the end that God has for us in Christ, the relation of "one's identity to a determination that exists beyond oneself without excluding oneself." That determination is transformation and redemption, participation in "the new body God is creating through the salvation of the world in Christ."[87] It is "the perfection of the creature," that is, "the creature coming to be itself, without restriction, complete in fellowship with God."[88]

Christ presents the first step of that life-giving movement as death—the denial of the self, the bearing of one's cross, the loss of life (Mk 8:34-35). When Christ calls us, Bonhoeffer says, "his call leads us to death." He "summons us away from our attachments to this world."[89] It is important to consider why Christ's call to life includes an initial and ongoing call to death, the daily taking up of one's cross. In order to "take hold of that which is truly life" (1 Tim 6:19), we have to let go of that which is uncertain, deceptive, and deadly. We have married ourselves to such things, but death is release "from the law of marriage" (Rom 7:2). When Christ calls us to lay down our lives, he is calling us away from those things that lead to death. He is calling us to retreat from the dangers of self-will, self-delusion, and cheap temptations, whatever entices us with life and safety but brings death and destruction.

Christ's aim for his disciples is life. He calls them to lay aside those things that entangle them so that they are free to live. It is the "freedom of self-denial given in faith," and it stands in opposition to "the world of self-assertion."[90] The modern world asserts itself against the life of discipleship and the ethical implications of self-denial because, as Brock says, "the belief that one has heard God fosters certainty and banishes the fear of men." Brock says that late-modern humanity, in the face of such certainty, "prefers

---

[86]Webster, "Discipleship and Obedience," 16.
[87]Hovey, *To Share in the Body*, 23.
[88]Webster, "Discipleship and Obedience," 16.
[89]Bonhoeffer, *Discipleship*, 87.
[90]Wolf, *Sozialethik*, 157. "Der im Glauben geschenkten Freiheit der Selbstverleugnung. Diese Freiheit der Selbstverleugnung ist der Ausdruck für die Spannung, in der der Christenmensch sich zur Welt der Selbstbehauptung befindet."

the safer language of decision making and planning," language that does not appeal to divine authority and in so doing, presumably, cuts itself off from all criticism.[91] O'Donovan recognizes this modern concern as well, saying that the church should uphold the truth "definitely but modestly," and "respectful of the eschatological 'not yet,'" that will surely purify our comprehension of the truth. Yet, he expresses concern about "the late-modern idea of a public truth" that is established through assertion by a "society that prides itself on 'knowing the science,'" but is incapable of acknowledging "that the fear of the Lord was the beginning of wisdom."[92] The secular objection to the divine call of Christ, because it is divine, falls flat. The language of decision making and planning divinizes itself and asserts its own authority that its disciples, in turn, would prefer not to be questioned.

I have entered briefly back into critical dialogue with the contemporary pursuit of safety here because of Christ's simple point that you cannot serve two masters (Mt 6:24). When safety is master, the claim that something is not safe becomes an ethical trump card, a means of cutting off thoughtful deliberation on how to live with others and before God in this world full of dangers. The goal to which Christ calls his disciples is not the fickle safety that our world so intensely pursues, but freedom and life in fellowship with him. Discipleship is a pursuit of wholeness and life marked by inexpressible freedom because that wholeness and life have already been secured by the one who "loved us and gave himself up for us" (Eph 5:2).

The freedom that Christ bestows on his disciples often invokes trepidation. A storm at sea makes us "afraid," but encountering the one who commands the wind and the waves fills us "with great fear" (Mk 4:39-41). In the face of the grace of God, we often fall victim to the temptation: "Throw yourself down from here, for it is written, 'He will command his angels concerning you, to guard you'" (Lk 4:9-10). We wonder, "Are we to continue in sin that grace may abound?" (Rom 6:1). But this is a small, self-interested question. It is timidity, motivated by attachment to those things that Christ calls us to separate from, another version of the question, "How far can I go before I get in trouble?" In Luther's idiom, those who ask such questions remember that "insofar as a Christian is free, no works are necessary," while

---

[91]Brock, *Christian Ethics*, 173.
[92]O'Donovan, *Finding and Seeking*, 110-11.

conveniently forgetting that "insofar as a Christian is a servant, all kinds of works are done."[93] Christ sets us free to walk in obedience, to bear one another's burdens in love, to bear witness to the crucified Christ as Lord. This freedom is not license to walk away from God or the ends for which he created us, but to walk with him and in fulfillment of those ends. Christ's call of discipleship is "the outworking of the eternal divine purpose."[94] The shape of that purpose is set forth in Scripture, which presents Christ "as an example, whose pattern we ought to express in our life."[95] Christ reveals God as our Father and calls us to show ourselves his children.

When safety is subjected to Christ's call of discipleship, it is seen in its proper light as a creational good that the Christian is free to enjoy with thankfulness to God and therefore also as something that the Christian is free to let go of in pursuit of Christ. As a creational good, physical safety is given by God to be enjoyed in its own right and to be used in service of God and others. More importantly, though, when safety is subjected to Christ's call of discipleship, life itself—that which we are trying to keep safe—is seen in its proper light as a gift from God, something to be joyfully devoted to the sake of Christ, something to be laid down in order to be received back from God, something that closes and shrivels and shrinks when we seek to save it, something that evades our attempts at anxious preservation, but overflows with abundance when poured out sacrificially and spent generously. If we think past safety as an activity in itself to what we truly hope to get from it—wholeness, freedom, and a favorable path through this world—we find that Christ offers all of that and more in fellowship with him. He does not promise a cheap and easy life, free from pain or struggle, but one in which all that we lose for his sake is returned to us in abundance. Eternal life awaits us in the age to come, but Jesus also has good things in this life for those who lose their lives for his sake (Mk 10:29-30).

---

[93]Luther, *The Freedom of a Christian*, 71.
[94]Webster, "Discipleship and Calling," 143.
[95]Calvin, *Institutes*, III.6.3, p. 686; see also Webster, "Discipleship and Obedience," 6.

TEN

Putting Safety in Its Place

Fear of danger is ten thousand times more terrifying than danger itself, when apparent to the eyes.

DANIEL DEFOE, *ROBINSON CRUSOE*

THERE IS AN OLD piece of advice for snowboarding or skiing through trees: Don't look at the trees, look at the spaces between them. Your body follows your eyes. If you focus on the tree trunks, you will find yourself heading toward them. If you focus on the open, white spaces between the trees, that is where you will go. The world's pursuit of safety is often nothing more than the avoidance of harm, a deliberate exercise in focusing on the trees and trying as hard as possible not to run into any of them. It is demanding and unrewarding. Christ calls his church to pursue him, to pursue life by way of the cross. Then life opens up before us. When we lose our lives for the sake of Christ, fears melt, dangers shrink down to size, and safety finds a rightfully subservient place in our lives.

At the beginning of this work, I said that I wanted to follow the tokens of safety to the fundamental conceptions that lie behind them and consider what is found in light of the lordship of Christ. I said that my task of developing a theology of safety was motivated by a series of historical and ethical questions that are raised by the prominent position safety occupies in our society. The historical questions had to do with understanding the current form and status of safety in the late-modern world: How is safety pursued? Why is it pursued in the ways that it is? Why does it have such an elevated moral status? The ethical questions had to do with the church's relationship to the pursuit of safety: How should the church engage with this pursuit? To what extent should the church affirm and participate in it? How should the church engage with the uncertainties of safety in this age in light of the certainty of safety in the age to come? How do we navigate between the pursuit of physical safety as a creational good and the need to relativize it in light of eternal salvation?

I also said that discussions about safety can easily go in various directions. It is a topic that tugs at our affections and resolve in perplexing ways. One of the reasons for developing a theology of safety is to find theological and biblical anchor points for those conversations, as well as the deliberations and decisions they involve—the important ways that safety shapes our lives. These anchor points are built on important themes that emerge from theological engagement with the contemporary pursuit of safety and faithful responses based on the teachings of Scripture.

Diminished Imaginaries

The first of these themes is the diminished imaginative or conceptual capacity for the spiritual realities of the world that is found in the contemporary pursuit of safety. It is not that the spiritual realities of the world have been removed or fundamentally changed, but that there have been major shifts in commonly shared perceptions of such realities, or what Taylor calls "social imaginaries."[1] In one sense, a social imaginary is social because it is shared by a society as a whole. According to Taylor, it is "the way we collectively imagine." In another sense, imaginaries are social because they have to do with how we imagine society, for example, "our social life in the contemporary Western world." In this latter sense, imaginaries are not just social. They are cosmic and natural as well: the ways we are able to think of or imagine the whole of the cosmos, the whole of nature. They include the ways people are able to imagine themselves in relation to each other and nature but also God and spiritual realities.

The historical development of the concept of risk and the contemporary pursuit of safety reveal some things about late-modern social imaginaries. They show that imaginations have been trained to look for safety within the

---

[1] Charles Taylor, *A Secular Age* (Cambridge, MA: Harvard University Press, 2007), 146-56.

processes of history and nature, apart from God or one's relationship to him. Imaginations have also been trained to disassociate the processes of history and nature from the actions and purposes of God, and especially from the influences of spiritual powers. If the effect of modernity has been "to banish the divine, it has even more emphatically been to banish the demonic," and, we may add, the angelic. The church's imaginative and conceptual capacities have also diminished in this area. To some degree, the church has "lost the sense of a cosmic battle which emerges visibly on to the stage of world events."[2]

Everyday conceptions of safety in the late-modern world generally correspond with this diminished imaginative capacity. Physical, temporal safety has an elevated moral status because all that is good, enjoyable, true, and valuable must fit within the constraints of physicality and temporality. Physical, temporal safety is pursued by physical, temporal means because such approaches are conducive to this diminished understanding of life. The problem with such a pursuit is not the desire for physical, temporal safety nor the use of probabilities, technologies, or procedures in themselves. The problem is that safety is pursued apart from the lordship of Christ. It is pursued based on fear of the destruction of the body but without regard for the destruction of the soul (Mt 10:28). It is pursued to the exclusion of the spiritual realities of humankind as created by God, fallen in sin, and redeemed by Christ. This exclusion is more than a mere strategic error, as if there are spiritual resources to be harnessed for the pursuit of safety in just the same way as material resources. That is the logic of magic, not the Christian faith. Instead, the exclusion of spiritual realities is indicative of eyes, heads, and hearts bent down toward this earth, striving for daily bread but not asking for it from our Father in heaven, fighting to avoid and overcome risks but not looking to him to be delivered from evil.

In a world obsessed with safety, something like Wittgenstein's absolute safety as a state of mind, a philosophical ideal, lies at the murky edges of present social imaginaries. How much more is this the case for Jesus' prayerful deliverance from evil or the apostle Paul's renewal of the inner self in the face of outward harm (Mt 6:13; 2 Cor 4:16)? The contrast between the

---

[2]James S. Stewart, "On a Neglected Emphasis in New Testament Theology," *Scottish Journal of Theology* 4, no. 3 (1951): 292-93; see also Paul G. Hiebert, "The Flaw of the Excluded Middle," *Missiology: An International Review* 10 (January 1982).

outer and inner self corresponds to the contrasts between the present and coming age, the visible and invisible, the transient and eternal, the earthly and heavenly.[3] Safety has an elevated moral status and is pursued in the ways that it is because it is imagined exclusively in the present age, the realm of the visible, transient, and earthly. Paul's contrast between the outer and inner self also corresponds to his contrasts between being afflicted but not crushed, perplexed but not despairing, persecuted but not forsaken, and struck down but not destroyed (2 Cor 4:8-9). The diminished imaginary of our age cannot account for this. Within an imaginary that is constrained by the horizons of time and materiality, with no room for the strength and comfort of the Holy Spirit, no resurrection power, and no age to come, there is little room for such paradoxes. There is even less room, if any, for paradoxes that extend beyond the hard line of death.

Present social imaginaries are deficient because of the absence of spiritual realities. This does not mean that any acknowledgment or conception of spiritual realities will be sufficient. Throughout this work, I have sought to present a biblical understanding of humanity's condition in this world before God. Such a world is neither the cosmic sandbox of superstition, where the course of history is a game of the gods, nor is it the cosmic machine of naturalism, where the course of history is an impersonal combination of determinism and randomness. Instead, it is a world in which all things, "visible and invisible," were created through and for Christ (Col 1:16), a world under the sovereign rule of God, made to know and worship him, a world in which we will have troubles, but one in which we may "take heart" because Christ has overcome it (Jn 16:33).

In response to this diminished imaginary, Christians ought to open their eyes, minds, and hearts to all the textures and layers of the cosmos that God brought into existence by the power of his word. This is not an invitation to speculation, superstition, or magic, but to see the world through biblical eyes. There is an enemy prowling about, seeking whom he may devour. There are angels sent to minister to God's children. The events that take place in time and space are neither fully contained within themselves nor merely the aftereffects of what happens elsewhere on some inaccessible spiritual

---

[3]Paul Barnett, *The Second Epistle to the Corinthians*, NICNT (Grand Rapids, MI: Eerdmans, 1997), 246.

plane. History is driven by things visible and invisible, by things good and evil.

With eyes opened to the fulness of God's creation, the most immediate and practical step that Christians can take in relation to the dangers of this world is to pray, lifting up their eyes, heads, and hearts toward their heavenly Father. He knows our days. He has numbered the hairs on our heads. Nothing escapes his view. The cosmos is embattled, but prayer is a mighty weapon. It is the means by which God casts light into darkness and brings peace into chaos. In prayer, the wisdom of serpents and the innocence of doves come together. It is where tension between the foresight of the ant and the faith of the lilies and ravens is put at ease, where conflicts between childlike faith and prudent maturity disappear. In prayer, we make our needs known to God. He listens. He acts.

Harm is caused in this world through the collisions of moving bodies, but the movements of those bodies depend on more than mechanics. The ways that people anticipate the future, engage with technology, and act in this world are often shaped by faithlessness, immorality, and sin. The pursuit of safety is often excessive and idolatrous, motivated by desires of the flesh such as greed, pride, and envy. Think of how often people harm others because of envy. Think of how often people put others in danger because of greed. Think of how often people put themselves in danger because of pride. Think of how much safer it is to be generous, humble, and kind.

With a widened imaginary, the realities of the spiritual realm come into focus, as do the power of prayer and the dangers of sin. A widened imaginary also draws attention to things that are valuable but are not strictly physical, things like the welfare of nations, the bonds of families, the beauty of the world, and the consolation of moral clarity. These are good things that should be part of our shared conceptualizations of life. They should be taken into account as we consider what we give up in pursuit of safety and what we are seeking to keep safe.

Existential Consistencies

The second theme is the consistency of human existence. I presented the first theme—a diminished imaginative capacity for spiritual realities—negatively, as a deficiency in human conceptions of safety. Within the contemporary pursuit of safety, such a view of the world is presented positively, as a step forward in relation to the dangers of this world. By discarding the dead weight of religious beliefs, humanity could observe, anticipate, and manipulate movements and objects in this world directly. Sources of danger could be met head on, without the complications of invisible spiritual forces or the constrictions of immovable moral orders.

Important historical developments coincided with these conceptual changes. The modern rise of the probabilistic approach to the future, the technological approach to creation, and the procedural approach to action set a new direction for the pursuit of safety. For some, these developments signaled fundamental and lasting change to human existence. Humanity could now master risk. Humanity no longer needed to suffer helplessly but could do something about the dangers it faced. The course of history could be anticipated. The forces of nature could be controlled. Actions could produce their intended results. Safety became an attainable state of being. The right tools were now, at long last, available. The right frame of mind was also at hand. It was no longer necessary to believe that the future was in the hands of higher spiritual beings, nor to feel helpless before the powers of nature. The future, creation, and action were controllable. A strand of pessimism accompanied this optimism. There was concern that humanity's ability to exert such power signaled a change to human existence that is, or could be, harmful. However it was viewed, though, claims could be found within the contemporary pursuit of safety that there has been a fundamental and lasting change to humanity's condition in this world.

The claim that humanity's condition in this world has changed depends on an accurate assessment of the starting condition, but descriptions of humanity's earlier state of existence are often exaggerated or incomplete. Premodern humanity is presented as incapable of assessing risks, unaware that something can be done in the face of danger, and helpless before the forces of nature. The dangers of the premodern world, as supposedly perceived by premodern humanity, are chaotic, irrational, and disorienting. Certainly, there are elements of truth to these claims, but life in the premodern world entailed more than misery, suffering, and death. Some forces were controllable and controlled. Some situations were well-ordered and enjoyable. Some risks were adequately assessed. Some dangers were successfully navigated.

The claim that humanity's condition has fundamentally changed also depends on an accurate assessment of its current condition. Yet even today, there are risks that humanity is incapable of assessing rightly, forces that people are helpless to stop, dangers that are beyond human control. The modern world itself often seems chaotic, irrational, and disorienting. Similarities between the premodern and late-modern world were acknowledged with the late-modern understanding of risk, but those similarities were located at the level of perception. The late-modern world sometimes seems as if it were beyond human control, but in reality, according to these claims, it is not.

There are good reasons to deny the claim that humanity's condition in this world has undergone a fundamental and lasting change and to affirm a consistency of human existence in relation to the dangers of this world. Late-modern humanity has not mastered risk. Safety is not now attainable as an abiding condition in this world. I have been critical of such apocalyptic claims. Instead, I sought to establish a basic theological understanding of the pursuit of safety that adequately accounts for humanity's standing in this world in relation to creation, fall, redemption, and consummation. This world is created, sustained, and loved by God, yet it is a world in which dark powers are in destructive rebellion against him. It is a world in which humanity is enslaved to sin and folly apart from the redemptive work of Christ. Even those who have been redeemed by Christ have the abiding presence of sin and folly at work within them and the world in which they live.

The consistency of humanity's condition in this world full of dangers can therefore be affirmed within certain theological boundaries. Descriptions of this condition are applicable to the present age, not to Eden nor to the age to come. Humanity's condition is grounded in certain creational realities. God created a world with other beings and forces besides humanity. Humanity lives in relation to and in dependence on these other things. Humanity has certain capacities in relation to creation, but those capacities have limitations. Humanity's condition in this world, including its relation to other things and the capacities that it exercises, has been affected by sin. Sin and evil are humanity's fundamental sources of danger, whatever era or stage in history. Humanity's condition in this world is also shaped by the grace of God and his redemptive work in Christ. God extends mercy to those who are in danger. He offers wisdom to those seeking to do what is right. He forgives those who have erred. His work of redemption in Christ points forward to the age to come, and that is when there will be a significant and lasting change to the human condition: "He will wipe away every tear from their eyes, and death shall be no more, neither shall there be mourning, nor crying, nor pain anymore, for the former things have passed away" (Rev 21:4).

In response to the existential consistencies of this age, Christians can acknowledge that historical developments do not lead to fundamental and lasting change in humanity's condition in this world. We will not return to Eden nor advance to heaven by the work of our own hands. Death and danger are part of life in this world. Historical developments may be better or worse, but danger will never be categorically tamed. We can work to make the world better but remain hopeful when it becomes worse. Either way, we can step forward. We can obey God, understanding that there will be risks, without being overly optimistic or pessimistic.

After the destructive power of the flood, God promised Noah, "While the earth remains, seedtime and harvest, cold and heat, summer and winter, day and night, shall not cease" (Gen 8:22). The constancies of human existence help to keep us sober minded about our place in this world, but they also bring relative stability to our lives. The repeated patterns of time shape our anticipations of the future. The constancies of physical properties and forces are the basis of our technological endeavors. The regularity of harvest following seedtime gives significance to our actions. It is hard not to take it for granted that the sun will rise tomorrow or that your car will stop when you hit the brake pedal. But each moment, each sunrise, each safe journey is a gift from him. When we contemplate the level of stability in this world, we ought to be thankful to God for his wisdom, care, and provision.

It is wrong to take the consistencies of our existence in this world for granted. It is also wrong to hold them too tightly. The relative stability of this world is a gift from God, but Satan would use it to lull us into complacency. He would have us be so consumed with the matters of this life that we cannot let them go. One of the consistencies of life in this age is that it is occasionally inconsistent. These inconsistencies are also gifts from God. He promised bountiful harvests, political stability, health, and long life to Israel when they walked in obedience to the law. He used wars, famines, captivities, and catastrophes to call them back to repentance. Jesus used the shock of the political deaths of some Galileans and the accidental deaths at the tower of Siloam to warn people of the need to repent, lest they perish (Lk 13:1-5). We ought to view seemingly random or meaningless accidents as reminders of the coming judgment and our need for the mercy of God.

Inherent Limitations

The final theme that emerges in this development of a Christian theology of safety is safety's inherent limitations. Humanity's condition in this world remains fundamentally consistent, yet the scientific, mathematical, and technological developments that accompanied the advent of modernity have been momentous. Those who look to the past, to the far side of modernity, see a world with no conception of molecules, cells, or bacteria, a world without electricity, self-powered machinery, or quantifiable probabilities. When they look to this side of modernity, they see a world of antibiotics and genetic analysis, a world of light bulbs, cars, and airplanes, a world of surgeries, airbags, radars, and cameras. They greet these developments with exuberant praise because they allow humanity to do and see things it had not done or seen before.

Such accomplishments are impressive, yet they carry within themselves the same basic limitations that are inherent in all human endeavors. These accomplishments are highlighted in the contemporary pursuit of safety. The limitations, constraints, and failures of such means of relating to this world are also revealed. The contemporary pursuit of safety fails to live up to its own demands. By its own standards, it has shortcomings and limitations that ought to be apparent and accepted by those who engage in it. Humanity's probabilistic, technological, and procedural extensions of itself can only go so far. They can only bear so much weight. They have hidden costs and unanticipated outcomes. But humanity's hope in its own progress obscures what ought to be obvious.

The limitations of the contemporary pursuit of safety extend beyond its own logic. There are also instances in which it fails to live up to the commands of Scripture, instances where it neglects the promises and wisdom of Scripture, instances where it ignores the teachings of Scripture regarding humanity's condition in this world before God. In light of safety's inherent limitations, theological and ethical reflection presents a number of tensions that are resistant to formulaic or simplistic resolutions. There is tension between passivity and activity in response to probable harm. There is tension between the costs and benefits of technological devices. There is tension between the goodness of safety and other good things that are forgone for its sake. There is tension between the successes and failures of our efforts to be safe.

Safety's inherent limitations reflect humanity's condition before God. Humanity's capacities to anticipate the future, manipulate creation, and direct its own actions cannot be considered hypothetically or theologically in the abstract. They can only be considered theologically in light of reality as portrayed at the cross. From the darkness of the cross, these human capacities are seen to be undeniable instruments of wickedness and death. When faced with the person of Christ, humanity's assessment of him was that he would be a risk, a danger, a threat. He was a risk to human righteousness because he ate with tax collectors and sinners. He was a danger to the people because he misled the nation (Lk 23:2). He was a threat to earthly empires because he claimed to be king. This assessment of Christ was met with expediency and action. The religious leaders, the political leaders, and the crowds of people conspired together to identify and manage the risk, and humanity's pursuit of safety at that exact and all-important moment could not have been more of a failure. Even the disciples fled from their Savior as if they were running for their lives.

From the light that shines out through the darkness of the cross, though, these human capacities are instruments of worship and service. Mary preemptively anointed Jesus for burial (Jn 12:3-7). Joseph of Arimathea met the practical, albeit temporary, need to prepare Christ's body and lay it in a tomb (Lk 23:50-56). The disciples had rightly anticipated that Christ "was the one to redeem Israel" (Lk 24:21). On the road to Emmaus, he showed them that their hope was accurate, though incomplete. Their hearts burned within them. Hearts burning with joy because of hope surpassed—in Christ, God orients our lives toward such a goal.

In response to the inherent limitations of the world's pursuit of safety, Christians ought to be decidedly under-impressed with both the dangers that so frequently cause alarm and the tools of safety that rise up to bring security and comfort. We ought to be under-impressed with the dangers of this world because we know the extent of their power. We know that joy, hope, and courage rise up in the midst of danger. We know that God uses trouble and harm to draw us into closer fellowship with each other. We know that a sparrow does not fall to the ground apart from God's knowledge. We ought to be under-impressed with the tools of safety for a number of reasons. To begin, many of them are foolish, ridiculous, and useless. Many others would be unnecessary to those who pursue a relationship with the physical world around them that is grounded in patience, diligence, self-control, and prudence. We ought to develop those qualities. We also ought to be under-impressed with the tools of safety because even if they are useful and effective, even if they perform exactly as designed and save our lives, we owe them no allegiance. They have no allegiance to us. We owe our allegiance to Christ. Our affections should be captured by him and nothing less. Anything else will disappoint.

As we follow Christ in delivering up our lives to God, he will give specific shape to our days. His calling on our life and the circumstances in which we find ourselves will help us determine which means of safety to make use of, and which ones to let go of for his sake.

In light of safety's diminished view of life, false hopes, and inherent limitations, it is unworthy of the pursuit that it has been given in our age. This world is in the hands of the sovereign God who cares for his children. Inasmuch as the church is secure in its relationship to him, it can look to the future with hope. It can acknowledge discrepancies between anticipations of the future and the actual future without allowing those discrepancies to become anxieties. It can receive safety as a gift from God without clinging to it as an idol. It can stand amid the perplexities of life without falling into despair. Christ's disciples are not called to pursue their own safety, but, in love for God and neighbor, to lay down their lives at the foot of the cross, the one true token of safety.

Bibliography

Abraham, William J. *Divine Agency and Divine Action: Exploring and Evaluating the Debate*. Vol. 1. New York: Oxford University Press, 2018.

"Accidents are Logical." *Safety Engineering* 37 (March 1919): 143.

Achtemeier, Paul J. *1 Peter*. Edited by Eldon Jay Epp. Hermeneia. Minneapolis: Fortress, 1996.

Aldrich, Mark. *Safety First: Technology, Labor, and Business in the Building of American Work Safety, 1870–1939*. Baltimore: Johns Hopkins University Press, 1997.

Althaus, Catherine E. "A Disciplinary Perspective on the Epistemological Status of Risk." *Risk Analysis* 25 (2015): 567-88.

Alvarez, Maria, and John Hyman. "Agents and Their Actions." *Philosophy* 73 (April 1998): 219-45.

Angehrn, Emil. "Das Streben nach Sicherheit: Ein Politisch-Metaphysisches Problem." In *Zur Philosophie Der Gefühle*, edited by G. Lohmann and H. Fink-Eitel, 218-43. Frankfurt am Main: Suhrkamp, 1993.

Aquinas, Thomas. *ST*. 61 vols. London: Eyre & Spottiswoode, 1964–1981.

———. *Super epistolas S. Pauli*. Turin: Marietti, 1953.

Aradau, Claudia, and Rens Van Munster. "Governing Terrorism Through Risk: Taking Precautions, (un)Knowing the Future." *European Journal of International Relations* 13 (March 2007): 89-115.

Aristotle. *Nicomachean Ethics*. Translated by Roger Crisp. Cambridge: Cambridge University Press, 2000.

Arnobius. *The Case Against the Pagans*. Translated by George E. McCracken. ACW 7. Westminster, MD: Newman, 1942.

Askonas, Jon. "How Tech Utopia Fostered Tyranny." *The New Atlantis* 57 (Winter 2019): 3-13.

Athanasius. *Defense of His Flight*. In *St. Athanasius: Select Works and Letters*, edited by Archibald Robertson, translated by Archibald Robertson, 4:254-65. NPNF[2]. New York: Christian Literature, 1892.

Atkinson, Gary M. "Theological History of Catholic Teaching on Prolonging Life." In *Moral Responsibility in Prolonging Life Decisions*, edited by Donald G. McCarthy and Albert S. Moraczewski, 95-115. St. Louis: Pope John Center, 1981.

Augustine. *City of God*. Translated by George E. McCracken. Vol. 1. LCL 411. Cambridge, MA: Harvard University Press, 1957.

———. *Confessions*. Translated by Carolyn J.-B. Hammond. Vol. 2. LCL 27. Cambridge, MA: Harvard University Press, 2016.

———. *Expositions of the Psalms*. Edited by John E. Rotelle. Translated by Maria Boulding. Vol. 2. WSA III/16. New York: New City, 2001.

———. *Homily VII on the First Epistle of John*. In *St. Augustine: Homilies on the Gospel of John; Homilies on the First Epistle of John; Soliloquies*, edited by Joseph H. Myers, translated by H. Brown. NPNF[1] 7. Buffalo: Christian Literature, 1888; reprint, Grand Rapids, MI: Eerdmans, 1978.

———. *On Christian Doctrine*. Translated by J. F. Shaw. Mineola, NY: Dover, 2009.

———. *The Retractations*. Translated by M. Inez Bogan. FC 60. Washington, DC: Catholic University of America Press, 1968.

———. *Saint Augustine Letters*. Translated by Wilfrid Parsons. Vol. 2. FC 18. New York: Fathers of the Church, Inc., 1953.

———. *A Treatise Concerning Man's Perfection in Righteousness*. In *St. Augustine: Anti-Pelagian Writings*, translated by Peter Holmes and Robert Ernest Wallis. NPNF[1] 5. Buffalo: Christian Literature, 1891; reprint, Grand Rapids, MI: Eerdmans, 1975.

Bacon, Francis. *The New Organon*. Edited by Lisa Jardine and Michael Silverthorne. Cambridge: Cambridge University Press, 2000.

Bailey, Lloyd R. *Leviticus-Numbers*. Smyth & Helwys Bible Commentary. Macon, GA: Smyth & Helwys, 2005.

Bailey, Michael D. *Fearful Spirits, Reasoned Follies: The Boundaries of Superstition in Late Medieval Europe*. Ithaca, NY: Cornell University Press, 2013.

Barbour, Ian. *Ethics in an Age of Technology*. San Francisco: Harper, 1993.

Barnett, Paul. *The Second Epistle to the Corinthians*. NICNT. Grand Rapids, MI: Eerdmans, 1997.

Barth, Karl. *Church Dogmatics: The Doctrine of Creation*. Vol. III/1. Edited by G. W. Bromiley and T. F. Torrance. Translated by J. W. Edwards, O. Bussey, and Harold Knight. Edinburgh: T&T Clark, 1958.

Bauer, W., F. W. Danker, W. F. Arndt, and F. W. Gingrich. *Greek-English Lexicon of the New Testament and Other Early Christian Literature*. 3rd ed. Chicago: University of Chicago Press, 1999.

Bauman, Zygmunt. *Community: Seeking Safety in an Insecure World*. Malden, MA: Blackwell, 2001.

Bavinck, Herman. *Reformed Dogmatics*. Edited by John Bolt. Translated by John Vriend. 4 vols. Grand Rapids, MI: Baker Academic, 2008.

Beck, Matthias, and Beth Kewell. *Risk: A Study of Its Origins, History and Politics*. Hackensack, NJ: World Scientific, 2014.

Beck, Ulrich. *Risk Society: Towards a New Modernity*. Translated by Mark Ritter. London: Sage, 1992.

———. *World at Risk*. Translated by Ciaran Cronin. Malden, MA: Polity, 2008.

Becker, Hollee Actman. "Science Says Kids Shouldn't Cross a Busy Street Solo Until They're 14." *Parents*, April 21, 2017.

Benjamin, Walter. *Illuminations*. Translated by Harry Zohn. New York: Schocken, 1968.

Bernstein, Peter L. *Against the Gods: The Remarkable Story of Risk*. New York: Wiley, 1998.

Berthiaume, Lee. "Woman Arrested for Not Using Métro Escalator Handrail Awarded $20,000." *Montreal Gazette*, November 30, 2019. https://montrealgazette.com/news/local-news/woman-arrested-for-not-using-metro-escalator-handrail-awarded-20000.

Bianchi, Francesco. "Qohelet 10,8-11 or The Misfortunes of Wisdom." *Bibbia e Oriente* 40 (Spring 1998): 111-17.

Bock, Darrell L. *Acts*. BECNT. Grand Rapids, MI: Baker Academic, 2007.

———. *Luke 9:51–24:53*. BECNT. Grand Rapids, MI: Baker Academic, 1994.

———. *Mark*. New Cambridge Bible Commentary. New York: Cambridge University Press, 2015.

Boholm, Åsa. *Anthropology and Risk*. New York: Routledge, 2015.

Boholm, Max, Niklas Möller, and Sven Ove Hansson. "The Concepts of Risk, Safety, and Security: Applications in Everyday Language." *Risk Analysis: An International Journal* 36 (February 2016): 320-38.

Bonhoeffer, Dietrich. *Creation and Fall*. Edited by John W. De Gruchy. Translated by Douglas Stephen Bax. Dietrich Bonhoeffer Works 3. Minneapolis: Fortress, 2004.

———. *Discipleship*. Edited by Geffrey B. Kelly and John D. Godsey. Translated by Barbara Green and Reinhard Krauss. Dietrich Bonhoeffer Works 4. Minneapolis: Fortress, 2003.

———. *Ethics*. Edited by Clifford J. Green. Translated by Reinhard Krauss, Charles C. West, and Douglas W. Stott. Dietrich Bonhoeffer Works 6. Minneapolis: Fortress, 2005.

Brock, Brian. *Christian Ethics in a Technological Age*. Grand Rapids, MI: Eerdmans, 2010.

———. "Culture as Flight from God: Jacques Ellul on the Fall." In *Fall Narratives: An Interdisciplinary Perspective*, edited by Zohar Hadromi-Allouche and Áine Larkin, 37-47. New York: Routledge, 2017.

Brown, F., S. R. Driver, and C. A. Briggs. *A Hebrew and English Lexicon of the Old Testament with an Appendix Containing the Biblical Aramaic*. Oxford: Clarendon, 1977.

Bultmann, Rudolf. "Jesus Christ and Mythology." In *Rudolf Bultmann: Interpreting Faith for the Modern Era*, edited by Roger A. Johnson, 288-328. Minneapolis: Fortress, 1991.

Burns, Robert. "To a Mouse: On turning her up in her Nest with the Plough, November 1785." In *The Complete Poems and Songs of Robert Burns*, 83-84. Glasgow: Gresham, 2015.

Byrne, Edmund F. *Probability and Opinion: A Study in the Medieval Presuppositions of Post-Medieval Theories of Probabilities*. The Hague: Martinus Nijhoff, 1968.

Caesarius of Arles. *Sermons*. Translated by Mary Magdaleine Mueller. Vol. 2. FC 47. Washington, DC: Catholic University of America Press, 1964.

Calvin, John. *Commentary on the Book of the Prophet Isaiah*. Translated by William Pringle. Vol. 4. Edinburgh: Calvin Translation Society, 1850.

———. *Institutes of the Christian Religion*. Edited by John T. McNeill. Translated by Ford Lewis Battles. LCC 20-21. Philadelphia: Westminster John Knox, 1960.

———. *2 Corinthians and Timothy, Titus & Philemon*. Edited by David W. Torrance and Thomas F. Torrance. Translated by T. A. Smail. Calvin's Commentaries. Grand Rapids, MI: Eerdmans, 1996.

———. *Supplementa Calviniana*. Edited by Hanns Ruckert. Neukirchen, Germany, 1961.

Campbell, Robert W. "President's Address." *Proceedings of the NSC Third Annual Safety Congress*, 7-15, Chicago: NSC, 1914.

"Canada's Medical Assistance in Dying (MAID) Law." *Department of Justice Canada*, June 19, 2023. www.justice.gc.ca/eng/cj-jp/ad-am/bk-di.html.

Chaney, Lucian W. "Federal Session." *Proceedings of the First Co-operative Safety Congress*, 7 Princeton, NJ: Princeton University Press, 1912.

Childs, Brevard S. *Biblical Theology of the Old and New Testaments: Theological Reflection on the Christian Bible*. Minneapolis: Fortress, 1992.

———. *Old Testament Theology in a Canonical Context*. Philadelphia: Fortress, 1989.

Christoffersen, Mikkel Gabriel. "Living with Risk and Danger: Studies in Interdisciplinary Systematic Theology." PhD diss., Copenhagen: University of Copenhagen, 2017.

Clancy, Gerard. "Foreword to Our Strategic Plan." In *Strategic Plan 2017–2022: Building the Foundation for a Great Story and a Greater Commitment at the University of Tulsa*. Accessed January 11, 2020. https://utulsa.edu/about/strategic-plan/.

Cockerill, Gareth Lee. *The Epistle to the Hebrews*. NICNT. Grand Rapids, MI: Eerdmans, 2012.

Collins, Raymond F. *Second Corinthians*. Paideia. Grand Rapids, MI: Baker Academic, 2013.

Conze, Eckart. "Sicherheit als Kultur. Überlegungen zu einer 'modernen Politikgeschichte' der Bundesrepublik Deutschland." *Vierteljahrshefte für Zeitgeschichte* 53 (2005): 357-80.

Core Elements for Vision Zero Communities. Vision Zero Network, November 2018.

Cortez, Marc. *ReSourcing Theological Anthropology: A Constructive Account of Humanity in the Light of Christ*. Grand Rapids, MI: Zondervan, 2018.

Corvellec, Hervé. "The Narrative Structure of Risk Accounts." *Risk Management* 13 (2011): 101-21.

Covello, Vincent T., and Jeryl Mumpower. "Risk Analysis and Risk Management: An Historical Perspective." *Risk Analysis: An International Journal* 5 (1985): 103-20.

Craigie, Peter C. *The Book of Deuteronomy*. NICOT. Grand Rapids, MI: Eerdmans, 1976.

Craver, Carl, and James Tabery. "Mechanisms in Science." In *The Stanford Encyclopedia of Philosophy*, edited by Edward N. Zalta, November 18, 2015. https://plato.stanford.edu/archives/sum2019/entries/science-mechanisms/.

Crittenden, Phyllis, ed. *Supervisors' Safety Manual*. 10th ed. Itasca, IL: NSC, 2009.

Cronin, Daniel A. *Ordinary and Extraordinary Means of Conserving Life*. Philadelphia: The National Catholic Bioethics Center, 2011.

Daase, Christopher. "Die Historisierung der Sicherheit. Anmerkungen zur historischen Sicherheitsforschung aus politikwissenschaftlicher Sicht." *Geschichte und Gesellschaft* 38 (2012): 387-405.

Dahlberg, Rasmus. "The Roots of Risk: A Brief Conceptual History of Predictability, Uncertainty and Statistics." Copenhagen Center for Disaster Research, Copenhagen, October 7, 2016.

Dattani, Saloni, Fiona Spooner, Hannah Ritchie, and Max Roser. "Child and Infant Mortality." *Our World in Data*, 2023. https://ourworldindata.org/child-mortality.

David, F. N. *Games, Gods, and Gambling: A History of Probability and Statistical Ideas*. Mineola, NY: Dover, 1998.

Dekker, Sidney. *The Safety Anarchist*. New York: Routledge, 2018.

Dekker, Sidney, Robert Long, and Jean-Luc Wybo. "Zero Vision and a Western Salvation Narrative." *Safety Science* 88 (October 2016): 219-23.

"Delaware and Hudson Coal Mine Disaster." *Safety Engineering* 37 (June 1919): 286.

Dillon, Richard J. "Ravens, Lilies, and the Kingdom of God (Matthew 6:25-33/Luke 12:22-31)." *CBQ* 53 (October 1991): 605-27.

Doolittle, William H. "Condition of Factories of Our Members." *Proceedings of the First Co-operative Safety Congress*, 276. Princeton, NJ: Princeton University Press, 1912.

Douglas, Mary. *Purity and Danger: An Analysis of the Concepts of Pollution and Taboo*. New York: Routledge, 2003.

Douglas, Mary, and Aaron Wildavsky. *Risk and Culture: An Essay on the Selection of Technological and Environmental Dangers*. Berkeley: University of California Press, 1983.

Ecola, Liisa, Steven W. Popper, Richard Silberglitt, and Laura Fraade-Blanar. *The Road to Zero: A Vision for Achieving Zero Roadway Deaths by 2050*. Santa Monica, CA: NSC and the RAND Corporation, 2018.

Edwards, A. W. F. *Pascal's Arithmetical Triangle: The Story of a Mathematical Idea*. Baltimore: Johns Hopkins University Press, 2002.

Edwards, Jonathan. "Sinners in the Hands of an Angry God." In *The Sermons of Jonathan Edwards: A Reader*, edited by Wilson H. Kimnach, Kenneth P. Minkema, and Douglas A. Sweeney, 49-65. New Haven, CT: Yale University Press, 1999.

"Elevator Accidents in Detroit." *Safety Engineering* 38 (August 1919): 96.

Elliot, David Michael. "Institutionalizing Inequality: The Physical Criterion of Assisted Suicide." *Christian Bioethics* 24, no. 1 (April 2018): 17-37.

Ellul, Jacques. *The Meaning of the City*. Translated by Dennis Pardee. Grand Rapids, MI: Eerdmans, 1970.

———. *On Freedom, Love, and Power*. Translated by Willem H. Vanderburg. Expanded. Toronto: University of Toronto Press, 2015.

———. *The Presence of the Kingdom*. Translated by Olive Wyon. New York: Seabury, 1967.

———. "Technique and the Opening Chapters of Genesis." In *Theology and Technology: Essays in Christian Analysis and Exegesis*, edited by Carl Mitcham and Jim Grote, 123-37. Lanham, MD: University Press of America, 1984.

———. *The Technological Society*. Translated by John Wilkinson. New York: Vintage, 1964.

"FARS Data Tables." National Highway Traffic Safety Administration. *Fatality Analysis Reporting System (FARS) Encyclopedia*, 2017. www-fars.nhtsa.dot.gov/Main/index.aspx.

Ferré, Frederick. *Philosophy of Technology*. Englewood Cliffs, NJ: Prentice Hall, 1988.

Ferrier, Kathleen, Leah Shahum, Louisa Gag, and Stacy Thompson. *Vision, Strategies, Action: Guidelines for an Effective Vision Zero Action Plan*. Vision Zero Network, December 2017.

Fonda, George T. "Response to 'Efficiency in Safety Work.'" *Proceedings of the NSC Third Annual Safety Congress*, 134-37 Chicago: NSC, 1914.

Forster, H. W. "Practical Results Obtained in Safety." *Proceedings of the NSC Third Annual Safety Congress*, 137-42 Chicago: NSC, 1914.

Foucault, Michel. *Discipline and Punish: The Birth of the Prison*. Translated by Alan Sheridan. 2nd ed. New York: Vintage, 1995.

Fredericks, Daniel C., and Daniel J. Estes. *Ecclesiastes and the Song of Songs*. Apollos Old Testament Commentary. Downers Grove, IL: IVP Academic, 2010.

Galilei, Galileo. *Discoveries and Opinions of Galileo*. Translated by Stillman Drake. 24th ed. New York: Anchor, 1957.

Giddens, Anthony. *The Consequences of Modernity*. Stanford, CA: Stanford University Press, 1991.

Gigerenzer, Gerd. *Calculated Risks: How to Know When Numbers Deceive You*. New York: Simon & Schuster, 2002.

Gillespie, Michael Allen. *The Theological Origins of Modernity*. Chicago: University of Chicago Press, 2009.

Ginzburg, Carlo. *The Cheese and the Worms: The Cosmos of a Sixteenth-Century Miller*. Translated by John Tedeschi and Anne C. Tedeschi. Baltimore: Johns Hopkins University Press, 1992.

Graunt, John. *Natural and Political Observations Made upon the Bills of Mortality*. Edited by Walter F. Willcox. Baltimore: Johns Hopkins University Press, 1939.

Green, Gene. *Jude and 2 Peter*. BECNT. Grand Rapids, MI: Baker Academic, 2008.

Green, Joel B. *The Gospel of Luke*. NICNT. Grand Rapids, MI: Eerdmans, 1997.

Gregersen, Niels Henrik. "Faith in a World of Risks: A Trinitarian Theology of Risk-Taking." In *For All People: Global Theologies in Context*, edited by Else Marie Wiberg Pedersen, Holger Lam, and Peter Lodberg, 214-33. Grand Rapids, MI: Eerdmans, 2002.

———. "Risk and Religion: Toward a Theology of Risk Taking." *Zygon* 38 (2003): 355-76.

Gregory of Nyssa. *Contra Eunomium I: An English Translation with Supporting Studies*. Edited by Miguel Brugarolas. Boston: Brill, 2018.

Gros, Frédéric. *Le Principe Sécurité*. Paris: Gallimard, 2012.

Gunkel, Hermann. *Genesis: übersetzt und erklärt*. Göttingen: Vandenhoeck & Ruprecht, 1922.

Guttmacher Institute. "Induced Abortion Worldwide." March, 2018. www.guttmacher.org/fact-sheet/induced-abortion-worldwide-2018.

Hacking, Ian. *The Emergence of Probability: A Philosophical Study of Early Ideas about Probability, Induction and Statistical Inference*. 2nd ed. Cambridge: Cambridge University Press, 2006.

Hagan, Philip E., John F. Montgomery, and James T. O'Reilly, eds. *Accident Prevention Manual for Business & Industry: Administration & Programs*. 14th ed. Itasca, IL: NSC, 2009.

Hald, Anders. *A History of Probability and Statistics and Their Applications Before 1750*. New York: Wiley, 1990.

Hamilton, Victor P. *The Book of Genesis: Chapters 1–17*. NICOT. Grand Rapids, MI: Eerdmans, 1990.

———. "הָגָשׁ." In vol. 2 of *TWOT*, edited by R. L. Harris, G. L. Archer Jr., and B. K. Waltke, 904. Chicago: Moody Press, 1999.

Hansson, Sven Ove. *The Ethics of Risk: Ethical Analysis in an Uncertain World*. New York: Palgrave Macmillan, 2013.

Healy, Edwin F. *Moral Guidance*. Chicago: Loyola University Press, 1942.

Heidegger, Martin. *Being and Time*. Translated by Joan Stambaugh. Revised edition. New York: Suny, 2010.

———. "The Question Concerning Technology." In *The Question Concerning Technology and Other Essays*, translated by William Lovitt, 3-35. New York: Garland, 1977.

Helm, Paul. *The Providence of God*. Downers Grove, IL: IVP Academic, 1994.

Hidden, Anthony. *Investigation into the Clapham Junction Railway Accident*. London: Department of Transport, September 27, 1989.

Hiebert, Paul G. "The Flaw of the Excluded Middle." *Missiology: An International Review* 10 (January 1982): 35-47.

Hobbes, Thomas. *Leviathan*. Edited by Edwin Curley. Indianapolis: Hackett, 1994.

Honecker, Martin. "Sicherheit, Gewissheit, Geborgenheit: Suche nach Verlässlichem in einer verunsicherten Welt." *ZTK* 112 (2015): 229-53.

Hovey, Craig. *To Share in the Body: A Theology of Martyrdom for Today's Church*. Grand Rapids, MI: Brazos, 2008.

Hughes, J. Donald. *Environmental Problems of the Greeks and Romans: Ecology in the Ancient Mediterranean*. 2nd ed. Baltimore: Johns Hopkins University Press, 2014.

Ide, William S. "Safety Education in Textile Industry." *Safety Engineering* 38 (November 1919): 284-85.

Ireland Road Safety Authority. "Going to School: A Parent's Guide to Getting Children to School Safely," 2017. www.rsa.ie/docs/default-source/road-safety/r3-education/rsa-going-to-school-guide.pdf.

Irenaeus. "Selections from the Work *Against Heresies*." In *Early Christian Fathers*, edited by Cyril C. Richardson, translated by Edward Rochie Hardy, 358-97. LCC 1. Westminster, 1953.

Jacobs, Alan. "After Technopoly." *The New Atlantis* 58 (Spring 2019): 3-14.

Janowski, Bernd. "Die Tat kehrt zum Täter zurück: Offene Fragen im Umkreis des 'Tun-Ergehen-Zusammenhangs.'" *ZTK* 91 (1994): 247-71.

Jaskolla, Ludwig. "Der Mensch als 'homo faber'?: Überlegungen zur Philosophie der Technik." *Stimmen der Zeit* 233 (June 2015): 385-92.

Jenkins, Richard. "Disenchantment, Enchantment and Re-Enchantment: Max Weber at the Millennium." *Max Weber Studies* 1 (November 2000): 11-32.

Jenson, Robert W. *Systematic Theology*. Vol. 2. New York: Oxford University Press, 1999.

Johnson, Allan Chester, Paul Robinson Coleman-Norton, and Frank Card Bourne. "Law of Caesar on Municipalities." In *Ancient Roman Statutes: A Translation with Introduction, Commentary, Glossary, and Index*, 93-97. Austin: University of Texas Press, 1961.

Jones, John N. "'Think of the Lilies' and Prov 6:6-11." *HTR* 88 (January 1995): 175-77.

Josephson-Storm, Jason A. *The Myth of Disenchantment: Magic, Modernity, and the Birth of the Human Sciences*. Chicago: University of Chicago Press, 2017.

Kamppinen, Matti. "Playing Against Superior Beings in Religion, Technology and Economy." In *Religion, Economy, and Cooperation*, edited by Ilkka Pyysiainen, 83-98. Religion and Reason 49. Berlin: De Gruyter, 2010.

Karmel, Jonathan D. *Dying to Work: Death and Injury in the American Workplace*. Ithaca, NY: Cornell University Press, 2017.

Kaufmann, Franz-Xaver. *Sicherheit als soziologisches und sozialpolitisches Problem*. 2nd ed. Stuttgart: Enke, 1973.

Keener, Craig S. *1–2 Corinthians*. New Cambridge Bible Commentary. Cambridge: Cambridge University Press, 2005.

Kelly, Gerald. "The Duty of Using Artificial Means of Preserving Life." *Theological Studies* 11 (June 1950): 203-20.

Kemp, Martin. *Leonardo da Vinci: The Marvellous Works of Nature and Man*. Revised. Oxford: Oxford University Press, 2006.

Kennedy, D. R. "Efficiency in Safety Work." *Proceedings of the NSC Third Annual Safety Congress*, 129-34. Chicago: NSC, 1914.

Kierkegaard, Søren. *Purity of Heart: Is to Will One Thing*. Translated by Douglas V. Steere. New York: Fontana Books, 1961.

Kilner, John F., ed. *Why the Church Needs Bioethics: A Guide to Wise Engagement with Life's Challenges*. Grand Rapids, MI: Zondervan, 2011.

Klein, George L. *Zechariah*. NAC 21B. Nashville: B&H Academic, 2008.

Krüger, Thomas. *Qoheleth*. Edited by Klaus Baltzer. Translated by O. C. Dean Jr. Hermeneia. Minneapolis: Fortress, 2004.

La Mettrie, Julien Offray de. *L'Homme Machine*. Paris: Galerie D'Orléans, 1865.

"Lacquers, Shellacs, Enamels and Japans." *Safety Engineering* 38 (July 1919): 15-23.

Lane, William L. *Hebrews 1–8*. WBC 47A. Grand Rapids, MI: Zondervan, 2015.

———. *Hebrews 9–13*. WBC 47B. Grand Rapids, MI: Zondervan, 2015.

Laplace, Pierre-Simon. *A Philosophical Essay on Probabilities*. Translated by Frederick Wilson Truscott and Frederick Lincoln Emory. London: Chapman & Hall, 1902.

Latour, Bruno. *We Have Never Been Modern*. Translated by Catherine Porter. Cambridge, MA: Harvard University Press, 1993.

Lavoie, Jean-Jacques. "Ironie et ambiguïtés en Qohélet 10:8-11." *Studies in Religion* 41 (September 2012): 455-78.

Leroi-Gourhan, André. *Milieu et Techniques*. Paris: Albin Michel, 1973.

Lévy-Bruhl, Lucien. *Primitives and the Supernatural*. Translated by Lilian Ada Long Clare. New York: E. P. Dutton, 1935.

Lewis, C. S. *The Abolition of Man*. New York: HarperCollins, 2001.

Lloyd, Clive. *Next Generation Safety Leadership: From Compliance to Care*. Boca Raton, FL: CRC Press, 2020.

Lombard, Peter. *The Sentences, Book 2: On Creation*. Translated by Giulio Silano. Mediaeval Sources in Translation 43. Toronto: Pontifical Institute of Mediaeval Studies, 2008.

Long, D. Stephen. "Does God Have a Future? Theology and the 'Future' of God." In *Theology and the Future: Evangelical Assertions and Explorations*, edited by Trevor Cairney and David Ian Starling, 27-44. New York: T&T Clark, 2014.

Longman, Tremper. *The Book of Ecclesiastes*. NICOT. Grand Rapids, MI: Eerdmans, 1998.

———. *Proverbs*. Grand Rapids, MI: Baker Academic, 2006.

Louth, Andrew. *Maximus the Confessor*. New York: Routledge, 1996.

Lugo, Juan de. "De iustitia a iure." In *Disputationes scholasticae et morales*, VI: Paris, 1868.

Luhmann, Niklas. *Risk: A Sociological Theory*. Translated by Rhodes Barrett. New York: Routledge, 2017.

Lupton, Deborah. "Introduction: Risk and Sociocultural Theory." In *Risk and Sociocultural Theory: New Directions and Perspectives*, edited by Deborah Lupton, 1-11. Cambridge: Cambridge University Press, 2000.

———. *Risk*. 2nd ed. New York: Routledge, 2013.

Luther, Martin. "A Brief Explanation of the Ten Commandments, the Creed, and the Lord's Prayer." In *Works of Martin Luther: With Introductions and Notes*, edited by Lane Hall, 2:351-386. Philadelphia: A. J. Holman Company, 1915.

———. "Exposition of Psalm 127, for Christians at Riga in Livonia (1524)." In *The Christian in Society II*, edited by Walther I. Brandt, 317-38. LW 45. Philadelphia: Muhlenberg, 1962.

———. *The Freedom of a Christian*. Translated by Mark D. Tranvik. Minneapolis: Fortress, 2008.

———. "Larger Catechism." In *The Book of Concord: The Confessions of the Evangelical Lutheran Church*, edited by Robert Kolb and Timothy J. Wengert, translated by Charles P. Arand, 377-480. 2nd ed. Minneapolis: Fortress, 2000.

———. "On the Councils and the Church." In *Church and Ministry III*, edited by Eric W. Gritsch and Helmut T. Lehmann, 9-178. *LW* 41. Philadelphia: Fortress, 1966.

———. "Whether One May Flee from a Deadly Plague." In *Devotional Writings II*, edited by Gustav K. Weinke, 119-38. *LW* 43. Philadelphia: Fortress, 1968.

Mabee, Charles. "Biblical Hermeneutics and the Critique of Technology." In *Theology and Technology: Essays in Christian Analysis and Exegesis*, edited by Carl Mitcham and Jim Grote, 157-69. Lanham, MD: University Press of America, 1984.

Malthus, Thomas. *An Essay on the Principle of Population*. Mineola, NY: Dover, 2007.

Marcuse, Ludwig. *Das Märchen von der Sicherheit*. Zürich: Diogenes, 1981.

Marshall, I. Howard. *Acts: An Introduction and Commentary*. TNTC 5. Downers Grove, IL: IVP Academic, 1980.

Mathews, Kenneth. *Genesis 1–11:26*. NAC 1A. Nashville: B&H Academic, 1996.

Mawson, Michael G. "Suffering Christ's Call: Discipleship and the Cross." *The Bonhoeffer Legacy* 3, no. 2 (2015): 1-18.

Mbiti, John S. *African Religions and Philosophy*. 2nd ed. Portsmouth, NH: Heinemann, 1990.

McCall, Thomas H. *Against God and Nature: The Doctrine of Sin*. Wheaton, IL: Crossway, 2019.

McFarland, Ian A. "Original Sin." In *T&T Clark Companion to the Doctrine of Sin*, edited by Keith L. Johnson and David Lauber, 303-18. New York: T&T Clark, 2016.

Merton, Robert K. "The Matthew Effect in Science." *Science* 159 (1968): 56-63.

Mitcham, Carl, and Jim Grote, eds. *Theology and Technology: Essays in Christian Analysis and Exegesis*. Lanham, MD: University Press of America, 1984.

Mlodinow, Leonard. *The Drunkard's Walk: How Randomness Rules Our Lives*. New York: Pantheon, 2008.

Möller, Niklas, Sven Ove Hansson, and Martin Peterson. "Safety Is More Than the Antonym of Risk." *Journal of Applied Philosophy* 23 (November 2006): 419-32.

Moltmann, Jürgen. *The Crucified God*. Translated by R. A. Wilson and John Bowden. Minneapolis: Fortress, 2015.

Moo, Douglas J. *The Letter to the Romans*. 2nd ed. NICNT. Grand Rapids, MI: Eerdmans, 2018.

Muchembled, Robert. *Popular Culture and Elite Culture in France, 1400–1750*. Baton Rouge: Louisiana State University Press, 1985.

Muller, Richard A. *Dictionary of Latin and Greek Theological Terms: Drawn Principally from Protestant Scholastic Theology*. Grand Rapids, MI: Baker, 2006.

Münk, Hans J. "Technik, Technologie." In vol. 9 of *Lexikon für Theologie und Kirche*, edited by Walter Kasper, Konrad Baumgartner, Horst Bürkle, Klaus Ganzer, Karl Kertelge, Wilhelm Korff, and Peter Walter, 1310-11. Freiburg: Herder, 2000.

Musculus, Wolfgang. *In Mosis Genesim plenissimi Commentarii, in quibus veterum & recentiorum sententiae diligenter expenduntur*. Basil: Johann Herwagen, 1554.

National Center for Statistics and Analysis. *Pedestrians: 2014 Data*. Traffic Safety Facts Report No. DOT HS 812 270. Washington, DC: National Highway Traffic Safety Administration, May 2016.

Noldin, H., and A. Schmitt. *Summa Theologiae Moralis*. Vol. II. 27th ed. Innsbruck: Rauch, 1940.

O'Donovan, Oliver. *Finding and Seeking: Ethics as Theology, Volume 2*. Grand Rapids, MI: Eerdmans, 2014.

———. *Resurrection and Moral Order: An Outline for Evangelical Ethics*. 2nd ed. Grand Rapids, MI: Eerdmans, 1986.

———. *Self, World, and Time: Ethics as Theology, Volume 1, An Induction*. Grand Rapids, MI: Eerdmans, 2013.

Olofsson, Peter. *Probabilities: The Little Numbers That Rule Our Lives*. Hoboken, NJ: Wiley, 2007.

O'Neal, Elizabeth E., Yuanyuan Jiang, Lucas J. Franzen, Pooya Rahimian, Junghum Paul Yon, Joseph K. Kearney, and Jodie M. Plumert. "Changes in Perception–Action Tuning over Long Time Scales: How Children and Adults Perceive and Act on Dynamic Affordances when Crossing Roads." *Journal of Experimental Psychology: Human Perception and Performance* 44 (January 2018): 18-26.

Oppenheim, A. Leo. *Ancient Mesopotamia: Portrait of a Dead Civilization*. Revised edition. Chicago: University of Chicago Press, 1977.

Pacioli, Luca. *Summa de Arithmetica, Geometria, Proportioni, et Proportionalita*. Venice, 1494.

———. "Summa de Arithmetica Geometria Proportioni et Proportionalita: F. 197 R. and 198 V." Translated by Richard J. Pulskamp. Unpublished, 2009. https://citeseerx.ist.psu.edu/pdf/31cb02840db91b43d719c9cf94f38a328baf2f63.

Pannenberg, Wolfhart. *Systematic Theology*. Translated by Geoffrey W. Bromiley. Vol. 2. Grand Rapids, MI: Eerdmans, 1994.

Parsons, Mikeal C. *Acts*. Paideia. Grand Rapids, MI: Baker Academic, 2008.

"Past Seasons Estimated Influenza Disease Burden," Centers for Disease Control and Prevention, November 22, 2023, www.cdc.gov/flu/about/burden/past-seasons.html.

Percival, Henry R., ed. *The Seven Ecumenical Councils*. NPNF[2] 14. New York: Christian Literature, 1900.

Perdue, Leo G. *Proverbs*. Louisville, KY: John Knox, 2012.

Perrow, Charles. *Normal Accidents: Living with High-Risk Technologies*. Princeton, NJ: Princeton University Press, 1999.

Pinnock, Clark H., Richard Rice, John Sanders, William Hasker, and David Basinger. *The Openness of God: A Biblical Challenge to the Traditional Understanding of God*. Downers Grove, IL: InterVarsity Press, 1994.

Plato. *Apology*. Translated by Harold North Fowler. LCL 36. Cambridge, MA: Harvard University Press, 1914.

———. *Phaedrus*. Translated by Harold North Fowler. LCL 36. Cambridge, MA: Harvard University Press, 1914.

Pliny. *Natural History*. Translated by H. Rackham. Vol. 2. LCL 352. Cambridge, MA: Harvard University Press, 1952.

Polhill, John B. *Acts*. NAC 26. Nashville: B&H Academic, 1992.

Power, Michael. *The Risk Management of Everything*. London: Demos, 2004.

Poythress, Vern S. *Chance and the Sovereignty of God: A God-Centered Approach to Probability and Random Events*. Wheaton, IL: Crossway, 2014.

Pritz, Ray. *The Works of Their Hands: Man-made Things in the Bible*. New York: United Bible Societies, 2009.

Quetelet, Adolphe. *Sur L'Homme et Le Développement de Ses Facultés*. Vol. 2. Paris: Bachelier, Imprimeur-Libraire, 1835.

Rabinovitch, Nachum L. "Studies in the History of Probability and Statistics. XXII: Probability in the Talmud." *Biometrika* 56 (August 1969): 437-41.

Rammstedt, Otthein. "Risiko." In vol. 8 of *Historisches Wörterbuch der Philosophie*, edited by Joachim Ritter and Karlfried Gründer, 1045-55. Basel: Schwabe, 1992.

Rausch, Chester C. "The Safety Engineer—His Qualifications and Duties." *Safety Engineering* 38 (November 1919): 261-62, 297-302.

"Recent Fires and Their Lessons." *Safety Engineering* 37 (January 1919): 46-49.

"Recent Fires and Their Lessons." *Safety Engineering* 37 (March 1919): 148-52.

Reiterer, Friedrich V. "Arbeit I, Biblisch-theologisch." In vol. 1 of *Lexikon für Theologie und Kirche*, edited by Walter Kasper, Konrad Baumgartner, Horst Bürkle, Klaus Ganzer, Karl Kertelge, Wilhelm Korff, and Peter Walter, 917-18. Freiburg: Herder, 1993.

Reno, R. R. *Genesis*. Brazos Theological Commentary on the Bible. Grand Rapids, MI: Brazos, 2010.

Rispalje, P. O. "The Fourteen Points of the League of 'Safety Last.'" *Safety Engineering* 37 (April 1919): 192-93.

"Robert S. Payne." *The Weekly Nashville Union*. Nashville, January 6, 1847, sec. Obituary.

Roberts, J. C. "Safety Measures in the Rocky Mountain Mining District." *Proceedings of the First Co-operative Safety Congress*, 98-103. Princeton, NJ: Princeton University Press, 1912.

Robertson Ishii, Teresa, and Philip Atkins. "Essential vs. Accidental Properties." In *The Stanford Encyclopedia of Philosophy*, edited by Edward N. Zalta, October 26, 2020. https://plato.stanford.edu/archives/win2020/entries/essential-accidental/.

Rondet, Henri. "Arbeit II, Theologisch." In vol. 1 of *Lexikon für Theologie und Kirche*, edited by Josef Höfer and Karl Rahner, 803-5. Freiburg: Herder, 1957.

Rooker, Mark F. *Leviticus*. NAC 3A. Nashville: Broadman and Holman, 2000.

Rose, Nikolas. "The Politics of Life Itself." *Theory, Culture & Society* 18, no. 6 (2001): 1-30.

"Roundtable Discussion." *Proceedings of the NSC Third Annual Safety Congress*, 146-60, Chicago: NSC, 1914.

Ruskin, John. *Modern Painters*. Vol. 3. London: Routledge, 1856.

"Safety News and Comment." *Safety Engineering* 38 (September 1919): 161-65.

Sambursky, Samuel. "On the Possible and the Probable in Ancient Greece." In *Studies in the History of Statistics and Probability: A Series of Papers*, edited by Maurice G. Kendall and R. L. Plackett, 2:35-48. London: Griffin, 1970.

Sanders, John. *The God Who Risks: A Theology of Divine Providence*. 2nd ed. Downers Grove, IL: InterVarsity Press, 2007.

Sarton, George. "Preface to Volume XXIII of Isis (Quetelet)." *Isis* 23 (1935): 6-24.

Schlegel, Jean-Louis. "L'eschatologie et l'apocalypse dans l'histoire: un bilan controversé." *Esprit* 343 (March 2008): 88-103.

Schleiermacher, Friedrich. *Christian Faith*. Edited by Catherine L. Kelsey and Terrence N. Tice. Translated by Terrence N. Tice, Catherine L. Kelsey, and Edwina Lawler. 2 vols. Louisville, KY: Westminster John Knox, 2016.

Seow, C. L. *Ecclesiastes: A New Translation with Introduction and Commentary*. Anchor Bible Commentary. New York: Doubleday, 1997.

Seuft, Charles M. "Take a Think of Safety." *Safety Engineering* 37 (March 1919): 136.

Silver, Nate. *The Signal and the Noise: Why So Many Predictions Fail—But Some Don't*. New York: Penguin, 2015.

Skenazy, Lenore. *Free-Range Kids: How to Raise Safe, Self-Reliant Children*. San Francisco: Jossey-Bass, 2010.

Sklar, Jay. "Sin and Atonement: Lessons from the Pentateuch." *BBR* 22 (2012): 467-91.

Smith, Walter Chalmers. "Immortal, Invisible." In *The Hymnal for Worship and Celebration*, edited by Tom Fettke and Ken Barker, 25. Waco, TX: Word Music, 1986.

Sonderegger, Katherine. "Creation." In *Mapping Modern Theology: A Thematic and Historical Introduction*, edited by Kelly M. Kapic and Bruce L. McCormack. Grand Rapids, MI: Baker, 2012.

Sophocles. *Electra*. In *Sophocles*, edited and translated by Hugh Lloyd-Jones, vol. 1. LCL 20. Cambridge, MA: Harvard University Press, 1994.

Spiegel, James S. "Does God Take Risks?" In *God Under Fire: Modern Scholarship Reinvents God*, edited by Douglas S. Huffman and Eric L. Johnson, 187-210. Grand Rapids, MI: Zondervan, 2002.

Stewart, James S. "On a Neglected Emphasis in New Testament Theology," *Scottish Journal of Theology* 4, no. 3 (1951): 292-301.

Stigler, Stephen M. *Statistics on the Table: The History of Statistical Concepts and Methods*. Cambridge, MA: Harvard University Press, 2002.

Stivers, Richard. *Technology as Magic: The Triumph of the Irrational*. New York: Continuum, 2001.

Sylva, Dennis D. "The Meaning and Function of Acts 7:46-50." *JBL* 106, no. 2 (1987): 261-75.

Taleb, Nassim Nicholas. *The Black Swan: The Impact of the Highly Improbable*. New York: Random House, 2007.

Tarbell, Ida M. "Effects of Safety on the Community." *Proceedings of the NSC Third Annual Safety Congress*, 119-25. Chicago: NSC, 1914.

Taylor, Charles. *A Secular Age*. Cambridge, MA: Harvard University Press, 2007.
Tertullian. *Apology*. Translated by T. R. Glover and Gerald H. Rendall. LCL 250. Cambridge, MA: Harvard University Press, 1931.
———. *A Treatise on the Soul*. Edited by Alexander Roberts, James Donaldson, and A. Cleveland Coxe. Translated by Peter Holmes. ANF 3. Buffalo: Christian Literature, 1885; reprint, Grand Rapids, MI: Eerdmans, 1963.
Tetens, Holm. "Der Glaube an die Wissenschaften und der methodische Atheismus: Zur religiösen Dialektik der wissenschaftlich-technischen Zivilisation." *NZSTR* 55 (2013): 271-83.
Thiel, Winfried. "Das 'Werk der Hände.'" In *Houses Full of All Good Things: Essays in Memory of Timo Veijola*, edited by Juha Pakkala and Martti Nissinen, 201-23. Göttingen: Vandenhoeck & Ruprecht, 2008.
Thompson, John L. *Genesis 1–11*. Reformation Commentary on Scripture. Downers Grove, IL: IVP Academic, 2014.
Thucydides. *History of the Peloponnesian War*. Translated by C. F. Smith. Vol. 1. LCL 108. Cambridge, MA: Harvard University Press, 1919.
"Time for 'Human Engineering.'" *Safety Engineering* 37 (May 1919): 255.
Todhunter, Isaac. *A History of Probability from the Time of Pascal to That of Laplace*. Cambridge: Macmillan, 1865.
Toly, Noah. "Risk and Responsibility in Global Environmental Governance." *Christian Scholar's Review* 42 (Spring 2013): 261-75.
Toppo, Greg. "Solar Eclipse Fears Prompt Schools to Cancel Class, Keep Kids Inside." *USA TODAY*, August 17, 2017. www.usatoday.com/story/news/2017/08/17/teachers-schools-eclipse-fears-drive-kids-inside/578050001/.
Tracy, Thomas F. "Creation, Providence and Quantum Chance." In *Philosophy, Science and Divine Action*, edited by F. LeRon Shults, Nancey Murphy, and Robert John Russell, 227-62. Philosophical Studies in Science and Religion 1. Leiden: Brill, 2009.
Treier, Daniel J. *Proverbs & Ecclesiastes*. Brazos Theological Commentary on the Bible. Grand Rapids, MI: Brazos, 2011.
Twaalfhoven, Simon F. M., and Willem J. Kortleven. "The Corporate Quest for Zero Accidents: A Case Study into the Response to Safety Transgressions in the Industrial Sector." *Safety Science* 86 (July 2016): 57-68.
Verkerk, Maarten J., Jan Hoogland, Jan van der Stoep, and Marc J. de Vries. *Philosophy of Technology: An Introduction for Technology and Business Students*. New York: Routledge, 2016.

Vitoria, Francisco de. "De temperantia." In *Relectiones theologicae*, relectio IX. Lyon, 1587.

Vitruvius. *On Architecture*. Translated by Frank Granger. Vol. 2. LCL 280. Cambridge, MA: Harvard University Press, 1934.

Waltke, Bruce K. *The Book of Proverbs, Chapters 1–15*. NICOT. Grand Rapids, MI: Eerdmans, 2004.

Walton, Steve. "An Introduction to the Mechanical Arts in the Middle Ages." Paper presented at the International Congress for Medieval Studies, Kalamazoo, MI, May 1993, AVISTA, revised 2014.

Waterfield, Robin, trans. *The First Philosophers: The Presocratics and Sophists*. Oxford World's Classics. New York: Oxford University Press, 2000.

Watt, Jeffrey R. "Calvin on Suicide." *Church History* 66, no. 3 (1997): 463–76.

Webster, John. "Discipleship and Calling." *SBET* 23 (Autumn 2005): 133–47.

———. "Discipleship and Obedience." *SBET* 24 (Spring 2006): 4–18.

Wenham, Gordon J. *The Book of Leviticus*. NICOT. Grand Rapids, MI: Eerdmans, 1979.

Westermann, Claus. *Genesis 1–11: A Commentary*. Translated by John J. Scullion. London: SPCK, 1984.

Winch, Peter. "Can a Good Man Be Harmed?" *Proceedings of the Aristotelian Society* 66 (1965): 55–70.

Wittgenstein, Ludwig. "A Lecture on Ethics." *The Philosophical Review* 74 (1965): 3–12.

Wolf, Ernst. *Sozialethik: Theologische Grundfragen*. Göttingen: Vandenhoeck & Ruprecht, 1975.

Wolff, Hans Walter. *Anthropology of the Old Testament*. Translated by Margaret Kohl. London: SCM Press, 1981.

Wolters, Albert M. *Creation Regained: Biblical Basics for a Reformational Worldview*. Grand Rapids, MI: Eerdmans, 1985.

Wolterstorff, Nicholas. *Art in Action: Towards a Christian Aesthetic*. Grand Rapids, MI: Eerdmans, 1980.

Wright, Christopher J. H. *Old Testament Ethics for the People of God*. Downers Grove, IL: InterVarsity Press, 2013.

Yocum, John. "A Cry of Dereliction? Reconsidering a Recent Theological Commonplace." *IJST* 7 (January 2005): 72–80.

Ziegler, Philip. "Discipleship." In *Sanctified by Grace: A Theology of the Christian Life*, edited by Kent Eilers and Kyle C. Strobel, 173–86. New York: T&T Clark, 2014.

Zwetsloot, Gerard I. J. M., Markku Aaltonen, Jean-Luc Wybo, Jorma Saari, Pete Kines, and Rik Op De Beeck. "The Case for Research into the Zero Accident Vision." *Safety Science* 58 (October 2013): 41-48.

Zwetsloot, Gerard I. J. M., Pete Kines, Jean-Luc Wybo, Riikka Ruotsala, Linda Drupsteen, and Robert A. Bezemer. "Zero Accident Vision Based Strategies in Organisations: Innovative Perspectives." *Safety Science* 91 (January 2017): 260-68.

General Index

abortion, 53
abuse, 28, 32
accidents, 4, 9, 18, 28, 45, 50, 55-56, 68, 70, 108, 112-13, 130, 134, 175, 178-98, 201-3, 206-16, 222, 247, 259
action, 7, 11, 17-18, 20, 28, 32, 46-48, 52-53, 67-68, 75, 79, 96, 108, 111, 113, 115-17, 124-25, 127, 139, 142, 164, 174-76, 183-85, 191-92, 195-96, 199-206, 209-11, 215-17, 234, 236, 239, 243-44, 253, 256, 258, 260
age
    coming, 116, 122, 127, 149, 163, 170, 223, 225, 228-30, 242, 250, 252, 254, 257-58
    present, 19, 116-17, 122, 150, 162-63, 170, 198, 215, 225, 228-30, 235, 242, 252, 254, 257-58,
agency, agents, 17, 28, 45-46, 52, 61-62, 75, 113-14, 116, 147, 164, 175, 195
angels, 4, 38, 45, 47-48, 60-63, 65, 87, 95, 126, 129, 141, 229, 236, 249, 254
animals, 28, 37, 42, 47-48, 50, 79, 153, 155, 159, 215, 246
anticipate, anticipation, 4, 12, 15, 17-18, 27-28, 30, 52, 57, 92, 96-98, 113-14, 116-23, 125-27, 130, 175, 203-4, 210, 221, 241, 255-61
anxiety, anxious(ness), 4, 17, 19, 30, 51, 118, 124-26, 128, 134, 178-79, 204, 215, 222, 234, 245, 250, 261
Aquinas, Thomas, 33-34, 101, 164-67, 171-72, 241
Aristotle, 34, 48, 101
art(s), 132, 148
    mechanical, 58
    practical, 132-33
artificial (as opposed to natural), 102, 129, 133-34, 139, 168-69, 181
Augustine, 64, 94, 96-97, 140, 167
Bayes, Thomas, 105-6

behavior, 8, 17, 19-21, 29, 32, 39, 42, 69, 71, 75, 76, 81, 93, 102, 107, 111, 120, 176, 192, 200, 202, 208-9, 234-35
behaviorism, 199
body, bodies, 19, 24-25, 31-33, 68, 122, 124, 145, 165, 167, 198-201, 205, 210, 225, 241, 243, 245, 248, 251, 253
Bonhoeffer, Dietrich, 114, 119, 227-29, 232, 236, 241
Brock, Brian, 156, 198-201, 211, 232, 248
calculations, calculative rationality, 7, 42, 44, 63, 70, 74, 78, 91, 94, 97-108, 127, 130, 170, 172, 176, 189-90, 238-40
Calvin, John, 12, 27, 34, 65, 118, 120, 145, 166-67, 178, 185, 216, 225, 241, 244
cancer, 4, 55-56, 108, 128
car seats, 134
carelessness, 12, 28, 120, 180, 184, 187, 189, 194, 197, 206, 208-9, 212-13, 216
certainty, 14, 44, 93, 98, 100-102, 105, 107, 116, 127, 166, 168, 176, 204, 213, 240, 248, 252
chance, 8-9, 26, 29, 44, 69, 100-102, 106, 128, 138, 178, 183, 196, 214
chaos, chaotic, 7, 12, 28, 80-81, 138, 150, 255-57
children, 3-5, 8-9, 12-13, 21-22, 26-27, 48, 53, 55, 73, 81, 100, 103, 109-10, 111-15, 127, 130, 134, 182, 184, 234
Christian life, 18, 162, 223-24, 226, 228-29, 231, 233, 235
church, 8-11, 13, 15, 17, 32, 92, 112, 129, 149, 161, 196-97, 216, 224, 226, 229-40
Code of Hammurabi, 42, 44
control, 12, 17, 21, 25-26, 30, 49-50, 63, 70-71, 85-87, 92-93, 97, 111, 133-37, 141, 163, 173, 175-76, 180, 183, 199-202, 204, 206, 208-9, 227, 256-57
Covid-19, 6, 8, 11, 163-64, 169, 196
craftsman(ship), 132, 156, 160, 207-8

crashes, 4, 7, 9, 26, 28, 30, 56, 73-74, 188, 197
creation mandate, 153-54, 156
cross of Christ, 10, 18, 33, 94-95, 110, 119, 152, 171, 205, 216, 223-26, 227-31, 234-35, 237, 239, 240-41, 248, 251, 260-61
cry of dereliction, 94
death, 19, 23, 33-34, 67, 87, 94-95, 103, 110, 112, 115, 121, 128, 132, 149, 160, 163, 165-66, 170, 173, 177-79, 185, 188-89, 192, 194-97, 205-6, 211, 215-16, 222-23, 229, 232, 236-37, 243-45, 248, 254, 256, 258, 260
decisions, decision-making, 11, 52, 70, 101, 108, 113, 128, 198, 210, 223, 249
gods, 16, 46-53, 56-59, 61-64, 68, 72, 76, 79-81, 83-86, 136, 146-47, 149, 226, 228, 237, 254
deliver up, 18, 238-39, 242-47
demons, demonic, 45-48, 61-63, 80, 87, 136, 237, 253
demythologize, 60, 62-64, 103
Descartes, René, 20, 67-68
discipleship, 18-19, 221-41, 247-50
disease, 6, 15, 25-26, 44, 48, 51, 53, 71, 74, 139, 179, 192, 196
disembedding, 60-61, 63, 103
disenchantment, 47, 57-58, 60-63, 65, 72, 103
dominion, 12, 130, 153-56, 160
economics, economy, 44, 50, 57-58, 61, 69, 71, 75, 79, 106, 181-83
Eden, Garden of, 14, 61, 153, 155-57, 190, 257-58
efficient, efficiency, 53, 109, 155, 157-58, 181-83, 198-99, 201-2
Ellul, Jacques, 136, 154-58, 201-2
eternal, eternity, 12, 24, 46, 67-68, 91-93, 95, 122-23, 145-46, 149, 151, 162, 165, 175, 178, 224-26, 228-30, 235, 237, 246-47, 250, 252, 254
faith, 13, 15, 24, 57-59, 116, 119, 125, 127-28, 140, 145, 173, 195, 224, 241, 245, 248, 255
Fall, the, 155-56, 159, 190-91
fatalities, fatality rates, 104, 107, 109, 115, 177, 187, 196-97, 208-11
fate, 52, 58, 80, 87, 178-80, 196
fire, 7, 26, 80, 98-99, 161, 169, 195, 235
flesh, the, 13, 145, 147-48, 190, 241, 255
flourishing, 33, 49, 57, 79, 154, 162, 177
food, 10, 25, 75, 78, 83, 118, 121, 123-27, 133, 150, 153-55, 164-65, 168, 174, 177-78, 234
foolproof, 203, 217
forecast, 38, 42, 100, 104, 106-8, 114-15, 239
forgiveness, 18, 186-87, 189, 192, 194, 197-98, 215-17, 223, 247, 258

Foucault, Michel, 76, 82, 200-201
freedom, 9, 13, 18, 66, 72, 106-7, 123-24, 127-28, 131, 139, 149, 155, 158, 162, 171, 173, 179, 186, 189, 191, 202, 209, 211, 223, 232, 248-50
gambling, 44-45, 99-100
God's fatherly care, 11, 94-95, 122-24, 129, 150, 152, 179, 205-6, 222, 234, 237, 243-44, 253, 255
gods, 16, 46-53, 56-59, 61-64, 68, 72, 76, 79-81, 83-86, 136, 146-47, 149, 226, 228, 237, 254
guns, 28, 200
healing, 4, 27-28, 34, 47, 123, 139, 166, 168, 192, 237
health, healthy, 25, 28, 32-33, 48-49, 51, 163-64, 180-81, 192, 221, 245, 258
Hobbes, Thomas, 65, 67-68
hope, 4, 11-12, 18, 24, 34, 41, 50, 71-72, 110, 115-18, 122-23, 131, 134, 138, 141-42, 144, 148-49, 158-62, 165, 168-69, 172-73, 192, 198, 210, 216-17, 225, 239, 241, 250, 259-61
idolatry, idols, 12, 17, 64, 122, 135, 142-44, 146-48, 157, 159-61, 173, 175, 191, 214, 222, 230, 233, 237, 255, 261
industry, industrialization, 9-10, 14, 23, 38, 56-57, 70-71, 78, 80, 83, 86, 106, 110, 123, 126, 136, 180-81, 183, 184-85, 187-89, 197-99, 201-3, 208-11, 222
injuries, injury rates, 25, 28, 56, 109-10, 115, 179-84, 187, 208-9, 211, 213
insurance, 44, 51, 69, 72
judgment of God, 12, 24, 95, 116-17, 119-22, 152, 161-62, 170, 176, 178, 227, 235
labor, 56, 121-22, 124-27, 203, 211-12, 222, 230
Laplace's demon, 102, 106-7, 183
law of God, 15, 18, 32, 42, 138, 142, 147, 151, 186, 191-93, 195-97, 204-5, 211, 245, 258
laws of nature, 52, 56, 60, 64, 65, 67-68, 74, 85
love
 of God, 24, 123, 155-58, 237, 243-46
 for God, 33, 114, 155, 165-66, 170-71, 261
 for neighbor, 10, 112, 114, 161, 185, 195, 197, 216, 224, 232-33, 235-37, 244-46, 250
 for one's own life, 33-34, 162, 164-65, 171, 229, 241-42
Luther, Martin, 48, 68, 126, 185-86, 226, 226, 245, 249
machinery, machines, 70-71, 79, 133, 135, 155, 190, 192, 200-202, 207, 209-10, 259
magic, 46, 49, 51, 57, 62, 66, 80, 215, 253-54
martyrdom, 10, 230, 245
mathematics, 42, 44-45, 57, 62, 82, 84, 97-101, 118, 259

General Index

mechanics, mechanism, mechanistic, 20-21, 44, 49, 51-52, 58, 60, 68, 84, 103-4, 106, 180, 199-202, 211, 255
medical, medicine, 43-44, 53, 71, 75, 106, 128, 133, 163-64, 168-70
missions, 10-11, 223, 230, 233, 238-40
moral theology, 164, 193
mortality, 103, 177, 189, 192
  infant, 53, 55, 103
murder, 28, 55, 94, 113, 185-86, 193, 195, 216
National Safety Council, 30, 180-82
O'Donovan, Oliver, 115-17, 140, 161, 193, 195, 231, 244, 249
open theism (theologies of risk), 15, 92-93
pedestrians, 5, 42, 109-11
Pelagianism, 190-91
persecution, 10, 186, 228, 235-36, 238-39, 246, 254
plague, 48, 56, 103
prayer, 38, 46, 50, 58, 95, 141, 144, 149, 161, 186, 236, 246, 253, 255
predictability, 58-59, 62, 76, 80, 85, 92, 98, 104, 106-8, 115, 120, 134, 181, 202, 209, 213, 228
predictions, 17, 91, 105-7, 116, 127-28, 131, 176
probability, theory of, 44-45, 52, 59, 62, 97-99, 101, 106, 113, 130
promises, 11, 21, 92, 131, 194, 215
  of God, 17, 19, 95-96, 116-17, 128, 142-43, 147-48, 259
providence, providential, 15, 34, 65, 93, 138, 176, 192, 241
prudence, prudential, 18, 38, 70, 111, 115, 118, 127-28, 203-6, 211, 216-17, 222, 229-30, 236, 255, 261
randomness, 59, 93, 103-5, 107, 111, 113, 178, 183, 196, 247, 259
resurrection, 121, 145, 149, 216, 223, 225, 229, 231, 235, 254
retribution, 120, 152, 212-14
risk society, 23, 75-78
sacrifice, 46, 50, 68, 86, 112, 145, 148, 197, 205-6, 216
safety first, 123, 181, 183, 202-3
school shootings, 4, 111, 127
security, 13, 16, 28-29, 49-51, 74, 104, 123-25, 155-56, 228, 261

sickness, 51, 53, 103, 173, 177, 246
signs, 5-7, 38-39, 76, 96, 98-99, 103, 118-20, 125-27, 145, 147, 195
sin, 12, 33, 96, 118, 138, 152, 154, 156, 160, 176, 177, 186, 188, 190-98, 211, 216, 234, 253, 255, 257
social imaginaries, 87, 252-55
Socrates, 23, 43, 101
spirits, spiritual powers, 11-12, 16, 18, 28, 45-49, 58, 62-63, 79, 86-87, 126, 133, 252-56
statistics, 20, 43, 53, 102-6, 109-11, 181, 239
streets, roads, 6-7, 32, 41-42, 73, 85, 109-10, 112-13, 115, 117, 127, 188, 247, 260
suffering, 19, 23, 30-31, 47, 50-51, 109, 111, 120, 134, 163, 177, 179, 189, 192, 197-98, 202, 205, 213, 225, 231, 237-38, 240, 245, 256
  of Christ, 94, 241, 243, 245
suicide, 163-67, 171
symbols, 6, 11, 18, 47, 75-76, 121, 212, 234
Taylor, Charles, 46, 84, 87, 200, 252
technique, 154-58, 201
techniques, 38, 45, 53, 111, 182, 198, 200
tower of Siloam, 46, 259
traffic, 5, 24, 41, 51, 72, 104, 109, 114, 117, 134, 188
unintentional harm/sin, 28-29, 84, 176, 179, 184, 186, 189, 193-97, 211, 215
violence, 10, 26, 32, 50, 53, 55, 111, 117, 134, 156-57
walking to school/crossing streets, 12-13, 79, 110, 113-15, 127-28
war, 4, 28, 43, 50, 53, 56, 77, 113, 135, 181
wealth, riches, 76, 78, 82, 108, 122, 124, 222, 227, 230
wholeness, 4, 18, 27, 32-33, 53, 221-22, 232, 236-37, 249-50
wisdom, 7, 11-12, 18, 98, 113-14, 117-18, 121-22, 149, 153, 171, 195, 203-5, 211-17
workers, 7, 53, 56, 207-9, 214
worry, 3, 13, 29-30, 117-18, 122-28, 131, 151, 195, 245
worship, 11, 32-34, 49-51, 126, 146-49, 157, 163, 199, 223, 237, 254, 260
zero accidents, 187-89, 210

Scripture Index

OLD TESTAMENT

Genesis
1, *154*
1–2, *153*
1–11, *153, 154*
1–11:26, *153*
1:22, *153*
1:26, *153*
1:26-28, *154*
1:28, *153*
1:29, *153*
1:30, *153*
1:31, *145, 153*
2:7, *144*
2:15, *153, 154*
2:16, *153*
3, *47*
3:7, *158*
3:14-19, *159*
3:21, *159*
4:7, *193*
4:17, *156*
4:17-22, *158*
8:22, *138, 258*
9:11, *138*
10:11, *159*
11:2-8, *159*
11:4-8, *161*
12:3, *160*
18:32, *190*
26, *154*
27:2, *206*
34:19, *114*
35:29, *115*
37:2, *114*
40:17, *146*

Exodus
2:6, *114*
14:9-10, *135*
20:3, *226*
20:13, *185*
21:28-32, *15*
25–30, *205*
26:1, *146*
27:4, *146*
31:2-6, *160*
32:20, *161*
35:10-35, *146*

Leviticus
1–6, *205*
4–5, *193*
4:2, *193*
4:3-12, *194*
4:13-14, *194*
4:14, *197*
4:22, *193*
5:1, *194*
6:1-7, *194*
13, *15*

Numbers
15, *193*
15:24, *194*
15:26, *197*
15:27-29, *197*
15:27-30, *194*
15:28, *197*
15:30-31, *194*
22:23, *141*
35, *193*
35:11, *195*
35:16-21, *195*
35:23, *195, 211*
35:28, *197*

Deuteronomy
2:7, *143, 146*
4:6, *205*
4:28, *142, 146*
5:17, *185*
6:7, *197*
10:16, *147*
13:4, *16*
19:4-6, *15*
19:5, *195, 211*
22:8, *15, 42, 193*
24:19, *143*
24:21, *15*
27:15, *142, 143, 146*
28:12, *146*
30:1-10, *142*
30:6, *147*
30:9, *142, 143*
31:29, *142, 146*
32:35, *85*
32:39, *178*

Joshua
4:5-7, *96*

Judges
6:21, *141*
16:30, *167*

1 Samuel
2:6, *178*

2 Samuel
1:20, *117*
1:23, *175*
4:4, *175*
11:25, *112*
12:9, *113*

18:5, *114*
24:16-17, *141*

1 Kings
10:5, *135*
15:4, *160*
16:7, *146*

2 Kings
1:2, *175*
19:18, *146*
25:13-17, *159*

1 Chronicles
12:8, *175*
21:16, *141*
22:10, *147*

2 Chronicles
5:1, *159*
26:15-16, *135*
34:25, *146*

Ezra
8:22, *86*

Esther
8:7, *212*

Job
1:21, *178*
11:13–12:6, *120*
12:5, *120*
12:6, *120*
12:7-8, *120*
12:9, *144*
12:9-10, *120*
12:23, *177*

14:15, *144*
33:19-20, *172*
33:29-30, *177*
38:4, *136*
38:18, *77*

Psalms
1:3, *33*
2:1, *177*
6:4-5, *177*
6:5, *34*
7:15, *212*
8:1-3, *145*
8:3, *144*
8:5, *213*
8:6, *130, 144, 153, 160*
9:15, *177, 212*
10:16, *177*
18:36, *128*
19:1, *143, 144*
20:7-8, *173*
22:1, *94*
22:5, *173*
23:2, *33*
28:4, *143*
33:10, *177*
33:13-15, *145*
34:12, *162*
40:2-4, *157*
42:10, *26*
44, *94*
46:6, *177*
47:8, *177*
49:14, *179*
55:4-5, *177*
56:1-8, *24*
56:11, *24*
63:3, *34, 165*
63:4-5, *34*
65:7, *175*
74:23, *175*
80:8, *177*
83:4, *177*
87:5, *160*
88:5, *177*
88:15, *177*
90:4, *95*
90:17, *141, 142, 143, 149, 161*
91:11, *38*
91:11-12, *141*
92:4, *144, 148*

102:4, *172*
102:23, *115*
102:25, *144*
104:15, *33*
104:27, *150*
104:27-29, *127*
107, *34*
107:4-7, *34*
107:10-16, *34*
107:17-22, *34*
107:23-32, *34*
107:36, *34*
111:4, *96*
111:5-7, *144*
111:7, *142, 143, 144*
118:17-18, *177*
119:9, *114, 118*
127, *124, 126*
135:10, *177*
138:7-8, *144*
143:5, *144*

Proverbs
1:4, *203, 204*
1:7, *121*
1:20-21, *117*
2:20, *117*
3:5-8, *123*
3:16, *222*
3:17, *117*
3:18, *121*
3:18-26, *222*
3:21-23, *117*
3:26, *123*
5:3-6, *222*
6, *122, 127*
6:6, *118*
6:6-11, *17, 118, 121, 122, 126, 127*
6:9, *123*
7:8, *117*
7:12, *117*
8:5, *203, 204*
8:35, *122*
8:35-36, *222*
9:6, *16, 122*
10:27, *121*
11:4, *222*
11:28, *222*
14:16, *189, 195*
14:27, *121*
14:30, *222*

18:11-12, *222*
22, *222*
22:3, *205, 222*
22:4, *222*
22:6, *197*
22:13, *115*
24:11-12, *185*
26:1, *222*
26:4-5, *204*
26:8, *222*
26:18, *115*
26:19, *115*
26:27, *212*
27:12, *222*
28:10, *212*
29:23, *222*
31:12, *33*

Ecclesiastes
1:2, *213*
1:3, *215*
1:11, *96*
2:11, *215*
2:13, *215*
2:16, *215*
2:21, *121*
3:1-8, *139*
3:9, *215*
4:4, *146*
5:6, *146*
5:16, *215*
7:10, *96*
7:12, *215*
7:16, *211*
7:17, *211*
8:7, *96*
9:2, *178*
9:3, *192*
9:10, *144, 149*
9:11, *211, 213, 214*
9:11–10:15, *213*
9:12, *213*
9:14-15, *213*
9:18-10:1, *213*
10, *214*
10:4, *204*
10:8, *212, 213*
10:8-9, *212*
10:8-10, *114*
10:8-11, *18, 211, 213*
10:9, *213*
10:10, *214, 215*

10:10-11, *212*
10:11, *212*
12:1-8, *115*
12:8, *213*
12:8-14, *214*
12:14, *176*

Song of Solomon
3:2, *117*
7:1, *143, 146*

Isaiah
2:8, *142*
2:12-21, *161*
2:18, *144*
5:25, *117*
10:6, *117*
15:3, *117*
17:7-8, *148*
19:25, *144*
24:11, *117*
29:23, *144*
31:1, *135*
40:6, *178*
41:23, *33*
42:17, *173*
45:21, *95*
46:11, *175*
60:21, *142, 144*
63:1, *15*
64:8, *144*
64:8-9, *144*
65:22, *142, 148, 149*

Jeremiah
1:16, *142, 143*
5:22, *129*
10:3-4, *148*
10:8-9, *146*
11:6, *117*
17:11, *222*
21:10, *33*
25:6, *146*
32:30, *146*

Lamentations
4:2, *143, 146*

Daniel
1:7-16, *237*
3:15, *237*
3:18, *237*

Scripture Index

3:27, *206*
6:22, *206*

Hosea
6:6, *205*
10:12, *112*
13:2, *146*
14:3, *142, 148*

Jonah
1:2, *159*
3:5, *159*

Micah
5:13, *143, 148*
6:8, *196, 205*

Nahum
3:5, *159*

Habakkuk
1:5-10, *129*

Zechariah
5:5-11, *159*
8:4-5, *115*
13:7, *231*

Malachi
1:4, *161*

APOCRYPHA

Sirach
40:1-5, *178*

NEW TESTAMENT

Matthew
5:29-30, *188*
5:44, *186*
5:44-45, *237*
5:47, *236*
6:1, *222*
6:2, *117*
6:12, *197*
6:13, *253*
6:19-20, *125*
6:20, *120*
6:24, *198, 249*
6:25-33, *126*
6:25-34, *118*

6:27, *222*
6:33, *222*
6:33-34, *96*
7:11, *234*
7:13-14, *231*
9:9, *16*
10:16-42, *237*
10:17-22, *246*
10:28, *24, 225, 253*
10:29, *129*
10:30, *24, 129*
10:38, *237*
12:1-14, *205*
12:36, *176*
13:12, *59, 108*
17:22, *242*
18:8-9, *237*
18:12, *190*
20:18-19, *242*
23:5-12, *222*
23:23, *205*
25:14-30, *204*
26:2, *242*
26:15, *242, 243*
26:21-25, *242*
26:38, *95*
26:45, *242*
27:2, *242*
27:3, *242*
27:18, *243*
27:24-26, *243*
27:26, *242*
27:46, *94*
27:50, *243*

Mark
1:10-11, *226*
1:13-16, *230*
1:17, *230*
1:18-20, *231*
4:39-41, *249*
7:1-13, *205*
8:21, *226*
8:31–9:1, *19*
8:34, *18, 230, 241*
8:34-35, *228, 248*
8:35, *18*
8:36, *227*
8:37, *227*
8:38, *227, 229, 237*
10:2-9, *205*
10:21, *230*

10:29-30, *228, 237, 250*
10:52, *237*
13:9, *246*
13:9-12, *246*
14:10, *242*
14:27, *231*
14:50, *230*
14:58, *144, 147*
15:34, *94*
16:6-7, *231*

Luke
4:9-10, *249*
6:9, *33, 185*
6:45, *199*
7:47, *192*
8:2-3, *230*
9:51–24:53, *125*
9:57-58, *241*
9:57-62, *228, 237*
10:25-37, *235*
10:29, *232*
10:30-35, *117*
11:39-41, *205*
12, *122, 125*
12:4-5, *122*
12:4-12, *237*
12:15-21, *122, 124*
12:16-19, *108*
12:17, *124*
12:22, *122, 124, 165*
12:22-31, *17, 118, 126*
12:24, *119*
12:24-26, *124*
12:27, *119, 122*
12:27-28, *125*
12:29, *124*
12:31-33, *122*
12:33, *125*
12:54-56, *119*
12:56, *120*
12:57-59, *120*
13:1-5, *46, 237, 259*
13:4, *120*
13:32-35, *95*
14:27-28, *240*
21:12-16, *246*
22:3-4, *242*
22:4, *242*
22:43, *95*
22:48, *242*

23:2, *260*
23:25, *242*
23:46, *94, 152, 243*
23:50-56, *260*
24:21, *260*
24:32, *117*

John
1:10-11, *150*
10:10-11, *236*
12:3-7, *260*
13:27, *242*
15:13-15, *226*
16:33, *254*
17:4-5, *206*
17:21, *247*
20:17, *226*
21:22, *238*
21:23, *238*

Acts
3:13, *243*
3:18, *243*
4:27-28, *246*
4:29-31, *246*
5:15, *117*
7, *147*
7:41, *141, 142*
7:46-50, *148*
7:47, *147*
7:48, *144, 147*
7:49, *147*
8:3, *246*
12:1-4, *246*
13:2-3, *240*
13:34-37, *206*
13:49-50, *238*
14:5-6, *238*
14:19, *238*
14:20-22, *238*
14:22, *225*
14:27, *239*
14:27-28, *238*
15:26, *238, 239, 246*
17:24, *144, 147*
17:24-25, *147*
17:26-28, *161*
17:28, *152*
21:11, *246*
22:4, *246*
23:8, *65*
27, *38*

27:10, *38*
27:14, *246*
28:3, *246*
28:3-5, *206*
28:17, *246*

Romans
1:24-28, *246*
1:25, *163*
2:5, *120*
2:29, *147*
4:25, *244*
5:3-4, *225*
6:1, *198, 249*
6:12, *198*
7:2, *248*
7:13, *194*
7:15, *191*
8:29, *226*
8:32, *242, 244*
8:35, *24*
8:35-37, *216*
12:1, *206*
12:2, *150*
14:5, *13*

1 Corinthians
3:9, *161*
3:11, *161*
3:13, *161*
4:12, *144*
8:4, *64*
8:6, *150*
9:4, *151*
9:9, *151*
10:12, *192*
13:3, *246*
15:25-27, *160*

2 Corinthians
4:8-9, *254*

4:16, *24, 225, 253*
4:17, *225*
5:1, *144, 145*
5:4, *160*
6:4-10, *112*
6:6, *112*
7:6, *112*
11:31, *93*
12:9, *93*
13:4, *112*

Galatians
2:20, *242, 244, 245*
6:9, *127*

Ephesians
2:11, *144, 147*
3:5, *62*
4:1, *117*
4:19, *246*
4:28, *15, 144, 149, 245*
4:32, *197*
5:2, *242, 243, 245, 246, 249*
5:25, *242, 245*

Philippians
2:3, *235*

Colossians
1:10, *117*
1:16, *254*
1:17, *150*
2:11, *144*
2:11-12, *145*
2:20, *11*
2:20-21, *3*
2:21, *11*
2:23, *11*
3:23-24, *122*

1 Thessalonians
4:11, *144*

1 Timothy
1:11, *93*
6:6, *128*
6:17, *222*
6:19, *248*

2 Timothy
2:21, *161*
4:20, *246*

Hebrews
1–8, *178*
1:1-5, *145*
1:2, *149*
1:3, *118*
1:10, *141*
2:2-3, *213*
2:5-9, *160*
2:14-18, *179*
2:15, *178, 222*
3:6, *94*
3:12-14, *170*
4:15, *94*
9–13, *145, 147, 148*
9:11, *144, 145*
9:23-26, *160*
9:24, *144, 146*
9:27, *176*
10:4, *197*
10:12, *197*
11:1, *116*
12:22, *160*
13:14, *195*

James
1:3-4, *225*
1:27, *15*
2:9-12, *192*

3:2, *192*
3:13, *205*
4:1, *108*
4:10, *222*
4:13-15, *96*
4:14, *108*

1 Peter
1:18, *163*
2:5, *161*
2:8, *163*
2:11, *162*
2:16, *162*
2:21, *245*
2:23, *243*
3:10, *162*
3:20, *162*
3:20-21, *161*

2 Peter
3, *162*
3:5-6, *162*
3:7, *161*
3:8, *95*
3:9-10, *95*
3:10, *161*
3:11, *162*
3:13, *162*
3:14, *162*

1 John
3:4, *193*

Revelation
8:4, *141*
9:20, *141, 142, 148*
14:13, *149*
19:6-9, *223*
20:1, *141*
21:4, *258*

THE STUDIES IN CHRISTIAN DOCTRINE AND SCRIPTURE SERIES

Studies in Christian Doctrine and Scripture promotes evangelical contributions to systematic theology, seeking fresh understanding of Christian doctrine through creatively faithful engagement with Scripture in dialogue with catholic tradition(s).

Thus: We aim to publish **contributions to systematic theology** rather than merely descriptive rehearsals of biblical theology, historical retrievals of classic or contemporary theologians, or hermeneutical reflections on theological method—volumes that are plentifully and expertly published elsewhere.

We aim to promote **evangelical** contributions, neither retreating from broader dialogue into a narrow version of this identity on the one hand, nor running away from the biblical preoccupation of our heritage on the other hand.

We seek fresh understanding of Christian doctrine **through creatively faithful engagement with Scripture.** To some fellow evangelicals and interested others today, we commend the classic evangelical commitment of engaging Scripture. To other fellow evangelicals today, we commend a contemporary aim to engage Scripture with creative fidelity. The church is to be always reforming—but always reforming according to the Word of God.

We seek **fresh understanding of Christian doctrine.** We do not promote a singular method; we welcome proposals appealing to biblical theology, the history of interpretation, theological interpretation of Scripture, or still other approaches. We welcome projects that engage in detailed exegesis as well as those that appropriate broader biblical themes and patterns. Ultimately, we hope to promote relating Scripture to doctrinal understanding in material, not just formal, ways.

We promote scriptural engagement **in dialogue with catholic tradition(s).** A periodic evangelical weakness is relative disinterest in the church's shared creedal heritage, in churches' particular confessions and more generally in the history of dogmatic reflection. Beyond existing efforts to enhance understanding of themes and corpora in biblical theology, then, we hope to foster engagement with Scripture that bears upon and learns from loci, themes, or crucial questions in classic dogmatics and contemporary systematic theology.